The Resourceful Writer

The Resourceful Writer

A Basic Writing Course

William H. Barnwell

HOUGHTON MIFFLIN COMPANY   Boston

Dallas   Geneva, Illinois
Lawrenceville, New Jersey   Palo Alto

Cover photo by David Caras.

The author gratefully acknowledges the following sources for their permission to reprint copyrighted material.

Maya Angelou. From *And Still I Rise,* by Maya Angelou. Copyright © 1978 by Maya Angelou. Reprinted by permission of Random House, Inc.

George Gipe. The following article is reprinted courtesy of *Sports Illustrated* from the September 15, 1975 issue. © 1975 Time Inc. "Yesterday by George Gipe. Did the Crash of a Stanley Steamer in 1907 Influence U.S. Foreign Policy?"

John Holt. "On Discipline," from *Freedom and Beyond* by John Holt. Copyright © 1972 by John Holt. Reprinted by permission of the publisher, E. P. Dutton, a division of New American Library.

Julie Price. From *Reflections*, by William H. Barnwell and Julie Price. Copyright © 1985 by Houghton Mifflin Company. Reprinted by permission.

Gabrielle Rico. From *Writing the Natural Way*, by Gabrielle Rico. Copyright © 1983 by J. P. Tarcher Inc. Reprinted by permission.

Robert Thigpen. "Merit Pay," from *Reflections*, by William H. Barnwell and Julie Price. Copyright © 1985 by Houghton Mifflin Company. Reprinted by permission.

Robert Thigpen. "Political Parties in Democracies," from *Writing for a Reason*, by William H. Barnwell. Copyright © 1983 by Houghton Mifflin Company. Reprinted by permission.

Vicki Williams. "The View from $204 a Week," by Vicki Williams. Copyright 1982 by Newsweek, Inc. All Rights Reserved. Reprinted by Permission.

Richard Wright. From *Black Boy* by Richard Wright. Copyright, 1937, 1942, 1944, 1945 by Richard Wright. Renewed 1965, 1970, 1972, 1973 by Ellen Wright. Reprinted by permission of Harper & Row, Publishers, Inc.

This book was published in 1983 in a previous edition under the title *Writing for a Reason*.

Printed in the U.S.A.

Library of Congress Catalog Card Number 86–81303

ISBN: 0-395-35915-5

EFGHIJ-A-93210

Contents

To the Instructor   *xv*

PART ONE
Writing from Experience   **1**

1   **A Place to Begin**   *3*

You and Your Audience: Writing a Letter   *3*

Writing Assignment 1   *3*
"Dear Classmates" (three student samples)   *6*

The Classroom Interview   *8*

Writing Assignment 2   *8*
"Gregory Nunn"   *10*
"Dawn Hubbard"   *10*
"Tracy Friedler"   *10*

The Outside Interview   *12*

Writing Assignment 3   *12*

Interviewing Yourself: Keeping a Journal   *13*
"A Lifeless Afternoon"   *14*

Journal Entries   *14*
"A Dramatic Day"   *14*
"The Person I Hardly Know"   *15*
"In the Midst of Decay"   *15*
"Waking Up"   *15*
"The Squirrel"   *16*
"The Jumping Dream"   *16*
Writing Assignment 4   *16*

2   **Using Paragraphs to Shape Your Writing**   *19*

The Paragraph   *19*

Writing a Single-Paragraph Essay   *20*
Writing Assignment 1   *23*
Writing Assignment 2   *24*

Writing Essays of Two or More Paragraphs   *24*
"United We Roll"   *25*

Revising the Paragraph   25

"A New Stereo" (first draft)   26
"A New Stereo" (revised)   27
"Jake" (first draft)   27
"Jake" (revised)   28

Paragraph Form   28

Revising Assignment 1   29
"Officer Mary Kennedy"   29
Revising Assignment 2   29

3 Gathering More Ideas and Information for Writing   *31*

Brainstorming   31

"The Watcher at the Gate"   32
Writing Assignment 1   33
"My Cadillac 999 Triple X"   34
Writing Assignment 2   35
"My Room"   35
Writing Assignment 3   36
"A Riddle"   36
"What Am I?"   36
Writing Assignment 4   37

Free Writing   37

Writing Assignment 5   37
"The Red Boat"   39
"The Day I Want to Forget"   40
Writing Assignment 6   42
"The Road of My Life"   43
"The Child in Me"   44
Writing Assignment 7   45

Clustering   45

"Summer"   47
"Fear"   49
Writing Assignment 8   49
Writing Assignment 9   50

Intentional Discussions   50

Writing Assignment 10   50
"He Always Wanted to Explain Things"   51
"Still I Rise"   52

Listening to Others   54

Writing Assignment 11   55
"The Conversation"   55

"*I Heard a Conversation*"   56
Writing Assignment 12   57
"*Jailbird*"   57

4 Six Steps to Writing Well   59

The Steps Described   59

Step One: Gather Ideas and Information   60
Step Two: Analyze the Ideas and the Information   61
Step Three: State Your Purpose   61
Step Four: Make Your Plan   62
Step Five: Write   62
Step Six: Evaluate, Revise, and Edit   62

"*My Home in the Country*"   63
Writing Assignment 1   64
"*My Home in the Project*"   72
"*At Home in the City*"   73

Transition Sentences to Join Paragraphs   74

Writing Assignment 2   75
"*Those Were the Days*"   82
"*A Rose for My Father*"   83
Writing Assignment 3   84

The Purpose or Thesis Statement   84

Introductions, Conclusions, and Titles   88

Introductions   88
Conclusions   89
Titles   90

Revising and Editing Papers   91

An Example of Revision   92

"*The Zoo*" (first draft)   93
"*The Zoo*" (evaluation)   95
"*The Zoo*" (revised)   95
Writing Assignment 4   96

5 Steps to Writing Description, Narration, and Process ("How To") Essays   97

Description   97

Writing a Description Essay   98

"*Molly*"   99
"*Pie*"   100
Writing Assignment 1   101
Writing Assignment 2   106

Using the Most Exact Word in Your Essays   107

Narration   *108*

Writing a Narrative Essay   *109*

"Black Boy" (Richard Wright)   *110*

Writing Assignment 3   *112*

Process ("How To") Essays   *116*

Writing a Process Essay   *117*

"How to Change the Oil in Your Car"   *118*

Writing Assignment 4   *119*

6 Steps to Writing Example Essays, Comparison and Contrast Essays, and Classification Essays   *125*

Example   *125*

Writing an Example Essay   *126*

"A Student's Life"   *127*

Writing Assignment 1   *128*

Comparison and Contrast   *131*

Writing a Comparison and Contrast Essay   *131*

Two Methods of Planning the Essay   *132*

"Two Medical Jobs"   *135*

"The Coon and the Coon Dog"   *136*

"The City Mouse"   *138*

Writing Assignment 2   *139*

Writing Assignment 3   *144*

Writing Assignment 4   *145*

Classification   *145*

Writing a Classification Essay   *146*

Transition Sentences in Classification Essays   *147*

"Roaches and Social Class"   *148*

"A Time to Live and a Time to Die"   *149*

Writing Assignment 5   *151*

PART TWO
Writing with Outside Resources   157

7 Reading and Summarizing   *159*

Writing Summaries   *159*

Writing Assignment 1   *160*

Writing Assignment 2   *161*

Summarizing Reading Material   *161*

"Yesterday" (George Gipe)   163
"The Wreck of the Stanley Steamer"   166
Writing Assignment 3   *167*
"The View from $204 a Week" (Vicki Williams)   168
Writing Assignment 4   *169*
"On Disciplining Children" (John Holt)   170
"Political Parties in Democracies"
(Robert Thigpen)   173
Writing Assignment 5   *175*
Writing Assignment 6   *176*

8   Finding Resource Material in the Library   177

The Library's Resources   *178*
Writing Assignment 1   *183*
Writing Assignment 2   *183*
Writing Assignment 3   *184*
Writing Assignment 4   *185*
Writing Assignment 5   *185*

9   Writing Persuasively   187

Forming an Argument   *187*

The Argument Essay   *190*

Writing an Argument Essay   *191*
"Arguments Against Capital Punishment"   193
"A 'Yes' for Capital Punishment"   194
Writing Assignment 1   *195*
"Merit Pay" (Robert Thigpen)   199
Writing Assignment 2   *200*
Writing Assignment 3   *200*
Writing Assignment 4   *200*
"Dear Editor: Support the ERA"   201
Writing Assignment 5   *202*

**PART THREE
A Writer's Workbook   205**

10   Parts of Speech   207

10.0 Introduction   *207*

10.1 Nouns   *208*

10.2 Verbs   *210*

10.3 Objects and Prepositions   *215*

10.4 Pronouns   *218*

10.5 Adjectives   *224*

10.6 Adverbs   *228*

10.7 Conjunctions   *230*

10.8 Interjections   *232*

10.9 Review Exercise   *233*

11   Writing Effective Sentences   235

11.0 Introduction   *235*

11.1 The Simple Sentence   *236*

11.2 The Compound Sentence   *238*

11.3 The Compound Sentence with a Conjunctive
Adverb   *242*

11.4 The Complex Sentence with a Subordinating
Conjunction   *243*

11.5 The Complex Sentence with an Adjective
Clause   *249*

11.6 The Sentence with an Appositive   *255*

11.7 Review Exercises   *261*
"Tons of Fun"   *262*

12   Preventing Sentence Errors   265

12.0 Introduction   *265*

12.1 Preventing Fragments   *265*

12.2 Preventing Run-on Sentences   *270*
"A Sunday Morning Revelation"   *275*
"The Weekend Camper"   *279*

12.3 Preventing Adjective and Adverb Confusion   *280*

12.4 Preventing Dangling Modifiers   *281*

12.5 Preventing Misplaced Modifiers   *283*

12.6 Preventing Faulty Parallelism   *285*

12.7 Review Exercises   *287*
"An Experience I Would Like to Forget"   *287*

13 Subject-Verb Agreement   291

13.0 Introduction   *291*

13.1 Verb Conjugation   *293*

13.2 Irregular Noun Subjects   *295*

13.3 Verb Endings   *297*

13.4 *Have* and *Has*   *300*

13.5 The *Be* Verbs   *301*

13.6 Subject and Verb Reversed   *302*

13.7 Verbs with Two or More Subjects   *305*

13.8 Verbs with Pronoun Subjects   *307*

13.9 Present-Tense Essays   *310*

13.10 Review Exercises   *313*
 "Uptown Versus Downtown"   *314*

14 Verb Tense   *317*

14.0 Introduction   *317*

14.1 Irregular Verbs   *318*

14.2 The Base Form   *323*

14.3 The Simple Past Tense   *325*

14.4 The Past Participle   *329*

14.5 The Progressive Form   *337*

14.6 Using the Dictionary for Verbs   *339*

14.7 Avoiding Tense Shifts   *341*
 "A Christmas to Remember"   *342*

14.8 Verbals: Infinitives, Participles, and Gerunds   *343*

14.9 Review Exercises   *349*
 "Two Children—Two People"   *350*

15 More Practice Using Verbs   *353*

15.0 Introduction   *353*

15.1 Subject-Verb Agreement   *353*

15.2 Third-Person Endings   *355*

15.3 The *Be* Verbs   *356*

15.4 Subjects with Two or More Verbs   *358*

15.5 Subjects and Verbs Separated   *360*

15.6 Verb Tense   *363*

15.7 Tense Shifts   *367*
 "Lynette's Baby"   *369*

15.8 Review Exercises   *371*
 "Sweet Albert Dee"   *372*
 "The Good Old Days"   *373*

16   Using Pronouns Correctly   *375*

16.0 Introduction   *375*

16.1 Avoiding Errors in Pronoun Case   *375*
 "My Summer at Nantucket"   *376*

16.2 Avoiding Pronouns with Unclear Antecedents   *377*

16.3 Avoiding Errors in Pronoun Agreement   *378*

16.4 Avoiding Pronoun Gender Confusion   *381*

16.5 Avoiding Pronoun Person Shifts   *384*

16.6 Avoiding Other Pronoun Errors   *385*

16.7 Summary of Common Pronoun Errors   *386*

16.8 Review Exercise   *389*

17   Spelling Skills   *391*

17.0 Introduction   *391*

17.1 Plurals of Nouns   *392*

17.2 Verb Endings   *394*

17.3 Contractions and Possessive Pronouns   *396*

17.4 Other Sound-Alike Words   *399*

17.5 Using the Hyphen   *401*

17.6 Words Often Misspelled   *402*

17.7 Review Exercise   *407*

18   Capitalization, Punctuation, and Numbers   *409*

18.0 Introduction   *409*

18.1 Capitalization   *409*

18.2 End Punctuation   *412*

18.3 The Apostrophe   *413*

18.4 The Comma   *417*

18.5 The Semicolon   *426*

18.6 The Colon   *428*

18.7 Quotation Marks and Underlining   *428*

18.8 Other Punctuation: The Hyphen, the Dash, and Parentheses   *432*

18.9 Numbers and Numerals   *433*

18.10 Review Exercises   *435*

   "A Letter to Gina"   *435*

Appendix A: **Preparing the Research Paper**   ***437***

Appendix B: **Reading for Pleasure**   ***459***

Appendix C: **Answers to Practice Exercises in Part Three**   ***463***

Index   ***499***

To the Instructor

Approach

The Resourceful Writer is based on the premise that beginning college writers have a great deal to say in their writing and the potential for saying it well. Given this premise, I have designed a course to help students write meaningful paragraphs and essays as they move from personal, expressive writing to more formal, academic discourse. Students begin by writing about what they know best: their own experiences and their perceptions of the world around them. They begin writing immediately in the course, learning early on how to put together a paragraph: how to structure it, how to use convincing details, and how to maintain their own voices in writing the paragraph. Throughout the book, students use a six-step writing method to guide them through the prewriting, writing, and revising process. As they practice this kind of writing in Part One of the text, "Writing from Experience," they can also work on mastering sentence structure and the mechanics of English by completing the many exercises that appear in Part Three, "A Writer's Workbook." Students learn the most from their own writing— but the workbook exercises, which can be assigned in any order, are a useful resource.

As students master paragraph writing and writing from their own experiences, they begin to learn how to draw from outside resources—primarily the reading they do—to write effectively about a variety of subjects. In Part Two of the text, "Writing with Outside Resources," students learn how to summarize reading material, how to draw on outside resources, how to refer to these resources in their own writing, and how to express agreement or disagreement with opinions expressed in outside resources. "Writing with Outside Resources" helps prepare students for writing a research paper; if you include research writing in your course, you can have students move on to the material in Appendix A, "Preparing the Research Paper."

Throughout the text, numerous student samples and eight professional samples show students what is expected of them and offer opportunity for reading and ideas for writing.

Organization

The Resourceful Writer is organized in three parts with a total of eighteen chapters.

Part One Part One, "Writing from Experience" (Chapters 1 through 6), guides students step by step through paragraph writing to short essay writing. Chapter 1, "A Place to Begin," asks students to plunge in and write: their first assignment is a letter about themselves, addressed to their classmates. Then students progress through various other writing assignments, including the classroom interview, the outside interview, and keeping a journal. This chapter also introduces the six-step writing method that will guide students through most of the writing assignments in the book. Chapter 2, "Using Paragraphs to Shape Your Writing," concentrates on helping students to write structured, thoughtful paragraphs. Chapter 2 also introduces revision, encouraging students to develop the habit of revising their work early on. In Chapter 3, "Gathering More Ideas and Information for Writing," students learn how to use brainstorming, free writing, clustering, class discussions, and conversations with others to enrich their writing. Chapter 4, "Six Steps to Writing Well," describes the six-step writing method in detail, walking/talking students through the various steps of the writing process. A substantial section on revision reinforces the importance of students' evaluating and revising their own writing with an example of a student paper taken through the revision process. Chapters 5 and 6 introduce various rhetorical and organizational strategies: description, narration, process, example, comparison/contrast, and classification. Students use the six-step method to write their own essays and are supported by plenty of student essays in these chapters.

Part Two   Part Two, "Writing with Outside Resources," helps students move from writing about their own personal experiences to writing with outside resources. In Chapter 7, "Reading and Summarizing," students learn how to summarize material they read. Chapter 8, "Finding Resource Material in the Library," describes the various resources available to most students and then has them write short essays about reading material they have obtained from the library (thus employing summarizing skills as well). In Chapter 9, "Writing Persuasively," students learn how to form an argument and write a persuasive paper supporting their argument, using outside resources. Preliminary exercises at the beginning of the chapter help students formulate arguments and present them clearly.

Part Three   Part Three, "A Writer's Workbook," is designed to be used throughout the course in conjunction with parts One and Two. While students write paragraphs and essays in parts One and Two, they can work on their mastery of grammar and mechanics in Part Three. Chapter 10, "Parts of Speech," offers a review of the parts of speech. Chapters 11 and 12 help students write correct, whole sentences. Chapters 13, 14, and 15 concentrate on verb use, including subject-verb agreement and correct use of tense. Chapter 16 guides students in proper use of pronouns, and Chapters 17 and 18 offer practice and instruction in spelling, capitalization, punctuation, and numbers. All of the chapters in Part Three contain brief instruction and lots of practice exercises for students. Answers to the practice exercises appear at the back of the book; answers to review exercises (which appear at the end of each chapter in Part Three) are provided in the Instructor's Support Package. Many of the exercises concentrate on students' own writing by asking them to write their own sentences.

Appendixes   Appendix A, "Preparing the Research Paper," provides instructions for constructing a research paper. Appendix B, "Reading for Pleasure," consists of a list of books—with a brief précis of each—that college students generally like to read, thus further encouraging beginning college writers to read as much as they can.

For interested instructors, there are three ancillary works available from the publisher: an *Instructor's Manual* with sample syllabi and teaching suggestions; an *Instructor's Support Package* with additional assignments, exercises, and answers to Review Exercises in the text; and, upon adoption, a set of acetate overhead transparencies for those who like to employ visuals.

Acknowledgments

This text has evolved with the help of my students and my former colleagues at the University of New Orleans. Various instructors with different teaching styles have contributed their ideas and at times provided me with exercises that appear here after having been tested in the classroom. I wish to thank Byrd Gibbens; Nancy Regalado, of New York University; and David Shroyer and Robert Thigpen, both of the University of New Orleans. I owe special thanks to Julie Price, of the University of New Orleans, with whom I coauthored *Reflections*, a thematic reader for beginning college writers.

The following reviewers contributed many good ideas to *The Resourceful Writer:*

Bonne August, Kingsborough Community College
Robert Dees, Orange Coast College
C. R. Embry, Truckee Meadows Community College
Toni Empringham, El Camino Community College
David Fear, Valencia Community College
Joan Fedor, Highlin Community College
DeLois Gates
Emory D. Jones, Northeast Mississippi Junior College
Robert Lawrence, Triton College
Dennis May, Northern Virginia Community College
David Skwire, Cuyahoga Community College
Stack Sutton, Polk Community College

But it is to my students that I owe my greatest thanks. Not only did they contribute the many samples of writing that appear in the text, but they also taught me, along the way, a lot about writing and a lot about life.

W. H. B.

The Resourceful Writer

PART ONE

Writing from Experience

Dear Students,

   The primary goal of this course is to help you say in writing what you want to say, with clarity and with style, and to say it correctly. The assumption is that you have much to say that is worth communicating. During the semester your instructor will lead you through various activities and exercises that are designed to help you relax in your writing and to bring forth your strengths.

   An important objective of Chapter 1 is to help you begin to know your classmates. They, along with your instructor, will be your audience for most of the writing assignments. In Chapter 2 you will study paragraphs and how they can help shape your writing. Then, in Chapter 3, you will discover and develop new resources for writing. By the time you finish that chapter, you should never have to worry about having something to say when you are asked to write an essay. In Chapter 4 you will learn a step-by-step writing method that will be helpful to you in all of your college writing. The next two chapters show how you can apply this method to different types of writing.

   Throughout Part One you will be the chief resource for your writing—what you see, what you hear, what you can remember. Then, in Part Two, you will learn how to draw on outside resources for writing—reading material and the library. You will discover that the same method you used for the personal writing in Part One will work well for the more objective writing in Part Two.

   Part Three is a writer's workbook that provides instruction and practice in the mechanics of writing: how to write in complete and interesting sentences, how to use tricky verbs and pronouns correctly, how to punctuate, and how to overcome spelling problems.

   Your instructor may ask you to work through Part Three from beginning to end while you are completing selected writing assignments in Part One and Part Two. Or your instructor may ask you to do particular assignments in Part Three that will help you learn certain skills. Either way, Part

Three can serve as a reference handbook for you. When you need to know how to write particular constructions, you will be able to find the appropriate rules (with examples and practice exercises) in Part Three.

I hope you enjoy this course and learn to say exactly what you want to say as you learn the craft of writing.

Sincerely yours,

William H. Barnwell

William H. Barnwell

CHAPTER 1

A Place to Begin

You and Your Audience: Writing a Letter

You will begin this course by writing a letter to your classmates. You are the writer. Your classmates are the audience. Your classmates and your instructor will be your audience for most of the writing in this text. The better you get to know them the more you will have a sense of writing *to* someone.

Here, and in many of the writing assignments in this book, you will be given step-by-step suggestions for writing. When you finish this first assignment, you should have written a 200- to 300-word letter about yourself in which you have said what you wanted to say to your classmates.

WRITING ASSIGNMENT 1

Step One: Gather Ideas and Information   Fill out one of the two work sheets below to use as a guide for your letter. Or, if neither work sheet helps you say what you want to say, make up your own outline for the letter, but plan to group your thoughts in paragraphs, as illustrated by the work sheets.

WORK SHEET A

_____
                              (date)

Dear Classmates,

FIRST PARAGRAPH
(PAST)

[When and where did you last go to school (or work)?]

_____

_____

[What did you like best (or least) about your school or job, and why?]

_____

_____

_____

[Give an example of what you liked best (or least).] _____

_____

SECOND PARAGRAPH
(PRESENT)

[When and why did you decide to come to this college or university?]

_____

_____

[How do you feel about your decision now?] _____

_____

[Name one particular thing that makes you feel this way and explain why.]

_____

_____

_____

_____

THIRD PARAGRAPH
(FUTURE)

[What do you hope to do when you finish school?] _____

_____

_____

[What has influenced you in your career choice?] _____

_____

_____

_____

FOURTH PARAGRAPH
(OPTIONAL)

[Add anything else you would like to say to your classmates.] _____

_____

_____

_____

Sincerely yours,

_____

WORK SHEET B

_____
(date)

Dear Classmates,

FIRST PARAGRAPH

[Describe the things that most people know about you.]

_____

_____

_____

SECOND PARAGRAPH

[Describe some things that very few people know about
you.] _____

_____

_____

THIRD PARAGRAPH

[What would you like people to know about you, and
why?] _____

_____

_____

_____

FOURTH PARAGRAPH
(OPTIONAL)

[Add anything else you would like to say to your classmates.] _____

_____

_____

Sincerely yours,

_____

Step Two: Develop Your Ideas   Read the student letters below to get more
ideas for your letter.

SAMPLE A

Dear Classmates

Dear Classmates,

Hi! My name is Karen, and I attended two high schools. First there was Grace King, then Slidell High, and then I quit and enrolled in John Jay Beauty College. I loved beauty college because I could relate so well to everyone there. A few of us became good friends and would go everywhere together. There was a college atmosphere. In other words, you could do as you pleased. The teachers took a special interest in everyone. If you weren't sure of a cut or the solution for coloring hair, they came running to your aid. While I liked John Jay, I thought I should get a couple of years of regular college while I still had the chance.

I picked this community college because I've always heard it was a hard but good school. My family warned me that people here would be unsociable, and they are. People will look you right in the eye and not speak, as if you weren't even there. Yesterday, when I said hello to a girl about my age, she didn't even look at me. I hope this class will be different, and we will get to know each other.

I want to be a teacher when I finish school because I love children.

Sincerely yours,

Karen

SAMPLE B

Dear Classmates

Dear Classmates,

It all started on December 14, 1965, and is still going on. I know you are wondering *what* started, so I will satisfy your curiosity and tell you that on that day, I was born. I grew up in a middle-sized city of about 50,000 people, where I went to a good high school. At Greenwood High I played basketball for a while but could never be as good as I wanted. There were five other guys who kept me on the bench. So I went on to boxing and was given the name "Windmill" because people said that I swung my arms like a windmill.

Now that I have graduated from high school, I want to pursue bigger and better things. Everything at this moment is just great as far as my studies go, but the dorm where I stay is too noisy. My roommate is a jazz lover and is the noisiest of all. He plays his music constantly and it really annoys me. I suppose he doesn't know that he is rooming with Windmill Will.

In four years I hope I have graduated and am on my way to becoming another Walter Cronkite. My intended major is communications, and being the best is what I want. I want to excel in my work, and I feel that if I do not have a condominium, drive a Mercedes, and have a Swiss bank account, I will be a failure. Maybe I am setting my goals for my standard of living too high, but if I don't I may not work hard enough.

Classmates, I hope that each of you will one day turn on your television set and see my smiling face in your living room.

Sincerely yours,

Will Myles

SAMPLE C

Dear Classmates

Dear Classmates,

I am thirty-three years old and probably the senior member of this class. I am a single parent with two main interests in life: to be a good mother to my seven-year-old son and to succeed in my work.

As a single parent, I have to play the role of mother and father and set all the rules for my son. He must keep clean because to me cleanliness is next to godliness. He must be well behaved and treat adults with respect. And finally, he must work hard at school because education is the most important means to a productive future. In order for my son to become successful, he must know who he is and where he is going.

At present I am employed as a licensed practical nurse in the recovery room at West Jefferson General Hospital. After working as a practical nurse for three years, I discovered that there is no upward mobility in this job. So I decided to further my education and become a registered nurse with a B.S. degree. I love people, and I love helping them, especially those who cannot help themselves. In addition to the good feeling nursing gives me, the salary is excellent.

My future and my son's future will depend on our positive attitude toward education and personal success.

Sincerely yours,

Gustavia Pritchard

Step Three: Write Your Letter   Study the following rules for writing a letter and then write the letter to your classmates.

1. Place the date at the top right-hand corner of the paper.
2. At the left-hand margin, a couple of lines below the date, begin the letter with "Dear" and the name of the person or persons to whom you are writing, followed by a comma.
3. Group your thoughts in paragraphs. (See the two work sheets and student samples above for ideas.)
4. When writing by hand, indent your paragraphs about an inch and a half; when typing, indent five spaces.
5. Begin your closing on the right-hand side of the paper, a few lines below your last sentence. In your closing, capitalize the first word only, for example, "Very truly yours" or "Love always."

Step Four: Read Your Letter   Read your letter aloud to a small group of four to seven people. After each person has read his or her letter, take turns answering the following questions:

1. What about the person interested you the most?
2. What, if anything, could you identify with? Explain.
3. What would you like to know more about?

Try to give equal time to each member of the group. If your group becomes stuck on any particular point, call on your instructor for help.

The Classroom Interview

A good writer must have a keen ear for what people say. The better you listen, the more you will have to write about. Much of the skill of active listening is simply deciding to concentrate on what other people are saying. In this exercise, you will practice active listening as you interview one of your classmates for five to ten minutes. After the interview, write a paragraph of about 150 words introducing your classmate to the rest of the class.

Here are some characteristics of a good listener. Can you think of others?

good eye contact _____   _____
shows interest _____   _____
puts own agenda aside _____   _____

Check your list against the observer checklist at the end of Step One below.

WRITING ASSIGNMENT 2

Step One: Gather Ideas and Information   Form yourselves into groups of three, preferably with students you do not yet know well. Each person will function in turn as a speaker, a listener, and an observer. The listener will ask questions and try to help the speaker say just what he or she wants to say. At the end of the interview, the observer will use the checklist that follows to evaluate how helpful the listener was to the speaker. When it is your turn to be the listener, you will need to learn enough about the person you are interviewing to write a full paragraph introducing that person to the class. Here are three suggestions for the listener:

1. Do not take extensive notes while you are interviewing; instead, wait until the interview is over.
2. Invite the speaker to answer each question in detail, but do not push the speaker to answer any question. The object of the exercise is not to embarrass anyone but instead to help others say what they want to say.

3. From time to time, summarize what you have heard the speaker say. Your summary will show that you are listening and will give the speaker a chance to correct anything you misunderstood.

You may want to ask the speaker some of the questions listed below, but do not feel that you must ask them in the order given. Take a few moments to study the list of questions before you begin your interview.

1. What are some of the nicknames you have had in the past? What did you think of them?
2. What are your hobbies? Which is your favorite, and why?
3. What is your zodiac sign? Does it have any significance for you?
4. What feature of your personality are you most proud of?
5. How important is religion in your life?
6. What is your favorite television program, and why?
7. What emotions do you find most difficult to control?
8. Do you consider yourself a political liberal or a conservative?
9. What are your favorite jokes or expressions?
10. What sorts of jobs have you had in the past? Which did you like the most, and which the least?
11. What is your intended career? Are you having any second thoughts about it?
12. What things frighten you the most?
13. How are you enjoying this college (or university) now?
14. What are some things you have not mentioned that very few people know about you?

After the interview, the observer should evaluate how helpful the listener was to the speaker. The following checklist will assist the observer in making this evaluation:

1. Did the listener seem interested in what the speaker had to say?
2. Did the listener ask too many questions, not enough questions, or just the right number of questions?
3. Did the listener summarize what the speaker said in a helpful way?
4. Did the listener seem relaxed?
5. Did the listener maintain good eye contact with the speaker?
6. In short, did the listener help the speaker say what the speaker wanted to say?

Before leaving your three-person group, jot down as much as you can remember of what the person you interviewed said. These notes will serve as the raw material for your paragraph about that person.

Someone from each group should report to the rest of the class on how well the interviews went. Were the active listeners effective? Did the speakers give a good portrait of themselves?

Step Two: Develop Your Ideas Read the following student samples for ideas about how to use the notes from your interview in writing the assigned paragraph.

SAMPLE A

Gregory Nunn

I interviewed Gregory Nunn, who believes nicknames tell a lot about a person. He has several nicknames himself. Some people call him "Lover Man" because he is always flirting. Others call him "Bleep Man" because he is good at basketball. (Bleep is just a term used when the basketball goes through the hoop.) Most call him "Beach Bum" because during the summer he spends more time in Florida than at home. But there is more to Greg than just nicknames. He is eighteen years old and a graduate of Saint Mark's High, and his hobbies are playing tennis, woodworking, and cracking bad jokes. (He managed to tell a few of these during our interview.) He wants to be a lawyer when he finishes school but is not expecting to become a millionaire. Greg mainly wants to be surrounded with good friends who enjoy having a good time. Someday he would like to have a wife, two children, and a great big dog, but he says he is not going to rush into that kind of life.

SAMPLE B

Dawn Hubbard

Dawn wants us to know two things about her: First, she wants to make a career of music. She has been singing with a band for the last three years and practices many hours a week. She is taking music at the university and is thinking of majoring in it. The band she sings with is called Pryntz. They have written ten songs of their own and hope to record some soon. Dawn herself wrote the lyrics for seven of the ten songs. The other thing she wants us to know about her is that she is very interested in psychology. She spends many hours with her family and friends talking about the ways people relate to each other. Psychology catches her attention because she enjoys helping people with the different problems they face. I enjoyed talking to Dawn and was particularly interested in her background in music.

SAMPLE C

Tracy Friedler

During my interview with Tracy, I found out that she and I are alike in many ways. One thing we both enjoy is laughing. As I interviewed her, I found that she laughs at just about anything and that it is sometimes hard for her to stop. Each time she began to laugh, I started to laugh as well. I also found out that we are both shy, but I am a little more shy than she is. It is too bad that we are shy because we both like meeting people. We have problems making conversation even though we are friendly to almost everyone. As we continued talking, I found out that we also have our differences. I found out, for example, that Tracy is quick tempered but cools down easily. I am the opposite. I do not get mad often, but when I do, it takes me a long time to get over it. I also found out that her favorite hobby is eating and that she does not gain a lot of weight. You can look at me and tell that when I eat I gain weight. In my opinion Tracy is a very nice person and would make a great friend to anyone. Even though we both may be shy, we talked as if we had known each other for years.

Step Three: Write Your Paragraph   In a paragraph of about 150 words, introduce the person you interviewed to the class. Do not try to tell everything that you learned in the interview. Instead, emphasize those things that seemed most important to you. Here are some suggestions:

1. Begin the paragraph with one sentence that names the person you interviewed and states generally what the paragraph will be about.
2. In the rest of the paragraph, tell at least two things about the person that seemed important. Support each item with enough information for your audience to understand the points you want to convey.
3. As you move from point to point in your paragraph, make sure you use smooth transitions. (In writing, *transitions* are the words that connect different thoughts.) Note how the students in the samples above used transitions:

    SAMPLE A

    To move from Greg's nicknames to other information about him: "But there is more to Greg than just nicknames."

    SAMPLE B

    To move from the first thing Dawn wants the class to know about her to the second: "The other thing she wants us to know about her is that she is very interested in psychology."

    SAMPLE C

    To move from the ways the writer and Tracy are alike to the ways they are different: "As we continued talking, I found out that we also have our differences."

4. Do not leave your audience dangling. Bring the paragraph to a close in one sentence. Note how the students in the samples brought their paragraphs to a close:

    SAMPLE A

    "Someday he would like to have a wife, two children, and a great big dog, but he says he is not going to rush into that kind of life."

    SAMPLE B

    "I enjoyed talking to Dawn and was particularly interested in her background in music."

    SAMPLE C

    "Even though we both may be shy, we talked as if we had known each other for years."

Step Four: Read Your Paragraph   Your instructor may ask you to read your paragraph to a small group or to the class. Reading papers aloud can be helpful in developing a sense of audience. Donald Murray, a teacher of writing at the University of New Hampshire, makes this argument for reading papers aloud:

> When students read their papers aloud, they hear the voices of their classmates without the interference of mechanical problems, misspellings, poor penmanship. . . . They laugh with the author, grieve with the author, nod in understanding, lean forward to try to learn more. That's how the writing class begins, and that is what carries it forward.

As you read your papers in class and hear others read theirs, you will discover that writing essays is not only an exercise but also a way of communicating ideas that are important to you.

After you have read your paragraph aloud, first ask yourself if it sounded like you. Then, when others have read theirs, address the following questions:

1. Did the writing sound natural?
2. Was it clear? If not, what was confusing?
3. Was the writing convincing? Did the writer support his or her points with examples?
4. What more would you like to know about the person described in the paragraph?

Step Five: Rewrite Your Paragraph   Using what you learned from reading your paper aloud, rewrite your paragraph. Consult the person you are writing about if you need more information.

The Outside Interview

Conducting an outside interview is very similar to conducting the classroom interview. You should listen actively and concentrate on what your subject is saying.

WRITING ASSIGNMENT 3

Following the relevant steps described above for the classroom interview, write a paragraph of about 150 words on one of these subjects:

1. Your oldest relative or the oldest person on your block
2. Your priest, minister, or rabbi
3. Your college dean
4. A high school or college teacher

5. A police officer or mail carrier
6. A coach
7. A foreign student
8. A student of the opposite sex (from outside this class) you would like to know

As you write, remember that you are writing *to* your classmates.

Interviewing Yourself: Keeping a Journal

One of the best ways to learn how to write effectively is to do a lot of it. What is true for an artist, a musician, or an athlete is also true for you as a writer: You become skilled through practice. Keeping a diary or personal journal is perhaps the single best way to practice your writing. Take twenty minutes at the beginning or the end of each day to write about something that caught your attention during the previous twenty-four hours. Besides giving you practice in writing, keeping a journal will give you an abundant supply of material for the various essays you will write for class.

The key to keeping a journal is learning how to interview yourself, that is, learning how to ask yourself the kinds of questions that start you talking about yourself and your experiences. You may want to begin by asking yourself questions such as these:

1. What made today different from other days? How did I feel about it?
2. What has been on my mind today? Why?
3. What new understanding about my life did I gain today? What happened to give me that insight? (For example, perhaps you learned that many old people have a certain wisdom about death that is beyond the comprehension of the rest of us or perhaps you learned that the old saying "When one door closes, another opens" is either true or not true. Maybe you learned that how much fun children have at their play has little to do with their material possessions.)
4. In what conflict did I find myself today? (Be sure to consider conflict within yourself as well as conflict with others.) What happened in this conflict?
5. What was the most unusual thing that I saw (or heard, smelled, touched, or tasted) today?
6. What did I dream last night? How was it significant to me?

Keep asking yourself similar questions that force you to give more and more detail about particular experiences. One student, in answering the first question listed above, said that sitting in a hospital waiting room was the thing that had been different that day. He then went on to ask these questions as he wrote his paragraph:

What was it like inside the waiting room?
What did the room smell like?

What caught my attention in the room?
How did I feel about what I smelled and saw?
What did I do while I was there?
What brought the experience to an end?

SAMPLE

A Lifeless Afternoon

I spent a lifeless afternoon in the hospital waiting room waiting for Granny. The room was dimly lit, and I could sense the sickness throughout the hospital by breathing the clean, cold air that smelled like rubbing alcohol. Sitting on the blue and red cloth-covered couch, I began to wonder what I would do if I became sick and actually had to come to this place. Opposite me were pictures on the wall that honored the founders of the hospital. They all looked the same, dressed in black or dull gray suits with white shirts and black ties. I tried to imagine what kinds of people they were and what kinds of lives they led. An artificial green plant and medical magazines were on a low table under the pictures. For some reason they depressed me. Off to my right was the receptionist's desk with her sign, "Give me your name and the patient you want to see." I finally got tired of sitting and took a walk up and down the pale gray floors that had been expertly mopped and waxed. I could see my shadow on the floor and little designs in the tile that looked like clouds on a clear day.

Journal Entries

Read the sample journal entries that follow, and note how the writers tried to answer each question.

SAMPLE A: WHAT MADE TODAY DIFFERENT FROM OTHER DAYS?

A Dramatic Day

Today was a dramatic day in my Drama and Communications 1000 class. The class usually starts at eleven o'clock, but today it did not. There was no teacher. At twenty after eleven I was about to leave when our teacher came storming through the door. She was sweating, out of breath, and looking very tired. She said, "Class, I am sorry for being late, but I just had a car accident." She was still out of breath but managed to continue, "I was planning to give you a pop quiz, but I left the test in my car. I was going to give you a lecture, but I left the notes in my car. I guess I will have to give the lecture off the top of my head." I could tell she was emotionally upset and not prepared to teach a class.

I admire her because even though she had just been through a bad experience she was committed to doing her job. Other teachers would have just dismissed their classes. But instructor Anne Collins is a real professional. After she took a moment to compose herself, she began her lecture.

She discussed theater from the sixth century B.C. to the year 1520. She talked about the Romans and Greeks and the church in medieval times. What I liked most was the part about a Greek god named Dionysus. She said Dionysus was god of fertility and wine and that people honored this god with rituals of sex and wine. Later today I told my girlfriend that we should go worship Dionysus, but she did not know what I meant.

SAMPLE B: WHAT HAS BEEN ON MY MIND TODAY?

The Person I Hardly Know

My father is a person I hardly know. Whenever I want to talk about something important, he is too busy to listen. I do not hate my father. I just want him to be with me more often. Is that too much to ask of someone you love? Sometimes I want to tell him all kinds of things, such as what I did during the weekend. But I always get the same old response—"I'm too busy now," or "I'll be back tomorrow. We'll talk then." *Then* never comes.

Today I finally got my father to talk to me, but I was very disappointed. It was like talking to a stranger. I hope that when I have children, I will be a good listener and not always say, "I'm busy right now." Too many kids have problems with their lives because of not enough love from their parents. I hope my father will some day learn what it would mean to me just to hear him say, "I understand." I want him to understand the joy, tears, mistakes, and love that I want to share with him. Maybe when I am older I will think about how much I really loved him.

SAMPLE C: WHAT NEW UNDERSTANDING ABOUT THE MEANING OF LIFE DID I GAIN TODAY?

In the Midst of Decay

In the midst of this decay there are children between the ages of five and ten playing with plenty of vitality. As they toss the football around, their bodies are full of energy, their clothes look like rainbows. The colors mix together and one is given the impression of being in a psychedelic dream, beautiful, active, and alive with unity. They yell to each other, increasing their morale. They have the sound of an organized alto section. At the sidelines are the girls who are shy, with the shyness that belongs to the very young. They are embarrassed when their dresses are raised by the wind. As their feet rise above pavement, they cheer for their boyfriends. In the midst of decay, children will continue to play.*

SAMPLE D: WHAT CONFLICT DID I FIND MYSELF IN TODAY?

Waking Up

This morning was another gloomy Saturday morning. It began about 8:00 A.M. when I felt a cold hand around my ankle jerking my tired body up and down in bed. It was my mother. Frowning and fussing, she said, "I told you not to stay out too late after that dance, didn't I?" I gave a huge yawn and ignored her unpleasant voice. I rolled over in my soft, warm bed and went back to sleep, but I dreamed that it was

---

* I am indebted to Mina P. Shaughnessy of the City University of New York for this example. It comes from her book *Errors and Expectations* (New York: Oxford University Press, 1979), p. 278.

already nine o'clock and I had just shown up for work in my nightgown, stale make-up, and hair standing straight up on my head. So this time, I woke up for good and began hurrying through my routine so that I wouldn't be late for work. Suddenly, I realized I felt bad, so, with a mouth full of toothpaste, I called, "Mom, will you call work for me and tell them that I'm sick and can't come in today?" "No!" she yelled back. "Because if I call, I'm going to tell them just why you don't want to go in." With that I dried my mouth and began searching for the car keys.

SAMPLE E: WHAT WAS THE MOST UNUSUAL THING I SAW (OR HEARD, SMELLED, TOUCHED, OR TASTED) TODAY?

The Squirrel

I was sitting at my desk this morning, typing away, when I did something I hardly ever do: I looked out of the window and actually saw what was there. About fifteen feet away in a neighbor's yard stands a tall, scrawny pine tree that is hardly worth noticing. But on the first limb of the pine a squirrel was busily shaking his tail while looking right at me. I seldom pay attention to the hundreds of squirrels in our neighborhood, unless of course our cat, Halloween, gets one of them. But this morning I could not take my eyes off the squirrel. Suddenly it occurred to me that the squirrel was making his tail keep time to the fast music that I was playing on the stereo. "This cannot be," I said to myself, so I began to play slower music to see if the squirrel would shake his tail more slowly. When I looked out of the window, however, the squirrel was gone. I guess I will never know for sure if squirrels keep time to music.

SAMPLE F: WHAT DID I DREAM LAST NIGHT?

The Jumping Dream

Last night I had my jumping dream again. This time I was jumping up and down on my parents' king-size bed. Each time I jumped, I bounced higher. At first I was enjoying myself and kept hearing myself say, "Higher some more. Higher some more." But then I realized that I was bouncing so high I could not control myself. I bounced higher than the ceiling, or rather where the ceiling should have been. I then bounced higher than where the roof should have been. Finally, I realized that I had bounced a mile up into the air. Then I began to panic. I could not even see the house below. "How will I get down this time?" I wondered. "I'm in big trouble."

When I woke up, I thought my dream was telling me that I had better find a way to "get my feet on the ground."

WRITING ASSIGNMENT 4

Begin keeping your own journal, following the suggestions outlined in this section. In addition to asking yourself the questions that the students who wrote the samples in this section asked themselves, here are some other questions you may want to ask yourself as you write your journal (they all relate to the newspaper and will give your journal more variety):

1. If you were writing to Dear Abby or Ann Landers (columnists to whom many people write for advice), what would you ask? Explain the problem in detail. Now play the part of Abby or Ann and write an answer to yourself. (For example, you may want to ask what you should do about a boyfriend who drinks too much or a girlfriend who drives too fast. Or you may ask for advice on how you should respond to a parent whom you can never please, *no matter what you do.* Or, you may want to ask how in the world you can get a child to eat vegetables: You have tried to set a good example by eating many vegetables yourself; you have tried gentle persuasion; you have sent the child to her room; you have even tried spanking. Nothing works. You are afraid the child will become ill from a vitamin deficiency.)

2. What headline would you most like to see in tomorrow's newspaper? Write an article explaining the headline. (You may choose a headline that might appear in the sports or entertainment section as well as in the front section of the newspaper.)

3. What would you like your obituary (death notice) to say? Write this article, explaining what you had accomplished before reaching the age of ninety-four.

CHAPTER 2

Using Paragraphs to Shape Your Writing

The Paragraph

A paragraph expresses some thought or point that is complete in itself. Paragraphs are usually 50 to 200 words in length, although in newspaper articles they may be shorter.

In your college writing you will sometimes want to write a single-paragraph essay, for example, to answer discussion questions on exams. At other times you will want to write several (or many) paragraphs on one topic. Each paragraph should have an organizing principle. Think of the organizing principle as one idea that you state and then explain by defining or illustrating. It is this idea that determines how you structure your paragraphs.

The writing assignments in Chapter 1 called for one-paragraph compositions of about 150 words in which you were asked to introduce to the rest of the class someone you had interviewed. Had these assignments called for longer compositions, you would have needed more paragraphs. Longer essays are broken into paragraphs because they are much easier to understand that way. The paragraph breaks, marked by indention, help the reader to grasp and assimilate one idea before going on to the next. Paragraphs also help the writer maintain organization.

If, for example, you were writing a letter to an employer asking for a job, you would need to write several paragraphs. You might structure your letter this way:

Paragraph 1: how you heard about the position

Paragraph 2: why you are interested in the position
Paragraph 3: why your education and experience qualify you for the position
Paragraph 4: your request for an interview

Notice how the content of each paragraph is distinct from the contents of the other paragraphs.

Writing a Single-Paragraph Essay

1. Begin with a sentence that points your reader toward the subject matter—the main idea—of the paragraph. (This is usually called the *topic sentence.*) If you were writing a short description of someone, you might begin with one of these topic sentences:

> In her work and in her play, Madeline Foster is the most competitive person I know.
>
> Elena Rodriguez has overcome her great handicap.
>
> Dan Daniels is, above all, a family man.

If you were writing about some insight you gained today, you might begin with one of these topic sentences:

> Today I learned that I do not have to yell at terrible drivers.
>
> Today I learned that some people like me more than I like myself.
>
> Today I discovered that my father is right—this is a "dog-eat-dog" world.

2. Your topic sentence should sound like you; that is, it should be natural, not contrived. Notice how contrived this sounds:

> The characteristic of Madeline Foster that stands out most is her competitiveness, which one can observe both in her work and in her play.

3. Do not announce what you are going to write about. For example, you do not need to say

> In this paragraph I will describe how Dan Daniels is, above all, a family man.

You can simply say

> Dan Daniels is, above all, a family man.

4. Support each point you make in your paragraph with enough information so that your reader will understand—and believe—what you are saying. Readers are convinced by detail and examples, not by general, abstract statements. If you were writing about how Elena Rodriguez had overcome her handicap, you would need to be specific. Instead of just saying that she gets around well in a wheelchair, you would need to say how she gets around and where she goes: for example, how she travels downtown, how she wheels over curbs that do not have curb cuts, and how she crosses busy

streets. Instead of just saying that Elena has a positive attitude toward life, describe the things she does with her life that make others know she has such an outlook.

If you were writing about how you learned today that you do not have to yell at terrible drivers, you would first need to explain your past behavior in some detail. You could describe how you ordinarily shake your fist at drivers who run stop signs, how you holler out the window at truck drivers who follow you too closely, and how on one occasion you stopped the car and got out ready to fight only to find out that the other driver was at least twice your size. You would then need to describe how today was different because in following the advice of a good friend you only smiled when someone backed his car into yours. You would also need to point out how you felt as you smiled. Perhaps you counted to ten five times. Perhaps you squeezed the steering wheel so hard that you sprained your hand. But you did not lose your temper.

5. If you make more than one point in a paragraph, be sure that your reader can smoothly follow from point to point. You can help your reader follow what you are saying by writing effective *transition sentences*. Here are examples of transition sentences:

TOPIC SENTENCE

Elena Rodriguez has overcome her great handicap. (The writer first explains what the handicap is.)

TRANSITION SENTENCE

But Elena has learned to deal with her handicap and can do just about anything she wants to do. (The writer now explains exactly what she has learned to do.)

TOPIC SENTENCE

Today I learned that some people like me more than I like myself.

TRANSITION SENTENCE

Lately I have been very down on myself, feeling pretty depressed. (The writer next explains the nature of the depression.)

TRANSITION SENTENCE

But today I was surprised to find out that some people actually do care about me. (Here the writer introduces the next part of the paragraph.)

TRANSITION SENTENCE

The first surprise came when I received a letter from my father telling me how much he missed me. (The writer briefly explains what his father said.)

TRANSITION SENTENCE

The next surprise came when my math tutor told me that she liked working with me. (The writer explains.)

TRANSITION SENTENCE

But the best surprise came when I went home and found two friends waiting for me, ready to take me out to dinner. (The writer explains.)

If you were asked to write a one-paragraph answer to a question on the unique qualities of American political parties for a political science exam, you might write the following:

TOPIC SENTENCE

American political parties are unique among the world's democracies.

TRANSITION SENTENCE

First, the members of American political parties do not have to pay dues. (The writer then explains how this is different from the situation in political parties in countries like England and France.)

TRANSITION SENTENCE

Second, the members may switch easily from one party to another. (The writer next explains that changing parties is fairly common in the United States but seldom done in other countries.)

TRANSITION SENTENCE

Third, the party members do not have to support the nation's leader. (The writer explains how the members of the United States Congress can vote against the wishes of the president, even when the president belongs to their party.)

If you were asked to write a paragraph on fuel consumption, you might write the following:

TOPIC SENTENCE

Each of us should make an effort to cut down on the use of fuel.

TRANSITION SENTENCE

We can reduce fuel consumption by driving less. (The writer explains.)

TRANSITION SENTENCE

We can *further* reduce our use of fuel by insulating our homes. (The writer explains.)

TRANSITION SENTENCE

Finally, we can cut down on fuel by using less electricity and gas in our homes. (The writer explains.)

In the examples above, *further* and *finally* served as transition words to help the reader follow as the writer moved from point to point.

Other transition words or phrases that help you tag several points within a paragraph include the following:

one way	one example of	the first reason
another way	a second example of	the second reason
still another way	a third example of	the third reason

If you were asked to write a paragraph on your views of the American space program, you might write this:

TOPIC SENTENCE

Despite the problems, we should continue our commitment to the space program. (The writer first discusses the problems of the space program.)

TRANSITION SENTENCE

But on the other hand, the space program promises great benefits to society. (The writer now explains the benefits and shows why they are greater than the disadvantages.)

Other transition words useful in joining just two points include:

however or *nevertheless* (The writer makes a second point that contrasts with the first.)

consequently or *thus* (The writer shows how the first point leads to the second point.)

moreover or *also* (The writer makes a second point that gives more information than the first.)

6. End your paragraph with a clincher statement that lets your reader know you are through, a sentence that brings together all the points you have been making. Think of the ending of the paragraph as the end of a conversation and let your final statement flow naturally from what you have just said. Be brief. Here is how you could conclude the paragraph on the competitive Madeline Foster:

With her extremely competitive nature, Madeline will accomplish a lot in her life, but I wonder how long that life will be.

You could conclude the "dog-eat-dog" paragraph this way:

For a long time I did not want to believe my father, but he is right—this is indeed a "dog-eat-dog" world.

You could conclude the paragraph about the political parties as follows:

Only in America do members of political parties have so much freedom.

And finally, you could conclude the fuel consumption paper this way:

There is a good deal each of us can do to reduce fuel consumption.

WRITING ASSIGNMENT 1

Write a paragraph in which you describe someone you know. Here are some suggestions:

Step One   Ask yourself what main thing comes to your mind when you think of the person. Is he or she timid? Aggressive? Religious? Does the person spend more time with animals than with people? Does the person have very strange eating habits? Exactly what is it that stands out the most when you think of this person? Write one sentence (your topic sentence) in which you describe that characteristic.

Step Two   Make a list of the reasons you chose that particular characteristic. Choose at least two of these reasons to write about.

Step Three   Write your paragraph, beginning with the topic sentence. As you develop your paragraph, be sure to use convincing details. You may want to reread the student samples in Chapter 1 to see how other students used details in their compositions. Also, as you write, pay attention to your transitions. End your paper with a clincher statement that brings your points together.

WRITING ASSIGNMENT 2

Write a paragraph in which you tell about something you learned recently or some insight you gained.

Step One   Make a list of several things you learned recently. Consider such topics as how you learned that life can be tough, not for the weak; how you learned that you are your own worst enemy; how you learned that you can play basketball or do something else that you never thought you could do. Choose one of the items from your list and state in one sentence (your topic sentence) exactly what you learned.

Step Two   Ask yourself what helped you learn this. Jot down notes that summarize what happened.

Step Three   Beginning with your topic sentence, write your paragraph. As you develop your paragraph, use details so that your reader will believe that you did learn something new. Also, as you write, pay attention to your transitions. End your paper with an appropriate clincher statement.

Writing Essays of Two or More Paragraphs

Chapter 4 deals with longer essays. For now, use the suggestions for the single paragraph when you write essays of two or more paragraphs. Note, however, that the first paragraph of an essay should point to what the whole essay is about. The beginning sentences of succeeding paragraphs should both introduce those paragraphs and relate to the other paragraphs in the essay. (In this text, these sentences are called *transition sentences between paragraphs.*)

Here is a student essay that was too long to be written in one paragraph. Notice how the writer used transition sentences to introduce his paragraphs. They are very much like the transitions you have been studying that introduce points within a single paragraph. Notice also how he developed his points with details and how he brought his essay to a close.

SAMPLE

United We Roll

A person in a wheelchair faces many barriers. Some of them can be overcome, but some cannot. I am working on those things we can change.

One barrier we wheelchair users face every day relates to transportation. Although there are a few buses equipped for wheelchairs, they are not dependable. They run only on certain streets in the city, and the hoisting equipment does not always work. Even if a person overcomes the problem of getting from place to place in a wheelchair, that person must then worry about getting up on the sidewalks. I have had the experience of actually turning over, upside down, trying to wheel over a curb on French Street. I was not hurt, but the experience was very embarrassing.

Another barrier to the wheelchair user is the stairs in front of the public buildings downtown. No one should be deprived of entering a public building. Some of these buildings do not even have elevators, and I know of one in which a person has to go up a flight of stairs to get on the elevator. (This shows just how intelligent people can be.) Stairs and wheelchairs do not go together very well.

The worst barrier of all, however, and the meanest one, is the occupational barrier. When wheelchair users go looking for a job, they often get discouraged. Nine times out of ten, employers do not give wheelchair users a chance to prove themselves. I can do a job just as well as the next person, but I, too, have difficulty finding work. Last summer I filled out an application for a job as a tow-truck dispatcher at a tire shop. The shop manager told me that the job had been filled by someone else. Later I found out that the manager was still looking for someone to fill the opening. I went back to the shop and again asked the manager for the job, but again he told me that the position had been filled. People in wheelchairs are a minority, and minority groups are often discriminated against.

These are only a few of the many barriers that wheelchair users face. Some day we will break through these barriers. We need everyone's help, but first we must organize ourselves. Divided we stall; united we roll.

Revising the Paragraph

You should revise all your papers. *Revision* means more than rewriting. The word itself means "re-seeing," that is, seeing your paper afresh. You may find that you need to add, change, or delete several sentences to make your paper work. Or you may find that you must begin all over again. The more you revise, the more you will learn about writing. Revising helps you not just with a particular assignment; it also helps you to learn the craft of writing.

Chapter 4 gives many suggestions for revising longer essays, but for now ask yourself these evaluation questions before you revise a paragraph or a short essay:

1. Did you write a *topic sentence* that points your reader toward the subject matter of the paper? Did you avoid making a statement that announces what the paper is about? (You do not need to say, for example: "In this essay I will write about fuel consumption." Instead, get right to the point: "If we make up our minds to do so, we can reduce our huge fuel consumption considerably.")
2. Did you support your ideas with enough *details* so that your reader will understand—and believe—what you are saying? If you have already used effective details, can you use more?
3. Did you move from point to point smoothly by using *effective transitions*? If the paper is two paragraphs long, did you begin the second paragraph with a smooth transition?
4. Did you end with an appropriate sentence so that your reader will know you are through—a *clincher statement*?
5. Should your paper be one or more paragraphs? A good rule is to divide papers of 200 or more words into two or more paragraphs.

Here is the first draft of a paragraph on an experience a student had on a particular day. An evaluation of the essay and the revised essay follow.

SAMPLE A (FIRST DRAFT)

A New Stereo

This is a paragraph about why I felt a little sad and guilty today when my parents gave me a new stereo. When I receive nice presents, I always think about how much I have and how little my mother had growing up. When my mother was a girl, the other children made fun of her because of her shabby clothes. They laughed at her also because of how she lived. She had never owned a bike, but when she was eleven years old, she got one for Christmas. It wasn't brand new, but to her it seemed like the best thing in the world. After the holidays she returned to school hoping the other girls would notice her bike. A girl named Tammy asked my mother what she was doing with *her* old bike. Tammy said that her father had taken it to a place where poor people buy second-hand things. She was standing in a group of four, and all the girls began to laugh at my mom and the gift she was so proud of. My mom never went to classes that day.

EVALUATION

1. The topic sentence announces what the paragraph is about. Since such an announcement is unnecessary, rewrite the topic sentence.

2. The story about the bike gives excellent details, but can you give more? Can you describe, for example, the shabby clothes? Can you say more about *how* your mother lived?
3. The sentences flow together smoothly. The word *also* helps join the first example of your mother's humiliation with the second. Even though you give three examples of why people laughed at your mother, you do not need to say: *one example, a second example, a third example*. The paragraph is clear and less awkward the way it is written.
4. You need to bring the paper to a close with a clincher statement.
5. When you expand the details, you will probably need two paragraphs. Where would be a good place to begin the second paragraph?

SAMPLE A (REVISED)

A New Stereo

REVISED
TOPIC
SENTENCE

DETAIL

DETAIL

My parents gave me a new stereo today, but instead of feeling happy, I felt a little sad and guilty, as I always do when I receive nice presents. I always think about how much I have and how little my mother had growing up. When my mother was a girl, the other children made fun of her because of her shabby clothes. Her dresses were often rumpled and hung on her like limp pillowcases. She had to take whatever second-hand clothes she could get at the thrift shop. The other children also laughed at her because of her home. She lived with her brother and sister in a one-room shed in the back of their uncle's house until the day she married my father.

NEW
PARAGRAPH
FOR LONGEST
EXAMPLE

CLINCHER
STATEMENT

She had never owned a bike, but when she was eleven years old, she got one for Christmas. It was not brand new, but to her it seemed like the best thing in the world. After the holidays she returned to school hoping the other girls would notice the bike. A girl named Tammy asked her what she was doing with *her* old bike. Tammy said that her father had taken it to a place where poor people buy second-hand things. She was standing in a group of four, and all the girls began to laugh at my mom and the gift she was so proud of. My mom never went to classes that day. I wish I could go back in time and give my mom the stereo she and my dad gave me today.

SAMPLE B (FIRST DRAFT)

Here is the first draft of an interview with Jake of Jake's Wrecker Service. An evaluation of the paragraph and the revised version follow.

Jake

Jake, the owner of Jake's Wrecker Service, says he loves his work and will probably stay in the wrecker business for the rest of his life. But he says that sometimes he is afraid of going out on a call. He never knows what he is going to see. Maybe somebody has been seriously injured or even killed. Once he was called to an accident on an interstate that caused him nightmares for weeks. A car couldn't stop and ran under a semitrailer truck. The truck cut the driver in two. Worst of all, the driver was still alive when Jake got there.

EVALUATION

1. The topic sentence successfully points to the subject of the paragraph. It mentions Jake and how much he likes his work. The problem is that the paragraph does not describe why he likes his work so much.
2. The story about the automobile wreck is good detail, grim as it is. But before you get into what Jake fears about his work, you need to say precisely *why* he likes it.
3. The transitions seem smooth:

   In the second sentence, *but* introduces a contrasting thought.
   In the fifth sentence, the word *once* introduces the example. This is less awkward than saying *for example*.
   In the final sentence, *worst of all* leads the reader to further detail of the wreck.

4. There is no clincher statement.
5. Unless the composition is considerably expanded, one paragraph should be enough.

SAMPLE B (REVISED)

Jake

DETAIL-
EXAMPLE/
TRANSITION
WORDS

Jake, the owner of Jake's Wrecker Service, says he loves his work and will probably stay in the wrecker business for the rest of his life. He likes to help people. When he arrives at the scene of an accident, he tries to calm people down and tells them he will do anything he can for them. For example, he calls relatives when asked and tells people how to talk to the police. Moreover, he likes the pay. But, he says, sometimes he is afraid to go out on a call. He never knows what he is going to see. Maybe somebody has been seriously injured or even killed. Once he was called to an accident on an interstate that caused him nightmares for weeks. A car could not stop and ran under a semitrailer truck. The truck cut the driver in two. Worst of all, the driver was

TRANSITION
WORD
CLINCHER
STATEMENT

still alive when Jake got there. Jake says, however, that such accidents are rare. Most of the time, he just does his job, and he likes what he does.

Paragraph Form

When you write the final version of your paragraph, keep in mind the following points:

1. When writing by hand, indent the first line of each paragraph about one and a half inches from the left; when typing, indent the first line five spaces.
2. Keep your left-hand margin completely straight.
3. Do not divide a word at the end of a line if you can avoid it (your right-

hand margin need not be straight). But, if it is necessary, divide the word between syllables as follows:

> . . . with these qualifi-

cations.

> . . . a government that is central-

ized.

If you are not sure where the syllables begin and end, consult a dictionary.

4. Do not end a line with an opening quotation mark.
5. Do not begin a line with a comma, a semicolon, a dash, or any end punctuation mark.

REVISING ASSIGNMENT 1

Evaluate the following paragraph, writing answers to the questions on page 26. Then revise it, writing a paper of about two hundred words.

Officer Mary Kennedy

When Officer Mary Kennedy is not patrolling the streets for crime, she works as a recruiter for the Greenville Police Force. She was the first female police officer with whom I actually sat down and talked. She spends most of her day on the lookout for crime. Usually, things are quiet, but every now and then she finds herself in dangerous situations. Officer Kennedy seems angry that so many people in our city say such critical things about the police force. She says that on the whole the Greenville police do an excellent job. Besides patrolling the streets, Officer Kennedy tries to recruit young men and women for "The Force," as she calls it.

REVISING ASSIGNMENT 2

Choose one of the assignments you completed for this chapter or for Chapter 1 and revise it: the classroom interview, the outside interview, or one of the journal entries. Evaluate your composition by writing your answers to the questions on page 26. Then revise your paper, being willing to add, change, or delete several sentences or even to start over, if that seems necessary. As you revise, follow the rules for paragraph form. Your revised composition should be about 200 words.

CHAPTER 3

Gathering More Ideas and Information for Writing

"What am I going to write about?" "What can I possibly say in 500, 400, or even 300 words?" These questions are very common among English students. This chapter is an attempt to give you so much to write about that you will begin to worry not about what to say, but rather about what to leave out. You will learn and practice the techniques of brainstorming, free writing, and clustering. You will then practice gathering ideas and information during class discussions and also by listening carefully to conversations.

Your own experiences are the best resources to draw upon for your writing. Your feelings, your ideas, your perceptions of the world, and your memories are all excellent resources. One definition of the word *experience* is "the act of living through an event." You have experienced anything you have seen, heard, touched, smelled, or tasted. The word *awareness*, on the other hand, means "knowing or being conscious of what is happening." In this chapter you will become more conscious of your experiences, ideas, and feelings—in short, more aware and more able to use yourself as a resource for writing. Awareness can be developed. You can choose to become aware—to observe closely, to notice fine details, to remember vivid images and exactly what happened.

Brainstorming

We all have more ideas and know more information than we are willing and able to express. Before writing anything at all, students often start worrying about what others will think of their thoughts, afraid they will sound stupid to the instructor, to other students, or even to themselves. As a result of their worry, many of these students sit back and write only what is "safe"—things that will not be criticized or laughed at. But what you do not say is sometimes the most interesting thing that you are thinking.

The poet W. H. Auden called the internal force that keeps us from expressing ourselves freely "the Watcher at the gate." The Watcher always wants to make sure that we do not say the wrong things, always wants us to say things perfectly, and is thus always ready to close the gate on what we are capable of saying. The Watcher performs a valuable service when it comes time to proofread and revise. But if the Watcher is allowed to close the gate on what we could say too soon, we may find that we have very little to write about. A second-semester freshman wrote the following essay explaining how the Watcher at the gate prevents him from writing what he wants to write.

SAMPLE

The Watcher at the Gate

My Watcher at the gate is a built-in critic who is tougher on the writer than Rex Reed is on movie producers. I often imagine my Watcher as a duplicate of my eleventh-grade English teacher, a slightly balding man in his early thirties, always wearing a doorman's uniform. He sits in a straight-back chair in front of the gate and lets nothing escape his discriminating eyes.

I believe that deep inside me is a writer, as well as a Watcher, who is waiting to surface. This writer is very small compared to my Watcher. The writer strives to be original and let the thoughts flow from my mind to the paper without stopping at the gate. Only at certain times, however, can my Watcher be caught off guard. One of these times is at three o'clock in the morning. While my Watcher is dreaming away, I am left alone, free to express myself. The Watcher can also be caught off guard in the closing moments of a deadline. At this point, the Watcher is frantic about making the deadline, so he becomes less critical and allows thoughts to flow freely.

My Watcher hates to take chances. He would rather block my thoughts and copy the style of another than risk failure. Because of this, most of my writing sounds as if it were taken from the pages of an English text instead of from my own mind. When all is taken into account, however, the Watcher at the gate is necessary in the writing of proper English. He does make me look up words in the dictionary and insists that each of my "sentences" is a sentence. Who knows? He may even have helped me in this essay about him.

Brainstorming is a technique that helps a writer open the gate, allowing all the thoughts—perfect, imperfect, silly, beautiful, or ugly—to flow freely from the brain to the paper, without stopping at the gate. This technique asks simply that the writer make a decision to open the gate and to jot down as many thoughts as possible on paper. Later, once all the thoughts are written down, the writer can pick and choose which ones to use. Here is how one student brainstormed when asked to describe the ideal mate. The student made her first list in the left-hand column and then, once she could think of nothing else, went back to see if any of her items reminded her of other characteristics of the ideal mate. These she wrote in the right-hand column.

—six feet tall, dark hair   ← big dreamy eyes that melt my heart
—good sense of humor   ← likes practical jokes played on him
—sensitive to problems I   ← willing to do anything for me
  bring to him   and others as well
—jogs every morning   ← muscular, lean, great shape
—doesn't mind doing dishes   ← willing to sweep, dust, scrub, etc.
—a little crazy & wild at times   —in short, just like
—has style and grace   Harry

WRITING ASSIGNMENT 1

Step One Imagine that you are being given a brand new car with everything on or in it you could possibly want. As quickly as you can, without stopping to think twice, write down everything you could possibly want on or in this car. *Don't censor your thoughts!* Express them all—creative, silly, brilliant, stupid, beautiful, ugly—everything. If you bog down, see if any items you listed remind you of other items.

_____   _____

_____   _____

_____   _____

_____   _____

_____   _____

_____   _____

_____   _____

Since brainstorming usually works better when done with others because one thought often inspires another, share your most original ideas with the rest of the class. Someone should volunteer to write the ideas on the chalkboard. As you hear the ideas of others, you will think of new ideas for your own list. Write these down as well.

_____   _____

_____   _____

_____   _____

_____   _____

_____   _____

Step Two   Now give some order to your brainstorming ideas. In your mind's eye, place yourself outside the car but close enough to see inside. From this position, make a list of what you see, using one of these two methods:

1. Describe the outside, starting at the front and moving toward the back, and then describe the inside, again moving from front to back.
2. Describe five eye-catching features of the car, starting with the one that demands your attention right away. When you write your paragraph, you should explain the value of each of these features.

Step Three   Reread Chapter 2 on writing paragraphs, and then, using your brainstorming list, write a paragraph of about 150 words on the perfect car. Here is how one student described his ideal car:

SAMPLE

My Cadillac 999 Triple X

Let me introduce you to my new Cadillac 999 Triple X. This car can hit fifty miles per hour in 2.3 seconds. For that reason and many others, it has been my dream car for quite a while. The outside is black with gold racing stripes flowing across both sides of the car. They match the fourteen-carat gold spoke wheels that cost me a considerable amount of money. All of the windows on my car are tinted light blue. But the best part is the inside of the car. The first thing you notice is the tilt steering wheel. The second thing is the cruise control, which is located on the turn signal collar. The dash contains the usual gauges and also an altimeter to let me know how high I am above sea level, an AM-FM cassette stereo, a two-inch built-in television, and four vents for air conditioning. Both seats are upholstered in soft, light gold leather. The floors are covered with a one-inch-thick carpet. But the fanciest thing about my car is the computerized remote control. By punching the right button, I can make virtually anything happen.

QUESTIONS FOR DISCUSSION

1. Does the first sentence effectively introduce the paragraph?
2. The writer first describes the outside of the car. What transition sentence does he use to move the reader to the next part of the paragraph? Is the transition smooth?
3. The writer collected most of the details for his paragraph in a brainstorming session. How successful is he in using the details? Can you get a good picture of the car in your mind's eye?

WRITING ASSIGNMENT 2

Step One   Form an image in your mind of your room at home, your dormitory room, or some other room you have strong feelings about. Make a brainstorming list of all the details of the room you can remember. What furniture is in it? What colors do you see? What little items catch your eye? What about the room is known only to you? What is out of place?

Step Two   Study the student sample below for ideas on how you might use your brainstorming list for writing a paragraph on a room.

SAMPLE

My Room

My room is usually clean, but when I left this morning, it was so messy that my dog wouldn't come in. My pink silk robe and pajamas were thrown across my unmade bed. My slippers were lying there in the middle of the floor, and I hate to admit it, but the floor was covered with big gobs of lint. Off to the right, my bureau top was piled high with caps from lotions, old empty bottles, hair curlers, deodorant, and many purses. And finally, my closet was overflowing with dirty clothes left over from last week and maybe even the week before. When I think of my room, it makes me glad I am not there.

Step Three   Plan your paragraph. Here are some suggestions:

1. In your first sentence, state when you were last in the room and summarize its general appearance in a word or two.
2. Choose at least five things that stand out for you as you think of the room.
3. Decide on some method for ordering your writing. Will you describe the room from left to right, from right to left, or from the most eye-catching features to the least eye-catching ones?

Step Four   Review Chapter 2 on writing paragraphs, and then, using your brainstorming list, write a paragraph of at least one hundred words on the room. Describe the details as precisely as possible. In your last sentence, give the one word or expression that best describes how the room makes you feel.

WRITING ASSIGNMENT 3

In this assignment you will write a paragraph of at least 100 words saying five or more things about an object without ever naming it. Choose something that is not too large, preferably something you can get your arms or perhaps even your hands around. Brainstorm a list of all the characteristics of the object that you can think of. Your description should be so exact that your audience can guess what you are describing. (However, do not make it too obvious. If you are describing your grandmother's teeth that sit by the bed at night, for example, do not describe them as something she bites with.) Study the following two student samples:

SAMPLE A

A Riddle

It is huge, dark brown, inexpensive, and weighs a ton. It is also at times the family joke. Everyone cannot get over the fact that it contains so many different items and is so heavy to carry around. Often my husband has said that if our country were bombed, our family would survive on the contents of my object. It contains headache pills, stomach-ache pills, and back-ache ointments, and if you dig deep enough, you can even find dental floss for those once-a-year emergencies. It contains chewing gum, a date book, a mini-umbrella, a checkbook, and several other things I cannot tell you about because then my object would be a dead giveaway.

SAMPLE B

What Am I?

I am to be admired for what I am. I grow and I die along with the seeds of life. People love me and those who give me. I bring life to dull and shady corners. I bring warmth and smiles to the hearts of my owners. I dress up many major dinners and decorate great celebrations. I am the color of a fair lady's blush and contrast with the blue in the eyes of the one who wears me. I must be seen only, for if I am touched, I will fall to pieces. What am I?

When you finish writing your paragraph, read it to the class to see if they can guess your object.

WRITING ASSIGNMENT 4

Using the brainstorming method to gather ideas and information, write a paragraph of about 150 words describing one of the following topics:

1. The ideal mate
2. Your most unusual teacher
3. The meanest coach you know personally or have heard about
4. The most peaceful place you can think of
5. The most unusual person you saw today
6. A scene from nature, such as a mountaintop, a beach, or a desert

Now, using the suggestions in Chapter 2, revise your paragraph.

Free Writing

Free writing is an excellent warm-up exercise you can use any time you are having trouble thinking of what to write or how to say it. The principle of free writing is quite simple: You just plunge in and *write*. Write whatever comes to mind without stopping to worry about phrasing, grammar, or spelling. However, do try to free write in complete sentences.

Free writing usually works best when you set a time limit—say, five or ten minutes—within which to write. If you are writing at home, you may even want to set the alarm clock. Simply keep writing at a pace that is comfortable for you until the time is up.

If your mind goes blank, write "my mind has gone blank" a few times until something else occurs to you. Do not be surprised if you stray from your original idea before you finish or if you write down words that may be nonsensical to someone else, maybe even to you. The mere act of putting words down on paper is relaxing and often puts you into a better frame of mind for moving on to more focused writing later. Peter Elbow, author of *Writing with Power*, observes, "Writing almost always goes better when you are already started; now [after the free writing] you'll be able to start off already started."

The writing assignments that follow all ask that you make use of free writing.

WRITING ASSIGNMENT 5

Step One   For this assignment, write an essay of several paragraphs (that should total 300 words or more) in which you recall an event from your past that you would like to forget. As an introduction to this assignment, read the following folk tale:

Once upon a time a handsome young prince offended the King and Queen of his land. They condemned him to be beheaded. When he pleaded to be forgiven, they offered him an alternative. They said that if within fourteen days he could find the answer to a very complicated riddle, he could not only have his freedom but their beautiful daughter as well.

The young prince went out and searched everywhere for the answer to the riddle, but by the fourteenth day he still had no answer. Worn out and depressed, he headed back to the castle. Near the gate, however, he met a bent, shriveled-up old hag. She motioned to him with her bony, crooked fingers and whispered in a croaking voice that she could tell him the answer to the riddle, but in return he must promise to grant her request if she ever needed a favor. Desperate, he agreed.

To the surprise and delight of everyone, the young prince returned to the court with the answer to the complicated riddle. True to their word, the King and Queen gave him both his freedom and also their daughter.

Just before the wedding ceremony was about to take place, the old hag appeared and said she was ready to make her request. She pointed her finger at the prince. "I want you to marry me," she said and then cackled. The prince was horrified, but being a noble young man, he did as he had promised and married the old hag.

On their wedding night, though, he was so repulsed by the old hag's grotesque appearance that he lay in bed with his back to her, keeping as far away as possible. But she nudged him with her bony fingers and insisted that he embrace and kiss her.

The prince gathered all his courage, turned to the hag, took her in his arms, and—taking a deep breath—kissed her on the lips. At that very moment, to his sheer amazement, the prince felt her body grow soft and graceful. He saw that the person in his arms was no longer a loathsome old hag, but the beautiful young princess, the woman of his dreams.

Step Two   The storytellers who passed this story down from one generation to another thought that life was like the story of the prince and the loathsome lady. They believed that what seemed ugly and repulsive was often the very thing that would turn into a beautiful source of growth and life if it were embraced.

In your own life, you can surely think of some loathsome ladies, or sad or unpleasant experiences you would like to forget. In this assignment, you will recall one or more of them as you write on the topic "What I Would Most Like to Forget." Perhaps you too will find that your loathsome lady is a fine source of growth.

Brainstorm to create a long list of the things you would most like to forget. Use the following headings:

My saddest experiences   My most embarrassing moments

_____   _____

_____   _____

_____   _____
_____   _____
_____   _____

My greatest goofs (errors or
mistakes)   My greatest disappointments

_____   _____
_____   _____
_____   _____
_____   _____

Now choose one topic for the subject of your essay.

Step Three   First determine when your story begins. If you are telling about the death of a loved one, perhaps you should begin with the moment you first heard the news. If you are writing about the time you showed up for a party in shorts when everyone else was in a dress or in a coat and tie, perhaps you should begin when you first received the invitation and tell how excited you were about going.

Using the technique of free writing, tell your story from beginning to end, writing as fast as you can. Try to write in whole sentences, but do not worry about grammar and punctuation for this draft. If you get sidetracked, do not worry, for you may be uncovering important parts of your story.

Step Four   Read the student samples that follow for ideas about how you might write your finished paper.

SAMPLE A

The Red Boat

Every Thursday in my hometown in Italy, the local marketplace would be filled with gypsy merchants. That day was no exception. They set up in the street between my block and the main market. Their tables were filled with products for every possible need. Everything from shirts to socks to plants to mirrors in leather cases could be seen massively piled on the tops of the temporary counters.

As on every other Thursday, I was pushing and shoving my way through the agitated market crowd. Being only ten years old and short for my age, all I could see from my eye level were elbows swinging, bellies flopping, and hands grabbing. Finally, I managed to see some of the things for sale in the spaces between the arms and the bodies.

All of a sudden my eyes fell upon it. There it was, gleaming in all of its beauty. Its hull was fire-engine red. At the bow hung two white anchors. The control room was also white, but the chimney was fire-engine red. Quickly I tunneled through some legs and worked my way right up to it. Then we touched. Ah, it was love. Gently I caressed it with my hands while I scrutinized it with my eyes. The shocker was tied to a porthole: a price tag that said 2,000 liras.

One month of allowance I would have to save before 2,000 liras would be possible. I had to get an advance. Climbing over boxes and crawling under tables, I got myself out of the mob of people. Then I sprinted home.

Mother was tough, but I was cute. I got the advance. In a flash I was back, but the boat was not. It was gone, sold for a mere 2,000 liras, probably to some tourist for her spoiled kid. My boat was probably headed to France, Spain, England, or even America.

I remember how I sat there, all alone. The street was empty and so was my heart. Mother was calling. I knew I had better go.

QUESTIONS FOR DISCUSSION

1. How does this student give you a good picture of the market?
2. How does he make you know just how disappointed he was that the boat had been sold?
3. What is the organizing principle (the controlling idea) of each paragraph? Should he have joined any of his paragraphs?
4. Do you think the title of this paper is the best one? Why or why not?

SAMPLE B

The Day I Want to Forget

I would most like to forget the day my godfather died. I was seven years old when it happened, and it was my first experience with death. My godfather and I had a very close relationship. He used to joke about how I was his princess and he was my knight in shining armor.

I will never forget September 22, 1970. That morning, I found out he had died. When my mother told me, I began to cry. Questions seemed to pour out of me. I wanted to know why he died and what was going to happen to him. Mother told me that God does not like to see people suffer and that he had suffered enough from his illness. She said he was going to heaven. I then asked her what he was going to do there. She took a long pause, but her answer was brief. She told me he was going to be my guardian angel. As fast as the questions began, they stopped. I stood there looking at my mother with a feeling of emptiness. I did not believe her.

Later, I went to the wake. As we walked into the funeral home, I could see the coffin from a distance. Tears began to fill my eyes, and I started to shake. My mother put her arm around me and led me into the room. Everything from that point on was a blurred vision. The only thing I can remember is my godmother taking me to the coffin. While I was looking at him, memories began to fill my mind: how he used to let me "ride the horsey" on his knee, how he always "dunked" his bread in his milk, how he called me Ba-ba-hop-along-too because I was always running after my sister. I was hoping that he would wake up, but I knew it was not going to happen.

The funeral the next day was the worst part of this whole experience. The sun was hidden by dark clouds, rain came down in sprinkles, and cold breezes passed through me. Everybody was standing in a circle. The priest said a few words, and we bowed our heads to pray. The next thing I saw was my four cousins picking up the coffin and placing it in a big hole in the ground. I knew that this was the end.

By bringing back this experience, I understand a little better the meaning of death. It is becoming clear to me that we are born to serve a purpose. After our purpose is fulfilled, we die. But just because a person dies does not mean that he is forgotten.

QUESTIONS FOR DISCUSSION

1. What did the student learn by recalling her childhood experience?
2. What is the organizing principle (the controlling idea) of each paragraph?
3. Beginning with the second paragraph, look at the first sentence of each paragraph. Is each an effective transition sentence? That is, does it help you move from one paragraph to the other smoothly? Do you think the title of this paper is the best one? Why or why not?

Step Five   Using your free writing as the basis for your paper, write an essay of 300 or more words on your own loathsome-lady experience. Most students need three to six paragraphs for this assignment. The suggestions below are similar to the revision strategies discussed in the next chapter.

1. Be willing to add to, delete, or change any of your free writing.
2. Plan your paper in a logical way. In deciding how to form paragraphs, refer back to the student samples to see how those writers set up their paragraphs. Have an organizing principle for each paragraph.
3. In your first paragraph, move your reader into the story as quickly as possible. You may want to begin your paper with "I would most like to forget . . . ."
4. Use smooth transition sentences to begin your second paragraph and those following.
5. In your last paragraph, tell your readers what you learned by bringing back your experience.
6. Give your paper a title. Keep it short. Use proper capitalization as explained in Chapter 18.1.

WRITING ASSIGNMENT 6

Step One   This assignment calls for your instructor to read aloud the following selection, which is designed to take you on a fantasy trip into a kind of twilight zone. As your instructor reads, close your eyes and listen closely. Clear your desk of everything except paper and pen or pencil so that you will not be disturbed.

It is early morning, just after sunrise. You find yourself alone, relaxed, happy, walking along a winding country road (or a street in the city with lots of trees on it). You are walking in the general direction of the sun, which is still not too bright but is trying to shine through the early morning haze or fog. On either side of you are tall, green trees. Try to get a picture of what they look like. (*Pause*) Dew is still on the grass and the leaves.

You begin to notice everything around you, becoming aware of the slightly damp morning breeze, the feel of your feet as you walk along, the birds' singing, the fresh smells, the sun's warmth on your face. (*Pause*)

As you walk along, you begin to have a sense that something rare and special is going to happen. (*Pause*) Up ahead to the right of the road, you see a large clearing, an open field. As you walk closer, you see at the far end of the clearing, a living creature. Moving closer still, you see that the living creature is a small child, about six years old, quietly playing in its own private world.

You are irresistibly drawn to this child. (*Pause*) There is something familiar. You are tuned in to the child's movements and expressions. You recognize the clothing the child is wearing. The child is playing the way you used to play, smiling the way you used to smile. Try to get a picture of the child at play. (*Pause*) Suddenly, you realize that the child in the clearing is you! You are flooded with memories from age six: how large everything seemed, how much you liked and cared for certain things, what you wore, the games you played.

Take yourself back to age six. Become aware of yourself at that age. (*Pause*) Now let yourself and the child have a conversation. Keep your eyes closed for another two or three minutes. (*Pause*) In a moment I will ask you to open your eyes and to write as fast as you can about what happened from the time you first found yourself alone on the road until you met yourself at age six. When you write, include the following information:

What you saw, heard, and felt along the road

What you saw as you looked at the child: the clothes, the facial expressions, the movements

What you saw the child doing

What you and the child said to each other

How you felt encountering yourself at age six

Now slowly open your eyes and write as fast as you can.

Step Two   Read your free writing aloud in a small group (but feel free to pass over any part of your paper that seems too personal). Address the following questions as you hear each of the other papers read:

1. What do you like best about the paper?
2. What details stand out the most?
3. What descriptions could be made more precise? How?
4. What else would you like to know about the child?

Step Three   Read the following student samples for ideas on how you might use your free writing to write a more finished paper.

SAMPLE A

The Road of My Life

I am walking down the road of my life. Its sights are vivid as my mind wanders aimlessly. It is quite cold. A light mist brings on the appearance of another world. As I walk along the edge of the road, the crunch of the pebbles beneath my feet is barely audible. A slight breeze whispers through the tall pines, causing the needles and the tall grass beneath the trees to sway in rhythmic motion. The sun is a brilliant orange as it clears the horizon. I know the cool moisture in the air will soon disappear. The birds sing in unison but with different calls, letting me know that they are seeking breakfast. The road is like a tunnel of serenity because all is so peaceful here. Because of the upgrade of the road, I am taking my time, breathing deeply of this dream. The fragrance of the pines and the green grass give off an aroma unmatched by any man-made perfume.

As I walk further along the road, I notice a clearing to the right. As I near it, I see a little boy standing beside the road as if he is waiting for someone, but he does not look my way. I am only a short distance from the boy now, and I can see that the clearing is paved with concrete. The little boy is wearing old clothes, like those I used to wear when I was a child, mostly hand-me-downs. Then he turns around with a blank expression on his face, and suddenly it hits me: He looks exactly like me in every detail. He reaches out his hand in a begging gesture. Because my senses are trained on him, I have not noticed what is to my right. It is a ghetto. I keep walking fast.

QUESTIONS FOR DISCUSSION

1. What are three pictures or details that stand out for you in this essay?
2. What was the six-year-old trying to say when he held out his hand in a begging gesture? What unnamed feeling was being expressed?
3. Why did the author keep walking fast? What feeling was being expressed?
4. What more would you like to know about either the boy or the adult?
5. What tense (present time or past) did the author use for his story? Why did he choose that tense?

SAMPLE B

The Child in Me

As I was walking along a country road, I looked up and saw lonely birds, flying high, flapping their wings, against an early morning pink sky that looked like soft and sweet cotton candy. I continued my walk down the road until out of nowhere a little girl appeared.

The little girl had two long pigtails with blue barrettes at the end of each. She had glowing white teeth, except for the one that was missing in the front. She was skinny and she wore a pair of blue shorts and a white blouse. I smiled at the little girl, asking her her name. She answered, "You should know my name." She said I should follow her, and she would help me find out her name. She then took my hand and led me to a playground where I used to play. There were lots of kids playing games: jump rope, jacks, dolls, and hopscotch. The little girl joined the other children as I sat on the bench. I watched the child closely and suddenly saw her fall. When I ran over to help, she began to cry and the other kids called out, "Crybaby, crybaby, ha, ha, ha." At that moment, I realized that the child was me, the one who cried over everything and was teased for it. As I picked her up and carried her over to the bench, she said with a sad face, "Now you know who I am." I looked at her and smiled. We both gave each other a big hug and laughed. The little girl said that when we met again, she hoped I would not forget who she was.

I realize now that the nice things in life and the bad things will always be a part of my thoughts and dreams. I knew when I saw the child that I could never be alone no matter what I was doing, no matter where I was. She would always be with me. I will always know her name.

Step Four   Using your free writing, write a two- or three-paragraph paper of 200 to 300 words. Make use of the small group discussion. In the next chapter you will learn more complete techniques for revising your papers. But for now here are some suggestions:

1. Be ready to add to, delete, or change any of your free writing.
2. Plan your paper in a logical way, letting your paragraphs express complete thoughts. In the first paragraph, you may want to describe your experience on the road before meeting the child. In the second, you may want to describe your encounter with the child. In the last sentence of the second paragraph (or in a short third paragraph), you may want to tell your readers how you felt about the experience.
3. Make sure you move from paragraph to paragraph with smooth transitions. Notice how the students in the samples above began their second and third paragraphs.
4. There are two mechanical errors you should especially try to avoid in this assignment: the run-on sentence and confusion of tense. When you are writing in the past tense, as when you are telling a story, it is very easy to

join sentences incorrectly because they are often so closely related in content. Study the rules for preventing run-on sentences in Chapter 12.2. Also, when you are writing in the past tense, make sure you end your regular verbs with *d* or *ed* and use the correct verb form for irregular verbs. For help in this area, study Chapter 14.

5. Give your paper a title. See Chapter 18.1 for rules on the capitalization of titles.

WRITING ASSIGNMENT 7

Begin your writing with one of the following statements, and then let your imagination take you wherever it wants to go. Use the free writing technique.

1. I found myself at age twenty on the outskirts of Chicago with no money in my pockets and no relatives or friends to turn to. It was getting dark, and I was chilly in the early fall air. I was hungry and I did not know what to do, but I knew I had to do something fast, so I . . . .

2. I have always believed that somewhere in the world there lives the perfect mate for me. I was at a small party the other night, and when I happened to look up toward the door, I saw him [or her] standing there alone. I knew, as I have never known anything so definitely before, that this was the right person for me. I gathered my courage and I . . . .

3. I was walking along the beach last summer and happened to see an old bottle with barnacles growing all over it. As I approached, I saw a piece of paper—a letter—inside the bottle. I had to break off the end of the bottle to get to the letter, and then I read these words: . . . .

4. I am a sick man. . . . I am a spiteful man. I am an unpleasant man. I think my liver is diseased. However, I don't know beans about my disease, and I am not sure what is bothering me. I don't treat it and never have. Yesterday on the way home from work I fell down on the sidewalk and a little boy offered to help me up and . . . . (These lines, except for the last sentence, are the first words of *Notes from Underground* by Fyodor Dostoyevsky. Feel free to substitute "woman" for "man.")

Now rewrite your paper using the suggestions listed above.

Clustering

Several years ago, writing teacher Gabrielle Rico devised a method to help her students get back in touch with the creative, inventive part of themselves. She calls her method "clustering."

In the explanation below Rico gives a name to that part of ourselves that is always trying to be logical and correct, that part of our mind that is always trying to put things in the right order. She calls this the "Sign mind." She also believes that we have a creative part of ourselves that is longing to express our well-hidden imagination and artistic ability. She calls this the "Design mind." She believes this side of us is playful and curious as well as creative and artistic. Here is how Rico summarizes her technique of clustering in *Writing the Natural Way:*

> To create a cluster, you begin with a nucleus word circled [see page 47], on a fresh page. Now you simply let go and begin to flow with any current of connections that come into your head. Write these down rapidly, each in its own circle, radiating outward from the center in any direction they want to go. Connect each new word or phrase with a line to the preceding circle. When something new and different strikes you, begin again at the central nucleus and radiate outward until those associations are exhausted.
>
> As you cluster, you may experience a sense of randomness or, if you are somewhat skeptical, an uneasy sense that it isn't leading anywhere. That is your logical Sign mind wanting to get into the act to let you know how foolish you are being by not setting thoughts down in logical sequences. Trust this natural process, though. We all cluster mentally throughout our lives without knowing it; we have simply never made these clusterings visible on paper.
>
> Since you are not responsible for any particular order of ideas or any special information, your initial anxiety will soon disappear, and in its place will be a certain playfulness. Continue to cluster, drawing lines and even arrows to associations that seem to go together, but don't dwell on what goes where. Let each association find its own place. If you momentarily run out of associations, doodle a bit by filling in arrows or making lines darker. This relaxed receptivity to ideas usually generates another spurt of associations until at some point you experience a sudden sense of what you are going to write about. At that point, simply stop clustering and begin writing. It's as easy as that.
>
> There is no right or wrong way to cluster. It is your Design mind's shorthand and it knows where it is headed, even if you don't. Trust it. It has a wisdom of its own, shaping ends you can't really evaluate yet. This wisdom has nothing to do with logic; should you try to apply logic to what you have just clustered, this sense of knowing where you're headed will be destroyed. Then you simply begin to write. The words will come; the writing takes over and writes itself.

Here is how two students used the technique of clustering, the first starting with the nucleus word *summer,* the second starting with the nucleus word *fear.* Both went on to write paragraphs saying what the words meant to them. (The paragraphs follow.)

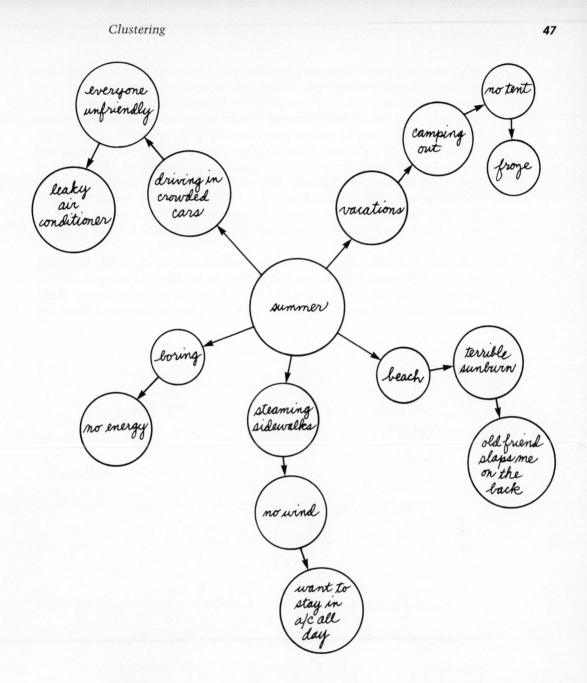

SAMPLE A

Summer

Each spring I look forward to summer vacation. School will be out. I will have a break from work, everyone will be in good humor, thinking of fun things to do. Then summer comes; there is one disaster after another. I go on a camping trip in the mountains and the wind blows my tent down; then it begins to rain. My flashlight does not work. There is nowhere to go, I cannot even see my hand in front of my face, and I shiver for five hours. I go to the beach and get so sunburned that I can hardly put a shirt on over my back. When I see my long-lost friend, he slaps me on the shoulders so hard that I think I am going to die. My family goes on a trip across the country in our subcompact car. Everyone in the car is cramped and unfriendly. The air conditioner begins to leak inside the car and the water drips onto our sandwiches. My dad says we have to eat the sandwiches anyway. We rebel. The baby starts crying. Then the air conditioner quits working altogether. It is so hot that steam rises from the highway. Give me school any time, let me work on a garbage truck if it is cool, just please, no more summer vacations. Next year I would like to move right from spring to fall.

In the clustering sample above, the writer began by recording thoughts, feelings, experiences, and images that came to his mind in connection with the nucleus word, *summer*. Whenever one string of associations "dead-ended"—that is, when he could not think of any more to write along one

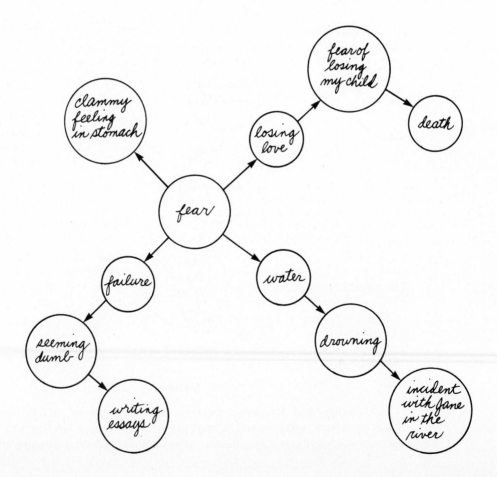

clustering path—he simply returned to the nucleus word and began in a new direction. Before beginning the clustering, he thought he would be writing about the pleasures of summer, but to his surprise each path pointed him toward miserable experiences. In his paragraph, he used most but not all of his clustering.

In the second clustering sample, the writer began with the word *fear*, as shown by the diagram on the facing page.

SAMPLE B

Fear

To me, being afraid is associated with loss—loss of love, loss of pride, loss of life. When I was a child, my sister Jane and I nearly drowned in the Calcasieu River. While we were playing a game we called "dragons," Jane was pulled into the undertow and reached out to me, the clumsy nonswimmer. I tried to help her and soon we were both fighting for air, for life, wondering if this was what it would be like to die. My greatest fear is of dying.

This writer focused most of her paragraph on one of the paths in the cluster, the near-drowning incident. In the first sentence of her paragraph, however, she generalized about fear, mentioning the different things fear meant to her. For this she used three of her four clustering paths.

WRITING ASSIGNMENT 8

Write a paragraph describing a "significant other"—someone you know well, such as a parent or your best friend. Limit your writing to about fifteen minutes. Then try clustering. Write the peson's name, circled, in the middle of a clean sheet of paper. Next, write down all the thoughts and associations about the person that come to mind. Do not censor any thoughts—just keep jotting them down, circling them, and connecting the related ideas with arrows. When you exhaust one set of possibilities, return to the nucleus word and begin again with a new string of associations. When you have clustered several connected thoughts, write a paragraph based on your cluster. (The whole process, including clustering, should take no longer than the fifteen minutes you set aside for the first paragraph.) Now compare your two descriptions. Did the clustering lead to any insights or important observations that were missing in the first paragraph?

Using the instruction in Chapter 2, revise your paragraph, using what Rico calls your Sign mind.

WRITING ASSIGNMENT 9

Choose one of the following words or phrases as your nucleus and use the suggestions for clustering to record whatever comes to your mind in association with the nucleus. When you finish, write a paragraph saying what the word or phrase means to you. (The topics are intentionally broad and abstract so that you will have plenty of freedom as you give your paper a focus and make it concrete.)

Summer, fall, winter, or spring
Fear
Happiness
Romantic love

Remember to let your creative side take over as you cluster. The idea is to play with your thoughts and writing possibilities.

Using the instructions in Chapter 2, revise your paragraph, using what Rico calls your Sign mind.

Intentional Discussions

Many students find that talking about a topic with classmates or friends is the best way to develop ideas for writing. Such discussions can also stimulate brainstorming, free writing, and clustering.

WRITING ASSIGNMENT 10

In this assignment you will be asked to discuss two poems that were chosen to bring out strong feelings in the reader. You will then be asked to write your response to one of the poems. If discussions help you to gather ideas and information for writing, talk over your writing topics with other people whenever you can.

As you write the various essays assigned in this text, it is important to reflect on how you feel about the subject matter and at times to explain your feelings to your readers. Responding to the following poems should be a good way to begin to practice these techniques. But notice, as you read the poems, that the writers' feelings are conveyed without mentioning such "feeling" words as *hate, happiness,* or *sadness.*

James Dickey, a well known poet, has written this about poetry: "The first thing to understand about poetry is that it comes to you from outside you, in books or in words, but that for it to live, something from within you must come to it and meet it and complete it. Your response with your own mind and body and memory and emotions gives the poem its ability to work its magic; if you give to it, it will give to you, and give plenty."

Step One . Read the following poems carefully and name the feeling or feelings each poem evokes in you. *Look up any words you do not understand.*

The first poem was written by an anonymous high school student. You will notice that in it and the poem that follows standard grammatical rules are sometimes broken. Poets claim the right to use nonstandard constructions, such as fragments, in their writing.

He Always Wanted to Explain Things

He always wanted to explain things.
But no one cared.
So he drew.
Sometimes he would draw and it wasn't anything.

He wanted to carve it in stone or write it in the sky.
He would lie out in the grass and look up in the sky.
And it would be only him and the sky and the things inside him that
   needed saying.
And it was after that he drew the picture.
It was a beautiful picture.
He kept it under his pillow and would let no one see it.
And he would look at it every night and think about it.

And when it was dark, and his eyes were closed he could still see it.
And it was all of him.
And he loved it.
When he started school he brought it with him.
Not to show to anyone, but just to have it with him like a friend.

It was funny about school.
He sat in a square, brown desk.
Like all the other squre, brown desks.
And he thought it should be red.
And his room was a square, brown room.
Like all the other rooms.
And it was tight and close.
And stiff.
He hated to hold the pencil and chalk.
With his arm stiff and his feet flat on the floor.
Stiff.
With the teacher watching and watching.
The teacher came and spoke to him.
She told him to wear a tie like all the other boys.
He said he didn't like them.
And she said it didn't matter!

After that they drew.
And he drew all yellow and it was the way he felt about morning.

And it was beautiful.
The teacher came and smiled at him.
"What is this?" she said, "Why don't you draw something like Ken's
    drawing? Isn't it beautiful?"
After that his mother bought him a tie.
And he always drew airplanes and rocket ships like everyone else.
And he threw the old picture away.

And then he lay alone looking at the sky.
It was big and blue and all of everything.
But he wasn't any more.
He was square inside.
And brown.
And his hands were stiff.
And he was like everyone else.

As you read the next poem, ask yourself if it is primarily about blacks
rising out of oppression. Or could it be about any minority group or any
individual person? On the other hand, could it be mostly about women? Is it
human nature to begrudge other people their victories?

Still I Rise

You may write me down in history
With your bitter, twisted lies,
You may trod me in the very dirt
But still, like dust, I'll rise.

Does my sassiness upset you?
Why are you beset with gloom?
'Cause I walk like I've got oil wells
Pumping in my living room.

Just like moons and like suns,
With the certainty of tides,
Just like hopes springing high,
Still I'll rise.

Did you want to see me broken?
Bowed head and lowered eyes?
Shoulders falling down like teardrops,
Weakened by my soulful cries.

Does my haughtiness offend you?
Don't you take it awful hard
'Cause I laugh like I've got gold mines
Diggin' in my own back yard.

You may shoot me with your words,
You may cut me with your eyes,
You may kill me with your hatefulness,
But still, like air, I'll rise.

Does my sexiness upset you?
Does it come as a surprise
That I dance like I've got diamonds
At the meeting of my thighs?

Out of the huts of history's shame
I rise
Up from a past that's rooted in pain
I rise
I'm a black ocean, leaping and wide,
Welling and swelling I bear in the tide.

Leaving behind nights of terror and fear
I rise
Into a daybreak that's wondrously clear
I rise

Bringing the gifts that my ancestors gave,
I am the dream and the hope of the slave.
I rise
I rise
I rise.

–Maya Angelou

Step Two In small groups, discuss both of the poems. The following suggestions may be helpful.

1. Reread the poem you are discussing. Perhaps someone will agree to read it aloud.
2. Discuss what the author is trying to say to you in the poem. For the time being, withhold your own response to the poem. Ask the following questions about the poem:

   What lines best capture the meaning of the poem?
   What is the message of the poem?
   What feeling does the poet convey? Anger? Sadness? Hate? Happiness? Arrogance? Hopelessness?
3. Discuss your reactions to the poem:

   What colors does the poem remind you of?
   What pieces of music?
   What would you like to say back to the author of the poem, or to any of the people in the poem?
   What one word best describes how you felt as you read it?

4. Try to relate the poem to your own life. Explain this relationship to the group.

What situation does the poem remind you of? Why?
Can you find yourself in the poem? Explain.
Does the poem remind you of someone you know?

Step Three   Write a two-paragraph paper on one of the poems, using the following questions to develop organizing principles for each paragraph. Make your transition from the first paragraph to the second as smooth as possible.

1. *Paragraph one:* What is the author trying to say in the poem? How does he or she say it? What images or pictures does the poet want you to see? What feeling is conveyed? What line says it best?
2. *Paragraph two:* What would you like to say to the author or any of the people in the poem? Why? How does the poem make you feel? Does the poem relate to your own experiences or the experiences of someone you know? Explain.

Listening to Others

Another way to gather ideas and information for your writing is by listening closely to others as they speak and by recording what they say. When you let people speak for themselves, you make your writing exact, specific, and interesting—always important goals in writing.

Mark Twain, the great American writer, was a master at recording dialogue, or what people say. Listen to one of his characters, Huckleberry Finn, describe his ne'er-do-well father, whom he had not seen in some time:

> He was most fifty, and he looked it. His hair was long and tangled and greasy, and hung down, and you could see his eyes shining through like he was behind vines. It was all black, no gray; so was his long mixed-up whiskers. There warn't no color in his face, where his face showed; it was white; not like another man's white, but a white to make a body sick, a white to make a body's flesh crawl—a tree-toad white, a fish-belly white. As for his clothes— just rags, that was all. He had one ankle resting on t'other knee; the boot on that foot was busted, and two of his toes stuck through, and he worked them now and then. His hat was laying on the floor—an old black slouch with the top caved in, like a lid.

Now listen to Huck's father speak to him, complaining about Huck's going to school:

> "Well, I'll learn her [the widow who had been taking care of Huck] how to meddle. And looky here—you drop that school, you hear? I'll learn people to bring up a boy to put on airs over his own father and let on to be better'n what *he* is. You lemme catch you fooling around that school again, you hear? Your

mother couldn't read, and she couldn't write, nuther, before she died. None of the family couldn't before *they* died. I can't; and here you're a-swelling yourself up like this. I ain't the man to stand it—you hear? Say, lemme hear you read."

In your college writing, you may never have to record a whole conversation for an essay. The following writing assignments ask you to do just that, however, so that you will gain skill in recording what people say. From time to time you will want to quote the people you write about. Also, by completing one or more of these assignments, you will learn to apply the tricky mechanical rules for recording dialogue.

WRITING ASSIGNMENT 11

Step One   Two people from the class need to volunteer for each of the following skits. After each skit has been performed, write down as much of the conversation as you can recall, as quickly as you can.

SITUATION 1

It is late afternoon. Player A has just finished the last class of the day and is ready to take the bus home, but discovers that he (or she) has no money. To make matters worse, a dark rain cloud is forming overhead. Everyone seems to have gone home except a student of the opposite sex (Player B), whom Player A does not know. Player A and Player B have a two- or three-minute conversation in which Player A asks Player B for the bus fare.

SITUATION 2

Same situation, except now Player B is an old friend of Player A.

Step Two   Several people should read aloud what they have written. Did they record the exact words that were spoken or did they substitute their own words? What did they leave out? Using information provided by other students, fill in any significant part of the conversations that you missed.

Step Three   Rewrite one of the above conversations, putting it in the correct form. Read the following sample conversation from a student paper, and study the relevant mechanical rules for dialogue that are presented:

SAMPLE

The Conversation

Speaker A: "Hey, how are you doin'?"
Speaker B: "Well, thank you."
"I'm glad. Hey, I have a little problem. You see, I spent all my money for lunch. And I

forgot to save any So could you lend me some money for the bus fare? I'll pay you back just as soon as I can."

"I'm afraid I'm not in the habit of lending money out."

"Hey, come on! I'll pay you back. Say, you're in Dr. Griffin's English class, right?" . . .

RULES FOR WRITING DIALOGUE

1. Use a colon (:) after the names of the speakers.
2. Use quotation marks at the beginning and end of each speaker's statements, but not after each sentence.
3. Always place the periods inside of the quotation marks.
4. If you quote an entire sentence that asks a question, place the question mark inside of the quotation marks. "How are you doing?"
5. If you drop a letter to make a word sound the way it was pronounced, use an apostrophe to show the omission. "How are you doin'?"
6. If there are only two people talking and it is clear which one is speaking, drop the names before each speech after you have introduced each speaker.
7. Begin a new paragraph each time the speaker shifts.

Step Four Now write the above conversation as part of a story, but first read the student sample below and study the mechanical rules.

SAMPLE

I Heard a Conversation

Player A walked up to Player B, a total stranger, outside of the Language Arts hall and said, "Hey, how are you doin'?"

"Well, thank you," Player B responded as she looked up from her book.

"I'm glad," Player A continued, looking away. "Hey, I have a little problem. You see, I spent all my money for lunch. And I forgot to save any. So could you lend me some money for the bus fare? I'll pay you just as soon as I can."

But Player B was not interested. "I'm afraid I'm not in the habit of lending money out," she said as she began to read her book again.

Player A was not about to give up, however. "Hey," he said, "come on! I'll pay you back. Say, you're in Dr. Griffin's English class, right?" . . .

RULES FOR WRITING DIALOGUE

1. Use speaker tags like those used above: *Player A . . . said, Player B responded, Player A continued.*
2. Use a comma (or commas) with each speaker tag:

   After: *Player A . . . said,* "Hey, how you doin'?"
   Before: "Well, thank you," *Player B responded.* . . .
   After and before: "Hey," *he said,* "come on!"

3. Begin a direct quotation with a capital letter: She said, *"Please don't bother me anymore."*
4. Begin a new paragraph each time the speaker shifts.

See Chapter 18.7 for more rules on the use of quotation marks.

WRITING ASSIGNMENT 12

Step One Position yourself near two or more people who appear to be having an interesting conversation: in the campus coffee shop, in the halls, outside the library, on the bus going home, or somewhere in your neighborhood. Write down as much of the conversation as you can. Be sure to use the speakers' words and not your own. If you object to listening to such a conversation, record a recent conversation in which you participated, or record a conversation from a radio or television talk show.

Step Two Study the rules for recording dialogue in Writing Assignment 11 and read this student sample for ideas:

SAMPLE

Jailbird

There were cops coming from every direction, shouting for us to put our hands against the wall. There was screaming, pushing, and shoving. About twenty of us were taken to Central Lockup.

When we arrived, we were allowed one phone call. Bernice and Sylvia made their calls first, and their parents agreed to come get them right away. I then called home. Of all the people in the house, my mother had to answer the phone. The conversation went something like this:

"Hello, Mamma," I said.

"Bernetta, what happened?" she asked.

"I'm in Central Lockup."

"Oh, my God! My child is in jail!"

"Come and get me out before it's too late and I have to spend the night."

"Bernetta, how did you get arrested?"

"The Blue Light got raided."

"You told me you were going to a party."

"I lied."

"Well, since you lied to me, Honey, I'm going to lie to you and say I'm coming to get you out."

"But Ma!"

The phone clicked off, and I thought the world was coming to an end.

The next morning my father picked me up and took me home. There was no conversation all the way home. When I opened the door, my mother was standing there, waiting.

"You are the first one to bring the family name down," she said.

My brothers and sisters were also waiting for me.

"What kind of birds don't fly?" my brothers asked.

"Jailbirds," my sisters answered.

Step Three   Write a paper of 200 to 300 words reporting your conversation. Begin with an introductory paragraph or two explaining the occasion for the conversation. Study the rules for recording dialogue in Writing Assignment 11 and observe how they are used in the student samples in both Writing Assignments 11 and 12. See Chapter 18.7 for more rules on how to use quotation marks.

Step Four   Read your writing in a small group. After each person has read his or her paper, answer the following questions:

1. Did the dialogue really sound like people talking? Explain.
2. What more would you like to know about the people talking or the conversation itself?

Exchange your paper with someone else to check for proper paragraphing, punctuation, and capitalization. Then, revise it.

CHAPTER 4

Six Steps to Writing Well

In the writing assignments in Chapters 1 through 3, you were learning a writing method. You gathered ideas and information to use as raw material for your writing, you reflected on your ideas as you read student samples, you sometimes made a plan for your writing, and you may have read some of your writing to the class or to a small group and heard their responses. But in this chapter you will concentrate on the writing method itself, which is made up of six steps and should help you in all your college writing.

First you will learn how the method works and practice using it in two writing assignments. Then you will study suggestions for writing transitions between paragraphs, you will practice writing purpose (or thesis) statements, and you will study suggestions for writing introductions, conclusions, and titles. Finally, you will study a method for revising and editing essays.

Instead of restricting your writing style, the suggestions on how to organize and develop your writing should give you an opportunity to express yourself more freely and clearly. Once you fully understand the structure of an essay, you can then concentrate on other elements, such as using the most precise word, writing a strong sentence, making a careful observation, developing a logical argument, and letting your imagination flow into your writing.

The Steps Described

Suppose a campus organization that you belong to—call it SOS (Students Organized for Service)—is planning an event to raise money for world hunger relief. The president of SOS might ask the members to make as many suggestions as they possibly can about what kind of event they would like to sponsor, while a recording secretary writes down the suggestions.

When the list is complete, the president asks the recording secretary to read the list aloud. The president then asks the members, "What do you think?"

As you analyze the suggestions, you realize that some are better than others. Some are probably duplicates. Perhaps someone has suggested a softball game between faculty and students as a way to raise money. Perhaps someone else has suggested a fair with a raffle for a television set. But it seems that most of the members of SOS want to sponsor a rock concert to raise the money.

Now the members begin to argue over what rock group they should engage and what kind of food and drink they should sell. Your president interrupts and says, "Wait a minute. You're jumping ahead. Just what is the purpose of the concert? What exactly do you want to achieve?" There may be several different responses to this question, until someone says the answer that is just right, a perfect way to describe what the group wants, such as, "While offering the maximum amount of entertainment, we hope to raise at least one thousand dollars for hunger relief." The next step is for SOS to plan the details of the concert: when and where it will be held, who will play, what food and drink will be sold, and so forth. You also must decide what each member will do in helping to stage the concert.

On the scheduled day at the scheduled place, your group has its rock concert, and at the next meeting, when all the money has been counted and all the expenses paid, your president asks, "Well, how do you think it went? Was the concert what you had hoped it would be? Did we raise enough money? Was everyone satisfied with the entertainment? If we do this again next year, what should we do differently?"

The writing method used throughout this text is very similar to the procedure the SOS group used. There are six steps to this method:

Step One: Gather Ideas and Information
Step Two: Analyze the Ideas and the Information
Step Three: State Your Purpose
Step Four: Make Your Plan
Step Five: Write
Step Six: Evaluate, Revise, and Edit

Step One: Gather Ideas and Information

When an instructor gives you a general topic for a writing assignment, the first thing you should do is collect as many ideas and as much information about it as you can. This will serve as your raw material. Chapter 3 explains three ways to gather ideas and information—brainstorming, free writing, clustering—and gives you practice in gathering ideas and information in class discussion and in exercises that require listening to conversations. After you have collected your ideas and information you should make a long list of what you have gathered. This step is like the first step the student organization took when it planned the fund-raising event. You will be like the recorder, writing as many ideas as you can think of on a sheet of paper.

Step Two: Analyze the Ideas and the Information

After you have gathered your ideas and information on the subject, sit back and ask yourself what items on the list stand out. This step is like the president asking the organization, after the recording secretary read the list of suggestions, "What do you think?" Here you begin to narrow down the ideas and information and to make your general topic more specific. What are the most important things on the list? What items could be omitted? Which are closely related? How might you order the material?

Step Three: State Your Purpose

After analyzing the ideas and information, you need to say *in one sentence* what you hope to prove in your paper, that is, the main idea you want to get across. The purpose (or thesis) statement is a statement of what you hope to achieve in your paper. The purpose statement for the fund-raiser was "While offering the maximum amount of entertainment, we hope to raise at least one thousand dollars for hunger relief." Ordinarily you should include the purpose or thesis statement in your first paragraph. Think of your preparation and writing as sand running through an hourglass, as illustrated below:

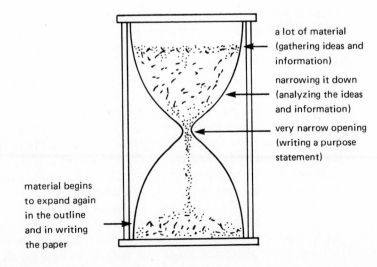

a lot of material
(gathering ideas and
information)

narrowing it down
(analyzing the ideas
and information)

very narrow opening
(writing a purpose
statement)

material begins
to expand again
in the outline
and in writing
the paper

Step Four: Make Your Plan

Just as the rock concert needed considerable planning, so will your paper. You have gathered and analyzed the ideas and information and stated your purpose; now you must figure out the best way to accomplish your purpose: to prove your point. In this step you will need to make a plan that helps you achieve this goal. Your plan should contain not just your general points but also a list of the details and examples that you will use in supporting your points. The list you made in Step One should be a rich source for your details and examples. While it is important to have a carefully made outline, you should be willing to change it as you write if you see that you can best accomplish your purpose in some other way. Plans for papers, like plans for activities, sometimes do and should change.

Step Five: Write

Look at your purpose statement—perhaps you will want to write it at the beginning of your first paragraph—look at your plan, and begin to write. New thoughts will come to you as you write, some of which you will certainly want to use. If you get stuck, make use of the free writing technique described in Chapter 3. Write "I am stuck" a few times until something else occurs to you.

Step Six: Evaluate, Revise, and Edit

At the meeting of the organization following the rock concert, the president asked for an evaluation: "Was the concert what you had hoped it would be? Did we raise enough money? Was everyone satisfied with the entertainment?" When you finish your paper, evaluate it. Were you able to carry out your purpose? Did each paragraph have an organizing principle? Did you use smooth transitions from paragraph to paragraph? Did you give enough examples and details to support the points you made? Did you bring the paper to a clear ending?

Evaluation is the first part of revision. As pointed out in Chapter 2, revision means a lot more than simply rewriting a paper. When you revise, you look at your paper afresh and ask yourself whether you should make major changes. You may have to add, delete, or change several sentences. You may have to reorganize your paper, or you may have to start over. Once you have evaluated your paper and decided on the changes, rewrite it from beginning to end incorporating the changes. As you rewrite, you will probably discover that you will want to make still other changes. (Revision is explained more fully in the last section of this chapter.)

Part of the sixth step is to proofread and edit your essay to correct as many mechanical errors as possible. Some students prefer to edit during revision, some afterward. Since it is difficult to look for all possible errors in just one or two readings, plan to proofread your paper at least three times: twice to catch any particular errors you are apt to make (such as sentence, verb, or pronoun errors), and once to catch any other errors.

Many students complain that they cannot identify errors in their essays because the writing is so familiar, especially if they have read a paper several times. If you have this problem, try the following for your last reading: Proofread and edit your paper a sentence at a time, starting with the last sentence and moving backward to the first sentence. Working this way will force you to look at each sentence separately.

A student wrote this paper while carefully following the six steps of the writing method. The questions at the end are designed to help you understand how to use the writing method.

SAMPLE
My Home in the Country

When I think of the sights, sounds, and smells of our place in the country, it makes me wish I were there right now. You see, I have been living in the high-rise student dormitory for the last few months and have heard nothing but the screaming sirens, screeching tires, roaring motors, and other boisterous sounds of the city.

There are many beautiful things to see around my home, for instance, blue and white cranes wading in ponds and dipping their heads in the water to catch fish, frogs, and other things to eat. In the spring, when the farmers are beginning to prepare the ground for planting, white egrets swoop down behind the tractors preying on bugs and insects harmful to crops. These egrets, along with white cranes, water turkeys, and various other birds, come each spring and nest in large cypress trees.

If you are lucky, you can probably see deer running across the fields with their tails sticking up and the whiteness of the hide underneath shining brightly. Also, you can see squirrels jumping and playing games in the tiptops of the trees. There is a large red squirrel with his half-rust, half-fire color and big fuzzy tail. There is also the elite gray squirrel who must think he is a smart little rascal, because each time you try to get a look at him, he moves around to the other side of the tree.

You can experience the seasons of the year by watching what happens to the lush green crops and the green woods around them. When the crops ripen and the fall steals the life from the trees, there is a beautiful blending of brown, gold, and rust colors. An old shack nearby hardly seems to notice the death and later the rebirth of the crops.

You can hear many different sounds around my home. To begin with, you can hear all those birds I have been describing, cawing and chirping, making you wonder if they have a distinct language of their own. Oil wells can be heard in the distance, with their "pop-pop-pop-pow" repeated over and over. It seems as though that sound will go on indefinitely. At nightfall, the crickets produce their chirping, which combines with the deep bellowing and croaking of the bullfrogs, sounding like beautiful music to someone who has heard these sounds all his life.

Finally, distinctive smells surround my home. My favorite smell is the indescribable smell of rain as it beats down on the raw earth after the soil has been plowed. There are also the bad smells, such as trash burning or a skunk that has emitted his device of self-defense. But when I get homesick, I miss those smells too.

My father tells me I should learn to like the city as much as I like the country, but I have a long way to go.

QUESTIONS FOR DISCUSSION

1. The student (a male) gathered a lot of details for his paper. Did he use too much of it? What particular detail stood out for you?
2. What is the purpose statement (the one sentence that says what the essay will be about)? Did the student accomplish his purpose in the essay? Explain.
3. In developing his paper, the student tried to build each paragraph on a controlling idea, an organizing principle. The organizing principle for the second paragraph, for example, was the birds he can see around his home. What is the organizing principle of the other paragraphs in the body of the essay? (The *body* is simply the main part of the essay; it is the essay less the introduction and conclusion.)

Paragraph 1: <u>Introduction (includes purpose statement)</u>

Paragraph 2: <u>*Things to see, especially birds*</u>

Paragraph 3: _____

BODY Paragraph 4: _____

Paragraph 5: _____

Paragraph 6: _____

Paragraph 7: <u>Conclusion</u>

4. Would you prefer to live in the city or the country? Why?

WRITING ASSIGNMENT 1

Write a paper of 300 to 500 words on your own neighborhood or another one with which you are very familiar. Use each of the six steps in the writing method as carefully as possible. The more you use the method, the easier it will be for you to use. At the end of this section are two samples of student writing. Before writing your paper, read these essays and the section that follows on writing transition sentences to join paragraphs.

Step One: Gather Ideas and Information   In this step you will first brain-storm to gather ideas and information about the neighborhood you are going to write about. (Later you can fill in any gaps by closely observing your neighborhood with a pencil and paper in hand.)

1. Imagine yourself across the street from your home or some place where you can get a good view of everything going on in the neighborhood. Conjure up a vivid picture of the neighborhood. Become aware of every detail before you. In the left-hand column below write down *every* detail that you see. Do not censor your thoughts. Take about five minutes.

_____	_____
_____	_____
_____	_____
_____	_____
_____	_____
_____	_____
_____	_____

2. To test just how precise your details are, share some of them with the class or with the instructor. Now go back and make your more general observations as exact as possible, this time writing in the right-hand column above. For example:

blue car parked in front	*baby-blue '52 Cadillac with 2 flat front tires, rusty fenders, for sale*
green hedge	*10' high green hedge hiding porch*
yellow cat	*yellow-and-white striped cat prowling over turf as if he was somebody*

3. You are still at the spot where you can see everything in the neighborhood. Only now imagine that you cannot see but have a keen sense of hearing. Become aware of everything you might hear over the course of a day—horns honking, mothers calling their children (what are their exact words?), boys arguing over a baseball, and so on. Make use of your skill in recording a conversation. Again, use the left-hand column.

_____	_____
_____	_____
_____	_____

_____   _____

_____   _____

_____   _____

_____   _____

_____   _____

_____   _____

4. Share some of your list with the class or check it with your instructor. In the right-hand column above, make your observations even more precise. For example:

Mother calling son to dinner   *Mrs. Sims bellowing, "Charles get in here right now before I come after you with the cattle prod."*

church bells   *church bells ringing every hour*

5. Imagine that you now have a superior sense of smell. You are still at the same place. Write down everything you might smell in the neighborhood in the course of a week—fumes from automobiles, your neighbor's cooking, burning trash, garbage, cows, newly cut grass, and so on. Make your observations as precise as possible.

_____

_____

_____

_____

_____

_____

6. If someone were to ask you how you felt about the neighborhood, how would you answer that person?

_____

_____

_____

_____

Step Two: Analyze the Ideas and the Information   Sit back, with pen in hand, and read over the information you have gathered so far and ask yourself what you think. Which detail is most interesting to you? Which items are closely related? Which items will you probably not want to use? How might you order the material? Write notes to yourself. Now might be a good time to read the student samples at the end of this section for ideas on how you might use your information. Be ready to add to your list if you notice any gaps.

Step Three: State Your Purpose   Try to say in one sentence what you really want to tell your reader about the neighborhood you are writing about. It usually takes several attempts before one can write an effective purpose statement. A later section of this chapter is devoted to the purpose statement. But for this essay, keep the following suggestions in mind as you try to come up with a purpose statement that is just right:

1. Does your purpose statement include your opinion about the neighborhood?
2. Is it narrow enough in scope so that you will not have to write about everything?
3. Is it at the same time broad enough so that you will have enough material on which to write three hundred or more words?

Here are some examples of purpose statements from successful papers:

> You can tell what time it is by the various noises in my neighborhood. (In this paper, the student used each paragraph in the body to discuss a different type of noise heard at different times during the day.)

> Only in swampy Saint Bernard could there be a neighborhood like mine. (The student showed what it was like living on the edge of a swamp and showed just how unique her neighborhood was.)

> If you want to see what my neighborhood is like, just pull up a chair outside the Poplarville General Store and watch the people coming and going. (The student wrote first about women carrying large bundles, then the farmers drinking colas, and finally the children carrying book bags.)

> The neighborhood I live in is plain, but the people in it are not. (In the first paragraph, the student described just how plain everything looked, but in the four paragraphs in the body of the essay he described four individuals who appeared on the sidewalk during the day and showed how unique each one was.)

> My neighborhood is a nightmare; it has everything to terrify you: junkies, police, child abuse, adult abuse, pistol shots at night. (The student described what she had actually seen and heard in her neighborhood at various times and showed how these things did indeed terrify her.)

Experiment with your purpose statement until you get it just right, and then write it here.

_____

_____

_____

Step Four: Make Your Plan   Study the following suggestions for planning an essay and then make an informal outline for your neighborhood paper. Your plan need not be rigid. The best plan is the one that helps you say what you want to say. You may need to change it once you begin your essay.

SUGGESTIONS FOR PLANNING AN ESSAY

1. Your plan should help you accomplish your purpose. Here are two examples:

   PURPOSE STATEMENT

   You can tell what time it is by the various noises in my neighborhood.

   POINT 1

   It is noisy in the morning.

   POINT 2

   It is noisy in the early afternoon.

   POINT 3

   It is noisy in the late afternoon.

   POINT 4

   It is noisy at night.

   PURPOSE STATEMENT

   My neighborhood is overrun by young people, but I enjoy them all.

   POINT 1

   The five Read children are in and out of everyone's house.

   POINT 2

   The eleven- and twelve-year-old set play catch football every afternoon of the week.

   POINT 3

   The Mushroom Cloud on the corner is a teenage hangout.

2. Your outline should be consistent; that is, each major point should fit in with the other major points. Here are two examples of abbreviated outlines whose points do fit together:

   1. Introduction
   2. Sights in the neighborhood

   1. Introduction
   2. Neighborhood in the fall

3. Sounds in the neighborhood
4. Smells in the neighborhood
5. Conclusion

3. Neighborhood in the winter
4. Neighborhood in the spring
5. Neighborhood in the summer
6. Conclusion

Which of the following abbreviated outlines are not consistent? Apply the "Sesame Street" test: Which of the things (organizing principles) is not like the others?

1. Introduction
2. Most eye-catching features
3. Next most eye-catching features
4. Crime in the neighborhood
5. Conclusion

1. Introduction
2. Neighborhood as viewed from the left
3. Neighborhood as viewed straight ahead
4. Neighborhood as viewed from the right
5. The people in the neighborhood
6. Conclusion

1. Introduction
2. One example that illustrates the purpose
3. A second example that illustrates the purpose
4. Why I like my neighborhood
5. Conclusion

3. It may be helpful to you to let your outline reflect the paragraph divisions in your paper. This way you can name the organizing principle of each paragraph in the outline itself. The student who wrote the paper on his country home set up his outline as follows:

Paragraph 1: Introduction

Paragraph 2: Things to see, especially birds

Paragraph 3: Things to see, especially animals

Paragraph 4: Things to see, especially vegetation

Paragraph 5: Things to hear

Paragraph 6: Things to smell

Paragraph 7: Conclusion

In deciding how to divide your paper into paragraphs, be sure you have enough information to make each paragraph. The paragraphs in the body of your essay should probably run between fifty and one hundred words each. In the outline above, the student divided the category "things to see" into three paragraphs, each of which turned out to be over fifty words, but he described "things to hear" in one paragraph, which turned out to be about one hundred words.

4. The introduction and conclusion should be designated in the outline as separate paragraphs, even though they may be short (fewer than fifty words).

5. Under each major point in your outline, include enough notes so that you will have before you, as you sit down to write, the details and other information necessary to support your point. If you cannot think of enough details, perhaps you need to rework your outline, changing your major points. The student who wrote the paper on his home in the country wrote detail into his outline in the following way:

PARAGRAPH 1   Introduction
_____
(organizing principle)

Purpose statement, how long in the city, contrast with the country
_____
(detail)

PARAGRAPH 2   Things to see, especially birds
_____
(organizing principle)

cranes in ponds, white egrets behind tractors, nests, birds eating bugs
_____
(detail)

harmful to crops
_____

Write your outline for your essay about the neighborhood in the space provided below. In a paper of between 300 and 500 words you will probably need five to seven paragraphs, including an introduction and conclusion. Include in your introduction such information as where you live, how long you have lived there, your purpose statement, and anything else that will capture the reader's attention. If you cannot think of a conclusion in the outline step, do not worry. The best conclusions often come to you after you have written the rest of the paper.

PARAGRAPH 1   Introduction
_____
(organizing principle)

_____
(detail)

_____

PARAGRAPH 2   _____
(organizing principle)

_____
(detail)

_____

PARAGRAPH 3 _____
(organizing principle)

_____
(detail)

_____

PARAGRAPH 4 _____
(organizing principle)

_____
(detail)

_____

PARAGRAPH 5 _____
(organizing principle)

_____
(detail)

_____

PARAGRAPH 6 _____
(organizing principle)

_____
(detail)

_____

PARAGRAPH 7 Conclusion _____
(organizing principle)

_____
(detail)

_____

Check your outline with your instructor before going on to the next step.

Step Five: Write   As you write, keep in mind the following suggestions:

1. Use smooth transition sentences to connect your paragraphs. (See Chapter 2 and page 74.)
2. Avoid words that are redundant, that is, words that repeat what you have already said.
3. Avoid the passive voice.
4. If you have stated a point clearly in one sentence, you need not repeat the same idea in another sentence.
5. Let your conclusion flow naturally from what you have said. Make sure your reader knows you are through.

Step Six: Evaluate, Revise, and Edit   Evaluate your paper by asking these questions:

1. Did the purpose statement meet the criteria given on page 67?
2. Did each paragraph help to carry out the purpose statement?
3. How can you better support each major point with more or different details?
4. Did you repeat yourself unnecessarily at any time?
5. Did the conclusion effectively bring the essay to a close?

Now revise and edit your paper. Be alert for two errors that often appear with this assignment: verb agreement and fragment errors. (See Chapter 13 for verb agreement and Chapter 12 for avoiding fragments.)

Share Your Writing   Read your papers in a small group and discuss the questions listed in step six above after each person reads.

SAMPLE A

My Home in the Project

When I think of the sights, sounds, and smells of my neighborhood, it makes me wish that I were living somewhere else instead of at the Bradley Housing Project. I have lived in this neighborhood all my life. When my family first moved there, the area was very pleasant and the apartments were recently built. The lawn was well cut, and the environment was clean. But things have changed.

There are no beautiful things to see. The project consists of brick apartments, which have faded in color. Outside, there is only a limited amount of grass. The grounds consist mostly of dirt. The streets have large holes and are covered with glass. If you are trying to avoid getting a flat tire, please do not visit. Many people pile up trash on the sidewalk, which is a sight to see. You can see paper flying all around on windy days.

There are no nice sounds to hear. You may hear gunshots when people are fighting. Obscene language is used frequently. Children are constantly playing and making noise with their bicycles and skates. Most of the parents call their children without using their names, using words I do not enjoy hearing. At night and during the day, it is very disturbing hearing police sirens and trains passing across the tracks. I really wish my neighborhood would quiet down.

There are no pleasant things to smell. You smell mostly the scent of marijuana. Guys walk the street and stand in hallways smoking grass. At times there are foul odors from trash burning and from urine, and sometimes there is no smell at all.

What I like most about my neighborhood is that the people in my building and I get along well. Even though I am not satisfied with the area in which I live, I am very comfortable inside our apartment. I feel as though I have most of the things I want inside my home, regardless of what is seen, heard, and smelled outside.

QUESTIONS FOR DISCUSSION

1. What details stand out for you? What else would you like to know?
2. What information does the student include in the introduction besides the purpose statement? Is it effective? Why?
3. In her conclusion, the student makes a different point from what she has been saying. What is it?
4. The first sentences in paragraphs two, three, four, and five are transition sentences. They are meant to join the paragraphs. Are they effective?
5. If you were describing this neighborhood to someone else, what would you say about it?

SAMPLE B

At Home in the City

<u>Peaceful</u> is the word that best describes my neighborhood. My neighborhood is named Kennedy Heights, and it is located on the west bank of the Mississippi River.

I see pleasant things in my neighborhood, such as beautifully kept, one-story brick houses. These houses have white iron bars covering the doors and windows. On the roofs of the houses, blue jays and robins pick at food that has fallen from the large trees that line the block. These trees have pink flowers and shade the entire fronts of the houses. The curved driveways are neatly trimmed. In front of my house, three little girls with jump suits on play jump rope, while four others play hopscotch. I can also see a Trans Am with a white vinyl top and a gold Mercedes parked right down from my house.

What I hear in my neighborhood may sound noisy to others, but to me the sounds are peaceful. There is music coming from car radios and stereos inside the houses, everything from Rick James to classical music. Mothers call their children inside to do homework or to get ready for bed. A mother will say, "Billy, it's time for you to come inside and get your bath for tomorrow." He will answer, "Can I please stay out for just five more minutes?" Freight and passenger trains make noise when they pass by in the distance. I guess those are peaceful sounds to me because I have heard them all my life.

My neighborhood has few smells. On Sundays the usual smell is that of barbequed chicken coming from a neighbor's backyard. On Saturdays there is the smell of grass being cut.

I have lived in my neighborhood for nineteen years, and I appreciate all of its sights, sounds, and smells.

QUESTIONS FOR DISCUSSION

1. Does the student successfully carry out her purpose statement in the body of her paper?
2. Could any of the transition sentences joining paragraphs together be improved? How?

3. What details stood out for you?
4. Was the dialogue in paragraph three effective?

Transition Sentences to Join Paragraphs

All of your paragraphs should be connected as smoothly as possible by transition sentences, as shown in the diagram below.

Transition sentences that join paragraphs have three functions: (1) to connect a paragraph with the previous paragraph, (2) to point to the content of the new paragraph, and (3) to help carry out the purpose statement. Keep these functions in mind, but remember the main purpose of the transition sentence is to help the reader move from point to point *smoothly*. You will often come up with the best transition sentences when you revise your paper.

Here are examples of transition sentences that might be used to carry out the following two purpose statements:

PURPOSE STATEMENT
When I think of the <u>sights</u>, <u>sounds</u>, and <u>smells</u> of our place in the country, it makes me wish I were there right now.

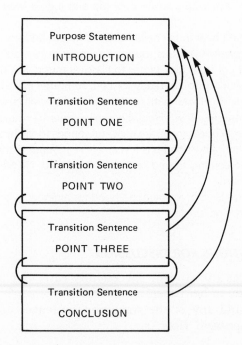

TRANSITION SENTENCES

There are many beautiful things to <u>see</u> around my home.

You can experience the seasons of the year <u>by watching</u> . . . .

You can <u>hear</u> many different sounds at our place in the country.

Finally, you can <u>smell</u> anything you want to smell around my home.

Notice how the underlined words in the purpose statement connect with the underlined words in the transition sentences.

PURPOSE STATEMENT

You can tell what time it is by the various noises in my neighborhood.

TRANSITION SENTENCES

I never have to use an alarm clock to wake up because at six o'clock each morning the train comes <u>clanging</u> by.

In the early afternoon, the children from Craft Elementary School <u>shriek</u> for a full hour as they pour out of their "prison."

By six o'clock in the evening most of the men are home from work and are <u>banging</u> on their cars as they try to repair them.

About eleven o'clock each night, just as things begin to get quiet, the Urban Decay Band next door starts practicing its <u>loud punk music</u>.

Notice how the underlined words in the transition sentences connect with the purpose statement. Clanging, shrieking, and banging are all disturbing noises to say nothing of the loud punk music played at eleven at night.

WRITING ASSIGNMENT 2

Write a paper of three hundred to five hundred words on the topic "Those Were the Days," using each step of the writing method described earlier in this chapter. Before writing your paper, read the samples of student writing that follow, as well as the section on the purpose or thesis statement and the one on introductions, conclusions, and titles.

Step One: Gather Ideas and Information In this step you will brainstorm, bringing back past memories from the years you were between the ages of six and eleven or twelve—your elementary school years. Before you actually write your paper, you may want to ask your parents or others who knew you then to help you fill in any information gaps. (If you prefer, use the clustering method described in Chapter 3 to gather ideas and information.)

1. As you think about yourself when you were in elementary school, what comes to mind when you hear the word *home*?

Do not censor your thoughts. Write down everything! (If you are using the clustering method, use *home* as your nucleus word.)

_____

_____

_____

_____

_____

2. What comes to mind when you think of the schools you attended during those years? (If you are using the clustering method, use *schools* as your nucleus word.)

_____

_____

_____

_____

_____

3. Who were your best friends over those years? Write down one or two things that stand out about each of them. (If you are using the clustering method, use *friends* as your nucleus word.)

_____

_____

_____

_____

_____

4. What setbacks (accidents, illnesses, deaths, parents' divorces, and the like) did you experience in those years? (If you are using the clustering method, use *setbacks* as your nucleus word.)

_____

_____

_____

_____

5. What special times do you remember (birthdays, awards, victories, vacations, and the like)? (If you are using the clustering method, use *special times* as your nucleus word.)

———————————————————————————————

———————————————————————————————

———————————————————————————————

———————————————————————————————

———————————————————————————————

Step Two: Analyze the Ideas and the Information   One of the tasks of this step is to narrow down the information you have gathered. Of the five categories above, pick the one that you would find the most meaningful (or fun) to write about. Look at the information you listed under the other headings and see if any of it relates to the category you have chosen. If so, add that information to the list, and add any other information you can think of. Use the blanks below.

———————————————————————————————

———————————————————————————————

———————————————————————————————

———————————————————————————————

———————————————————————————————

———————————————————————————————

Sit back and look at this revised list. What stands out? Which things relate to each other? How can you begin to give an even more narrow focus to your topic? Which things can be eliminated from the list? What information gaps can your parents or someone who knew you during those years help you fill in? At this point it may be helpful to read the student samples near the end of this section.

Step Three: State Your Purpose   You began with a very large topic, your elementary school years, you then narrowed it down to one of five subtopics—home, school, friends, setbacks, or special times, and you have now begun to give a more narrow focus to the subtopic. Now you will need to narrow down the subtopic even more and say in *one sentence* what you will try to show in your paper. The diagram on page 78 gives examples of this process.

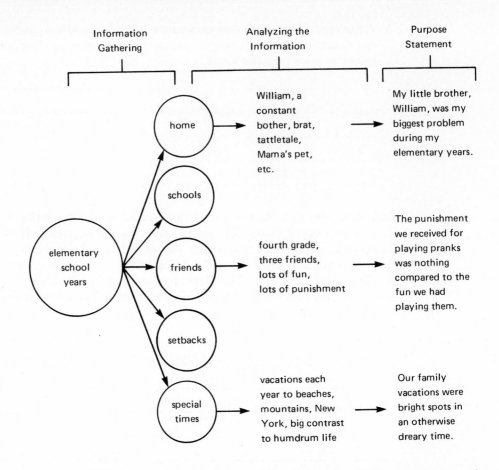

The purpose (or thesis) statement should not be simply a statement of what your paper is about, as these attempts at purpose statements are:

WEAK

In this paper I will write about my three best friends from the fourth grade.

WEAK

This paper is about the various vacation trips my family made when I was in elementary school.

Instead, include within your purpose statement your *opinion* about the topic. Your purpose statement should challenge you to be persuasive. The two purpose statements above could be revised as follows:

STRONGER

The punishment we received for playing pranks was nothing compared to the fun we had playing them.

STRONGER

Our family vacations were bright spots in an otherwise dreary time.

Now you have to write convincingly to persuade your reader that the fun you had with your friends really was worth the punishment, or that the vacations you and your family had really were bright spots in years that were otherwise dreary.

The diagram on page 78 shows how you can move from your information gathering to your purpose statement. Here are some more examples of effective purpose statements for this assignment. In each, the writer must convince the reader of something.

> The hard times of my youth were also times of great learning. (The writer must not only describe the hard times but also show *why* they were occasions of great learning.)
>
> The hobbies I became interested in when I was ten years old changed my life. (The writer must both describe the hobbies and show *how* they changed her life.)
>
> Whenever Mike, Tommy, Bean, and I are together, we begin to talk about and long for the good old days at Libson Elementary. (The writer must show just *why* he and his friends long for the good old days. What made them so memorable?)
>
> Even though we had our bad times as well as our good times, I will never forget Curtis Johnson as long as I live. (The writer must not only describe the good and bad times but also *make the reader believe* that his relationship with Curtis Johnson is unforgettable.)

Write your own purpose statement for this assignment below, and then check it with your instructor.

_____

_____

_____

Step Four: Make Your Plan   In the space provided, write an informal outline for your paper that effectively carries out your purpose statement. If you have difficulty making enough points and filling in enough detail, perhaps you need to rewrite your purpose statement. Your paper should probably consist of four to seven paragraphs. Study the instructions on writing introductions, conclusions, and titles in this chapter.

_____
(your title)

PARAGRAPH 1   Introduction (include purpose statement)
_____
(organizing principle)

_____
(detail)

_____

PARAGRAPH 2 _____
(organizing principle)

_____

(detail)

_____

PARAGRAPH 3 _____
(organizing principle)

_____

(detail)

_____

PARAGRAPH 4 _____
(organizing principle)

_____

(detail)

_____

PARAGRAPH 5 _____
(organizing principle)

_____

(detail)

_____

PARAGRAPH 6 _____
(organizing principle)

_____

(detail)

_____

PARAGRAPH 7 Conclusion
_____
(organizing principle)

_____

(detail)

_____

Before moving to the next step, check your outline with your instructor.

Step Five: Write   As you write, keep in mind the following suggestions:

1. Most of your paper will probably be written in the past tense. If you switch to the present tense, make sure you have a legitimate reason for doing so.
2. Let your sentences flow into each other as smoothly as possible.
3. Give your sentences variety. Write some as compound, some as complex, and some as simple sentences. (See Chapter 11.)

4. If you have stated a point clearly in one sentence, do not repeat the idea in another sentence that says just about the same thing.

Step Six: Evaluate, Revise, and Edit   Evaluate your paper by asking these questions:

1. Did the purpose statement express an opinion?
2. Did each paragraph help carry out the purpose statement?
3. How can you better support each major point with more or different detail?

Now, using your evaluation, revise and edit your paper. Look especially for two errors that often appear with this assignment, namely verb-tense errors and run-on sentence errors.

1. *Verb tense.* Be careful to give regular verbs a *-d* or an *-ed* ending when they refer to action in the past. Watch out especially for those verbs whose endings are hard to hear:

    She seem<u>ed</u> less nervous now.

    He help<u>ed</u> us all more than he knew.

    If you have any problem at all with irregular past-tense endings, check the list of irregular verbs in Chapter 14. Watch out especially for those that are often missed, such as:

    She <u>began</u> her work on time that day.

    He <u>laid</u> his pen on the table and refused to write.

    It <u>cost</u> more last year than it costs this year.

2. *Run-on sentences.* Be careful not to run your sentences together. In telling of events in the past, many of your sentences will be closely related in content. The more closely related they are, the easier it is to run them together. (See Chapter 12.2.)

    INCORRECT

    A friend of the family from across the street came over, he saw what had happened and rushed me to the hospital.

    CORRECT

    A friend of the family from across the street came over. He saw what had happened and rushed me to the hospital.

    INCORRECT

    I was finally admitted by the nurse, she x-rayed my arm in different positions.

    CORRECT

    When I was finally admitted by the nurse, she x-rayed my arm in different positions.

Share Your Writing   Read your paper in a small group and make use of the evaluation questions in step six above as each paper is read. Next, exchange papers with one other person and proofread the paper you receive. Be sure to check with the student before writing any changes on the paper.

This is one of the last times in this text that the suggestion will be made to share your writing. Your instructor, however, may ask you to read your papers in small groups for later assignments. If class time does not permit small group discussions, share your paper with a classmate outside of class when possible. It makes good sense to read your paper to the people for whom it was written and to listen to their papers as well. It is also a good practice to exchange papers for proofreading and editing.

Here are two student samples for the assignment "Those Were the Days."

SAMPLE A

Those Were the Days

The friend I can remember best from my childhood is Curtis Johnson. I met Curtis Johnson in Children's Hospital when I was there in 1969, but I have not seen him since. Even though we had our bad times as well as our good times, I will never forget Curtis as long as I live.

I entered Children's Hospital a year after my family had moved to this country from Cuba. Curtis used to come up to me and talk about many things. At first I would never talk because I did not speak English. I learned how to speak English in the hospital. There was a school room in the hospital, and every day the teacher, Mr. Manuel, would show me flash cards with different letters and words on them. Pretty soon I began to speak a little English. I started communicating with Curtis, and he would talk to me as though I were a native-born American. I think that is why I picked up English so fast. Curtis and I started hanging around each other. I depended on him, and he depended on me. I cannot use my legs, and he does not have arms.

Curtis and I did everything imaginable together. We played games, went to parties, chased all the female volunteers, hunted blue jays with slingshots in the park near the hospital, set up squirrel traps, and played tricks on people. The best times we had were when we tried to talk to pretty volunteers. Here were a couple of young punks, one ten and the other eleven, trying to make it big with girls seventeen and older. Curtis had a line that would get them every time. It went something like this: "Hi, my name is Curtis; I'm from Turtle Creek. Have you ever heard of it?" Then Curtis would drop something on the floor on purpose, knowing that the girl would feel sorry for him and pick it up. When she reached down, Curtis would stand near her. The moment she stood up he would kiss her smack on the lips. He tried to get me to do it a few times, but I did not have the nerve. With my luck, the girl would probably have slapped me. We did many things that were fun and sometimes got into trouble doing them.

Every now and then Curtis and I would get into fights. Our worst brawl happened one day when I had a visitor who brought me some chocolate-chip cookies. When my visitor was leaving, I escorted her out. When I returned, all my cookies were gone. Curtis had cookie crumbs on his lips, so I asked him, "Curtis, did you eat my cookies?" He said no. Then I said, "You're lying!" He answered, "Are you calling me a liar, Rudolfo?" I said "Yeah, you are a liar." That started feet kicking and fists swinging. To make a long story short, Curtis gave me a good beating with his feet. It was a real back-alley brawl with flying books, flying toys, and flying people (mainly me). We both got punished for three weeks.

During that time we made up and became good friends once again. I often wonder what Curtis is doing now.

QUESTIONS FOR DISCUSSION

1. What is the purpose statement? Is it effective? Is the student successful in carrying it out?
2. What is the organizing principle of each paragraph?
3. Look at the transition sentences that introduce the second, third, and fourth paragraphs. Could any of them have been written more effectively?
4. One of the best ways to develop your paragraphs is by giving examples. What examples does this writer give? What points do they illustrate?
5. Does the student give enough background information in the introduction for you to put his paper in some context?
6. Is the conclusion effective? Would you like the writer to say more? If so, what?
7. What might be a more exact title for this essay than the one the student used?

SAMPLE B

A Rose for My Father

I was twelve years old when my father died. I came home from the store on a Sunday morning at about 10:00 and got the news. I had lost someone I loved: my father.

As I walked up to our front door, I saw many people standing around in our house. I wondered what was going on because everyone was crying and whispering. I just knew something had happened. When my mother's best friend, Miss Rose, told me that my father had died, I cried and cried. At first it was hard for me to believe. We had eaten breakfast together earlier that morning. Miss Rose told me he had had a heart attack. When they took him out to the car to go to the hospital, he died.

That was one of the worst days of my life. Everybody in the house was weeping. I remember how all my aunts, uncles, and friends gave us their sympathy and brought us plates and plates of food. It was late that night before everyone left. I cried the whole night and wondered how much I was going to miss my father.

The funeral was at Illinois Funeral Home on North Clairborne Avenue, November 25, 1976. All the family was ready for the funeral, except me. I did not want to go because I knew this would be the last time I would see him. When I finally got to the funeral home, Mother and I said a prayer together. After we finished praying, the funeral director closed the casket. The chauffeur then drove us to the cemetery, where the preacher prayed and the people sang sad hymns. After all the family and friends had left, I picked a rose from the basket of roses nearby and dropped it on the casket. "Good-bye, Daddy," I said. "I will miss you. I love you very much."

Adjusting to life without him was not easy. I was too frightened to sleep in my bed, so I slept at my friend's house as much as I could. About six months after he died, I finally began to sleep in my bed, but I often woke up screaming. It was hard to grow up without my father. I had no one to help me with my homework, nobody's back to jump up on for rides. Now that I am older I have accepted his death, and I am going to try to make my daddy proud of his daughter.

QUESTIONS FOR DISCUSSION

1. The student is writing about an event that was very sad for her. Was she able to convey her sadness without sounding too emotional? Do you feel the sadness with her? If so, what did she say that made you feel that way?
2. What examples did the student give as she developed each paragraph?

WRITING ASSIGNMENT 3

Write another paper of 300 to 500 words on the same topic, "Those Were the Days," only this time focus on your high school years (or some other four-year period in your life).

The Purpose or Thesis Statement

A purpose statement, often called a *thesis statement*, is a short, to-the-point declaration of what you will try to convince the reader of in your paper. Unless your teacher gives you different instructions, include your purpose statement in the first paragraph. Sometimes it takes a long time to come up with just the right purpose statement. And when you revise your essay, you may find that you want to refine your purpose statement.

SUGGESTIONS FOR WRITING AN EFFECTIVE PURPOSE STATEMENT

1. The purpose statement should be narrow and specific enough in focus so that you do not have to write about everything related to your topic:

    WEAK

    Aunt Kathleen was a very interesting person.

    STRONGER

    Aunt Kathleen was poor but proud.

    WEAK

    To Kill a Mockingbird is an enjoyable book.

STRONGER

To Kill a Mockingbird is a story of both tenderness and courage.

2. However, the purpose statement should be broad enough so that you will have *enough* to write about. Sometimes you will not know if your purpose statement gives you enough to write about until you get to the planning step. If you find that you cannot think of enough points to write a good outline, perhaps you need to find another purpose statement.

3. The purpose statement should express an opinion or state a position, something you will have to convince your reader of. The following "tell-them-what-you-are-going-to-tell-them" statements are *not* strong purpose statements:

WEAK

In this paper I will write about three ways to improve study habits.

WEAK

In this essay I will discuss the times that Dr. Eugene Woods, my dentist, lectured to me on politics while I sat helplessly in the chair.

These kinds of sentences, if used at all, should be revised so that the *I will* is taken out. They should then be placed *after* the actual purpose statement, as follows:

STRONGER

Developing good study habits is simply a matter of self-discipline. There are a number of things you can do to improve your study habits, and you can begin now.

STRONGER

Dr. Eugene Woods, my dentist, should have been a politician. On several occasions he has lectured to me on politics while I sat helplessly in the chair.

4. The purpose statement should state just one thing, the one point you will need to prove. A good paper will often have secondary purposes, but they should not compete with the main point, the thrust of your essay. The student in the second example above may want to explain how Dr. Woods is a fine dentist, but the main point that must be kept before the readers is that the doctor lectures to his patients on politics when they are in no position to respond. Here is another example:

WEAK

The federal government should take steps to make cigarette smoking illegal and should actively seek nuclear disarmament.

STRONGER

The federal government should take steps to make cigarette smoking illegal.

or

STRONGER

The federal government should actively seek nuclear disarmament.

Both ideas could be combined in a sentence like the following:

STRONGER

The first two priorities of the federal government should be to make cigarette smoking illegal and to seek nuclear disarmament.

EXERCISE 1

Mark the following sentences *W* for weak purpose statement or *S* for stronger purpose statement. Be able to say why you answered as you did. Instructors as well as students may differ on a couple of responses.

_____   1. The reading texts we used in my elementary school taught us to dislike reading.

_____   2. Capital punishment should be abolished and long jail sentences should be shortened.

_____   3. John Steinbeck's *Of Mice and Men* is a story of maintaining hope when there was no hope.

_____   4. In this paper I will describe three types of high school teachers.

_____   5. The drivers in Washington, D.C., must be the worst in the nation.

_____   6. My boss, Mrs. Viola Wright, is nice.

_____   7. Learning to write well is largely a matter of developing self-confidence, and the same thing is true of reading.

_____   8. My two pets are as different as you can imagine any pets to be.

_____   9. I will describe discrimination against women, first in the United States and then in Russia.

_____   10. The only difference between my pet and me is that she has four legs and I have two.

EXERCISE 2

Write purpose statements expressing your views on the following topics. (Be sure to write in complete sentences.)

1. Your favorite relative

_____

_____

_____

2. The "Refrigerator" of the Chicago Bears or some other popular American

_____

_____

_____

3. Drunk driving

_____

_____

_____

4. Farmers

_____

_____

_____

5. The women (or men) on your college campus

_____

_____

_____

6. Single-parent families

_____

_____

_____

7. Saturday night

_____

_____

_____

8. Religion

_____

_____

_____

9. Divorce

_____

_____

_____

10. Cats

_____

_____

_____

Introductions, Conclusions, and Titles

Most students find that they need to spend a good bit of time writing introductions to their essays. Conclusions and titles usually come much more easily. Suggestions for writing introductions, conclusions, and titles are outlined below.

Introductions

You can usually introduce a one- or two-paragraph paper effectively with one or two sentences, but when you are writing a paper of several paragraphs, you will probably need a separate paragraph for the introduction. Writing a good introduction is often the most difficult and time-consuming part of writing an essay. While preparing for an essay to be written in class, it is wise to write your introduction as well as your outline ahead of time so that you will know exactly how to begin your essay when you sit down to write in class. The introduction is usually—though not always—shorter than the paragraphs in the body of your paper.

WHAT TO INCLUDE IN AN INTRODUCTION

1. Unless your instructor gives other directions, include your purpose statement in your introduction. Place it at the point where it is most effective. If it is a catchy purpose statement, like "My neighborhood is so noisy it disturbs the dogs" or "My cousin Cassandra has gone crazy over religion," use it as the first sentence.
2. Include enough background information so that your reader will be able to put your essay in some context. For the neighborhood paper assigned earlier, for example, you were asked to say in your introduction where your neighborhood was and how long you had lived there. In the introduction to the "Those Were the Days" paper, you might tell which of your early years you are talking about, where you were living at the time, and what school or schools you were attending.

3. Include a summary statement in your introduction only if you believe it will help your readers understand what you want to accomplish in the paper. This statement is often the last sentence of the first paragraph. It should come after the purpose statement. Keep it brief. Here are two examples of summary statements that could come after the purpose statement "Developing good study habits is simply a matter of self-discipline."

   WEAK

   First, I will write about how important it is to plan your study time carefully. Second, I will write about how important it is to use the library. Third, I will write about how important it is to keep up with all of your assignments.

   STRONGER

   There are a number of things you can do to improve your study habits, and you can begin now.

   In other words, when you are writing summary sentences, do not overdo it. Your transition sentences at the beginning of each paragraph should make your individual points clear.

4. Include anything else in your introduction that will stimulate your reader to continue to read. One effective way to begin a paper is with an example. If you were writing about how a student's life is a difficult one, you might begin with a short example that illustrates your point. (See the example essay on page 127.)

Conclusions

In each essay you write, you must make sure your reader knows you have come to the end of what you want to say. Like the introduction, the conclusion is usually—but not always—shorter than the other paragraphs in the body of the paper. If it is just one sentence long, you may want to hook it onto the last paragraph.

Your concluding statements will usually come naturally to you, much like ending a telephone conversation:

   And so you see, everybody gossips.

   If I had my way, I would live in this house at 42 Legare Street the rest of my life.

   The "good old days" were not so good after all.

   Thus, television should be outlawed.

OTHER IDEAS FOR YOUR CONCLUSIONS

In addition to bringing your essay to an end, you may want to include in your last paragraph one of the following:

1. *A contrasting idea.* The student who wrote the paper on the Bradley Housing Project (page 72), for example, used the conclusion to show what

she *did* like about her home after writing the rest of the paper about what she did not like about it. If you were writing about sad or difficult times, you could use your last paragraph to note that not *everything* was bad, beginning perhaps with a sentence like "But not everything was disappointing during those years."

2. *A statement of the significance of your topic.* When you finish making your points about why something is true, you may want to bring your reader up-to-date, saying what it all means. One student described the highlights of her fifth-grade year in her essay and then wrote the following conclusion, explaining the significance of what had happened to her that year:

> These experiences were important to me then, and they are still important to me. I continue to play the trumpet, first chair in concerts, and in the school marching band. Mary and I are still best friends. And would you believe, I still play baseball every chance I get?

If you were writing a paper about why sex education should be taught in high schools, you might conclude with a statement on the difference it would make to young people if your ideas were accepted.

3. *A call to action.* If you are arguing for a belief, you may want to ask your reader to join with you in trying to remedy a certain problem. For example:

> The best way for us to conserve energy is to make a decision—right now—that we will cut down on our driving, use less heat, and, if possible, insulate our homes.

> If you agree that capital punishment should be abolished, write your state and congressional representatives today.

4. *A summary.* Beware of this one. You will not need to repeat *each* point that you made in a separate sentence. Summary endings are useful if each point can be expressed in a word or two and if the summary takes only a single sentence. For example:

> Whether male or female, young or old, everyone likes to gossip.

> A young person will not go wrong if he or she goes into banking, computer science, or nursing.

Titles

Unless your instructor gives other instructions, practice giving titles to all of your papers, even the ones that are just one paragraph long. You may want to wait until you have completed your paper before you give it a title.

SUGGESTIONS FOR COMPOSING TITLES

1. Make your title relate to the main idea of your paper.
2. Try to pick a title that stimulates interest in your subject.

3. If possible, keep your title short: one to six words. Usually the title should not be a whole sentence.

RULES FOR WRITING TITLES

1. Do not underline or put quotation marks around your title when it appears at the top of your paper.
2. Always capitalize the first and last word and every other word except:

   articles (*a, an,* and *the*)
   short prepositions (such as *of, on, in,* and *for*)
   short conjunctions (such as *and, but,* and *or*)

   Here are some examples of properly capitalized titles:

   The Ghost of the Plantation   A Rose for Daddy
   When I Was Very Young   The Curse of My Childhood
   An Experience on the Road   Pranks and Punishments

   Explain why each word in the above titles was either capitalized or not capitalized.

Revising and Editing Papers

The word *revision* means "re-seeing," that is, looking at your paper with fresh eyes to see how it can be improved. When you revise an essay, be willing to change, delete, and add to material you have already written. If you can see that your essay is not working and probably cannot be corrected, be willing to start over, perhaps with a different topic.

Some students are disappointed when instructors keep asking them to revise papers; they think that this means they have somehow failed in writing the first drafts. But think of writing as a kind of art form or a craft: It takes a lot of practice and sometimes several drafts of a paper before you can say what you really want to say and what you are capable of saying. Revising will help you not only with the particular paper in front of you; it will also help you a great deal in mastering the principles of organization and the elements of style. *From now on, revise all your papers.*

Once you have written your first or second draft, let your paper sit for a while and then evaluate it, asking yourself how well your paper works. As you develop as a writer, you will learn to ask yourself better and better questions about your writing. (The questions for discussion following the student writing samples in this text are designed to help you evaluate not just the sample writing but your own writing as well.) For now, ask yourself the following ten questions as you evaluate your paper. You may need to read your paper several times before you can respond to all ten questions.

1. Did your paper say exactly what you wanted it to say? (Does your *purpose statement* properly reveal what you wanted to say?)

2. How convincing were you in making a case for what you wanted to say? (Did you use *effective detail*: description, examples, quotations, facts, and so forth? Could you use more detail? Were any of the details you used about something other than the subject?)
3. Did you help your reader to become involved in your paper right from the beginning? (Did your *introduction* give enough background information and begin to stimulate interest?)
4. Did you divide your paper into appropriate parts so that your reader could follow you? (Did you give your paper an appropriate *paragraph structure?*)
5. Did you move from one point to another smoothly? (Did you use *effective transitions* between and within paragraphs?)
6. Did the paper sound like you, or was it written in a stuffy, dull, mechanical voice? (Did you write in an *authentic voice*? Did you give your sentences variety?)
7. Did you bring the paper to an appropriate end so that your reader was not left hanging? (Did you write an *effective conclusion?*)
8. Did your paper make sense all the way through? (Was it always *logical*? Were there any contradictions?)
9. Could you leave out any words or sentences without taking away from what you wanted to say? (Were there any *redundancies*? Did you keep your paper from being *wordy?*)
10. Could you use any better or more exact words to make your points? (Did you make the *best word choice?*)

While you are evaluating your paper, show it to a friend to see if he or she understands what you meant to convey in the paper. Ask your friend to state to you what you were trying to say and to give evidence why your paper was convincing or unconvincing.

As you evaluate your essay, make notes either directly on it or on a separate sheet of paper or both, and then rewrite the essay. While you are rewriting, you will probably want to make even more changes.

The last step is to edit your paper to catch mechanical errors. As suggested earlier in this chapter, you should read your paper at least three times to catch such errors. Some students are able to edit as they evaluate and rewrite, but do not be timid about reading your paper over and over again: It does not take long, and it can only help.

An Example of Revision

In response to the neighborhood essay assigned earlier in this chapter, a student turned in the following imaginative paper. Even though the instructor was pleased, she asked the student to revise the essay. An evaluation and the revision itself follow. Note that the evaluation is written out under the ten questions and also on a copy of the essay itself. Although this example of revision does not include the editing process, Part Three of this text contains several editing exercises.

SAMPLE (FIRST DRAFT)

The Zoo

My neighborhood reminds me of a zoo because it is a zoo. The personalities of the people who live in my neighborhood are those of animals. There are three basic types of personalities: the chimps, the gorillas, and the giraffes.

The chimps are timid but playful creatures. They walk up and down the street in a very hip and boastful manner. When they gather on the street corners, they say things like, "Aw, Brother Lion, he's about nothin'. I pulled his tail yesterday, and he didn't do a thing." But when one of these young chimps is challenged by the simple roars of the lions and gorillas, he will flee for cover every time. That is what I mean by timid.

The gorillas are much more aggressive than the chimps. Often they stride and talk boastfully in the streets, but they have the power to back up their words. Thus, they seem to be the bosses. When they speak to the chimps, they might say, "Hey, you, come he-ah. Now what did you say 'bout me?"

Last and least of all are the giraffes. They are usually on the prissy side. Sometimes their tongues are just as long as their necks. They use their long necks to listen in on everything that is going on in the other cages. When they finish snooping, they use their long tongues to gossip all over the zoo about the most personal information. That is why on some days you might see a chimp or even a gorilla with his head down, a victim of a giraffe's gossip. Maybe the giraffes are the real bosses. Everyone in the other cages is afraid of them.

I am not ready to leave my neighborhood. I guess I like zoos.

THE EVALUATION

1. Does your purpose statement properly reveal what you wanted to say?

   Yes, but it could be stated more forcefully. To say in the first sentence that the neighborhood reminds you of a zoo "because it is a zoo" seems a bit weak. Also, the meaning of this statement is not clear until the second sentence. In the revision the meaning of the first two sentences is combined into one sentence.

2. Did you use effective detail: description, examples, quotations, facts, and so forth? Could you use more detail?

   For the most part the detail is very effective, but the paper needs to be expanded with more detail, for example:

   Describe more fully how the chimps walk up and down the street.
   Give examples of what the giraffes actually say instead of only generalizing about them.
   Create a class of animals to put the writer in. The writer does not seem to be like any of the other animals that are described. In the revision, the writer became an owl.

3. Did your introduction give enough background information and begin to stimulate interest?

   Yes. For most neighborhood papers, you would need to say something about the location of the neighborhood, but in this paper the location does not seem important, although it would not hurt if the writer gave some background information on the setting.

4. Did you give your paper an appropriate paragraph structure?

   Yes. It was easy: an introduction, a paragraph for each animal, and a conclusion. In the revision, the fourth animal is combined with the conclusion.

5. Did you use effective transitions between and within paragraphs?

   Yes. Note that it was not necessary to say, "First, the chimps . . .; Second, the lions . . .; Third, the giraffes . . . ." The transitions as written sounded natural and flowed smoothly.

6. Did you write in an authentic voice? Did you give your sentences variety?

   Yes. There was nothing stuffy or dull about the writing style. It did indeed sound like the student.

   On the whole, the student used a good variety of sentences, which sounded natural. However, the first two sentences in the fourth paragraph could be combined.

7. Did you write an effective conclusion?

   The conclusion was okay but could have been expanded, as demonstrated in the revision.

8. Is it logical? Are there any contradictions?

   One problem with the original essay is the mention of the lions in the second paragraph. Lions are not introduced as one of the animals in the neighborhood. In the revision, the lions replace the gorillas all the way through. Also, as pointed out above, the writer did not identify himself among the animals, so the category of owls was created for the writer and everyone else.

9. Are there any redundancies? Have you kept your paper from being wordy?

   Paragraph 1: Omit one sentence.
   Paragraph 2: Omit the last sentence; it does not add to the paper.
   Paragraph 3: Okay.
   Paragraph 4: Omit *and least of all* from the first sentence. The meaning is unclear.

10. Have you used the best word choice?

    Paragraph 2: In the first sentence, *timid* does not seem to describe the chimps.
    Paragraph 2: *Simple* does not describe the roar of a lion. Try *deep.*

SAMPLE (EVALUATION)

The Zoo

rewrite purpose statement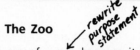

combine { My neighborhood reminds me of a zoo because it is a zoo. The
sentences { personalities of the people who live in my neighborhood are those of
animals. There are three basic types of personalities: the chimps, the
lions ~~gorillas,~~ and the giraffes. **add owls - the writer and everyone else**

good trans. → The chimps are timid but playful creatures. They walk up and down
more detail → the street in a very ~~hip~~ and boastful manner. When they gather on the *(wrong word)*
good detail → street corners, they say things like, "Aw, Brother Lion, he's about
nothin'. I pulled his tail yesterday, and he didn't do a thing." But when
But are all → one of these young chimps is challenged by the ~~simple~~ roars of the lions
of them young? and ~~gorillas,~~ he will flee for cover every time. That is what I mean by *(wrong word)*
timid. ← *— omit - wordy —* →

good trans. → The *lions* ~~gorillas~~ are much more aggressive than the chimps. Often they
more detail → stride and talk boastfully in the streets, but they have the power to back
up their words. Thus, they seem to be the bosses. When they speak to
good detail → the chimps, they might say, "Hey, you, come he-ah. Now what did you
say 'bout me?"
omit - wordy *who ← combine*
Last (~~and least of all~~) are the giraffes. They are usually on the prissy
expand with → side. Sometimes their tongues are just as long as their necks. They use
more detail, their long necks to listen in on everything that is going on in the other
cages. When they finish snooping, they use their long tongues to gossip
give examples → all over the zoo about the most personal information. That is why on
some days you might see a chimp or even a gorilla with his head down,
a victim of a giraffe's gossip. Maybe the giraffes are the real bosses.
Everyone in the other cages is afraid of them.
expand ending, I am not ready to leave my neighborhood. I guess I like zoos.
add "owls" →

SAMPLE (REVISED)

The Zoo

The people who live in my neighborhood are like the animals you see in a zoo. We
have chimps, lions, and giraffes. And then we have people like me, owls, who stay
inside and watch the others.

The chimps are lively, playful creatures, and all seem to be young. They walk up and
down the street, swinging their long arms from left to right in a very hip and boastful
manner. When they gather on street corners, they say things like, "Aw, Brother Lion,
he's about nothin'. I pulled his tail yesterday, and he didn't do a thing." But when

these chimps are challenged by the deep roars of the lions, they will flee for cover every time.

The lions are much more aggressive than the chimps. Often they stride down the street with their heads high and their manes bristling, daring anyone to get in their way. And they have the power to back up their words. Thus they seem to be the bosses. When they speak to a chimp, they might say, "Hey, you, come he-ah. Now what did you say 'bout me?" Chimps stay well out of the way of the lions.

Then there are the giraffes, who are usually on the prissy side. Sometimes their tongues are just as long as their necks. They use their long necks to listen in on everything that is going on in the other cages. When they have finished snooping, they use their long tongues to gossip all over the zoo about the most personal information. They might say, "That little light-colored chimp been slippin' in the back door after two every morning." Or, "Did you see how those lions treated Grandpaw Lion on his birthday? They don't care for anybody 'cept themselves." On just about any day of the year, you can see a chimp or even a lion with his head down—a victim of a giraffe's gossip. Maybe the giraffes are the real bosses. Everyone in the other cages is afraid of them.

Then there are the rest of us, the owls. We usually stay inside because we are afraid to go out. Wouldn't you be too? But we do enjoy watching from behind dark windows where no one can see us. You do not need to visit a zoo if you live in my neighborhood because you can see anything you want right here.

WRITING ASSIGNMENT 4

Choose one of the essays assigned in this chapter or one of the longer essays assigned earlier in the text and revise it, following this procedure:

1. Exchange your essay with a classmate and evaluate each other's essays, using the ten questions listed above.
2. Evaluate your own essay, again using the ten questions. This time write out the answers to the questions so that you can hand them in to your instructor.
3. Revise your essay on the basis of the evaluations, and make other needed changes as you rewrite.
4. Edit your essay, being sure to proofread it at least three times: twice to catch errors you are particularly apt to make, once to catch other errors. Rewrite a final time if your paper looks messy after you have made the corrections.

CHAPTER 5

Steps to Writing Description, Narration, and Process ("How To") Essays

This chapter and the one that follows teach special techniques for particular assignments you may receive in English classes and other courses that require essays. As the need arises, refer back to Chapter 4 for help in writing a purpose statement, planning a paper, writing introductions and conclusions, and revising an essay.

Description

To describe an experience, person, place, or object is to give a verbal account in detail. A good description helps the reader see, hear, and feel what you are describing; it also does more, for it helps the reader know the experience, person, place, or object you are describing. When you were describing a neighborhood in Chapter 4, for example, your task was to help your reader know something of what it is like to be there, to know the neighborhood from the inside. If you are describing a sunset, the task is not only to help your reader see as a camera "sees," but also to experience with you what it is like to see the sunset. Remember, no one sees, hears, and experiences something exactly as you do. Do not ever simply give in and say what you think others want you to say. Your descriptions should come from your own perceptions.

Learning to write descriptions will help you in courses other than this one. In a literature class you may be asked to describe George and Lennie's dream in *Of Mice and Men* by John Steinbeck. In a history class you may be asked to describe the reign of Louis XIV. In a philosophy class you may be asked to describe Plato's symbolic cave. Moreover, your skill in describing people and objects will be a most useful tool in paragraph development in all your papers because you will be able to make good use of detail.

Writing a Description Essay

Your main purpose in writing description is to convey to your reader your dominant impression of the person, place, object, or experience you are describing.

1. Stress details. Your paper can be only as strong as the details in it. Whether you are telling your reader what you see or hear, describe the details as precisely as you can. If, for example, you are describing a room, ask yourself the following kinds of questions to produce a detailed description:

What is the size of the room?
What small items does one see?
Do they have an odor?
Do they have rough edges? smooth?
Are they rusty? shiny?
Is the air dank and musty or fresh?
Are there cracks in the walls and old wax stains around the edges of the floor?
Is the wallpaper bright and colorful?

Once you have a long list of details, you can choose the most effective for your paper and omit those that are irrelevant.

2. Let yourself become involved with whatever you are describing. To a casual observer, the oak tree in the back yard may be just an oak. But when you are writing a descriptive essay, you are no longer a casual observer. Look at the tree closely and perhaps you will see ancient initials carved in the trunk, the bark where they were carved long ago now bulging like scar tissue. Listen carefully. Does the wind really whistle through the leaves, or is it more of a sweeping or brushing sound? And try to remember what the tree meant for you in the past. When you were very young, did you and your friends have tea parties in the shade of the great oak on hot, dry summer days? Did you ever build a tree house in the arms of the oak? If so, can you still see the nails? What memories come back to you when you think of that tree house you built (or always wanted to build)?

3. Do not feel that you have to conjure up spectacular people or things to write about. The ordinary, the everyday will do just as well. But always look for meaning in the ordinary. The grass that grows in the cracks of a downtown sidewalk need not be just grass: It can be a reminder that while people pollute, build pavement everywhere, and even bomb cities into wastelands, they cannot kill life altogether; it keeps coming back, like the grass in the cracks of a downtown sidewalk.

4. When describing people, let them speak for themselves when you can. A single parent, the mother of six, reveals pages about herself when she tells her children, "The Lord makes the back to bear the burden." The old man who sits in front of the television set every day watching the same programs and making the same one-word comment—"Stupid!"—at the conclusion of each program tells us quite a bit about himself, if not about television.

5. Tell stories that are a paragraph in length, or even shorter, to help convey your main point, your dominant impression. If you are writing about how your friend Ernesto is cranky, tell a short story to help illustrate his crankiness. If you are describing a typical mid-winter day in your icy climate, tell a short story about what you did once to protect yourself from the cold.

6. Sometimes you can best describe a subject by comparing it to something else. You can make this comparison by saying that your subject is *like* something else, or you can say that your subject *is* or *was* something else. If you say your subject is like or similar to something else, you are using a simile. If you say that your subject actually is or was something else, you are using a metaphor. One student used a simile to describe a chubby relative who "was shaped *like* a loosely rolled sleeping bag." Another used a simile to say that his uncle "was as mean *as* a pit bull." If the first student had said his relative "*was* a loosely rolled sleeping bag" and the second had said his uncle "*was* a pit bull," the students would have been using metaphors.

Do not settle for using similes and metaphors you have heard many times before. Instead of saying "he was as thin as a rail," one student wrote "he was as thin as capital *I*." Instead of saying that the ice on a pond was "as smooth as glass," one student wrote that "the frozen ice pond looked like grandmother's cloudy, cracked bureau mirror." The use of such similes and metaphors can make your description richer and more original.

Read the student essays below in preparation for writing a description essay on one of your relatives or friends. How effective are the students in helping you get to know the people they are writing about?

SAMPLE A

Molly

If you ever bumped into my grandmother, you would probably say she was the perfect picture of a mean, old, grouchy grandmother. But really deep down, she is not that way at all. You just have to get to know her.

Her name is Molly. Her hair is gray with white streaks and is usually combed into braids. She always walks with a cane, which she carries for protection. You can rarely understand what she is saying because she has very few teeth in her mouth. When you have just a few teeth, it is hard to get those words out. I guess you could say Molly is a small-framed woman. She weighs only one hundred ten pounds. But even though she is little, she is a woman who gets around.

An important thing for Molly is her routine of walking from the back of the house to the front. Molly makes this little journey at least five times daily. When she makes this trip in the late afternoon, she goes out the front door and sits on the porch. She is stationed there for the rest of the evening. As night falls, everyone comes out to greet a friend or visit a neighbor. People who pass in front of Molly's porch know to speak to her. If you don't happen to speak, you get a big argument from her and a lot of name calling.

It is not a good idea to do or say anything to offend Molly. If you do, there is a guarantee you will not hear the end of it. Once when I was combing my hair, I accidentally left my comb and brush on her dresser. When I finally remembered where I had left my belongings, I hastily went back to get them. But when I got there, to my surprise, everything was on the floor. There was a note on the dresser that read, "Don't ever leave your mess on my dresser again or your things won't be the same." When I finished reading the note, I was so angry I tore it up and threw it into the fireplace. I should never have done that because Molly was standing right behind me. She politely told me to go to her study and write another note and tear it into small pieces. Then she made me pick up the pieces and put them together like a puzzle. That was the last time I made a mistake like that.

Molly is not always a mean person. Usually on Sundays she is in a good frame of mind. Early in the morning she attends church service and then returns home to finish cooking dinner. After the dinner is eaten, we all sit down and talk. The evening ends with one of Molly's favorite desserts. Molly is really a wonderful person. You just have to understand her. She is now ninety-one years old. Those are a lot of years of sweet grouchiness.

QUESTIONS FOR DISCUSSION

1. What is the purpose statement of this essay? Does the student succeed in helping you get to know Molly? How? What else would you like to know about her? Does the student seem personally involved in her description?
2. What is the organizing principle of each paragraph?
3. Does the second paragraph help carry out the purpose statement?
4. Look at the transition sentences that join the paragraphs. Are they effective? Could they be improved? How?
5. What particular use does the student make of the concluding paragraph? Does the example she uses in that paragraph effectively illustrate her point?

SAMPLE B

Pie

If you ever go to Woodville, Mississippi, you may meet my grandfather. He is a very respected man in the town. People say, "Pie was a working man, and he still works when he can."

His real name is Johnson Tolliver, but he is known to everyone as Pie. The top of his head looks like a shiny bowling ball, except for the snow-white hair around the sides. Pie has a hard time getting the words out because he stutters so badly. He is a medium-framed man and weighs about one hundred eighty pounds. Even though he is eighty, he can move as fast as any twelve year old.

As a boy, Pie was alone. He had to work all the time because his mother was ill. He could not even attend school because he was working in the field. While other little children played, Pie worked. They would make fun of how he always worked and hardly ever played.

When Pie's mother finally passed away, he left home to make his own life, moving to a white man's plantation. Soon after that, he married. Years passed, and he and his wife had nine children. As soon as the children were able to walk, they too began working in the field. But Pie always worked harder than anyone else. He started at six in the morning and ended at eight at night, always trying to pay his debts and to save what he could. My mother told me one day, "Mary, my daddy worked me so hard at the age of six. You don't know just how lucky you are." He raised extra corn, cattle, hogs, and chickens and was able to pay his way out of the plantation and to have enough money to buy land.

On this new land was a shack that was about to fall down. That was where Pie and his family lived. They planted crops and continued to work from sunup to sundown. The rest of the black people were still on the white man's land, saying "I wish I had worked as hard as Pie and his family. Maybe I would be off this white man's land." Pie's first wife passed away while she was giving birth to their ninth child. Pie was sad but kept on with his work.

Pie finally did remarry. Now he has a home and acres of land, and he does not owe money to anyone. At the age of eighty, he races around in his new car, while other people say, "Pie was a working man, and he still works when he can." In Woodville, many blacks are still poor and uneducated. To see a black man with luxuries is like seeing a king. Pie is helping out some of the blacks in Woodville, but he has always said, "People, you have to work hard for what you want and make the best of it."

QUESTIONS FOR DISCUSSION

1. How effective was the student in helping you get to know Pie? If you were introducing Pie to someone else, what might you say about him?
2. What is the purpose statement of the essay? Did the student carry it out successfully?
3. The student used a chronological sequence in developing her paper. What is the organizing principle of each paragraph?
4. The student quotes Pie and others. How successful is her use of the quotations? Do they sound like real people talking?
5. What are the similes in the second and sixth paragraphs?

WRITING ASSIGNMENT 1

The task is to write a paper of several paragraphs describing a relative or friend. First, choose the person you will write about, and then follow the six steps of the writing method as you compose the paper.

Choose Your Topic   List some of your relatives or friends (living or dead) that you could possibly write about.

_____   _____   _____

_____   _____   _____

_____   _____   _____

_____   _____   _____

Look over the list and pick a person who is especially interesting to you. (Do not be too quick to pick your mother, father, boyfriend, girlfriend, or spouse. The people who are closest to you are often the most difficult to write about.) List your choice below:

_____

Step One: Gather Ideas and Information

1. Using the brainstorming method, write in the left-hand column below exactly what you see when you look at your friend or relative. What would a camera with color film pick up? What are the person's physical characteristics? What kinds of clothes does the person typically wear?

_____   _____

_____   _____

_____   _____

_____   _____

_____   _____

_____   _____

_____   _____

2. In the right-hand column above, make your description more precise, as shown in the following examples from different papers:

always smoking   *always smoking a long, thin cigarette*

bald head   *shining dome of a head with bushy hair around the ears*

white hair   *snow-white hair that matches the teeth he takes out at night short and chubby* _____   *shaped like a loosely rolled sleeping bag*

limps _____   *has a hernia that forces him to tilt left when he walks*

always bundled up _____   *wears two black, ankle-length coats buttoned to his chin*

red nose _____   *a cherry tomato of a nose*

3. How does your relative or friend spend his or her time? Think in terms of a typical day or week.

   _____

   _____

   _____

4. What are some of your relative's or friend's favorite expressions? Here are a few examples to get you started:

   "It is just no use trying to please everybody."

   "Whereya at, man?"

   "When I die, don't cry over me."

   "When one door closes, another opens."

   "I can't tell you how strongly I feel about that."

   "Tommydamnrot!"   "Horsefeathers!"   "Fiddlesticks!"

   _____

   _____

   _____

5. Think of as many incidents (events of short duration) as you can that would tell the reader something significant about your relative or friend. Use the fourth paragraph of the "Molly" paper as an example. Identify these events in just a few words.

   _____

   _____

   _____

6. Consult with someone who also knows your relative or friend and see what information that person can add to your lists.

Step Two: Analyze the Ideas and the Information   Read over the information you have gathered and check the items that seem most significant. Write down three or four of the most important things about your relative or friend. (For this step, the author of the "Molly" paper wrote, "old, grouchy, loving, determined.")

_____

_____

_____

Step Three: State Your Purpose   State in one sentence exactly what you would like to say about your relative or friend. (Review the criteria for the purpose statement in Chapter 4.)

_____

_____

_____

Here are some examples of purpose statements from successful papers:

> I have a hustler for a cousin.
>
> My Aunt Birdie is a rare species of aunt that will soon become extinct; she cares more for her family than for herself.
>
> Aunt Gerdie Mae, as she says, "doesn't take anything from anybody."
>
> Mr. Terry takes care of anything that is homeless—from dogs to human beings.
>
> Although Lloyd's life was short, the time we had with him was special.

Step Four: Make Your Plan   You will probably need four or more paragraphs to carry out your purpose statement. In your outline, include details you will write about. Brainstorm for more details and more examples for each paragraph, if you find yourself short. You may want to include the physical description in the introductory paragraph, or, like the author of the "Molly" paper, you may want to use a separate paragraph for it. Use the space provided below for your outline.

Here is part of an outline from one student's paper:

PARAGRAPH 2   Mr. Terry takes care of dogs.
_____
(organizing principle)

his four well-kept dogs (describe), people bring him dogs and he finds
_____
(detail)

homes for them, the time my dog was hurt
_____

PARAGRAPH 1   Introduction (include purpose statement)
_____
(organizing principle)

_____

(detail)

_____

PARAGRAPH 2   _____
(organizing principle)

_____

(detail)

_____

PARAGRAPH 3   _____
(organizing principle)

_____

(detail)

_____

PARAGRAPH 4   _____
(organizing principle)

_____

(detail)

_____

PARAGRAPH 5   _____
(organizing principle)

_____

(detail)

_____

PARAGRAPH 6   Conclusion
_____
(organizing principle)

_____

(detail)

_____

Before moving to the next step, check your outline with your instructor.

Step Five: Write　 Here are some suggestions to keep in mind as you write. First, pay attention to detail. Remember, the word _describe_ means to tell about something _in detail_. Use the information you have gathered. You will think of more as you write. Second, let yourself become involved with the person you are writing about. Show your reader through your writing why this person is important to you in either a positive or negative sense. Third, read over the suggestions for conclusions in Chapter 4, and use your conclusion to make a contrasting statement or a statement about the significance of the person for you.

Step Six: Evaluate, Revise, and Edit   Evaluate your paper using the ten questions listed on pages 93–94. Pay particular attention to the following questions:

1. Did each of your paragraphs help carry out your purpose statement? If not, did you have a valid reason for using each paragraph the way you did?
2. Did most of your details relate directly to your purpose statement? Did you use too little or too much detail?
3. Did you use dialogue? If so, did it sound like your relative or friend talking?
4. Can any of your sentences be omitted? Can any be shortened?
5. Did you use the most exact words possible? (For further help, see the suggestions that follow this section.)

Now revise and edit your paper. You should especially watch for errors that often appear on this assignment—errors in verb agreement, verb spelling, and punctuation of dialogue—as the following examples illustrate:

1. *Verb agreement*. In writing about what your relative or friend does each day, you probably need to use third-person singular, present-tense verbs. This form calls for using the *-s* or *-es* ending for regular verbs, *has* instead of *have*, and *is* instead of *are:*

Correct	Incorrect
She *acts* as if . . .	She *act* as if . . .

   If you have a problem with verb agreement, study Chapter 13.

2. *Verb Spelling*. When you add *-s* or *-es* to verbs that end in *-y*, follow the rules given in Chapter 17. The following forms are correct:

   Ricky *flies* around the house . . .

   She *tries* her best to please . . .

3. *Punctuation of dialogue*. Follow the rules given in Chapter 18.7.

WRITING ASSIGNMENT 2

Using the suggestions above for descriptive writing, write a paper of several paragraphs on one of the following:

1. Describe two animals fighting.
2. Describe the salesclerks who work in your favorite or least favorite store.
3. Describe people in busy shopping areas who are either selling things, preaching, or begging.
4. Describe the night before a combat mission.
5. Describe the worst storm you were ever in.
6. Describe the most beautiful place you have ever seen.
7. Describe a street corner and the group that gathers there each day.
8. Describe a jog in the park (or wherever else you jog).
9. Describe an automobile wreck that you either were in or witnessed.
10. Describe a particular tree (or any other plant) that is special to you.
11. Describe the four seasons where you live.

Using the Most Exact Word in Your Essays

As you proofread and then revise your paper, look at each word separately to see if you have chosen your words well and are saying what you want to say.

When in doubt, consult a dictionary or thesaurus. Besides giving the definition of a word, a good dictionary will also give synonyms (words of similar meanings) for many words. A thesaurus is a reference book consisting entirely of synonyms and antonyms (words of opposite meanings). Ask your instructor to recommend a complete dictionary and perhaps a thesaurus.

SUGGESTIONS FOR USING THE MOST EXACT WORD

1. Do not use a general word such as *good, bad,* or *interesting* when you can think of a more precise word. Instead of *good friend,* maybe you want to say *dependable friend, close friend, fun-loving friend.* Of course, maybe you do want to say *good friend.* If so, say it. The important thing is to make a decision about the words you use.
2. Avoid using inexact words. Words like *aspects, factors,* and *things* have their uses, but all too often they are used casually and, thus, misused.
3. Do not use a slang word unless it really is the best word to say what you mean. In writing about his cousin, one student used the slang expression *freaked out:* his cousin was *freaked out* over religion. He was looking for an expression that was negative but not too belittling, an expression that was not overly serious. Perhaps *freaked out* was his best choice. Ordinarily, however, avoid slang words. Later in the paper the same student spoke of women who were *into* religion. Certainly he could have found a word that was not slang that could replace *into* as used in that way.
4. It is important to try out new words from time to time, even though you

will not always use them correctly. But be careful. Everyday words are usually better than high-sounding words:

Choose	*Instead of*
spit	expectorate
his death	his demise
opening	aperture

Narration

A narrative is simply a story in which the writer tells of one event or a series of closely related events. In this section you will learn to write a narrative that will tell of a time when you learned something important to you. At the end of the section are suggested topics for writing other narratives.

Many students respond to narrative assignments by saying that they can think of nothing to write about. They are convinced that they have no story to tell. By the time you complete this assignment, however, you should find that you have in your memory many stories worth telling and writing down. You will discover that in its own way your life is full of drama, not necessarily the kind you see on television but rather the kind that grows out of situations that are *important to you.* The single best thing you can do in writing a narrative is to prod yourself to tell the whole story: give all the important details, report all the important dialogue, tell all the significant events within the main event.

One of our great American writers, Flannery O'Connor, has written about telling stories, "There is a certain embarrassment about being a storyteller in these times when stories are considered not quite as satisfying as statements and statements not quite as satisfying as statistics; but in the long run, a people is known, not by its statements or its statistics, but by the stories it tells" (*Mystery and Manners*). We know about Jews and Christians primarily from the stories they told, which were eventually written down to make one long story, the Bible. We know about the beginnings of Greek, and thus Western, culture from the stories the early Greeks told and Homer retold in the *Iliad* and the *Odyssey*. In this class you will learn more about each other and more about yourself if you will do the hard work of prodding yourself to recall some of your story so that you can tell it in detail. Learning to write narratives will help you in other courses in college also, especially when you are given such questions as the following:

1. In a history course: "Trace the events leading up to the Bolshevik Revolution." (In describing the events, you show how one thing led to another and then another and so on. Similarly, narratives show how one thing leads to another, and then another.)

2. In an economics course: "Tell what happened when the stock market crashed in October 1929."
3. In a literature course: "Tell what happened when Odysseus returned home after years of trying to find his way."

Writing a Narrative Essay

Your main purpose in writing narration is to tell in detail a story that has one main point.

1. Make sure you write a story, not reflections on a story. If you were in an automobile accident and went to see a lawyer about it, your lawyer would ask you to tell exactly what happened, not give your views on reckless driving or on how right you were and how wrong the other driver was. When you write your story, it is appropriate to use your introduction to give background information and your conclusion to discuss the significance of the story for you, but most of your paper should be an account of exactly what happened.

2. For short essays choose to write about events of limited duration that take place in an hour, half a day, or at most a day. Do not tell your reader what happened last summer or during the three weeks you worked at Sammy's Salmon Camp. Pick *one* event from last summer or *one* event from your work at the camp that illustrates what it was like.

3. In writing narration one often discovers the main point of the story as one writes. Be willing to revise your essay until you make the point you really want to make. By the time you write the final draft, however, you should have a main point or purpose in mind, although you may decide not to state it outright anywhere in the essay.

4. When possible, choose to write about an event in which conflict is present. Conflict is the stuff powerful stories are made of. Here are four kinds of conflict you can develop in narrative:

(1) *Conflict between people.* If you are writing about a disastrous canoe trip during which you and your friends argued heatedly about whether to stop and make camp or paddle to the next campsite, describe the argument.

(2) *Conflict between an individual and the environment.* Perhaps one of the reasons the canoe trip was a disaster was that it rained and turned much colder. Write about the conflict between the canoe party and the forces of nature.

(3) *Conflict within yourself.* Perhaps you really did not want to go on the canoe trip in the first place, knowing that there would be bad weather, but went because your friends put a lot of pressure on you. Write about the conflict within yourself between doing what they wanted you to do and what you wanted to do.

(4) *Conflict between an individual and society.* Sometimes it is appropriate to write about how an individual fights with society. In such cases you

may want to show how one person refuses to go along with what everyone else does.

5. Make use of your skills in presenting detail and, when it helps your story to come alive, recording dialogue.

The following is taken from Richard Wright's famous book *Black Boy*. As you read it, ask yourself what the main point of the story is.

SAMPLE

One evening my mother told me that thereafter I would have to do the shopping for the food. She took me to the corner store to show me the way. I was proud; I felt like a grownup. The next afternoon I looped the basket over my arm and went down the pavement toward the store. When I reached the corner, a gang of boys grabbed me, knocked me down, snatched the money, took the basket, and sent me running home in panic. That evening I told my mother what had happened, but she made no comment; she sat down at once, wrote another note, gave me more money, and sent me out to the grocery again. I crept down the steps and saw the same gang of boys playing down the street. I ran back into the house.

"What's the matter?" my mother asked.

"It's those same boys," I said. "They'll beat me."

"You've got to get over that," she said. "Now go on."

"I'm scared," I said.

"Go on and don't pay any attention to them," she said.

I went out of the door and walked briskly down the sidewalk, praying that the gang would not molest me. But when I came abreast of them someone shouted.

"There he is!"

They came toward me and I broke into a wild run toward home. They overtook me and flung me to the pavement. I yelled, pleaded, kicked, but they wrenched the money out of my hand. They yanked me to my feet, gave me a few slaps, and sent me home sobbing. My mother met me at the door.

"They b-b-beat me," I gasped. "They t-t-took the m-m-money."

I started up the steps, seeking the shelter of the house.

"Don't you come in here," my mother warned me.

I froze in my tracks and stared at her.

"But they're coming after me," I said.

"You just stay right where you are," she said in a deadly tone. "I'm going to teach you this night to stand up and fight for yourself."

She went into the house and I waited, terrified, wondering what she was about. Presently she returned with more money and another note; she also had a long heavy stick.

"Take this money, this note, and this stick," she said. "Go to the store and buy those groceries. If those boys bother you, then fight."

I was baffled. My mother was telling me to fight, a thing she had never done before.

"But, I'm scared," I said.

"Don't you come into this house until you've gotten those groceries," she said.

"Then stay in the streets; don't come back here!"

I ran up the steps and tried to force my way past her into the house. A stinging slap came on my jaw. I stood on the sidewalk, crying.

"Please let me wait until tomorrow," I begged.

"No," she said, "go now! If you come back into this house without those groceries, I'll whip you!"

She slammed the door and I heard the key turn in the lock. I shook with fright. I was alone upon the dark, hostile streets and gangs were after me. I had the choice of being beaten at home or away from home. I clutched the stick, crying, trying to reason. If I were beaten at home, there was absolutely nothing that I could do about it, but if I were beaten in the streets, I had a chance to fight and defend myself. I walked slowly down the sidewalk, coming closer to the gang of boys, holding the stick tightly. I was so full of fear that I could scarcely breathe. I was almost upon them now.

"There he is again!" the cry went up.

They surrounded me quickly and began to grab for my hand.

"I'll kill you!" I threatened.

They closed in. In blind fear I let the stick fly, feeling it crack against a boy's skull. I swung again, lamming another skull, then another. Realizing that they would retaliate if I let up for but a second, I fought to lay them low, to knock them cold, to kill them so that they could not strike back at me. I flayed with tears in my eyes, teeth clenched, stark fear making me throw every ounce of my strength behind each blow. I hit again and again, dropping the money and the grocery list. The boys scattered, yelling, nursing their heads, staring at me in utter disbelief. They had never seen such a frenzy. I stood panting, egging them on, taunting them to come on and fight. When they refused, I ran after them and they tore out for their homes, screaming. The parents of the boys rushed into the streets and threatened me, and for the first time in my life I shouted at grown-ups, telling them that I would give them the same if they bothered me. I finally found my grocery list and the money and went to the store. On the way back I kept my stick poised for instant use, but there was not a single boy in sight. That night I won the right to the streets of Memphis.

Richard Wright, from *Black Boy*

QUESTIONS FOR DISCUSSION

1. What is the main point of the story? How would you write a purpose statement for it?
2. Was Wright's mother acting responsibly in making him fight? Have you ever had a similar experience? Must violence always be met with violence?
3. Where is the conflict in the story?
4. How did Wright develop suspense in the story? What did he do in telling the story that made you want to read on?
5. Read some of the dialogue aloud. Does it sound real to you? Can you actually hear the boy and his mother talking?
6. Did you like the story? Why or why not?

EXERCISE

Name, in the order in which they occurred, the events that made up the story by Richard Wright. (You should be able to identify six to eight events.)

1. *Wright's mother showed him how to shop.*
2. _____
3. _____
4. _____
5. _____
6. _____
7. _____
8. _____

Before writing your narrative, you may want to read the student samples on pages 275 and 287.

WRITING ASSIGNMENT 3

Write a story about a time you learned something important to you. First, choose a particular event, and then follow the six steps of the writing method as you write your paper.

Choose Your Topic   Using the brainstorming method, name as many events from your past as you can think of in which you learned something important. The categories below should help you think of such events.

1. A time you learned that not all promises should be kept

_____

_____

_____

2. A time you learned a bitter lesson

_____

_____

_____

3. A time you learned something important about the opposite sex

_____

_____

_____

4. A time you learned never to do a certain thing again

_____

_____

_____

5. A time you learned to take care of yourself

_____

_____

_____

6. A time you learned that mothers (or fathers) are not always right (or wrong)

_____

_____

_____

7. A time you learned what the police are like

_____

_____

_____

8. A time you learned to "grin and bear it"

_____

_____

_____

9. Some other time you learned something important to you

_____

_____

_____

Pick one of the above events to write about. Ask yourself if you can write several paragraphs on that event. Write the name of the event here:

_____

Step One: Gather Ideas and Information   Write below at least six episodes *within* the main event, the time you learned something important. Use the exercise following the Richard Wright story as a guide.

1. _____

2. _____

3. _____

4. _____

5. _____

6. _____

Prepare the worksheet below, filling out as much of it as you can. Follow this order for each episode.

episode within the
main event _____   who did what _____

who said what _____

what you felt _____

_____   _____
(first episode)
_____

_____

_____   _____
(second episode)
_____

_____

_____   _____
(third episode)
_____

_____

_____   _____
(fourth episode)
_____

_____

_____   _____
(fifth episode)
_____

_____

_____   _____
(sixth episode)   _____
                                      _____

Step Two: Analyze the Ideas and the Information   Ask yourself the following questions:

1. Where is the conflict in the story? How can I develop it?
2. Where is the story going? What is it really about?
3. What dialogue might I use in my narrative? (Although dialogue is not essential, it often helps make a story come alive for the reader.)

Step Three: State the Purpose   The narrative is one kind of writing in which the purpose statement is often not revealed until the middle or the end of the paper or even left out altogether. But you should know where you are headed in your narrative and what you want to accomplish. Thus, you should have a purpose statement in mind even though it may not be expressed. Look over the work you have done so far and write your purpose statement below:

_____

_____

_____

One way to prepare your purpose statement for this assignment is simply to fill in the blanks in the following sentence:

I learned _____ the time _____

_____

A purpose statement for Wright's story could be "Richard Wright learned how to take care of himself the time his mother forced him to fight." (As pointed out above, once you begin to write you may find that you need to change your purpose statement and start your story again.)

Step Four: Make Your Plan   Write an informal outline that will help you to accomplish your purpose. If you quote a conversation with several exchanges, you may not be able to set up your outline in the usual paragraph form since you will have to begin new paragraphs each time the speaker shifts. Instead, let each episode within the event you are writing about constitute one of the main points in the body of your outline. You will want to use the information-gathering worksheet as you write your outline.

You may want to use the introduction to place the event you are writing about in a larger context by mentioning other events that led up to it. You may also want to use the conclusion to show the significance of the event for you.

Step Five: Write   As you write, make sure you are telling the whole story: Your narrative should have a beginning, a middle, and an end. Also, make sure you are not going off in directions that take you away from your purpose. If you can build suspense into your narrative, do so. If possible, emphasize the conflict. Concentrate on using detail and, when it seems helpful, dialogue. Finally, be careful to give your sentences variety.

Step Six: Evaluate, Revise, and Edit   Evaluate your paper by asking the following questions:

1. Did you tell what happened, or is your story mostly reflections on what happened or what could have happened?
2. Did you keep the main point of the story before you throughout the paper? If not, where did you go off in another direction?
3. Did your story take place within a short period of time? If not, what was the time span?
4. Did your sentences flow smoothly into each other or were they choppy? Did you use too many *ands* and *thens* to connect sentences and clauses?

Now revise and edit your paper. Watch especially for the following errors, which often show up in narrative essays:

1. Run-on sentences (see Chapter 12.2)
2. Tense confusion (see Chapter 15.7)
3. Errors in punctuating dialogue (see Chapter 18.7)

Process ("How To") Essays

A process essay is often called a "how to" essay because it tells you how to do or make a particular thing. The explanation of the six-step writing method in Chapter 4 is an example of process writing. You might be asked to write several process papers in college. In a political science class, for example, you could be asked to tell how a bill becomes a law. Here you would begin with the legislator or private citizen who first formulates a bill that he or she would like to see enacted into law, and then you would tell step by step what must be done until the president finally signs the bill and it becomes the law of the land. In a biology class you could be asked to show how photosynthesis works. In an education class you could be asked to explain how you would teach a blind person—step by step—to ride a bus.

The key point to remember in writing a process paper is that you tell how to do or make something a step at a time, from beginning to end. The form of a process paper is much like the form of a narrative, and that is why it comes after the narrative in this text. Both essays are based on a chronological sequence: one thing leads to another, and then to another, and then to another.

Writing a Process Essay

Your main purpose in a process essay is to explain clearly, step by step, how to do or make something.

1. Be clear. Keep in mind the audience to whom you are writing, and ask yourself if the people reading your paper could actually do what you are showing them how to do. In order to be clear, write your process essay in steps and define all terms that might be unclear to your particular audience. If, for example, you are writing to your class telling them how to master the skill of editing, you will need to define *editing* if the class has not yet talked about what it is. If the class has already discussed the term, you will not need to define it.

2. In your first paragraph, in addition to including your purpose statement, you may want to tell *why* it is important to do or make the thing you are explaining. You may also want to tell how you happened to learn this skill. One student began her paper as follows:

> If you want to decorate your living room for a special occasion, try making a flower arrangement. I have worked at a florist shop for the last three years and have discovered what a nice touch a flower arrangement can add to a room. You will see just how easy it is to arrange flowers.

3. In your purpose statement you should both indicate what you are going to explain how to do and also say something about the process of doing it. In the example above, the student not only stated that her paper would show how to make a flower arrangement, but also that arranging flowers was easy. Thus, she must accomplish two things in her paper: First, she must explain the steps of flower arranging, and second, she must persuade the reader to accept her point of view, namely, that it is easy. If she had a different point of view, she would need to state her purpose differently, perhaps as follows:

> Making a good flower arrangement can make your day.
>
> Arranging flowers is good therapy.
>
> Arranging flowers is an art.

4. If you need materials to do or make the thing you are explaining, list everything that is needed as your first step. If you are explaining how to make your favorite dish, for example, you should list the necessary ingredients first. But use common sense. In explaining how to shoot free throws in basketball, you do not have to tell your readers that they need a basketball and a basketball court.

5. Group your steps into logical units. There might be fifteen actual steps to changing a tire, but you do not need fifteen paragraphs to explain how to do it. You might want one paragraph on gathering the necessary equipment, another on jacking up the car, another on actually changing the tire, and a final paragraph on lowering the car from the jack and putting on the hubcap. Three to five paragraphs should be enough for the body of most process papers. Remember, you are writing an essay, not simply writing a list of instructions as you would in a recipe book.

6. Use smooth transition sentences to connect your paragraphs. If you have three paragraphs in the body of your paper, you may want to begin your transition sentences as follows:

> First, you . . .
>
> And then you . . .
>
> Finally, you . . .

(Note that a comma follows *first* and *finally* but not *and then*.) If you have four or more paragraphs in the body of your paper, you may want to use numbers—*first, second, third, fourth*, and so on—to introduce the paragraphs, perhaps substituting *finally* for the last number.

7. In the body of the paper, when you are giving instructions address your audience in the second person: "First, gather all of the necessary equipment . . . . Second, let your engine . . . . Third, crawl under . . . ." In each sentence *you* is understood.

As you read the following student essay, ask yourself if you could change the oil in an automobile by following these instructions. You may even want to try doing it.

SAMPLE

How to Change the Oil in Your Car

With prices as they are today, people are trying to figure out ways to economize. Americans want to learn how to do simple maintenance on their cars. Changing your own oil is one way you can save money. If you were to take your car to a garage for an oil change, you would find that a mechanic would charge you about fifteen dollars and maybe keep the car for a whole day. What many people do not realize is that you can change the oil yourself for about eight dollars and fifteen minutes of your time. So for those who do not know how to change their car's oil, this is how it is done.

First, gather all of the necessary equipment. You will need a jack, a blanket or a creeper to lie on, a wrench to fit the nut on the oil pan, an oil filter wrench, a bucket to catch the oil, an oil filter, and new oil. Ask a salesperson at an auto supply store to help you pick out the right wrenches, oil filter, and oil.

Second, let your engine run for about five minutes to get the oil hot. Turn the motor off and put the emergency brake on. Then jack the car up just high enough so that you can fit under it without any trouble. Before you get under the car, make sure that the bucket, the wrenches for the oil pan nut, and the oil filter are all close by. If you have a creeper, use it to slide under the car, but, if you do not, throw an old blanket on the ground to prevent your clothes from getting dirty.

Third, crawl under the car and look for the oil pan, behind the radiator, under the engine block. At the corner of the oil pan there is a nut about one-half inch wide. Put the bucket under the nut and loosen it. Be careful because the oil may be hot. After the nut is off, let the oil drain into the bucket for about five minutes. Put the nut back on and make sure it is very tight.

Fourth, look for the oil filter. It is next to the oil pan and is about the size of a man's wrist. It should be only hand tight, but if not, use the oil filter wrench to take it off. Some oil will still be in the filter; let it drain. Now you have the option of either keeping the old filter or using the new one. (You should change the filter at least every other oil change.) If you decide to put on the new filter, take a little of the old oil and rub it on the rubber gasket around the filter to make a better seal. Tighten the filter only hand tight as you screw it in.

Fifth, to put fresh oil in the engine, raise the hood and look on the side of your engine for a cap that screws into the engine block. It usually says "oil." Take the cap off and put the right amount of oil in your engine, usually four or five quarts. After the oil is in the car, run the engine for a few minutes and examine the nut and the oil filter to see if any leaks have formed. If not, lower your car from the jack and put the equipment away.

You see, changing your oil is not hard, and it can save you money.

QUESTIONS FOR DISCUSSION

1. Could you actually change the oil in your car from these instructions? Are any steps not clear? Is any step left out?
2. What is the purpose statement?
3. What is the organizing principle of each paragraph?
4. Did the author overuse transition words like *then*, *now*, or *next*?
5. Should the author have defined any terms? If so, which?

WRITING ASSIGNMENT 4

Choose Your Topic   Brainstorm for as many specific topics as you can think of under the following general headings:

1. How to do something relating to automobiles

   how to change oil _____   _____

   _____   _____

2. How to do or make something relating to music or art

   how to write a song _____

   _____   _____

3. How to do something relating to sports

   how to win the quarter mile   _____

   _____   _____

4. How to do or make something relating to homemaking

   how to make a blouse   _____

   _____   _____

5. How to do something relating to pets

   how to train a rabbit   _____

   _____   _____

6. How to do something relating to study skills

   how to edit an essay   _____

   _____   _____

7. How to do something relating to raising children

   how to teach your child to swim   _____

   _____   _____

Or, consider writing on one of these topics:

1. How to succeed (or not succeed) in the military
2. How to win over the opposite sex
3. How to survive in college
4. How to make your first million
5. How to spend a rainy weekend
6. How to catch a big fish
7. How to plan a party
8. How to plan a trip

Now choose a topic that you would enjoy writing on and that you know enough about. Make sure that your topic is not too technical on the one hand nor too general in scope on the other. Write your topic here:

_____

Step One: Gather Ideas and Information   In a process paper, information gathering is a short but important process. In the left-hand column below, list the steps that your reader must follow to do or make the thing you are explaining:

_____   _____

_____   _____

_____   _____

_____   _____

_____   _____

_____   _____

_____   _____

Now look at each step carefully and see if you need to include additional steps, steps within steps, or steps between steps. Write these in the right-hand column. Remember, your directions must be perfectly clear.

Look over your lists and see what equipment or materials, if any, your reader will need to gather before beginning. Write them below:

_____   _____

_____   _____

_____   _____

Step Two: Analyze the Ideas and the Information   See what steps you can group together in a logical way so that you will not have too many paragraphs in the body of your paper. Remember, you are writing an essay, not making a list. What terms will you need to define? What steps will be particularly hard to explain? Is there anything you can leave out and still be clear in what you have to say?

Step Three: State Your Purpose   What word or words best describe the process you are explaining? Choose words like *easy, difficult, fun, dangerous, important,* and *relaxing.* Write them below:

_____

As the examples below demonstrate, such descriptive words can help you construct a purpose statement. However, note that you need not use the descriptive word itself.

DESCRIPTIVE WORD
fun

PURPOSE STATEMENT
Preparing for a trip is almost as much fun as the trip itself.

DESCRIPTIVE WORD

difficult

PURPOSE STATMENT

Giving your dog a bath is more complicated than you might think.

DESCRIPTIVE WORD

dangerous

PURPOSE STATEMENT

In charging a battery with jumper cables, you must be very careful.

DESCRIPTIVE WORD

easy (if motivated)

PURPOSE STATEMENT

If you like to clap your hands and stomp your feet, you can learn to play the drums.

Keeping your descriptive word (or words) in mind, state your purpose below:

_____

_____

Step Four: Make Your Plan   Decide what you will include in your introduction, and then group the individual steps you are explaining in a logical way. (Three to five paragraphs in the body of your paper should be enough.) Instead of detail, under each of your paragraph headings list the individual steps. The student who wrote the paper on changing oil outlined his third paragraph this way:

PARAGRAPH 3   *steps before you crawl under the car*
(organizing principle)

run engine, jack up car, get bucket ready, wrenches,
(steps)

blanket or creeper

Write your outline in the space below. Try to use three to five paragraphs in the body of your essay.

_____
(your title)

PARAGRAPH 1   Introduction
_____
(organizing principle)

PARAGRAPH 2   _____
(organizing principle)

_____

(steps)

_____

PARAGRAPH 3 _____
(organizing principle)

_____

(steps)

_____

PARAGRAPH 4 _____
(organizing principle)

_____

(steps)

_____

PARAGRAPH 5 _____
(organizing principle)

_____

(steps)

_____

PARAGRAPH 6 _____
(organizing principle)

_____

(steps)

_____

PARAGRAPH 7   Conclusion
(organizing principle)

_____

_____

Step Five: Write   As you write, try most of all to be perfectly clear. If your audience is the class, write to them: Ask yourself if class members will actually be able to do the thing you are describing. Be sure to define any terms that your audience is not likely to understand.

Also, try to give variety to your sentences. Avoid the following kind of writing:

> First, you run around the track once. Then you do forty jumping jacks. Then you do thirty knee bends. Next, you do thirty back bends. Then you run around the track one more time. Finally, you catch your breath and relax.

One way to avoid such monotonous writing is to ask yourself *why* you should do the things you are writing about. The above passage could be written as follows:

> First, jog around the track once slowly to loosen up your leg muscles and to increase the flow of adrenalin in your body. Then, to loosen up other muscles,

do your warm-up exercises: forty jumping jacks, thirty knee bends, and thirty back bends. You should be breathing hard by now, but you are not quite through. Before you begin the race, run around the track one more time, at a slightly faster pace than before. Now catch your breath and relax completely.

Step Six: Evaluate, Revise, and Edit   Evaluate your paper by asking the questions below:

1. Is every step of your essay clear? If not, where is it not clear? What can you do to make it clear?
2. Does your purpose statement tell your readers what you want to say about your topic?
3. Does your paper sound choppy when you read it aloud? At what point do you notice any choppiness? How might you correct it?

Now revise and edit your paper. Two kinds of errors that often appear in this type of essay are pronoun person shifts and run-on sentences.

1. *Pronoun person shifts.* Do not change the person of a pronoun within the same sentence unless you have a valid reason for doing so. (See Chapter 16.5.) What is the error in the following sentence?

   One has to walk very slowly, breathing deeply, if you are going to make it to the top.

2. *Run-on sentences.* You cannot join two sentences or independent clauses with *then* or *next*, but you can join them with *and* or a semicolon. (See Chapter 12.2.) The following is a run-on sentence. Correct it.

   First, you make a white sauce, then you begin adding water slowly.

CHAPTER 6

Steps to Writing Example Essays, Comparison and Contrast Essays, and Classification Essays

One of the most important skills you can learn for developing an essay is how to write effective examples that illustrate your main point. In example essays, you illustrate your main point entirely by giving examples. You can make good use of your skill in giving examples when you write comparison and contrast essays (comparing two things), classification essays (comparing three or more things), and many other kinds of essays as well.

Example

An example essay is one in which you support your point of view on a particular topic simply by giving examples. Learning how to use examples in your writing will help you in writing not only an example essay but also practically every kind of essay. In writing about the civil rights battles in the 1960s, particular examples of the effects of segregation on black children will make your paper less abstract, more concrete, more real. In arguing against capital punishment, particular examples of people who were executed and then later proven innocent will certainly enhance your argument. In describing a particular character from a novel, examples of the character's actions in the story that illustrate your thesis or point of view will stengthen your essay.

Your readers will respond to examples because they make your writing interesting, easier to understand, and convincing. Notice how general—and how unconvincing—the following paragraph is:

> My parents mean the most to me because without the help of my mother and my father, I would not be where I am today. My parents taught me how to conduct myself around others. They have given me all the things I need and most of the things I want.

The author has given no examples of *how* her parents have helped her or *what* they have taught her and given her. With examples, the same thoughts could be expanded and expressed as follows:

> My parents mean the most to me because without the help of my mother and my father, I would not be where I am today. My mother stopped work when I was born just so that she could be with me. She made sure that I was held a lot, that I ate well, and that I got proper medical attention. She also taught me how to play softball. My father taught me how to swim, ride a bicycle, play the piano, and most important of all, how to do my school work. Together, my parents showed me how to conduct myself around others. They taught me to say "sir" and "ma'am" to adults. From them I learned to do unto everyone as I would have them do unto me. They have always provided me with clothing, food, and enough money to buy the essentials. Although my parents are not wealthy, they did buy me a piano, knowing how much I love music, and they did manage to send me to this community college.

Writing an Example Essay

Your main purpose in an example essay is to support your point of view on a particular subject solely by giving examples.

1. Offer at least three examples to illustrate your point of view. If you are making a particular point about children's television programs, give examples of at least three programs that prove your point. If you are making a general statement about high school teachers, give examples of at least three particular high school teachers who illustrate the point you are making.

2. Play fair with your reader. Do not make statements that are generally not true and then use unique examples to back them up. The statement "Teen-age marriages are usually successful" is statistically untrue. It is not playing fair for a writer to claim that the statement is true and then back up the claim by giving as examples a few teen-age marriages that were successful. However, the same writer could state, and state fairly, "Contrary to popular belief, teen-age marriages are sometimes successful." Then the writer could use several examples to back up that position.

3. For emphasis, and to catch your reader's attention, place your most convincing example first.

Example **127**

4. Consider using an example to begin your paper. One way to attract your reader's attention in the introduction is by giving an example of the point you will illustrate in your essay. See, for example, the first paragraph of the student sample below on "A Student's Life."

5. Even though you are writing an example paper, avoid the expression *for example.* When you give an example, it is usually clear that this is what you are doing. The test is simply to read what you have written without using *for example* and see if anything is lost by the omission.

SAMPLE

A Student's Life

A student's life is a difficult one. My Aunt Mary has decided to go back to school to get her college degree. It would not be so hard on her if she did not have a house to clean, children to raise, a family to feed, and a husband who does not help very much with these tasks. I do not see how she has any time for homework. Can you imagine trying to write an essay and yelling at children at the same time? Sometimes she has to make a choice of which is most important: the house, the family, or the homework. Being a housewife, mother, and student are three major jobs in themselves.

My friend Sue Laporte was complaining to me the other day about her teachers. She said they expect too much of her. Sue is studying accounting and therefore has a tremendous amount of homework. But to attend school she must maintain her job. To add to her troubles, her mother works, so after school Sue must babysit for her younger brother and two sisters. Her job is from six to ten-thirty, and by the time she arrives home and showers, it is around eleven. She limits herself to four hours of studying a night and goes to bed at about three in the morning. With the schedule Sue has, she has very little or no time for herself. But she has decided to commit herself to a few years of misery so that she can enjoy what she calls "the laughs of luxury."

Another friend, José Rodriguez, is attending the University of Colorado on a scholarship, which means he must keep his grades at a certain average. He is majoring in chemical engineering, he carries a total of seventeen credit hours, and he also plays baseball. Because he has little money, José has had to get a job. In one day he attends school, practices baseball, goes to work, and does homework. He wakes up at six-thirty every morning and does not go to sleep until very late at night. How he keeps up his grade point average is a mystery to me.

Sometimes teachers think that the only class you have is theirs. But it is not really their fault. No one ever said life was easy, especially at school!

QUESTIONS FOR DISCUSSION

1. Do you like the way the student began the paper? Should she have included any other material in the introduction? If so, what?
2. How do the transition sentences that begin the second and third para-

graphs serve to carry out the purpose statement? What particular words in the transitions relate to the word *difficult* in the purpose statement?
3. Are the three examples the student gives effective in illustrating her point? Does she need to expand any example? Explain.
4. Is the conclusion a contrasting statement, a statement of significance, a call to action, or a summary?
5. Can you identify with any of the students she writes about?

WRITING ASSIGNMENT 1

Choose Your Topic   Complete the following sentences, selecting the most exact words you can think of:

1. A college student's life is _____.

2. Most of my jobs have been _____.

3. Soap operas are _____.

4. One thing everyone loves to do is _____.

5. Teen-age marriages are _____.

6. Children's television programs are _____.

7. Most college (or high school) teachers could be described as

   _____.

8. The military could be described as _____.

9. People in _____ drive like _____.
   (name your town or city)

10. _____ is the most _____ sport.
    (name a sport)

   Discuss the above topics with others to stimulate more ideas and then choose one topic to write on. (Remember that this is not the title of your paper.)

Step One: Gather Ideas and Information   In the left-hand column below, list as many examples as you can think of that will support your statement.

_____   _____

_____   _____

_____   _____

_____   _____

Example **129**

_____   _____

_____   _____

Now, in the right-hand column, write as many supporting details as you can think of for each example.

Step Two: *Analyze the Ideas and the Information*   Which of the examples you listed above best support your purpose statement? Can any of the examples be combined? Can any be omitted without taking away from what you want to say? Do you need more examples?

Step Three: *State Your Purpose*   The sentence you chose to write on could serve as your purpose statement, but now that you have gathered and analyzed information about your topic, you may find that you need to write a new purpose statement.

Step Four: *Make Your Plan*   This time when you make your outline, write the transition sentences that will begin each paragraph in the body of your paper.

Introduction

PARAGRAPH 1   _____

_____

(detail)

PARAGRAPH 2   _____
              (transition sentence)

_____

_____

(detail)

PARAGRAPH 3   _____
              (transition sentence)

_____

_____

(detail)

PARAGRAPH 4   _____
              (transition sentence)

_____

_____

(detail)

PARAGRAPH 5   _____
                (transition sentence)

_____

_____

_____
(detail)

PARAGRAPH 6   Conclusion _____

_____
(detail)

Step Five: Write   As you write, make sure you give enough details to make each example convincing. If you are writing on gossip, do not just say someone is gossiping; give examples, preferably in dialogue, of the gossip. If you are writing on television programs, do not just say a particular program is violent; give particular examples that illustrate the violence. The more relevant details you give the more convincing your example will be.

Also, as you write, be aware of the verb tense you are using. If the example you are reporting happened in the past, use the past tense. If the example is still going on, use the present tense. When using present-tense verbs, be sure to add *-s* or *-es* in regular third-person singular constructions.

Step Six: Evaluate, Revise, and Edit   Evaluate your paper by asking the following questions:

1. Did you choose clear, relevant examples to prove your point? Do you need more?
2. Did you go into enough detail with each example you gave? Which is your best-written example? Which is your least well written example?

Now revise and edit your paper. Be on the lookout for three errors often found in this assignment: verb-tense confusion (see Chapter 15.7), verb-agreement problems (see Chapter 13), and errors in the use of *for example* or *for instance* to introduce an example. If *for example* introduces an independent clause, either capitalize *for* and write the clause as a sentence or use a semicolon before *for example,* as follows:

> I enjoy reading novels about the sea. For example, I really love *Moby Dick* and *The Old Man and the Sea.*

> *or*

> I enjoy reading novels about the sea; for example, I really love *Moby Dick* and *The Old Man and the Sea.*

If, however, *for example* introduces words or phrases, connect it to the preceding sentence with a comma, as follows:

> I enjoy reading novels about the sea, for example, *Moby Dick* and *The Old Man and the Sea.*

Notice that in all the above constructions, a comma comes after *for example.* To give your sentences variety, try using *for example* following the example you give:

> I enjoy reading novels about the sea, *Moby Dick* and *The Old Man and the Sea,* for example.

Comparison and Contrast

Much of our thinking is based on comparison and contrast. When we say a house is big, we mean it is big in comparison to other houses. The same house is quite small when compared to a skyscraper or a large industrial plant. When we say a diamond is small, we mean small in comparison to large diamonds or perhaps other precious stones. The same diamond may be very large when compared to a truly small diamond, such as one used for the tip of a phonograph needle. The words we use to describe many things are meaningful only when those things are compared and contrasted with other things.

Your assignment is to compare and contrast two people, two places, or two things in an essay of several paragraphs. Many essays assigned in college call for comparison and contrast. In a sociology class, you might be asked to compare the political views of white-collar workers with those of blue-collar workers. In a political science class, you might be asked to compare communism as practiced in the Soviet Union with communism in Yugoslavia. In a biology class, you might be asked to compare meiosis with mitosis. The two methods presented in this section for writing a comparison and contrast paper should be helpful for writing any such essay you might be assigned in the future.

Writing a Comparison and Contrast Essay

Your main purpose in a comparison and contrast essay is to show how two people, two places, or two things are alike or different or both.

1. Compare and contrast two things only. Use the classification essay format (discussed next) to compare and contrast three or more things.

2. In your purpose statement, give your views of the people, places, or things you are comparing. Do not just say that you will show in your paper how life in the suburbs is both similar to and different from life in the city. Offer an opinion as you compare the suburbs and the city. Here are several ways you could write your purpose statement:

> Life is easier (or more difficult) in the city than it is in the suburbs.
>
> The city is full of excitement, but the suburbs are boring.

The suburbs are clean and carefree, but the city is dirty and dangerous.

Life in the suburbs is surprisingly similar to life in the city.

Notice that both units to be compared are mentioned in each of these purpose statements.

3. In describing each of the two units, use your skill in giving examples, writing details, and when helpful, recording dialogue.

Two Methods of Planning the Essay

Method A   After your introduction, write one long paragraph about the first subject in your comparison, then write one long paragraph about the second subject, and then give your conclusion. (If your paper is much longer than three hundred words, you may want to subdivide each paragraph in the body into two or more paragraphs.) Here is an example of a Method A outline.

Introduction (include purpose statement)

PARAGRAPH 1

My two most opposite friends from the Air Force, how long
(detail)

I've known them, how they've influenced me.

PARAGRAPH 2   *James Evans*
(organizing principle)

1. General information: 6'7", lives in Tombstone, Arizona
(detail)

2. Married Ella Kentuck, whose father owns an auto repair shop

3. Runs sports supply store

4. Odd habits: always chews tobacco

5. Particular influence on me: convinced me that there was
a pot of gold at the end of the rainbow

PARAGRAPH 3   *Ted Spicer*
(organizing principle)

1. General information: 5'2", chubby, lives in Cowan, Tennessee
(detail)

2. Married to his fourth wife, Luella Writhe, whose father
left on a trip around the world when she was two

3. Works at odd jobs between marriages

4. Odd habits: dresses up on Sunday and sings in the church choir (for him that's odd)

5. Particular influence on me: taught me how to build a cabin

Conclusion

PARAGRAPH 4

How both have influenced me

(detail)

Note the following about the above outline:

1. The particular items of detail (1–5.) in paragraphs 2 and 3 are parallel to each other; that is, they follow the same pattern. If you use Method A, try to write your detail in a similarly parallel way. But not all of it has to be parallel. Perhaps you want to tell the reader that Ted Spicer has never voted but has nevertheless run for sheriff three times. Write this detail in your paragraph somewhere, even though you may not be able to provide parallel detail for James Evans.

2. When you are writing about the second subject in your comparison, try to refer back from time to time to the first subject so that your reader will be able to think of both subjects together. Otherwise, it may sound as though you are writing two separate essays. For example, you could introduce some of your detail describing Ted Spicer in the following way:

> While James has been married to the same woman for the last thirty years, Ted just got married for the fourth time to . . .

> James told me about the pot of gold, but Ted taught me how to build a cabin.

When using these "reminders," do not overdo it. Rely on what sounds right to you, or your paper may sound contrived.

3. Be careful to write your sentences so that they flow into each other smoothly, or your detail will sound like a list. Again, rely on your ear, on what sounds smooth to you as you read your writing back to yourself.

4. Method A is a good choice for comparison and contrast essays that are not too long. The more you say about each subject the more difficult it becomes for your reader to think of the two subjects together.

Method B As the organizing principle for each paragraph in the body of your paper, use the particular point of comparison or contrast. An abbreviated outline for the James Evans–Ted Spicer paper might look like this:

Introduction (include purpose statement)

PARAGRAPH 1

My two friends from the Air Force, how long I've known them

(detail)

PARAGRAPH 2   *General information*
                (organizing principle)

James Evans
(detail)

Ted Spicer

PARAGRAPH 3   *Marriages*
                (organizing principle)

James
(detail)

Ted

PARAGRAPH 4   *Employment*
                (organizing principle)

James
(detail)

Ted

PARAGRAPH 5   *Odd habits*
                (organizing principle)

James
(detail)

Ted

PARAGRAPH 6   *Particular influences on me*
                (organizing principle)

James
(detail)

Ted

PARAGRAPH 7   Conclusion

How they've both influenced me
(detail)

Note the following about the above outline:

1. In each paragraph in the body of the outline, the first subject in the comparison (James) is presented first. This helps make the paragraphs parallel to each other.
2. You will need to use a transition sentence in the middle of each paragraph as you move from the first subject in the comparison to the second. Here is an example. The transition sentence is italicized.

> James married Ella Kentuck thirty years ago. She is also from Tombstone, and her father has run an automobile repair shop there for the last fifty years. Ella is a very traditional housewife and has raised four children with

James. *Ted Spicer, on the other hand, has just married his fourth wife, Luella Writhe.* She is known mostly in Cowan, Tennessee, for being the woman whose father left home on a trip around the world when she was two and never came back. She does not like housework, but she has a good job in a neighboring town where she is a manager for Sears.

Here are two other ways the transition sentence could be written for this paragraph:

But Ted Spicer has different ideas about marriage. He has just married his fourth wife, Luella Writhe.

But Ted Spicer's wife is quite different.

Can you think of still other transitions? Try not to use the same transition words each time; instead give your writing variety.

3. Method B is a good choice for comparisons that are longer. But be careful not to write too many short paragraphs. You may need to combine two or more of your paragraphs with a new organizing principle. In the example above, paragraph 4 on employment might have been combined with other information in paragraph 2.

The three student samples below offer examples of using both Method A and Method B for writing comparison and contrast papers. Method A is demonstrated in the first two samples:

SAMPLE A

Two Medical Jobs

I have worked both as an x-ray technician in a hospital and as an assistant in a private physician's office. Working in the hospital is more fulfilling than working in a doctor's office.

In the hospital, where I am working now, there is never a dull moment. I work with many patients and doctors. Since the hospital is a nonprofit organization, no one makes me hurry, and I am able to take my time with each patient. I talk with the patients and learn their medical history. I do not feel as though I am the only person doing the work because the staff is large enough to do all the work required. Also the doctors are nice and compliment us often on a job well done. Lunchtime is no problem, for the cafeteria is convenient and the prices are reasonable. Parking costs employees only twenty cents a day. As long as I continue to work full time, my hospitalization insurance is fully paid. The best thing about the job is that I am not given a lot of extra work. All I am required to do is to x-ray the patients and show a lot of interest in each of them.

The doctor's office where I used to work was entirely different. Many times the doctor was not in the office and everything was delayed. Because the office was run to make a profit, the work was rushed, and I was not able to take my time with each patient. It was like an assembly line. "Get 'em in, and get 'em out," I was told. Lunchtime was a problem. If I did not bring my lunch, I had to go to a fast-food restaurant that was expensive and poor. There was no parking for the employees and no insurance plan. The worst thing was that I not only had to do x-ray work but almost everything else that came along, including bringing the doctor coffee.

I am glad that I had the chance to experience both places of work because now I know which is more fulfilling.

QUESTIONS FOR DISCUSSION

1. Does the purpose statement tell the reader what the writer wants to say about the topic? Does the student successfully carry it out in the essay? For practice, write another purpose statement for this paper.
2. Read the essay aloud and comment on how smoothly it reads. Is the detail successfully incorporated into the essay, or does it sound like a list?
3. Is the transition sentence at the beginning of the third paragraph effective? Should there be other "reminders" of the work in the hospital in the third paragraph? Or is the parallel structure sufficient for the reader to think of both jobs together?
4. What detail might the student have added to the introduction?

EXERCISE 1

List below the details in the second and third paragraphs of the student sample above and see if they are successfully presented in a parallel manner.

Paragraph 2

1. _____

2. _____

3. _____

4. _____

5. _____

Paragraph 3

1. _____

2. _____

3. _____

4. _____

5. _____

In this essay, another student also used Method A techniques to write a comparison and contrast paper:

SAMPLE B

The Coon and the Coon Dog

Out in the country, where I live, we train certain hound dogs to hunt raccoons. When you see a fight between a well trained coon dog, as we call them, and a raccoon, you are witnessing a contest between a force trained by humans and a force of nature. The savage desire of the raccoon for survival is pitted against the training in killing given the coon dog by a human.

Most raccoons form their habitats in or around sluggish swamps and marshes, beneath the mighty cypress trees. They build their dens in hollow logs or trees entangled with briar thickets and lush, gray moss. The average adult raccoon ranges from six to nine pounds; however, it is not at all unusual to see these roly-poly creatures weighing ten, fifteen or twenty pounds.

Raccoons have knifelike teeth with razor-sharp claws to match. Their eyes, ringed with black, make them look like masked bandits. It is appropriate that they look like thieves because these aggressive animals make their living by stealing food from other animals. The raccoon's fur is dark and bushy; its especially bushy tail is circled by black rings that match the rings around its eyes. A raccoon generally wobbles along very lazily as if it were an old, fat bear that is not in a hurry. Once it is frightened or cornered, however, the raccoon becomes amazingly swift. It is a beautiful sight to see a raccoon running at full speed with its large tail flowing in the breeze. The raccoon's ability to maneuver, its sharp teeth and claws, and its powerful desire to survive all prepare it for the challenge of its civilized enemy, the coon dog.

The coon dog is usually raised around the home of its devoted master. The dog is usually born in a pen and does not see the wilderness until it is old enough to chase coons. The average coon dog weighs about thirty pounds and stands about two and a half feet tall. If it is a good dog, it has probably been kept very lean. A good coon dog is agile and has a vicious set of teeth. Like the coon, it also has terribly sharp claws. A good coon dog learns to hate coons passionately. By taking a coon hide and rubbing it on the dog's face over and over again, the master instills in the coon dog a bloodthirsty vengeance for the raccoon and its smell.

After the coon dog has been trained, it finally meets the coon. The battle is vicious. Then the coon digs its teeth into the dog's neck and gnaws frantically until the dog drops dead. The coon almost always wins, even when fighting the best-trained coon dog.

Perhaps this fight shows us that even though the skill of the coon dog, who is trained by a human, is great, the force of the coon, who is trained only by nature, is greater.

QUESTIONS FOR DISCUSSION

1. What is the purpose statement?
2. The first subject in the comparison—the raccoon—is discussed in two paragraphs. Why?
3. Notice how the student used transition sentences between the third and fourth paragraphs and the fourth and fifth paragraphs. Are these transitions effective? Why or why not?
4. In comparing the coon and the coon dog, how does the student use a structure for the details that is roughly parallel? (See the suggestions presented for Method A above.)
5. In your view, what are some of the best details that the writer gives?

6. Is the conclusion effective? Does the student tie the conclusion to the introduction?

Method B was employed by the student who wrote the third sample essay of comparison and contrast:

SAMPLE C

The City Mouse

For over twenty-three years I lived in Jefferson. City life was all I knew since I was born and raised in the heart of the city. Thinking that the grass was greener somewhere else, I moved to the suburbs seven years ago. Only now do I appreciate the advantages of the city that I took for granted when I lived there.

Residents of Jefferson enjoy many conveniences that people in the suburbs miss. Bus service in the city is excellent. You can go just about anywhere if you are willing to change buses once or twice. With buses stopping at every second street corner and coming at intervals of every ten to fifteen minutes, city dwellers can depend on the transit system as their chief means of transportation. Unfortunately, bus service in the suburbs cannot compare to the city transit system. Suburban bus routes are few and a wait at a bus stop can last thirty minutes.

Jefferson is full of charm and beauty, which are both lacking in the suburbs. Huge oak trees line the avenues and boulevards of the city, and the public grounds are decorated with blooming oleanders and azaleas. The city's two giant parks are a great asset to Jefferson. People can spend enjoyable Sunday afternoons feeding the ducks that swim lazily on the ponds in the park. The suburbs, however, have no real parks. Small playgrounds are the most they have to offer. These playgrounds are naked compared to the city's parks with their huge moss-covered trees.

Another advantage of the city is that life there is neighborhood oriented. You can walk to a neighborhood grocery store in many parts of the city. Children usually grow up together, attending the same neighborhood school. Life in the suburbs is not as tightly knit as life in the city. People shop at large supermarkets. Children are bused all over the place to different schools. Suburban neighbors seldom take time to get to know one another.

I find myself constantly returning to the city. I reside in the suburbs, but my heart is in the city.

QUESTIONS FOR DISCUSSION

1. Why did the student choose "The City Mouse" as the title?
2. Read aloud the transition sentences *at the beginning* of each paragraph in the body of the paper. What words in these transitions relate back to the purpose statement?
3. Underline each transition sentence *in the middle* of the second, third, and fourth paragraphs. The author used these transitions to move from the first subject in each comparison to the second. Are they effective? If not, how could they be improved?

4. What is the organizing principle of each paragraph?
5. Did the author give enough detail to support the three main points?

WRITING ASSIGNMENT 2

Choose Your Topic Compare and contrast as many of the following subjects as you can in the blanks provided:

1. Two jobs you have held

_____   _____

2. Two of your relatives (two aunts, two cousins, or the like)

_____   _____

3. Two places you have lived

_____   _____

4. Two famous athletes from the same sport

_____   _____

5. Two churches or religious centers

_____   _____

6. Two famous singers or musicians

_____   _____

7. Two opposing political candidates

_____   _____

Choose one of the above to compare and contrast below:

Step One: Gather Ideas and Information In the left-hand column below, using the brainstorming method, write down everything that comes to mind when you think about the first subject in your comparison. In the right-hand column, write down everything that comes to mind when you think about the second subject. (Think of particular examples as well as descriptive details.)

_____   _____
(first subject)   (second subject)

_____   _____

_____   _____

_____   _____

_____   _____

_____   _____

———————————————   ———————————————
———————————————   ———————————————
———————————————   ———————————————
———————————————   ———————————————
———————————————   ———————————————

Now connect similar details. In the brainstorming for the first student sample above, the student wrote the following details and connected similar items in the comparison with numbers, as shown:

Work in the Hospital

lots of doctors ①
good lunches
time to work with patients ②
nonprofit organization
hospitalization
good parking facilities ③
professional treatment ④

Work in the Doctor's Office

one doctor ①
had to do any jobs (bring coffee to ④ doctor)
no parking ③
"Get 'em in and get 'em out." ②

Go back over your lists and see what items were not connected. See if you can think of details that correspond to the unconnected items and add those details to your lists. In the example above, three items in the left-hand column were not connected. The student added the following to the right-hand column to correspond to those items:

good lunches   poor lunches in fast-food restaurant
nonprofit organization everything for a profit
hospitalization   no hospitalization

Step Two: Analyze the Ideas and the Information   Look over both lists and see what items are most important, what items might be grouped together, what items might be omitted. Which of the two subjects in your comparison do you prefer? Why? Has your preference changed in recent months or years? If so, you may want to write about the reason for the change in your essay.

Step Three: State Your Purpose   Name both subjects of the comparison in your purpose statement, and state your opinion of the two subjects when you think of them together:

———————————————————————————————————

———————————————————————————————————

Here are some examples of purpose statements for a comparison essay:

Shopping without money is more exciting than shopping with money.

Except for the fact that my pet has four legs and I only have two, we are much alike.

No twins could be more opposite than Joshanna and Jovanna.

High school teaching was related to our experience, but college teaching is abstract.

Bill Walton is a good basketball player, but Wilt Chamberlain was great.

My children see me as serious minded, but actually I am full of fun.

Step Four: Make Your Plan   Using the criteria given above, choose either Method A or Method B to outline your paper. Use examples as well as descriptive details to support your main points.

METHOD A OUTLINE

In your outline, be sure to make your details in paragraphs 2 and 3 parallel when you can.

(your title)

PARAGRAPH 1   Introduction

_____

(detail)

PARAGRAPH 2   _____
(organizing principle)

1. _____
(detail)

2. _____

3. _____

4. _____

5. _____

6. _____

PARAGRAPH 3   _____
(organizing principle)

1. _____
(detail)

2. _____

3. _____

4. _____

5. _____

6. _____

PARAGRAPH 4   Conclusion _____

(detail) _____

METHOD B OUTLINE

In your outline, be careful not to use too many paragraphs in setting up your paper—three to five paragraphs in the body should be enough.

_____
(your title)

PARAGRAPH 1   Introduction _____

_____
(detail)

PARAGRAPH 2   _____
(organizing principle)

_____
(unit 1)

_____
(detail)

_____
(unit 2)

_____
(detail)

PARAGRAPH 3   _____
(organizing principle)

_____
(unit 1)

_____
(detail)

(unit 2) _____

(detail) _____

PARAGRAPH 4 _____
          (organizing principle)

(unit 1) _____

(detail) _____

(unit 2) _____

(detail) _____

PARAGRAPH 5 _____
          (organizing principle)

(unit 1) _____

(detail) _____

(unit 2) _____

(detail) _____

PARAGRAPH 6 _____
          (organizing principle)

(unit 1) _____

(detail) _____

(unit 2) _____

(detail) _____

PARAGRAPH 7   Conclusion _____

(detail) _____

Step Five: Write   Although a comparison and contrast paper is highly structured, your writing does not have to sound rigid or contrived. Use the suggested structure, write clear transitions, and whenever possible make your constructions parallel, but remember that you are speaking to your readers through your writing, so make sure it flows smoothly.

Step Six: Evaluate, Revise, and Edit   Evaluate your paper by asking the following questions:

1. What *opinion* did you express in your purpose statement?
2. If you chose Method A, did you present your details in a parallel manner?
3. If you chose Method B, check the transitions in the middle of the paragraphs in the body of your paper. Do they help the reader move easily from the first subject in your comparison to the second?
4. When you read your paper aloud, does it sound like you? If not, where in your essay does the writing not sound like you?

Now revise and edit your paper. As you do, keep in mind that the phrase *on the other hand* can function as a conjunctive adverb at the beginning of a new sentence or, after a semicolon, in a compound sentence:

> The bank did not pay well. On the other hand, it did provide an excellent introduction to the business world.

> The bank did not pay well; on the other hand, it did provide an excellent introduction to the business world.

Watch for fragments that begin with *while* or *whereas*. Correct these fragments, using commas to join them to the preceding sentences.

> My dog likes to be around people. While I like to go off by myself.

> Teachers in high school teach practical English. Whereas teachers in college teach "egghead" English.

Watch also for the misuse of *more* and *most* (see Chapter 10.5).

WRITING ASSIGNMENT 3

Choose another topic from the list on page 139 or from the following list. If you used Method A for structuring your first essay, use Method B for this one; if you used Method B, this time use Method A.

1. Teaching methods in high school and college
2. Yourself and your pet
3. Yourself when you are happy and yourself when you are sad or angry
4. Your parents' (or children's) view of you and your view of you
5. Shopping with money and "shopping" without money
6. The Democratic and Republican parties
7. Soldiers and sailors
8. Officers and enlisted personnel

9. Political "hawks" and "doves"
10. Foreign cars and American cars
11. Democracy and socialism

WRITING ASSIGNMENT 4

Using the two outlines on James Evans and Ted Spicer, write a paper on the two men, inventing the necessary facts as you write. Use either Method A or Method B.

Classification

Classification means the arranging or ordering of material. We use the principles of classification every day, for example, when we look up classified ads in the newspaper or use the yellow pages in the telephone book. The other name for the yellow pages is, in fact, the *classified telephone directory.* The items in the yellow pages are first classified alphabetically, but there are also classifications within some of the alphabetical listings. If you looked up churches under *C* in the yellow pages of a large city directory, for example, you would see that they are classifed by denomination. Under each domination, particular churches are listed. If you continued reading, you would probably see that churches are also classified by where they are located in the city.

A common form of classification is the organizational flow chart, which uses a diagram to show the particular functions within an organization. A community center, for example, classified the functions of its employees with the following flow chart:

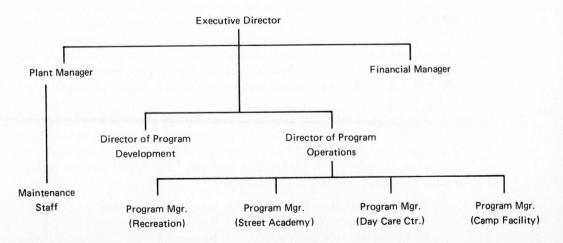

In a classification essay, your task is threefold: (1) to classify or arrange ideas and information on a particular subject in a logical way, whether the subject is contemporary music, college males or females, or the causes of the First World War; (2) to describe the classes or divisions within the subject area; and (3) to give your overall opinion of the subject area. If you were writing an evaluation of the Department of Program Operations for the community center shown in the diagram above, you would follow this procedure. First, you would divide your evaluation into four parts: Recreation, Street Academy, Day Care Center, and Camp Facility. Second, you would describe how each of these programs is functioning. And third, you would give your overall view on how well the entire Department of Program Operations is functioning, and why.

You have already been classifying material in your writing, especially in making outlines. In this assignment, however, you will concentrate on classification itself as you write a paper of several paragraphs. The skills you learn will help you not only in many college essays, but also in the sort of practical writing required in many jobs. For example, some day you may be required to make a written report evaluating departments within an organization or divisions within a department.

Writing a Classification Essay

Your main purpose in a classification essay is to divide a subject area into various classes, describe those classes, and state your overall view of the subject area.

1. Make your classification as comprehensive as possible. If you are writing on contemporary music, try to group all of the music into one class or another. If you are writing on college males or females, try to place each individual within a certain class. If you are writing on soap operas and other television serials, try to include each program in your classification. A shortcoming of the classification essay is that many subject areas cannot be easily or rigidly divided into classes. The intent of the essay, however, is to give your reader a *general* idea of the types of contemporary music one might hear on the radio, the types of males or females one might discover on your campus, or the types of soap operas or other serials that play each week on television.

2. If possible, limit your classes or divisions to three or four. If several items do not fall into one of the classes, you may have to describe them under the category "Other," but avoid using this category if you can.

3. Choose classes that fit together logically. You could classify college teachers logically in the following ways:

1. Those interested in students
   Those indifferent to students
   Those hostile to students

2. Graduate assistants
   Instructors
   Professors

3. Excellent teachers	4. Inexperienced teachers
Average teachers	Moderately experienced teachers
Poor teachers	Highly experienced teachers

In other words, use one principle of classification.

4. In your purpose statement give your overall view of the individual classes *when considered together.* What is your dominant impression of the subject area? Here are some examples using the subject of college teachers:

> Most of our teachers are interested in students, but some are indifferent and a few are even downright hostile to students.

> Teaching ability at our university has little to do with whether the teacher is a graduate assistant, an instructor, or a full professor.

> Most of our teachers are either too structured in their teaching or not structured enough, but some seem to use just the right amount of structure.

5. When possible, present detail for each class in a way that parallels the detail in other classes, as follows:

Inexperienced Teachers	*Moderately Experienced Teachers*	*Highly Experienced Teachers*
1. The way they lecture	1. The way they lecture	1. The way they lecture
2. The way they test	2. The way they test	2. The way they test
3. The way they deal with students	3. The way they deal with students	3. The way they deal with students
4. A particular example	4. A particular example	4. A particular example

6. Write about the same amount on each of the classes or divisions.

Transition Sentences in Classification Essays

As a general rule, the transition sentences that introduce the paragraphs in the body of classification essays should be roughly parallel to each other. Here are two examples:

> PURPOSE STATEMENT
> In spite of the large number of pitchers in the major leagues, there are basically only three types.

> TRANSITION SENTENCE
> The first type of pitcher relies on his fast ball.

> TRANSITION SENTENCE
> The second type throws the curve ball much of the time.

> TRANSITION SENTENCE
> The third type of pitcher throws the screw ball.

These transition sentences are roughly parallel because each begins with a type of pitcher followed by a description of what kind of ball he throws.

PURPOSE STATEMENT

My neighborhood reminds me of a zoo because the people in it are very much like some of the animals in a zoo: chimps, lions, and giraffes.

TRANSITION SENTENCE

The chimps are timid but playful creatures.

TRANSITION SENTENCE

The lions are much more aggressive than the chimps.

TRANSITION SENTENCE

The giraffes are known for their tongues, which are just as long as their necks.

Each transition sentence begins with a type of animal followed by a statement that characterizes it.

SAMPLE A

Roaches and Social Class

The cockroach has a great deal to teach us about ourselves. Just as there are three social classes of human beings, there are three classes of roaches.

First, there is the affluent class of roach, which is like the rich American businessman. This type of roach is a survivor because of its large size, which ranges from two to three inches. Roaches of this class will have nothing but the best. For instance, it is the only kind of roach daring enough to crawl over a delicious pot roast, recently set on the table in broad daylight, right before a person's eyes. Like the rich American businessman, this roach will go to any extreme to get what it wants, and it cares less about the fate of others than do any of the other roaches. A good example is when one of these creatures is found digging around the bottom of a sugar bowl on the kitchen table after everyone has just finished eating.

Second, just as there is a division of Americans called the middle class, there is also a middle class of roach, ranging from one to two inches in size, that makes up the bulk of the roach population. This type of roach is not as daring as the affluent class, and it usually settles for bread crumbs and other scraps as a food source. One may find this roach propped up on one's toothbrush in the morning. This roach will stand up for its rights, and the only way to get rid of it is to exterminate it. However, by staying alert and moving very swiftly, this roach has become highly resistant to being stomped on.

Third and last, there is the poverty class of roach. This type of roach ranges from one-half to one inch in size. One startling characteristic of this roach is that it is never seen in the daytime. Like bums and hobos, it moves about in a dark and dreary world, usually scavenging what it can from garbage bags. This is the kind of roach that a person lying in bed might find crawling up the covers. As long as this roach is in the dark, it is very brave and courageous, but it becomes frightened and runs when the light is flicked on.

Roaches, it seems, have social classes just as humans do. Many people ponder the theory of evolution. Just where have we, as humans, been? Or, should I ask, where are we going?

QUESTIONS FOR DISCUSSION

1. What is the purpose statement? How does the student attempt to carry it out?
2. What particular examples does the student give in the three paragraphs in the body of his paper?
3. Would you say that the transition sentences introducing the second, third, and fourth paragraphs are roughly parallel?
4. Does the writing meet all the criteria set forth above on the classification essay? Explain.
5. The ending seems a bit weak. How might you write a stronger ending?
6. Some students complain that the analogy between roaches and humans is so disgusting that it ruins the paper. Do you agree?

EXERCISE 2

List the detail as presented in the second, third, and fourth paragraphs of "Roaches and Social Class" to see how closely it parallels the detail in the other two paragraphs in the body of the essay.

Affluent Roach	*Middle-Class Roach*	*Poverty-Class Roach*
1.	1.	1.
2.	2.	2.
3.	3.	3.
4.	4.	4.
5.	5.	5.

In the following essay, the writer argues that the elderly have much to teach us about death. In making her argument, she classifies people into three groups: the young, the middle-aged, and the elderly.

SAMPLE B

A Time to Live and a Time to Die

The young person thinks little about death; the middle-aged person tends to fear death; oftentimes, however, the old person comes to accept death calmly, as part of life and the final point in the life cycle. The elderly can offer us a special gift as they pass on their wisdom about death.

For the young person, death is often an abstraction; it is like color to someone blind from birth. For a spirited adolescent barely able to deal with all the personal concerns that arise or a young adult desperately trying to succeed professionally, death has no place in life. It is something totally unrelated to what the person thinks or does. When a sudden death does occur, one that strikes close to home, the young person is stunned. "Why did it have to happen?" she asks in a demanding voice. "It's not fair. God is cruel," he says angrily. Depression often follows. But then the anger and the depression both pass, and the pressing agendas of the adolescent and the young adult again take over, pushing the very idea of death out of the conscious mind.

Eventually, the young person grows older and begins to see the body functioning less and less well. Hair falls out; teeth loosen; wrinkles can no longer be hidden under make-up; bifocals replace regular glasses; the memory slips, just a little, but slips nonetheless; aches and pains in the joints set in. The specter of death thus pushes its way into the consciousness like an unwelcomed visitor from a strange planet. "I don't want to get old. I don't want to die," the woman says. "I'm forty-seven," the man says. "It's more than half over. This must be happening to someone else. Why, I still feel like a little boy inside. 'Little Rufie,' my mother used to call me. To die? To cease to be? This is really going to happen to me, Rufus Craig, Little Rufie? For God's sake, not me!" Some people in their middle years start drinking when they think about death. Others revert to their adolescence, trying to relive their youth so they will not have to think about what is going on. Still others try to build monuments to themselves by achieving great wealth and power so that they will never be forgotten. But none of these things works in the long run. Denial simply postpones despair.

Gradually, almost imperceptibly, the middle-aged person becomes an elderly person—an old man or an old woman. In many ways life is harder than before. He says, "I can't stand any more losses. My family has moved away. I have given up my home. The corner grocery store has been turned into a parking lot. I can't even work part-time anymore. When my body works at all, it creaks." She says simply, "Old age is not for sissies." But with the breakdown of the body and in spite of—or maybe because of—all the losses, something remarkable happens.

Death joins the family table, not as a stranger now, but as an old acquaintance, not a friend exactly, more like your childhood doctor—strict but gentle. Death smiles and makes you know that one of these days it will be your turn, just as it has been the turn of everyone else before you. "It is going to be okay," Death says. "Don't worry." And the old person finds that he or she is ready. "No, I'm not afraid of death," he says to his grandson who bounces on the bed. "There are many things in the world worse than death," she explains. "When you get to be my age, you start counting your many blessings, and you come to realize that death is part of life. I wish I could help you understand."

When we learn about death from the elderly, we also learn about life.

QUESTIONS FOR DISCUSSION

1. What is the purpose statement? How does the writer carry it out?
2. In the transition sentences connecting the second, third, and fourth

paragraphs, what words refer to the three stages of life that the author is describing?

3. How does the writer describe each stage so that it is roughly parallel in form to the descriptions of the other stages?

4. Do you agree that the young, the middle-aged, and the elderly generally perceve death quite differently? If so, would you describe their perceptions of death differently than the writer did? Explain.

5. Should the ending be expanded or for this essay is one sentence long enough?

6. Is the title appropriate? Why did the writer give her essay this title?

WRITING ASSIGNMENT 5

Choose Your Topic   For the topics listed below, fill in as many blanks as possible. Choose classes that fit together.

1. Types of college males or females

   _____   _____

   _____   _____

2. Types of mothers or fathers

   _____   _____

   _____   _____

3. Types of teachers in your college or high school

   _____   _____

   _____   _____

4. Types of problems old people or teen-agers face

   _____   _____

   _____   _____

5. Types of pitchers in baseball, quarterbacks in football, or athletes in another sport

   _____   _____

   _____   _____

6. Types of social classes in America or your native country (try to focus on specific behaviors or traits, such as dress)

   _____   _____

   _____   _____

7. Types of television serials

   _____   _____

   _____   _____

8. Types of people in your neighborhood

_____   _____

_____   _____

9. Types of police officers, nurses, doctors, or other professionals

_____   _____

_____   _____

10. Types of music played on AM or FM radio stations or the types of music *within* a certain class, such as country music

_____   _____

_____   _____

11. Types of bosses

_____   _____

_____   _____

12. Types of opinions on subjects such as death, drugs, sex, or love

_____   _____

_____   _____

Discuss your classifications with others and check them with the instructor to see if they meet the criteria given on page 146. Choose one topic to write on.

Step One: Gather Ideas and Information   Brainstorm for details to describe and examples to illustrate each of the classes or divisions of the subject area you have chosen. In your brainstorming, include your opinions: what you like, what you do not like; what is most and least worthy of praise, and so forth.

Class One   *Class Two*

_____   _____

_____   _____

_____   _____

_____   _____

_____   _____

_____   _____

_____   _____

_____   _____

Class Three   *Class Four (Optional)*

_____   _____

_____   _____

_____   _____

_____   _____

_____   _____

_____   _____

General Brainstorming on the Topic

_____   _____

_____   _____

_____   _____

Step Two: Analyze the Ideas and the Information Have you chosen the best way to classify your material? Or do you need to rearrange your material in different classes? Check the information that is most important. What might you leave out? What might you add?

Step Three: State Your Purpose In one sentence, state your views on all of the classes when considered together.

_____

_____

Here are some examples of purpose statements for various topics listed above:

> All nurses perform valuable services.
>
> We sometimes forget about the many problems old people face.
>
> Of all the music played on AM stations, I like country music the most.
>
> The chief petty officers run the Coast Guard.
>
> Each type of boss is a tyrant in his or her own way.
>
> The unusual teen-ager is the one who does not have serious problems.

Step Four: Make Your Plan In outlining your paper, first try to make the transition sentences roughly parallel to each other; second, try to present the detail and examples in each paragraph in the body of the essay so that they are parallel to the detail and examples in the other paragraphs.

(your title) _____

PARAGRAPH 1   **Introduction** _____

_____

(detail)

PARAGRAPH 2   _____
           (transition sentence)

_____

1. _____   4. _____

(detail and examples)

2. _____   5. _____

3. _____   6. _____

PARAGRAPH 3   _____
           (transition sentence)

_____

1. _____   4. _____

(detail and examples)

2. _____   5. _____

3. _____   6. _____

PARAGRAPH 4   _____
           (transition sentence)

_____

1. _____   4. _____

(detail and examples)

2. _____   5. _____

3. _____   6. _____

PARAGRAPH 5   _____
           (transition sentence)

_____

1. _____   4. _____

(detail and examples)

2. _____   5. _____

3. _____   6. _____

PARAGRAPH 6   Conclusion
_____

_____

(detail)

Step Five: Write   Like the comparison and contrast essay, the classification essay is highly structured. As you make use of the suggestions for
parallel transitions and detail, be careful not to lose sight of the main task,
which is to say what you want to say in your writing. As you write, avoid
sentences that begin as follows:

> There are three types of . . .
>
> The three types of problems are . . .

The trouble is that when you go to name the types, your sentences often
become long and unwieldy, as shown below:

> The three types of problems old people face are that their children often desert
> them, they live on a fixed income and every time the cost of living goes up they
> lose money, and many old people have illnesses or at least they cannot get
> around very well.

Simply say in your introductory paragraph that old people face many problems. Each time you begin a new paragraph in the body of your essay,
introduce one of the problems, as the example here demonstrates:

> . . . Old people face many problems.
>
>   Many old people are lonely; often their children have deserted them.
>
>   A second problem many old people have to deal with is living on a fixed
> income, which means that every time the cost of living goes up they lose
> money.
>
>   A third problem that bothers many old people is that they sometimes
> cannot get around very well.

Step Six: Evaluate, Revise, and Edit   Evaluate your paper by asking the
following questions:

1. Did you state your opinion in your purpose statement?
2. Did you present your detail and examples in a roughly parallel way?
3. Does the writing sound like you talking? If not, where in the essay does
   the writing not sound like you?
4. Did the classes of things you chose to write about fit together?

Now revise and edit your paper.

PART TWO

Writing with Outside Resources

Part One concentrated on helping you to write from your own experience, but as you progress in college you will be asked more and more to write on topics that you cannot understand solely on the basis of your own experience. Thus you will need to find outside resource material that will help you in these areas. In Part One, for example, you were asked to write about a relative or friend. Probably all you had to do was bring to mind a picture of that person and recall some of your experiences with him or her. But if you are asked to write about your opinion on capital punishment, affirmative action, or drunken driving, you will need to learn more about these issues before writing your paper; you will need to know the facts and what the experts think about the issues even though you may already have strong feelings about them yourself.

Part Two will help you find and understand resource material that you can use in your writing. Chapter 7 focuses on developing reading skills and summarizing material that you read. Chapter 8 shows how to find resource material in the library. And finally, Chapter 9 teaches techniques for writing persuasively. In many subject areas, you must know how to find and summarize resource material before you can write persuasively.

CHAPTER 7

Reading and Summarizing

The more you read the better you will write. Without your even noticing, reading helps you learn how words fit together to make strong sentences. It greatly increases your vocabulary and general knowledge. Reading also helps you learn how to analyze a subject and order your thoughts.

The further you progress in college, the more you will need to incorporate material from your reading into your writing. This chapter focuses on summarizing reading material. Knowing how to give a concise, accurate account of a writer's thoughts is one of the most valuable writing skills. A student is often called upon to summarize: in taking an essay test, for example, or in compiling information from many sources for a research paper. Of course, you often summarize your own thoughts when you write a conclusion to an essay. The summary is especially useful in writing an essay in which you argue for a certain point of view. You may wish to summarize the essential points of an article or essay before you agree or disagree with the author's main point of view.

Writing Summaries

Imagine looking at a famous photograph, such as one taken after the first astronauts landed on the moon. You could state the main theme of the photograph as: "The first landing on the moon"; "The greatest event since Columbus discovered America"; or "Astronaut strolls on the moon." Looking more closely at the photograph, you would see important details that contribute to the main theme: the spacecraft, the moon's horizon in the background, and perhaps some scientific equipment that the astronauts have set out on the moon's surface. Looking still more closely, you would see the particular features of the space suit worn by the astronaut, the spacecraft, and the moon scape.

You could write a long essay about this photograph, including a description of all the minor details. Or, if you were writing just about your dominant impression of the photograph, you would state what you thought to be the theme of the picture and then describe *briefly* its major features: the spacesuit, the landing craft, the moon's surface, and the scientific equipment. Writing a summary of an article, a chapter, or a book is like writing about your dominant impression of this photograph. You state the author's main idea and then you describe briefly the major points that he or she gives to support that idea.

WRITING ASSIGNMENT 1

Choose a photograph from a magazine or newspaper in which something powerful is happening. What is the main theme? What major details help explain this theme? Write a one-paragraph summary of the photograph for a reader who has not seen it. How can you help him or her "see" the photograph by what you write?

WRITING ASSIGNMENT 2

Reread the narrative from Richard Wright's *Black Boy* beginning on page 110, and then write a one-paragraph summary, using these suggestions:

1. State the main point of the story in one or two sentences. A way of determining the main point in this story is to ask: What did Wright learn?
2. Outline all the various events in the story. You should be able to identify six to eight such events, beginning with:

    Richard's mother showed him how to shop.

3. Now write the paragraph, starting with a sentence that states the main point of the story. Be careful to use an effective transition between the first sentence and what follows, such as:

    One night when Richard Wright was a young boy living in Memphis, he learned . . . . The day before his mother had shown him how to shop at the corner grocery store.

As you summarize the story, follow your outline step by step. *Briefly* explain each event within the story.

Summarizing Reading Material

To write effective summaries, you need to read the material carefully with good comprehension. If you do not already have a good reading method, follow the suggestions below. (This is called the SRR reading method: S̲kim, R̲ead, and R̲eview.)

First, Skim the Material

1. Try to pick out the main idea of the piece you are reading. Often you can find it in the title or first paragraph.
2. Look for definitions and difficult words at the beginning that you must understand before you can understand what follows. Look them up in the dictionary if necessary.
3. Read all subheadings. They will help give you an overview of the material.
4. Read the first (and sometimes second) sentences of enough paragraphs so that you will know the general subject.
5. If something confuses you, stop and try to figure it out. If you still do not understand, move on.

6. Read the last paragraph or two.
7. Jot down the main point of the material. Also, write several questions that emerge from your skimming. When you read the material closely, be sure to answer these questions.

Second, Read the Material Thoroughly

1. Underline the main ideas. When possible, summarize the main points in the margin. (If you own the book, write all over it if this will help you learn.)
2. Relate the material to your own experience when possible. Make notes naming the experience the reading material reminds you of.
3. Write down questions to ask your instructor or another student on any important points that you do not understand.
4. Look up words that you do not understand in a dictionary. Keep a list of new words and their definitions.

Third, Review Briefly the Material

1. Without looking back, ask yourself: What was the main point of the material? What ideas and facts were presented to back up the main point? Write these down.
2. If you cannot answer the above questions, review the material and read over your notes.

EXERCISE 1

Using the SSR method, read the article below from *Sports Illustrated* (September 15, 1975). The following sample of underlining and notes in the margin will give you an idea of how to make notes as you read:

Stanley Steamer — Did the crash of a Stanley steamer in 1907 influence U.S. foreign policy?
a car operated — It is entirely possible that a little gully on a Florida beach 68 years ago had a weighty
by steam — influence on America's current foreign policy and environment. As of January 25, 1907, the American people were still undecided about what kind of automobile they
formative — wanted. The industry was in its <u>formative</u> stages, with a variety of models on the
means — market, including cars powered by gasoline, steam and electricity. From the beginning,
"pertaining — the limitations of the electric automobile were all too apparent, but <u>advocates of steam</u>
to growth" — <u>and gasoline vehicles debated</u>, sometimes genially and often furiously, the merits of
their favorites.

In 1907, the Am. people were trying to decide between steam and gasoline engines.

steam versus gasoline

Yesterday

Did the crash of a Stanley steamer in 1907 influence U.S. foreign policy?

It is entirely possible that a little gully on a Florida beach 68 years ago had a weighty influence on America's current foreign policy and environment. As of January 25, 1907, the American people were still undecided about what kind of automobile they wanted. The industry was in its formative stages, with a variety of models on the market, including cars powered by gasoline, steam and electricity. From the beginning, the limitations of the electric automobile were all too apparent, but advocates of steam and gasoline vehicles debated, sometimes genially and often furiously, the merits of their favorites.

Both engines had advantages. Perfected by twin brothers, F. E. and F. O. Stanley, the steamer was a quiet and smooth-running automobile. It also was capable of extraordinary speed and acceleration. To the astonishment of a large crowd at a race in Detroit on October 11, 1901, a steamer hit 30 mph and won the five- and 10-mile events. Thereafter, steamers won so regularly that they were sometimes banned from races with gasoline cars, despite the fact that competition was supposedly open to all autos of the same price range. (The ban was unofficial and inconsistent. Racing drivers had learned that Stanleys did less well when the distance was more than five miles. They were at their best in short distances.)

After establishing several speed records with their passenger machines, the Stanley brothers designed and built a car specifically for racing. Shaped like an inverted canoe, painted red and dubbed "Wogglebug" by the press, the racer made history in January 1906 by covering a mile in 28⅕ seconds—an average speed of 127.659 mph.

In addition to being fast, the steamer was a simple machine. "Our present car is composed of but 32 moving parts," the Stanleys said in their 1916 catalog, "which number includes front and rear wheels, steering gear, and everything moving on the car, as well as the power plant. This is about the number of parts contained in a first-class self-starter. We use no clutch, nor gear shifts, nor fly wheels, nor carburetors, nor magnetos, nor spark plugs, nor timers, nor distributors, nor self-starters, nor any of the marvelously ingenious complications which inventors have added in order to overcome the difficulties inherent in the internal-explosive engine and adapt it to a use for which it is not normally fitted."

The Stanleys also could have stressed the nonpolluting nature of their steamer. Not only did it not foul the air with unburned hydrocarbons, but it produced little or no noise. And it was capable of using fuels, such as kerosene, alcohol, coal gas and even coal, that were much cheaper than gasoline and more readily available.

On the other hand, operation of the steamer often could be troublesome, especially before the addition as standard equipment of a condenser permitting the vehicle to re-use its water supply. Until that step was taken, steamer owners had to carry a hose with them in order to raid horse troughs every 40 or 50 miles.

The biggest problem that confronted steamer manufacturers was fear. Americans had been through nearly a century of boiler explosions on boats and locomotives, and were extremely wary of high-pressure steam systems. The fact that early steamers trailed a light vapor as they moved along, giving the impression that the vehicles were already on fire or were smoldering preparatory to a massive explosion, did not build public confidence. Nevertheless, by 1907 the steamer had become a favorite of President Teddy Roosevelt and was making steady if not spectacular headway in the safety department. So close was it to winning acceptance that even the most avid partisans of internal-combustion engines would not have dared to predict its imminent demise.

Then came the international speed trials at Ormond Beach, Florida, on January 25, 1907. Expecting a new record, an unusually large crowd turned out to view such vehicles as the first Rolls-Royce entered in a U.S. race and, of course, the Wogglebug with ace driver Fred Marriott at the tiller.

Gradually warming up his car for the record run, Marriott made two dashes along a mile section of beach, the first in 32 seconds, the second in 29⅗, less than a second and a half slower than his world record.

On his third run, Marriott hit the starting line at full throttle and shot up the beach. Although running against the wind, the steamer's speed was approaching 150 mph when the accident occurred. "He was nearly out of sight, being almost at the end of the mile, when the machine upset," wrote a reporter in *The New York Times.*

No one knew exactly what had happened. Those nearest the car agreed that the hood appeared to come loose—"seemingly lifted by the wind while the front wheels were so tilted upward that they did not strike the sand of the beach by several inches. . . . The tubing broke and the car was enveloped in a cloud of steam."

By the time spectators had raced up the beach to the scene of the accident, a Rolls-Royce had arrived and Marriott had been picked up, "his face covered with blood and lying insensible across the laps of two men in the rear seat. . . . He was found well up on the beach, while the round boiler, four or five times the size of a cheese box, was rescued rolling around in the ocean. When the car broke in two it dropped the boiler as it did Marriott. . . . The debris was thrown into two piles, over which hundreds of amateur photographers hovered like seagulls and many souvenirs were carried away. . . ."

The Stanleys later argued that a gully in the sandy beach caused the racer to rise, but they accepted blame for their flat-bottomed design, which, even if the gully was responsible for the steamer's take-off, contributed greatly to its becoming airborne.

Although Fred Marriott survived the accident by more than half a century, the American public and the Stanley brothers were greatly discouraged. The twins never again used their automobiles for racing. The public, its fear of steam propulsion revived, leaned more and more to the gasoline engine, a preference that was clearly established within a decade. Although the Stanleys continued producing cars until 1927, those ripples in the sand at Ormond Beach effectively ended their dream of a steam-powered society that might have left us today with an environment relatively free of noise and air pollution and a foreign policy less vulnerable to the pressures of oil-producing countries.

–George Gipe

SUGGESTIONS FOR WRITING SUMMARIES

1. Identify the main idea of the material and state it in your own words in a sentence or two. Be sure that your statement is the main idea of the entire work, not just one section or paragraph. Do not assume that the opening sentence always states the thesis. Many writers delay giving the controlling idea, and some never state it directly. Often the main idea will be made clear in the concluding paragraph or paragraphs. If you are having trouble grasping the main idea, write a one-sentence summary of some of the paragraphs to see if the thesis begins to emerge.

2. List the various points that support the main idea as you have stated it. Analyze the list, weeding out less important details. Now make an informal outline showing how the author defends the main idea. Arrange the individual points in the outline in a logical order, which may or may not be the order of the author.

3. Write the summary. Here are some suggestions:

   a. In your first sentence, name the author and the work you are summarizing and give general information about the topic. For example: "In his article 'Yesterday' in *Sports Illustrated* (September 15, 1975), George Gipe explains why the crash of the Stanley steamer in 1907 had so much influence on us today." (Put quotation marks around titles of articles, essays, and short stories; underline titles of magazines, books, and newspapers.)

   b. State the author's main idea in the next sentence or shortly thereafter: "According to Gipe, the crash convinced the American automobile makers that they should invest in gasoline engines instead of steam engines." (Note the first name of the author is dropped after it is given once.)

   c. Be brief. Remember why you are writing the summary: to reduce the original material to its main points. You may want to use direct or indirect quotations, but do not get bogged down by extensive quoting. (Suggestions and rules for quoting reading material appear in Appendix A.) It may help to put the reading material aside while you are writing the summary. This way you will be less likely to retell everything.

   d. Write the summary in your own words, not the words of the author. Not only will this be much better writing practice for you, but it will also help you avoid the danger of *plagiarism*, which is the use of the words or ideas of another as though they were your own. If you need to use the exact words of the author, the proper way to do so is by using direct quotations.

   e. Do not offer your opinion in the summary itself. Often it is appropriate to write an additional paragraph or more in which you give your response to the material you are summarizing. But in the summary, present only the author's views. Thus, the writing should be as objective as possible, although stated in your own words.

   f. Summaries longer than two hundred words should be in two or more paragraphs.

   g. Evaluate, revise, and edit the summary. As you are evaluating, compare your summary with the original and ask yourself these questions: Have you conveyed the important points as briefly as possible? Have you rephrased without altering the author's original meaning?

Here is how one might write an outline and a two-paragraph summary of the Gipe article on the Stanley steamer:

OUTLINE

First Paragraph

Title, author, source, date, general content
Main point: why we use gasoline instead of steam
How people viewed the steamer before the crash

Second Paragraph

The great drawback of the steamer—fear of an explosion
Fear made worse by the wreck in 1907
Effects of the wreck

SAMPLE

SOURCE
TITLE
DATE
AUTHOR

GENERAL
CONTENT

MAIN POINT

HOW PEOPLE
VIEWED THE
STEAMER
BEFORE THE
CRASH

TRANSITION
WORD
DRAWBACK
OF THE
STEAMER

The Wreck of the Stanley Steamer

In his article "Yesterday" in <u>Sports Illustrated</u> (September 15, 1975), George Gipe explains why the crash of the Stanley Steamer in 1907 has had so much influence on us today. According to Gipe, the crash convinced the American automobile makers that they should invest in gasoline engines instead of steam engines. Before the crash of the steamer, many looked at the steam engine as the best source of power for automobiles. It was quiet, smooth-running, and capable of great speed, at least for short distances. Moreover, the steamer was a simple machine, and it did not pollute the air with hydro-carbons. Finally, it used fuels that were easily available.

The American people, however, feared the steamer because they had lived through nearly a century of boiler explosions on boats and trains. At the international speed

FEAR MADE
WORSE BY
THE WRECK

trials at Ormond Beach, Florida, on January 25, 1907, what many feared most about the steamer, occurred—a Stanley steamer, hitting ripples in the sand, blew up. The driver survived, but the public quickly lost interest and moved more and more toward the gasoline engine, which has caused us problems ever since. In Gipe's words,

EFFECTS OF
THE WRECK/
DIRECT
QUOTATION

"Although the Stanleys continued producing cars until 1927, those ripples in the sand at Ormond Beach effectively ended their dream of a steam-powered society that might have left us today with an environment relatively free of noise and air pollution and a foreign policy less vulnerable to the pressures of oil-producing countries."

The following writing assignments include a summary of a magazine article, a summary of part of a chapter from a book often assigned in college education classes, and a summary of a classroom lecture. Other summaries are assigned later in this book.

WRITING ASSIGNMENT 3

The following reading selection comes from the "My Turn" column in the January 18, 1982, issue of *Newsweek*. It was written by Vicki Williams, a factory worker in Huntington, Indiana. In this article Williams demonstrates the practical value of learning to express oneself in writing. Although she is not a professional writer, she is able to use writing to express effectively her point of view on a subject very important to her—taxes.

Read the selection carefully, using the SSR reading method described above. Then, using the suggestions for writing a summary, write a two-paragraph paper in response. In the first paragraph, of your essay, summarize the article. State the main idea and explain the author's reasons for holding this point of view. In the second paragraph, give your personal response to the article and explain why you hold this opinion. If you have not yet struggled over paying taxes yourself, consult friends, relatives, or others who have. You may want to show them the article and see how they react. Begin your second paragraph something like this: "More people should view taxes the way Vicki Williams does." Or, "Vicki Williams does not express my point of view about taxes. I believe . . . ."

Somewhere in your essay, practice using a direct quotation. See the suggestions and rules for this technique in Appendix A.

SAMPLE

The View from $204 a Week*

I consider myself the classic "poor overburdened taxpayer" that you hear so much about these days. I work for an electronics company and make $6.58 an hour which translates into $204 per week after deductions, $30.21 of which are Federal withholding taxes. I have a husband, laid off, whose unemployment compensation has run out, and a 13-year-old son who thinks he should have a leather coat, a P. K. Ripper motocross bike, a Pioneer stereo and an Asteroids game. It bothers me a lot that I can't afford to buy him any of these things. It also bothers me that I'm not sure how we're going to fill up the fuel tank often enough to stay warm this winter.

There is something else that bothers me, though not to the same extent as my son's unfulfilled desires or the ever-hungry fuel tank, and that is that every single politician and editorialist is positive he knows exactly what I think. Everyone seems to be wildly anxious to be my spokesman. Yet these people don't know a damn thing about how the "poor overburdened taxpayer" thinks or lives. I imagine it's been quite some time since most politicians or well-known journalists lived on $204 per week, though I've read plenty of complaints from congressmen about their meager salaries. One even said he had to sleep in his office because he couldn't afford to buy a house. Do you know how much pity I can spare for a senator who can't live on $60,000 a year?

Tired. I know I'm not as articulate as the people who write the editorials for newspapers and the speeches for politicians, but just once I'd like to have on the record the thoughts of an average taxpayer. I'm tired of these people putting their words in my mouth and their thoughts in my head.

One of the statements I read and hear most often is how fed up I'm supposed to be with the amount of my taxes that goes toward welfare, food stamps, programs for the elderly, subsidized school lunches and other supportive social services. Wrong! What the people "up there" don't understand is that I identify with the beneficiaries of these programs much more than I do with the politicians and the media people. "There, but for the grace of God, go I." So far, I have never had to rely on welfare, free lunches or Medicaid, but I very well might someday. When I was divorced, I could have qualified for welfare. Fortunately, I had parents who were in a position to help, but if I hadn't, you can believe I would have swallowed my pride rather than watch my son go hungry. People like me, who live only a hair-breadth from economic disaster, are glad these programs are out there, though we pray we'll never have to use them. We feel sympathy for the ones who do.

In 1977 my sister-in-law was abandoned by her husband. Her health did not permit her to work full time, so she drew $194 per month from the welfare department to support herself and her child. I doubt that anyone can think she lived extravagantly on $194 per month.

I think it's possible that at least one of the very same politicians who are now complaining about welfare recipients might have taken a political junket during one of the months that my sister-in-law and her son lived on $194. Believe me, I resent that

---

junket at my expense much, much more than I resent helping an ADC[1] mother, or buying eyeglasses for an elderly person or free lunches for a ghetto child. . . .

If there is even one child in this country who is hungry or one old person who needs medical care, then I want my $1,570.92 in taxes to go toward helping that child or that old person. I think this country is based on the philosophy that when that $1,570.92 is gone, we will find more to take its place, as long as the need is there.

I know about the cheaters. There are always cheaters. They are a part of life as surely as death and taxes. Certainly, if they are caught, they should be punished and denied aid, but I know we'll always support some cheaters along with the "truly needy." If we have to give a free lunch to one child whose parents could afford to pay in order to give free lunches to nine children who genuinely deserve them, so be it.

Benefits. The much-touted tax cut doesn't make sense to me. Perhaps there's a complicated economic formula that explains the logic of a tax cut at the same time we're slashing Federal programs because of lack of funds, but if so, I missed it. I pay $30.21 per week to the Federal government. As I understand it, when all the tax cuts are in effect, I will only pay $22.66, giving me $7.55 extra to save or spend. Well, I could do a few things with $7.55 a week but, had I been consulted, I would have just as soon paid it and kept the food-stamp program or veterans' benefits intact. I suspect that the government will give it to me with one hand and take it away with the other.

You see, I really believe that most politicians and media people think that those of us out here in America who work in the factories and offices are ignorant. I believe that they think we will never catch on to their sleights of hand. I believe that they think they can tell us the grass is black one day and white the next and we'll never trust ourselves enough to look down and say, "Why, that grass isn't black or white—it's green!" Well, we know the grass is green. We just don't know what to do about it.

We don't really believe that 56 oil companies recorded 98 percent of the increase in all corporate profits from 1978 through 1980 for *our* benefit. We don't believe the tobacco subsidy is for *our* benefit. We don't believe that congressmen who were violently anti-AWACS[2] magically changed their minds for *our* benefit. We know it's always us who pay the bills that result from the politicians' machinations.

I wish a politician would come along who'd tell me that the grass is green.

–Vicki Williams

WRITING ASSIGNMENT 4

The following selection comes from a book often assigned in college education classes, *Freedom and Beyond*, by John Holt, a famous but controversial educator. Although Holt wrote the book in 1972, the issues he raised are still prominent in the field of child development.

Read the selection carefully, using the SSR reading method. Then, using

[1]ADC: Aid to Dependent Children (a federal welfare program)
[2]Automatic Warning and Control System, used on military planes

the suggestions for writing a summary, write a two- or three-paragraph paper in response. In the first paragraph or two, summarize the selection. State the main point and explain how the author backs up his point of view. In the last paragraph, give your personal response to the selection and say why you hold your opinion. If you do not have children, it may be helpful to discuss the article with parents of young children. How is Holt's view of discipline similar or different from theirs? Begin your last paragraph something like this: "Every parent of young children should read John Holt." Or, "One cannot help but wonder if Holt ever had children himself."

For practice, use a direct quotation somewhere in your essay.

On Disciplining Children

If we give children freedom how will they ever learn discipline? This is a common question—really a statement. When people talk about their child "learning discipline," what is it that they really want him to learn? Probably, most or all of the following:

1. Do what you're told without questioning or resisting, whenever I or any other authority tell you to do something.
2. Go on doing what you're told for as long as you're told. Never mind how dull, disagreeable, or pointless the task may seem. It's not for you to decide.
3. Do whatever we want you to do, *willingly.* Do it without even having to be told. Do what you're *expected* to do.
4. If you don't do these things you will be punished and you will deserve to be.
5. Accept your life without complaining even if you get very little if any of what you think you want, even if your life has not much joy, meaning, or satisfaction. That's what life is.
6. Take your medicine, your punishment, whatever the people above you do to you, without complaining or resisting.
7. Living this way is good for your soul and character.

Rather like the sermon the rich used to preach to the poor in the early days of the Industrial Revolution: accept the station in life, however humble, to which God has called you, and there meekly and gratefully do your duty. This preaching still goes on, of course; the rich and powerful, for obvious reasons, always like to tell the poor and lowly about the virtues of duty, obedience, and hard work. Not long ago, after an evening meeting in a town of about 15,000 people, a man came up to me and said, "I run a bank here, and what I want to know is, if kids get the kind of education you're talking about, what are they going to do when I tell them that if they want to work in my bank they are going to have to get their hair cut and wear a suit and show up promptly at eight-thirty in the morning?" I said, "Well, I suppose if a young person really wants to work in your bank, he will accept those conditions as part of the deal." He walked away looking dissatisfied. What I might have said to him, but didn't, was that if willingness to obey his orders was all he was looking for in his employees, he would probably not be in the banking business for long. Also, that perhaps the way he and many like him felt and behaved toward young people might have something to do with a problem others had told me about that day—that all the young people in the town were leaving as soon as they finished high school.

Some people who worry about discipline may not necessarily want their children to believe all the ideas listed above. But most of the Americans who said in a recent nationwide poll that what they wanted above all else in schools was more discipline probably had all these ideas in mind. The Boston *Globe* reports that Vice-President Agnew recently said to a convention of farmers in Chicago, ''I would think restoration of discipline and order ought to be a first priority—even ahead of curriculum—in the schools of this country.'' They add that this statement won Agnew louder applause than anything else he said to the farmers. What those farmers want is more coercion, more threats, more punishment, more fear. Above all, more fear. Make them afraid! They experience their own life as a kind of slavery, and this is what they want for their (and everyone else's) child, perhaps on the theory that if it's good enough for them it's good enough for him, if they can put up with it then by God he will, perhaps on the theory that nothing else is possible.

The word ''discipline'' has more and more important meanings than just this. A child, in growing up, may meet and learn from three different kinds of disciplines. The first and most important is what we might call the Discipline of Nature or of Reality. When he is trying to do something real, if he does the wrong things or doesn't do the right one, he doesn't get the result he wants. If he doesn't pile one block right on top of another, or tries to build on a slanting surface, his tower falls down. If he hits the wrong key, he hears the wrong note. If he doesn't hit the nail squarely on the head, it bends, and he has to pull it out and start with another. If he doesn't measure properly what he is trying to build, it won't open, close, fit, stand up, fly, float, whistle, or do whatever he wants it to do. If he closes his eyes when he swings, he doesn't hit the ball. A child meets this kind of discipline every time he tries to *do* something, which is why it is so important in school to give children more chances to do things, instead of just reading or listening to someone talk (or pretending to). This discipline is a great teacher. The learner never has to wait long for his answer; it usually comes quickly, often instantly. Also it is clear, and very often points toward the needed correction; from what happened he can not only see that what he did was wrong, but also why, and what he needs to do instead. Finally, and most important, the giver of the answer, call it Nature, is impersonal, impartial, and indifferent. She does not give opinions, or make judgments; she cannot be wheedled, bullied, or fooled; she does not get angry or disappointed; she does not praise or blame; she does not remember past failures or hold grudges; with her one always gets a fresh start, this time is the one that counts.

The next discipline we might call the Discipline of Culture, of Society, or What People Really Do. Man is a social, a cultural animal. Children sense around them this culture, this network of agreements, customs, habits, and rules binding the adults together. They want to understand it and be a part of it. They watch very carefully what people around them are doing and want to do the same. They want to do right, unless they become convinced they can't do right. Thus children rarely misbehave seriously in church, but sit as quietly as they can. The example of all those grownups is contagious. Some mysterious ritual is going on, and children, who like rituals, want to be part of it. In the same way, the little children that I see at concerts or operas, though they may fidget a little, or perhaps take a nap now and then, rarely make any disturbance. With all those grownups sitting there, neither moving nor talking, it is the most natural thing in the world to imitate them. Children who live among adults who are habitually courteous to each other, and to them, will soon learn to be courteous. Children who live surrounded by people who speak a certain way will speak that way, however much we may try to tell them that speaking that way is bad or wrong.

The third discipline is the one most people mean when they speak of discipline—the Discipline of Superior Force, of sergeant to private, of "you do what I tell you or I'll make you wish you had." There is bound to be some of this in a child's life. Living as we do surrounded by things that can hurt children, or that children can hurt, we cannot avoid it. We can't afford to let a small child find out from experience the danger of playing in a busy street, or of fooling with the pots on the top of a stove, or of eating up the pills in the medicine cabinet. So, along with other precautions, we say to him, "Don't play in the street, or touch things on the stove, or go into the medicine cabinet, or I'll punish you." Between him and the danger too great for him to imagine we put a lesser danger, but one he can imagine and maybe therefore want to avoid. He can have no idea of what it would be like to be hit by a car, but he can imagine being shouted at, or spanked, or sent to his room. He avoids these substitutes for the greater danger until he can understand it and avoid it for its own sake. But we ought to use this discipline only when it is necessary to protect the life, health, safety, or well-being of people or other living creatures, or to prevent destruction of things that people care about. We ought not to assume too long, as we usually do, that a child cannot understand the real nature of the danger from which we want to protect him. The sooner he avoids the danger, not to escape our punishment, but as a matter of good sense, the better. He can learn that faster than we think. In Mexico, for example, where people drive their cars with a good deal of spirit, I saw many children no older than five or four walking unattended on the streets. They understood about cars, they knew what to do. A child whose life is full of the threat and fear of punishment is locked into babyhood. There is no way for him to grow up, to learn to take responsibility for his life and acts. Most important of all, we should not assume that having to yield to the threat of our superior force is good for the child's character. It is never good for *anyone's* character. To bow to superior force makes us feel impotent and cowardly for not having had the strength or courage to resist. Worse, it makes us resentful and vengeful. We can hardly wait to make someone pay for our humiliation, yield to us as we were once made to yield. No, if we cannot always avoid using the Discipline of Superior Force, we should at least use it as seldom as we can.

–John Holt

The following selection is a lecture presented to a freshman political science class. The underlined words and phrases were written on the chalkboard. Read the selection carefully, using the SSR method. Even though the selection was written as a lecture, this method should help you understand and remember its contents.

The instructor who gave this lecture asked his students to write a paragraph on one of two topics, both of which are given here as Writing Assignments 5 and 6. When you write these paragraphs, you will need to use your skills in summarizing. Be sure to review the suggestions for summarizing before you write.

SAMPLE

Political Parties in Democracies

I. Introduction
II. Functions of political parties in general
III. Unique features of American political parties

It is not easy for Americans to understand political parties in other countries, because our political parties are weak compared to those in other democracies, such as England, France, and other countries of Western Europe. Even our two large political parties, the Republican and Democratic parties, are weak compared to those of Western Europe. In Europe, being a member of a political party is more like joining a club. There are frequently dues to be paid, meetings to be attended, and duties to be carried out, such as campaigning for the parties' candidates in elections.

In the U.S., we ordinarily consider a person to be a member of a political party if he or she simply identifies with a party when registering to vote. But there are no dues to be paid, no meetings one must attend, and no duties one must perform. It is hard to point to the real party leaders because those with the highest titles often have little influence. For example, the national chairperson of the Republican or Democratic party has relatively little influence within the party.

Today, we will first talk about the functions of political parties in general; that is, we will talk about how political parties operate in democratic countries around the world. Then, we will talk about the unique features of American political parties.

There are seven basic functions of all political parties in democratic countries. First, political parties try to win votes for candidates in elections. In a representative government, the people choose government officials in elections. Political parties developed historically when the masses of people won the right to vote. This was not so long ago. The United States was the first country in the modern world to permit large numbers of its citizens to vote. But even here, during the early years of our history, the only persons who could vote were white, male property owners. Those who were not property owners gained the right to vote by the 1830s. Women won the right to vote through the 19th Amendment to the Constitution in 1920. Blacks achieved the constitutional right to vote in 1870, with the passage of the 15th Amendment, but it was not until the Voting Rights Act of 1965 that large numbers of blacks were actually permitted to vote in southern states. Once large numbers of people won the right to vote, political parties developed as organizations that attempted to win enough votes for candidates to get them elected.

A second function of political parties is to serve as a source of government personnel. The parties run candidates for elective office, candidates that are recruited from the party organization. Once elected, the candidates appoint other executive officials and sometimes judges as well. The American president, for example, appoints the top U.S. executive officials and federal judges. (Those officials and judges are almost all chosen from within the party of the president.)

A third function of political parties is to serve as a source of government policy. The parties propose general goals and specific programs as solutions to problems that face the nation. Those candidates who are elected try to make the goals and programs of their party the official policy of government. [The instructor asked if there were any questions on this point.]

A fourth function of political parties is to educate the public on political matters. As a party campaigns in elections, it tries to convince voters to choose its goals and programs over those of the other parties. To persuade the voters, a party must show why its goals and programs provide better solutions to the country's problems. Competition between parties develops interest in political issues and helps the voters to decide which policy alternatives they prefer.

A fifth function of political parties is to simplify voter choice. Because a party exists over a long period of time, from one election to another, voters come to associate certain goals and programs with each party. And they can identify themselves with the party whose goals and programs they most prefer. The choices of voters in elections are thus simplified. Voters do not have to make a choice between candidates running for every office. They can simply vote the <u>party ticket</u>; that is, they can vote for every candidate of their party. The party ticket is also called the <u>party slate</u>.

Sixth, parties help the public to hold public officials accountable for their actions. Since a candidate is chosen because the people prefer the goals and programs of the candidate's party, public officials are expected to enact those goals and programs into law. If they do not do so, the public can refuse to support these officials when they run for reelection.

Seventh, parties function to bring social unity. A major party is a coalition of many diverse groups, for a coalition is necessary if a party is to have a reasonable chance to elect its candidates to office. The diverse groups that are brought together within a party learn to cooperate and compromise, thus unifying the country to some degree. For example, in the U.S., the Democratic Party is a coalition of blacks, of labor and professional groups, of northerners and southerners, of the poor and the well-off.

So far we have been talking about the general functions political parties can perform. Now we turn to the unique features of American political parties. In the U.S., parties are relatively <u>uncentralized</u> and <u>undisciplined</u> and therefore are <u>nonprogrammatic</u>, in comparison to parties in other democracies.

U.S. parties are uncentralized because the real power in the parties lies at the local and state levels, not at the central or national level. Compared to local political parties, national parties accomplish little in between elections. [The instructor asked if there were any questions at this point.]

They are undisciplined because elected officials do not always support the party programs, even if the leader of the party is president. This contrasts sharply with England, which has centralized, disciplined parties. Power in English parties is centralized because the national party leaders have more power than local leaders. The members of the parties in the national legislature (called <u>Parliament</u> or the <u>House of Commons</u>) vote together in support of the parties' goals and programs. This insures that the programs of the majority party will pass the legislature intact. But American parties are undisciplined. Party members in Congress will even vote against the president on particular issues. [Any questions at this point?]

American parties are also nonprogrammatic. This means that they do not formulate a set of clearly distinguishable programs that the party is committed to enact into law if it candidates are elected. The parties do write a party platform before national presidential elections, and this platform is supposedly a statement of the goals and programs the party favors. But, because the parties are not centralized and disciplined, much of the platform cannot be enacted into law. Since party leaders realize the platform will not necessarily become public policy, they have little incentive to draw up a platform that is clearly distinguishable from the platform of the other principal party. [Any questions?]

Finally, we need to show *why* American parties are uncentralized, undisciplined and nonprogrammatic. Although the reasons are quite complicated, we can single out two. One reason is the federal system in the U.S. that gives substantial power to the individual states. Because state and local officials have important powers, these officials can be more independent of national party leaders than if there were no federal system. [Any questions?]

A more important reason for the uniqueness of American political parties is the voting habits and expectations of the people. In the U.S., voters decide which *person* they most prefer for a given office. The candidate's personal leadership abilities and positions on the issues are carefully considered. In some countries, such as England, voters decide which party they prefer, based on their assessment of the parties' goals and programs and the qualifications of the parties' *general* leadership. In England the persons who are running for each government position may not receive much attention as individuals, since these persons are simply expected to carry out the party goals and programs. In contrast, in the U.S. people often say, "I vote for the person, not the party." The result is that American politics tends to be personal politics rather than party politics. Political parties, therefore, tend to function quite differently in the U.S. than in other Western democracies.

–Robert Thigpen, The University of New Orleans

WRITING ASSIGNMENT 5

Write a paragraph on what in your view are the most important functions of political parties in democratic countries. Describe at least four functions. Use the following suggestions as you write:

1. First, determine which functions of political parties you believe are most important. They may not have been given first in the lecture.
2. Begin your paragraph with a sentence that immediately states your main point, such as "Political parties have at least four important functions."
3. Tag each point clearly, using something like this:

First, they . . .
Second, political parties . . .
Third, they . . .
Fourth, political parties . . .

Notice that the pronoun *they* is substituted for *political parties* to give the essay variety. What *they* refers to in the context of the essay must be made perfectly clear, however.

4. For each point, state the function in your own words as clearly and as briefly a possible, and then write a sentence or two summarizing what the instructor said about it, as the example below suggests:

> First, they get out the vote for their candidates. Political parties, in fact, only came into being when large numbers of people got the right to vote. Second, political parties . . .

WRITING ASSIGNMENT 6

Write a paragraph that explains how and why American political parties are unique. Here are some suggestions to use in your writing:

1. Begin with a sentence that appropriately introduces the paragraph, such as the following:

> American political parties are _____ compared to political parties in other democracies.   (fill in the best word)

2. Summarize what the lecturer said about the three unique qualities of American political parties.

3. Finally, explain why American political parties are unique, again summarizing what the instructor said.

CHAPTER 8

Finding Resource Material in the Library

Sometimes you can best learn about a topic you are going to write about by interviewing others who have had firsthand experience with your subject, sometimes by studying a textbook or by taking careful notes in class, and sometimes by watching the news or a documentary on television. But you can almost always find what you need to know on a topic in your college library.

This chapter gives suggestions for finding resource material in the library, and it offers several writing assignments that require library use. As you progress in college, you will be asked to use the library as the basis for research papers. But do not use the library only for research papers. Use it also to locate books that you will read for pleasure, to find magazines that will keep you informed about national and international news, and to learn current information in areas of special interest to you: sports, fashion, auto mechanics, music, and so forth. Also, use the library to find resource material for essays that you will write in English classes and other courses. You will probably be assigned many essays in college that are not full-length research papers but that will nevertheless require outside reading to gather information for them. More than likely, what you need to know for these essays can be found somewhere in your college library.

The library belongs to you, and you should learn your way around it as soon as possible. Check at the main desk to see if there is a handbook explaining where everything is. If you need assistance, do not hesitate to ask. Library staff are there to answer your questions and help you find what you need. Many college libraries offer orientation tours and classes to acquaint students with the organization of the books and other items (records, documents, periodicals, and so forth). Even without a formal tour, however, you can learn where things are located simply by studying the library plan and taking a stroll. In particular, you will want to investigate the reference room and locate the major indexes mentioned below. These simple steps may save you hours of frustration and aimless wandering later.

The Library's Resources

There are several main kinds of resources in the library that can help you find the things you need to know.

The Card Catalog   Most libraries have at least three kinds of collections: books, periodicals, and reference materials. The central index of information about books is the card catalog. This is a large cabinet full of many tray-like drawers that is usually located near the main desk. Each book the library owns is catalogued three ways in the file: by title, author, and subject. The title card is filed alphabetically according to the title of the book. (Books are not alphabetized by *a, an,* and *the.* Look up the next word in the title.) The author card is filed alphabetically according to the author's last name. In addition, one or more cards are filed alphabetically according to the subjects treated in the book. If you know the author or the exact title of a book, you will be able to check quickly to see whether the library owns a copy. If you are looking for a book on a particular subject, such as gymnastics, solar energy, French cooking, or public education, use the subject index.

When you are using the subject index, you will often find cards that read "See" or "See also." For example, if you look up "America" in the subject index, the card may say "See United States." If you look up "public education," the card may say "See also Education, public." ("See also" means that you will find cards under both subject headings.) Often students make the mistake of looking up a common-language word like "Car," which will in fact be listed in the card catalog as "Automobile." If you cannot find any card on your subject, ask your librarian for help. Sometimes the author and title indexes in the card catalog will be combined; sometimes all three indexes will be combined.

When you find the card for the book you want, write down the entire *call number* (the number printed in the top left-hand corner). The number will look something like this:

F
279
.C49N4

or this:

191.9
S233

In the first call number, the *F* designation is from the Library of Congress classification system. The call number in this system always begins with a letter.

In the second call number, the *191* designation is from the Dewey decimal system. The call number in this system always begins with a three-digit number between 000 and 999. The library directory or a diagram of the floor plan will show you which bookshelves (or stacks, as they may be called) have books labeled with a letter (in the Library of Congress system) and which have those labeled numerically (in the Dewey decimal system). The books will be shelved alphabetically and numerically. For example, to find the above book with the Library of Congress designation, you first find the *F* stacks, and then you look for the shelves labeled *279*. Next you look for the books designated *.C*. And finally, you look for the particular book with the designation *.C49N4*. If you have trouble finding your book, ask the library staff for help.

Periodicals (Magazines, Newspapers, and Journals)   Often you will want the very latest information about a particular subject, such as space travel, ecology, or nuclear power. Recent magazines are a good source for this information. You can find the latest edition of many popular magazines such as *Time, Newsweek, Scientific American,* and *National Geographic* in the magazine section of your library. You will also find many scholarly journals (usually shelved separately from the popular magazines), which contain more specialized articles on science, literature, philosophy, and art. Browse until you become familiar with the various periodicals your library receives.

Periodicals from previous years may be bound together in book covers, which are then shelved in order by year, or they may be preserved on microfilm. (Microfilm is a film on which printed materials appear, greatly reduced in size. You can view the microfilm of a magazine or newspaper by placing the film in a special viewer and advancing the film till it reaches the material you wish to read.) The best way to find particular articles is to use the large sets of indexes and bibliographies available in the reference room of your library.

An index that is especially valuable in locating articles in popular magazines is the *Readers' Guide to Periodical Literature*. It is bound in separate volumes by years and contains listings of articles from over 150 magazines. The articles are listed by both subject and author. Here is a sample entry from the 1981 volume of the *Readers' Guide:*

Education

Blackboard jumble
J. S. Siegel and E. J. Delattre
New Repub 184:17–18 Ap 18 '81

This tells you the following:

1. The article title: "Blackboard Jumble"
2. The authors: J. S. Siegel and E. J. Delattre
3. The magazine in which the article appears: *The New Republic*
4. Location: volume 184, pages 17 and 18 of the issue dated April 18, 1981

If any abbreviations confuse you, check the list of abbreviations and what they stand for at the beginning of the *Readers' Guide*. The magazine abbreviations are listed together. If you cannot find your subject listed, perhaps you are using a term different from the one used by the *Readers' Guide*. Ask for assistance if necessary.

Another useful reference tool for finding recent articles of popular interest is called *Hot Topics: The Magazine Index*. This is an article-finding machine and accompanying booklet, usually located in the reference section of the library, that can provide you with a long list of articles on a given subject published over the last five years. The articles are listed both by subject and by author, using a format similar to that in the *Readers' Guide*. The advantages of this machine are its speed and the fact that it allows you to see several years' accumulation of articles on one subject at a glance. Ask the reference librarian to show you how to use the *Magazine Index*. It is a simple procedure, and well worth your time.

If you need scholarly articles on subjects of historical or literary interest, however, the *Readers' Guide* and the *Magazine Index* are not likely to list them. To find an article on the writings of Mark Twain, for example, or one of the economic roots of the Great Depression, you should consult the *Humanities Index*. Organized much like the *Readers' Guide*, it lists scholarly articles pertaining to history and literature. For articles related to psychology, sociology, anthropology, political science, and economics, check the *Social Studies Index*. The library will also have a number of highly specialized indexes for more intensive research into a particular field. For instance, if you are looking for information for a paper on needed reform in our public schools, the *Education Index* would list many articles on the subject. Check with your reference librarian about these special indexes.

Whichever index you use, the next step is to see whether the library has the periodicals you need. The *Serials Catalog*, usually located at the reference desk, lists all the periodicals the library receives and their call numbers. The catalog will also indicate whether the article you need is on microfilm or in bound issues of the periodical. Once you have found the periodicals you need, write down their call numbers and consult the general plan of the library to see where the back issues are located.

Other Reference Tools   In addition to the indexes listed above, a few others may be especially useful in your research. The *Essay and General Literature Index* can help you find essays and chapters within books that relate to your topic, even if the title of the book gives no clue to this. This allows you to find valuable information that you would have missed if you had relied upon only a quick glance in the card catalog. The *New York Times Index* is the chief guide to newspaper articles on any event of note since 1851.

One extremely helpful guide to recently published articles on social issues is the *Social Issues Resources Series (SIRS)*. Although often located in the reference room, this series of books is actually far more than a tool for locating information. Each volume contains dozens of reprinted copies of articles on subjects of social concern written from many points of view. The volumes are continually updated as the library receives new articles. Using the *Resources Series* is quite simple. Each volume has a general subject heading: Abortion, Aging, Defense, Drugs, Religion, Schools, and so on. (The books are arranged alphabetically by subject.) An index at the front of each book breaks the subject into subdivisions so that you can easily locate the articles that are important to your study.

The reference shelves also contain many specialized dictionaries, as well as sets of encyclopedias. As with the other reference tools, usually these cannot be checked out of the library but are for reference room use only. Although the encyclopedia will probably be of limited use to you in writing college papers (it would be inadequate as a major source of information for a term paper, for example), it can be a good place to begin if you are not too familiar with a topic. Many encyclopedia articles contain excellent background and statistical information on general areas. Many also supply you with a bibliography for further reading on a given subject.

Publications on Reserve   Some instructors put certain books and periodicals "on reserve." That is, they ask the library staff to make these publications available only to a particular class for short periods of time so everyone has access to the material. Consult the library floor plan to find the location of the reserve section, or ask the librarian.

EXERCISE

Answer the following questions about your library:

1. What hours is the library open?

   _____

2. Check out a novel or autobiography you think *you* will enjoy reading. (You might try one of the books suggested in Appendix B.) Give the following information for your book:

   (1) Call number

   _____

(2) Title

_____

(3) Author

_____

(4) Publisher, place and date of publication

_____

_____

(5) Due date

_____

(6) Fine for each day the book is late

_____

3. If your name were in the card catalog, what name that is now in the catalog would come right before it?

4. Exactly where is the *Readers' Guide to Periodical Literature?*

_____

5. Locate an article on public education in a recent volume of the *Readers' Guide.* Give the name of the article, the author, and the periodical it appeared in, and the date it was published.

_____

_____

6. Does your library own *Hot Topics: The Magazine Index?* If so, ask the reference librarian to show you how to find a listing of articles printed over the last five years on cloning. How many articles have been printed on the subject? Write the title and source (name of magazine, date, pages) of one such article.

_____

_____

7. Does your library own the *SIRS?* If so, ask the reference librarian to help you find the set of volumes, which will be labeled by subjects on their spines. Give the title of the first article in the volume on drugs.

_____

_____

8. Exactly where is the *Serials Index?*

_____

9. According to the information in the *Serials Index*, does your library subscribe to *Political Theory*? If so, what is its call number?

_____

10. In which volume of the most recent edition of the *Encyclopedia Britannica* will you find an entry on African religions? What is the page number?

_____

11. Using the *Humanities Index*, locate the title of an article on the writings of Edgar Allan Poe and write it here.

_____

_____

12. Of all the magazines your library carries, which are your favorites?

_____

_____

WRITING ASSIGNMENT 1

In your library, locate the issue of *Newsweek, Time, Ebony,* or *U.S. News and World Report* that came out the week you were born. Find a news article that particularly interests you (anything from international news to sports) and write a two-paragraph essay on it. Here are some suggestions:

1. In the first paragraph, summarize the article, giving the most important information. (Before you begin your summary, study the suggestions in Chapter 7.) Begin with a one-sentence statement of what the article is about. Be sure to include the name and date of the publication, and since it is a magazine, underline the title. If you use the title of the article itself, enclose it in quotation marks but do not underline it.
2. In the second paragraph, say why you chose to write on that particular news article. Why did it interest you? What from your experience made you interested? If, for example, you choose an article on the Beatles, you may want to explain your interest in popular music. If possible, relate the news article to today's news.

WRITING ASSIGNMENT 2

Write summaries of two magazine or journal articles listed in recent volumes of the *Readers' Guide to Periodical Literature* under one of these headings (the exact wording of the topics may differ somewhat):

aging	drug abuse
capital punishment	the poor
civil rights	public schools
divorce	sexual ethics

Once you have picked a topic, read through the list of titles of relevant articles and choose several that interest you. Find them on the shelves or on microfilm and decide which two you would like to write on. If your library carries the *SIRS*, you may find the articles you would like to write on there.

In writing the summaries, use the suggestions in Chapter 7. For practice, use at least one direct or indirect quotation in each summary. In your first sentence be sure to include the title of the article and the name and date of the publication in which it appears, as well as the author's name if it is given.

WRITING ASSIGNMENT 3

Imagine that a very close friend has just been killed in an automobile wreck. The driver of the car in which your friend was riding was driving while intoxicated. You are naturally extremely upset that such a thing has happened. Everyone has been saying that the death was such an unnecessary loss of human life. To help prevent other deaths or injuries from drunken driving, you decide to write the editor of your college newspaper to try to convince other students to think twice before they drink and drive or before they ride with someone who has been drinking.

Since you want to be as informed as possible when you write this letter, go to the library and read about drunk driving. Find pertinent articles in the *Readers' Guide* under the heading "Alcohol and automobile drivers" and in the *SIRS* and read several of them. When you think you have done enough reading on the issue, write the letter to the editor. Here are some suggestions:

1. Begin your letter *Dear Editor:*
2. In the first paragraph, explain that your close friend has been killed because the driver of the car in which he or she was riding was intoxicated. Give a brief account of what happened.
3. In the following two or three paragraphs, describe how this unnecessary death underlines the national problem of drunk driving. Use your library research to explain just how serious this problem is. Give the titles of the articles that support your findings, their authors, and the dates and names of the publications in which they appeared.
4. In your final paragraph, ask your fellow students not to drive after they have been drinking or to drive with others who have been drinking. If you believe that additional laws need to be passed to help prevent drunken driving, you may want to state this as well, but be specific about the type of law or laws that should be passed.

WRITING ASSIGNMENT 4

Imagine that you have just received a letter from your friend Emily, who is in her first year of college, where she lives in a dormitory. She has recently discovered that she is pregnant. Her parents do not know about the situation, and her boyfriend has distanced himself from her, although he has offered to pay for an abortion. Emily knows that if she has the child she will have to drop out of college, go home to live with her parents, and get a job. She will have little chance of returning to college for years to come. Emily has always said that she did not think abortion was right, but now she faces giving up college and thus a professional career. Moreover, you know that her parents are not likely to be supportive if she does go home to have the child. They will probably feel shamed and treat Emily unkindly, although you believe they will let her live with them during the maternity period.

Your friend sounds desperate in her letter. She asks you for advice, saying that you are the one person who can help her think clearly about the situation. Your task is to write her a letter and give her your opinion on whether she should have the abortion. Before you write the letter, however, you need to become as informed as you possibly can on this important issue. Go to the *Readers' Guide* or *SIRS* in your library and search for recent magazine and journal articles on abortion. Study them carefully. Also consult one or more of the encyclopedias in your library.

When you write to your friend, compose a friendly, personal letter, giving her advice and explaining why you feel the way you do. You will probably not want to make reference to the reading you have done on the subject, but instead use it for background information on this very important matter. Remember that you are writing to a friend who needs help: She does not need to be lectured or scolded. (Also assume that the boyfriend's detachment and the parents' insensitivity will not change. For most of the letter, address the central question: Should Emily have the abortion?)

Use the suggestions for writing a personal letter in Chapter 1. Include with your letter on a separate sheet the research you did in the library. (Give the titles of the articles you consulted, their authors, and the dates and names of the publications in which they appeared.)

WRITING ASSIGNMENT 5

Imagine that your parents or perhaps close friends are considering putting an elderly relative in a nursing home. They would like the relative to stay with them, but it would be quite a hardship because they have so little extra room. Unfortunately, they know little about nursing homes. They have heard some terrible things about them and also some encouraging things. They write you asking your advice.

Go to the library and look for articles on aging or the elderly, especially as relating to nursing homes, in the *Readers' Guide* or the *SIRS*, which has many articles on the subject. Articles should be listed under the headings "Aging" or "Nursing homes."

When you think you have read enough of these articles, write a letter to your parents or friends about nursing homes, mentioning their strengths and weaknesses as well as your view. Should your parents or friends keep the relative with them in spite of the hardship? Or should they place the person in a nursing home if the right kind of home is available? (If you take this position you will need to define the "right kind of home.")

Assume that the relative is in fairly good health and mentally alert, but very old and not able to do much for him- or herself. Assume further that the relative has a modest income, which is enough to pay for a nursing home of average cost. Use the suggestions for writing a personal letter in Chapter 1. Include with your letter on a separate sheet of paper the reading you did in the library. Give the titles of the relevant articles, their authors, and the dates and names of the publications in which they appeared.

CHAPTER 9

Writing Persuasively

The purpose of this chapter is to help you learn how to convince your reader of the validity of your point of view on a particular subject. In most of the essays you wrote in Part One, you needed to persuade. You were asked to include your opinion on a topic in your purpose statement and then to support your opinion in the body of the essay. In this chapter, however, you will concentrate on using the techniques of persuasion and outside resources to write persuasively in an argument essay.

Forming an Argument

The exercises below should help you prepare to write argument essays. Before you can convince someone else of what you believe on a topic, you must be quite sure that you know what you believe. As you reflect on a certain subject and discuss it with others, you may find that you actually believe something quite different from what you had thought you believed. If so, this is fine; some people call this process of changing one's opinions "growth." Also, it is important that you understand the positions held by those who disagree with you. You must learn to address these positions as well as to state your own case.

EXERCISE 1

Let two opposite sides of yourself talk with each other about an important decision you have to make. Record the "conversation" and then revise it, using three hundred words or more. What you have to do is to persuade *yourself* on a course of action. Here are some examples of a decision you may want to write about:

> I have a great job offer. Should I take it, or should I stay in college and finish my degree?

I think one of my brothers (or sisters) is developing a serious drinking problem. Should I talk with him (or her) myself or ask someone else to do so? Or should I do nothing?

I have a choice of two jobs: One pays a lot of money, but I do not think I would like it very much. The other sounds more interesting but does not pay nearly as well. Which one should I accept?

I broke off an important relationship. Now I think I have made a mistake. Should I try to reconcile with the person or just leave things as they are?

In choosing a decision to write about, be sure that it would be a very hard decision for you to make.

When they are having their internal "conversation" for this exercise, some students find that it helps to set up two chairs and to switch seats each time they argue for the other position. Argue as convincingly as you can for each point of view—that's the trick! Keep going back and forth between the two sides as long as necessary; just be sure that you finally make a decision. You might begin to record your "conversation" as follows:

> For the twelfth time today I went to the phone, picked up the receiver and dialed six of the seven numbers. I am dying to accept the job my uncle has offered me as the lead auto mechanic at his service station. He told me that I would start at ten dollars an hour and that with my military experience I should do terrific work.
>
> One side of me has been saying, "Oh, go ahead. You can go back to college anytime. What job could you get after college that would pay you more than ten dollars an hour? That's over twenty thousand dollars a year. Call your uncle and . . . ."
>
> The other side has been saying, "Hold it. Not so fast. All those years you were in the military you planned to go to college so that you would have many career possibilities to choose from. You have planned your whole life around going to college, and now . . . ."
>
> Then the first side says, "Just think: Twenty thousand dollars a year! Why I could buy . . . ."

When you revise your internal conversation, use the rules for recording dialogue on page 56 and observe how they are used in the student samples on pages 56 and 57. See Chapter 18.7 for more on how to use quotation marks.

EXERCISE 2

Have a class discussion about all the examples of public persuasion that you can think of. Include examples from persuasive advertising (from television, newspapers, magazines, and so forth), military recruiting, religious proselytizing, and political campaigning. Your instructor may want to ask someone to write these examples on the chalkboard. Which are most persuasive? With the class, carefully analyze *why* they are persuasive.

Choose one example of persuasion, and write a paragraph explaining why it is particularly persuasive to many people. As an alternative exercise, choose a very persuasive political figure and in a paragraph analyze why he or she is so persuasive. You need not agree with this person's point of view. In fact, it may help to choose someone you do not generally agree with. Revise your paragraph before turning it in to your instructor. If class time permits, share your paragraph in a small group to learn what others think of effective persuasion.

EXERCISE 3

Write a paragraph explaining how someone changed your mind on a particular issue or how you changed someone else's mind. Be sure to state exactly what the original position was and what was used to cause the change: Logical arguments? Examples from experience? Appeals to morality?

EXERCISE 4

In preparation for this exercise, go to the library and read about capital punishment in an encyclopedia and in at least one of the articles indexed in the *Reader's Guide* or reprinted in the *SIRS*.

In class divide into groups of no less than five and no more than eight students. Listed below are five case situations in which someone was sentenced to die. After your instructor reads each case, indicate your reaction to the death sentence, not to the murder—ranging from absolutely wrong to absolutely right—by putting your initials in the appropriate box in the grid:

	Absolutely Wrong	*Wrong*	*Slightly Wrong*	*Slightly Right*	*Right*	*Absolutely Right*
CASE 1						
CASE 2						
CASE 3						
CASE 4						
CASE 5						

There should be no discussion until each person has responded to all five case situations. Then all participants should speak in turn as to why they put their initials in the particular boxes. Be sure to discuss the underlying values that led to the decisions. Only after everyone has given his or her reasons for the decisions should there be general discussion.

The purpose of this exercise is to help you appreciate the degrees of right and wrong on particular issues and to help you understand why others may disagree with your opinion. (Your instructor may want to replace capital punishment with some other issue of social importance.)

Here are the five case situations:

CASE 1

A skyjacker has been sentenced to die after trying to steal a commercial plane and killing one of the passengers. He claimed that his only objective was to call the world's attention to the plight of his badly oppressed people.

CASE 2

A woman has been sentenced to die after killing her husband in a fit of rage. She cried on the witness stand and said that she deserved to die and that she loved her husband.

CASE 3

A sixteen-year-old boy has been sentenced to die after shooting a grocery store owner who pulled a gun on him while he was robbing the store. This was the boy's first major offense.

CASE 4

A prison inmate has been sentenced to die after killing a prison guard. He claimed that the guard was always harassing him. Some witnesses agreed. The prisoner was serving a sentence for simple assault and would have been released in three weeks.

CASE 5

A paid gunman has been sentenced to die for killing three people. He was paid five thousand dollars to kill two of the victims and fifteen thousand to kill the third. He offered no defense at his trial, saying, "It doesn't matter anyhow."

After the discussion, choose one of the case situations and write a paragraph explaining why you made the decision on it that you did. It may be most helpful to choose a situation that forced you to make a truly difficult decision because of your conflicting values about the case. In your paragraph you can thus write about both why you think the person should be executed and why you think the person should be spared. Revise your paragraph before submitting it to your instructor.

The Argument Essay

Many college essays assigned in both English classes and other courses are arguments. You may be asked, for example, to defend your point of view on why some historical event occurred, why the labor movement is or is not a constructive force in our economy, why authors present the characters in novels in a certain way, why a poem is powerful, or why Plato was a greater philosopher than Aristotle.

The skills you learn in writing an argument will also help you in a practical way after college. Think of the many occasions when you might need to write a convincing argument. If you are concerned about a local or national issue, you may want to write a letter to your local newspaper or to your councilperson or representative in Congress. If you think your church, organization, or children's school should do something differently, you can argue for your position in a letter to the appropriate official. The library contains a vast store of information that will help you think through your positions on various subjects and develop sound arguments to promote your point of view.

Writing assignment 1 in this chapter asks you to defend a position on a subject of your choice that is well documented in your library. Writing assignments 2 through 4 ask you to use the library to respond to particular issues.

Writing an Argument Essay

The purpose of the argument essay is to express your opinion on a particular subject. Acknowledge the complexity of the subject if you like, but state a definite opinion. Think of yourself as a member of a jury. Consider the arguments on both sides of the issue, but then cast your vote one way or the other.

If you are permitted to choose your own topic, always pick one that is important to you so that you can make your essay a real argument.

As you develop an argument essay, ask yourself what kinds of arguments would convince you of a certain point of view. You would probably not be convinced by emotional arguments or by general statements that were not soundly supported. Your reader is no doubt very much like you. In your writing, emphasize arguments that are calm, rational, and not overstated. Qualifying words and expressions like *maybe, perhaps,* and *it seems to me* are often appropriate. For example:

> In spite of the many sound arguments for the Equal Rights Amendment, it seems to me that . . .

Take advantage of all the information-gathering resources at your disposal: Use the brainstorming or clustering technique, talk to others for ideas, and use the resources in the library such as encyclopedias, magazines, books, and newspapers. (See Chapter 8.)

State your position in the first paragraph. This will serve as your purpose statement.

Address the arguments on the other side of the issue somewhere in your essay. You want to avoid having your reader saying, "Yes, that sounds good, but . . ." You will do much to reduce the impact of such a response if you address reasonable arguments made by the opposition. Sometimes you can best address the opposing arguments in your introduction, sometimes as you make each of your own arguments, and at other times in a separate paragraph, perhaps the second.

Use the various writing methods discussed in Part One:

1. *Description.* Your skills in observing detail and listening to dialogue will help you support your arguments. Fine points and concrete details convince; the general and the abstract do not.

2. *Narration.* Use your skill in telling a story to illustrate certain arguments. If you are arguing that sex education should be taught in high school, you may want to tell in one paragraph what happened to someone you know who was not properly educated in this area.

3. *Examples.* Examples strengthen all arguments. In fact, many effective arguments are written as example essays: You first state your point of view; then you support it with three or four examples, using a paragraph or so for each one. You could write convincing essays on topics such as the following simply by giving examples:

    > Capital punishment takes innocent lives.
    >
    > Disabled pesons are often discriminated against.
    >
    > _____ has perhaps the worst drivers in the country.
    > (name a city)

4. *Comparison and contrast.* If you want to give full treatment to the other side of an issue, the comparison and contrast structure may work best. Here you would give the opposing arguments in the second paragraph and then state your own arguments in the third. (You may of course need to subdivide each of these two paragraphs in the body of the essay.) If you choose this structure, whenever possible make your arguments parallel to the arguments of the opposition. For example:

Paragraph 2: For Capital Punishment	Paragraph 3: Against Capital Punishment
deters crime, why	does not deter crime, why
"an eye for an eye"	"To err is human, to forgive, divine."
now administered justly, examples	now administered unjustly, examples

5. *Classification.* The most common method for writing an argument is to give several reasons why something is right or wrong. Your skills in classifying material will help you group your arguments together in a logical way.

In your introduction, consider telling why the issue under discussion is an important one. Also consider ending your paper with a call-to-action conclusion.

Support your main points with logical arguments and, when appropriate, statistics, quotations from reading material, examples, descriptive details, and one-paragraph stories. Here are two logical arguments that could be made about the effect of capital punishment on deterring other capital crime:

> Capital punishment is not likely to deter others from committing crime. Stop and think about it. What person is going to make a rational decision about whether to kill on the basis of possible punishment by death or life imprisonment? Both fates are terrible.

> Capital punishment is bound to reduce crime. If convicted murderers are executed, at least *they* will not kill again. Maybe ridding society of a few potential killers is reason enough to justify capital punishment.

Here are two other logical statements, this time on the legal drinking age:

> We should not raise the legal drinking age from eighteen to twenty-one. Someone who is old enough to vote and to fight and die for our country is old enough to decide when to drink.

> We must raise the legal drinking age from eighteen to twenty-one. A high percentage of motor vehicle deaths involve accidents caused by drivers under twenty-one. What is more important: saving human lives or giving eighteen year olds their so-called civil rights?

Throughout your essay keep your audience in mind. What will it take to persuade your readers that you are right?

As you read the two student essays below, notice how the writers have used outside resources to make their arguments and how they have addressed the arguments of the opposition. (Another argument essay—by a professional writer—appears on page 199.)

SAMPLE A

Arguments Against Capital Punishment

Capital punishment has been used since the beginning of human existence. However, in this century the number of people executed has been decreasing. In the 1930s, 1,667 people were executed, compared to 717 in the 1950s. Since 1977, 47 people have been executed. In spite of the fact that a majority of Americans advocate keeping the death penalty, I am glad it is being used less frequently. In my view it should not be used at all.

The first reason why we should abolish capital punishment is that it is ethically unacceptable. "Thou shalt not kill" is the fifth commandment that was given to us by God. An individual has no right to kill, no matter what another person has done. Only God can create, and God should be the only one to destroy.

The second reason we should not have capital punishment is that it has failed in its purpose. Supporters of the death penalty argue that it is a strong deterrent to people who could be criminals. They use the theory that a person will weigh the amount of the reward to be gained from killing someone against the pain of the punishment. If the punishment is great enough, they reason, the person will not commit the crime. But this is a false argument because most people who commit violent crimes are not rational at the time. A study by Dr. Gordon Grisby of the University of Florida showed that 75 percent of the males and more than 90 percent of the females who commited violent crime were under the influence of alcohol or drugs and not rational at the time.

The final reason we should do away with capital punishment is that it costs more than a life sentence. Most people think it is cheaper to execute a criminal than it is to supply him or her with room, clothing, and food, but they are wrong. The death penalty is very expensive because of the long, drawn-out process of jury selection, extended trials, maintenance of the prisoner on death row, and the appeals process. It cost the State of Utah nearly a million dollars to execute Gary Gilmore.

If you agree with me that capital punishment is not necessary and that we would be better off without it, write your legislator about changing our law.

QUESTIONS FOR DISCUSSION

1. Is the writing persuasive? If so, what in particular makes it persuasive? If not, what should be changed or added?
2. What logical argument does the writer use in the third paragraph to support his position?
3. How does the writer address the arguments of the opposition in the third and four paragraphs? Are you left saying "Yes, but . . ."? Why or why not?
4. The writer uses statistics in three of his five paragraphs. What are they? Are they effective?
5. What kind of conclusion does the writer use?

SAMPLE B

A "Yes" for Capital Punishment

Capital punishment is punishment by death, and it is sometimes given to those who are guilty of the most serious crimes. Few people have been punished by death since the 1950s, but there has been a terrible increase in crime in the United States in recent years. If capital punishment were used more often, crime would surely decrease significantly.

Some people argue against capital punishment because there used to be so much racial prejudice against blacks, and it was mostly blacks who were executed. There is no doubt that capital punishment was used unjustly in many cases, but today racial prejudice is not as great. Capital punishment could be given to all those who deserve such a sentence. Only 17 of the 47 men executed since 1947 were black. As a black American, I do not think the racial prejudice argument is valid anymore.

Others argue that capital punishment does not deter crime, but I disagree. Many people commit serious crimes because they know that the law will not be enforced as it once was. They know that they can get a good lawyer to defend them, or they can plead insanity, or they feel they can get out of jail early on probation or for good behavior. If capital punishment were enforced more often, people would know that if they are found guilty of serious crimes such as murder, they will be put to death. This is not a way to control all crimes, but it is a way to control some of the more serious ones.

Next, some argue that capital punishment is immoral, but my response is that murder and rape are also immoral. The law cannot be totally moral when criminals are not moral. As Walter Berns wrote in *For Capital Punishment: Crime and the Morality of the Death Penalty,* "The real issue is whether justice permits or even requires the death penalty. I am aware that it is a terrible punishment, but there are terrible crimes and terrible criminals." We simply cannot allow criminals to take advantage of the law, but instead must stand up to them sternly.

The last argument against capital punishment is that it is too expensive. However, the state spends millions of dollars on all types of programs that do not always benefit people, so why should it not spend money on enforcing capital punishment? It is a threat to innocent people to have murderers and rapists in the streets. The state should realize the significance of capital punishment and enforce it.

I hope you will join me in voting "yes" for capital punishment.

QUESTIONS FOR DISCUSSION

1. Is the writing persuasive? If so, what in particular makes it persuasive? If not, what should be changed?
2. The writer depends on logical arguments in making his points. What are they? Are they effective?
3. How does the writer address the arguments of the opposition? Are you left saying "Yes, but . . ."? Why or why not?
4. What statistics might the writer have used in the first and second paragraphs?
5. Is the quotation from an expert an effective one? Explain.
6. Are the transition sentences in the body of the essay effective?

WRITING ASSIGNMENT 1

The object of this assignment is for you to use the library to help you think through and support your views on a particular issue of national importance that is also a concern of yours. (Read Chapter 8 on using the library if you have not already done so.) Then, after you have finished your research, write an argument essay of several paragraphs on the subject you have chosen.

Choose Your Topic In your library, find a recent volume of the *Readers' Guide* and look up at least one of the following subjects:

aging
alcohol and automobile drivers
capital punishment
civil rights
divorce
drug abuse

the poor
public schools
sexual ethics

Read through the titles of the articles that are listed under the headings and read at least three on one of the topics. If these articles are not informative and thought provoking, try three more, and keep trying until you find the right articles. As you read, take notes. You may also want to summarize particular articles. It may be helpful to consult the encyclopedia for background information on your topic, but do not stop there.

As you study your subject, try to narrow it down so you will not be covering an issue too broad for a short essay. For example, if you are studying public schools, you may want to write on the proposed voucher system, discipline, or required courses. If you are studying sexual ethics, you may want to write on faithfulness in marriage.

When you are ready, write a statement in which you take a position on an issue. Here are possible statements on some of the subjects listed above:

> Capital punishment is cruel and unusual punishment.
>
> Society has a right to demand capital punishment.
>
> Alcohol is the most dangerous drug.
>
> The legal drinking age should be eighteen.
>
> Drugs are seriously damaging college sports.
>
> The welfare system is a disaster.
>
> At this time, the welfare system is the best we can devise.
>
> We can save the public schools.
>
> The voucher system is the only way to save our public schools.
>
> The voucher system will destroy public education.
>
> Faithfulness is vital in marriage.

Before you move on to the next step, check your purpose statement with your instructor.

Step One: Gather Ideas and Information   Think of as many reasons as you can why your position on the issue you have chosen is the right one, and write these reasons in the left-hand column on page 197. Then think of all the arguments that could be made for other positions on the issue, and write these in the right-hand column (this is a difficult but important step). In addition to using the brainstorming and perhaps the clustering techniques to gather ideas, be sure to discuss the issue with others. Now read through the notes you have taken from your reading and write down any information or quotations you may want to use. If you find that you need more information, go back to the library and explore your topic further.

Your Position   *Other Positions*

_____   _____

_____   _____

_____   _____

_____   _____

_____   _____

_____   _____

_____   _____

_____   _____

_____   _____

Relevant Information and Quotations

_____

_____

_____

_____

_____

_____

_____

_____

_____

_____

_____

_____

Step Two: Analyze the Ideas and the Information   Looking at both sides of the issue, which arguments are valid? Which are weak? Exactly where do you stand on the issue now that you have had time to reflect on it with resource material in hand? Has your position changed since you began to think about the issue?

Step Three: State Your Purpose   In an argument essay, the purpose statement is usually just a simple statement of what you believe. Any of the statements listed above could serve as a purpose statement. Be sure you state your thesis exactly as you want to defend it. You may want to qualify your statement to some degree, as follows:

> In spite of the strong arguments that can be made for teaching sex education in high school, I am against it.
>
> The advantages of teaching sex education in high school are greater than the disadvantages.

But be aware of qualifying your purpose *too much*. Take a position and argue for it. Too much qualifying will weaken your argument.

Step Four: Make Your Plan   Before writing an outline for your argument essay, review the various writing methods that are listed on page 192. Can you best develop your essay by using examples or comparison and contrast, or simply by stating several reasons why your position is the correct one? As you write your outline, plan to address the reasonable arguments of the opposition. It may help you to reread the student samples above to see how those two writers outlined their essays. You may want to read the argument essay called "Merit Pay," later in this chapter, as well.

Step Five: Write   As you write, keep reminding yourself of your audience. Is it your instructor and your class? The readers of your school newspaper? Or is it some other group? Also keep in mind the purpose of an argument essay, which is to convince your readers of the validity of your point of view. Would you yourself be convinced by your writing? Include at least one direct quotation in your essay.

Step Six: Evaluate, Revise, and Edit   Evaluate your paper, using the criteria in Chapter 4. Write a short paragraph, as though you were your instructor, commenting on the organization and style of the essay. Is it convincing? Why or why not? Now revise your essay. Finally, edit your writing.

Read the argument essay below carefully, and then complete the writing assignments that follow:

Merit Pay

Many people, including the members of the National Commission on Excellence in Education, argue that the quality of teaching in American public schools needs strengthening. One suggestion for improving the quality of teaching that has received wide support, including that of President Reagan, is the idea of merit pay for teachers. It is an idea that on the surface seems a good thing, but actually it would create more problems than it would solve.

Teachers are now generally paid on the basis of their university credentials and their seniority. A merit pay system would provide raises to teachers according to the quality of their teaching. Most merit pay plans have specified that a teacher's merit be determined by a written evaluation by the school principal. Supporters of merit pay argue that, by rewarding excellence, such a plan would encourage present teachers to teach better and make the profession a more desirable career choice for those with the potential to be superior teachers. These arguments are attractive to many people because of the widespread belief that those who do a better job should be paid more. Although merit pay proposals may seem desirable, there are three main reasons why they should not be adopted.

First, it is very difficult to determine merit in teaching. Most of us simply do not agree about the proper way to judge a teacher's merit. By contrast, people do agree about what constitutes merit in some jobs. For example, it is generally agreed that insurance salesmen should be judged according to the value of the policies they sell. But does the teacher who stimulates the curiosity of students or who brings students from diverse backgrounds to cooperate with one another have more or less merit than one who can get students to learn more facts? People disagree about the answer to this question.

Some argue that it is possible to determine merit in education because universities have based pay on merit for many years. But the way merit pay is distributed at universities actually illustrates the problem of determining merit. University professors are generally expected to do research as well as to teach. Because of the difficulty of evaluating teaching, the tendency is for professors to be evaluated mainly, sometimes solely, in terms of their research. Research, unlike teaching, can be quantified; that is, the number of research publications can be counted. There is a danger that a search for similarly "objective" standards for elementary and secondary teaching might lead to the evaluation of teachers in terms of the performance of their students on standardized tests. But such tests cannot measure aspects of good teaching such as the development of students' curiosity and cooperation. Moreover, a reliance on standardized tests may cause teachers to "teach the test." They would try to prepare students for the test and ignore other aspects of learning.

The second problem with merit pay is that it would cause damaging competition and divisions among teachers and between teachers and administrators. Competition may stimulate the performance of salesmen, but competition among teachers for pay would undermine the cooperation and mutual support that is essential if a school is to be a good learning environment. Teachers would be less likely to offer help and advice to one another. They would also be more distrustful of their principals.

The third shortcoming of merit pay is that it does not deal with the basic problems that stand in the way of effective teaching. Back in 1953 the San Diego, California, school district stated, "Merit programs too frequently presuppose that all improvement comes through changing the teachers." Writing in *The American Educator,* Daphne S. White quotes Gary Sykes, former head of the teaching policies team at the National Institute of Education: "I have never seen any evidence that shows merit pay promotes excellence in teaching."

The necessary changes in the professional conditions of teaching must begin with a general increase in the salaries of classroom teachers. It can no longer be assumed that teachers will be women who are supplementing the main family income provided by their husbands. Salaries sufficient to support a family must be paid if capable young persons are to be attracted to the teaching profession. Other needed reforms concern the classroom conditions that teachers face daily. Reductions in class size would reduce discipline problems and permit teachers to give students individual attention. A decrease in the number of classes taught would allow teachers more time to prepare their classes. Fewer interruptions and less paperwork would enable teachers to give undivided attention to their students. Genuine solutions to our educational problems will require a great national commitment. Merit pay for teachers is not the answer.

–Robert Thigpen, The University of New Orleans

WRITING ASSIGNMENT 2

Go to the library and find other articles on merit pay for teachers. Be sure to check both the *Readers' Guide* and the *SIRS.* Discuss the issue with at least one high school teacher if possible. Then, using the six-step writing method and the suggestions for the argument essay, write a response to Robert Thigpen's essay. You may want to summarize his essay in your first paragraph and then state your own view, which you can defend in the rest of the paper. Include at least one direct quotation in your essay.

WRITING ASSIGNMENT 3

Write a one-paragraph essay summarizing Thigpen's argument.

WRITING ASSIGNMENT 4

A first-year-English student wrote the letter below to the editor of her college newspaper. In it she called on her fellow students to support the Equal Rights Amendment (ERA). If the ERA had gone into effect, this statement would have been added to the Constitution: "Equality of rights under the law shall not be denied or abridged by the United States or by any state on account of sex." (The ERA, however, failed to receive the support of three-fourths of the state legislatures it needed to become law. But the ERA movement is slowly building once again.)

Your assignment is to write a letter to the same college newspaper either agreeing or disagreeing with the student's letter. Use the resources in the library to carefully support your arguments. You may want to begin with the *Encyclopedia Americana*. In the *Readers' Guide*, the ERA is listed under the "United States Constitution." Also look for articles in the *SIRS*. The student argued for the ERA from her experience. Your task is to agree or disagree with her on the basis of both your experience *and what you read on the subject.*

Dear Editor:

As you know our state legislature will soon vote on the ratification of the Equal Rights Amendment. I urge the readers of this newspaper to write their state representatives asking them to vote for ERA. Women are oppressed in our society, and the ERA, by providing "equality of rights under the law," will help us to gain our rights.

Women are victims of job segregation. Many people say that women should stay home and do domestic chores, but I believe they should have the same rights in choosing an occupation as men have. We often feel useless in the traditional role of housewives, and some of us must work to support our families.

Women want challenges. We want to work and use our minds. Unfortunately, no matter where we work, we are still paid less than men for the same job. I have heard that women receive only sixty-nine cents for every dollar men earn. Yet we have the same abilities as men and can do any job they can. There are even women welders and electricians. The ERA will help us receive the same salaries as men.

Women are also deprived of political equality in American society. Many people say that women cannot think for themselves and that men should talk about politics only to other men because such talk would bore women. I disagree. Women are very intelligent and have the same mental ability for political work as men. Many of us have gone to college and have vast amounts of knowledge to contribute to the rest of society. While the ERA cannot guarantee us more political power, it can help us to gain more respect in the community, and then we will be able to demand political power.

Women have progressed a great deal, but we have a long way to go. Please ask your representative to vote "yes" on ERA.

Sincerely yours,

Reina Bougere

WRITING ASSIGNMENT 5

Imagine that you have just received the following letter from your friend Ethel Rittenberg, a high school biology teacher. As she says in the letter, she has written several of her former students for advice on a matter of extreme importance to her: whether she should teach sex education in her classes. After you have read the letter closely, jot down your thoughts. Then go to the library and study the issue. You may want to begin by looking up the topic in the *Encyclopedia Americana*, the *Readers' Guide*, and the *SIRS*.

Next write Ethel a personal letter in which you give your advice. Try to present both sides of the question, but then take a position, using all of your skills in making an argument. Remember that Ethel Rittenberg is your friend and wants your advice, not a lecture.

> Dear _____,
>
> I am writing to a few of my former students to ask their advice on a matter that is very important to me. As you probably know, the state legislature has recently made it possible for biology teachers to offer sex education in our high school classes.
>
> I was delighted when I heard the news because I have long thought that sex education should be a part of the curriculum. In the last few weeks, however, there has been a loud public protest against teaching anything connected with sex in high school. I know a few of the people involved in this protest, and they seem like responsible, loving parents. While I disagree with them, I do respect their position. They are afraid that if we offer sex education in the schools, their young people will be tempted to indulge in sexual promiscuity.
>
> Because you did not receive sex education in high school, I thought your advice would be helpful. What I would like from you is your opinion on the importance of sex education to the high school student. If I am convinced that this subject really will help my students in their personal lives, I am going to teach it. If it does not seem to matter that much, however, I am not going to stick my neck out. Why fight a battle that does not have to be fought?
>
> Please write me as soon as possible and tell me, from your reading and your experience, just how important you believe it would be for me to offer sex education in my biology classes. Do you think the arguments against sex education in high school are valid? Thank you in advance for your help.
>
> Sincerely yours,
>
> Ethel Rittenberg

PART THREE

A Writer's Workbook

Many students have wondered aloud why some instructors stress the mechanics of English so heavily: "Isn't it much more important that you write well than it is to know what a conjunctive adverb is?" "Why should we learn all the rules about commas when everyone seems to use them differently anyway?" "Grammar is for grammar school."

It is true that many fine writers would be hard pressed to define a conjunctive adverb or to list ten rules for using commas. It is also quite possible that these same writers have not thought much about the mechanics of writing since their school days. Over time, avid readers pick up the mechanics of writing naturally without thinking a lot about them. If these readers also do a lot of writing, they gradually master the skills of Standard Written English.

If you are an avid reader, the mechanics of English will come easily to you as you practice writing the essays assigned in Parts One and Two. But even if you are not, you will learn better control over your writing by learning the vocabulary and rules for the mechanics of English presented in Part Three.

If you are just beginning to develop good reading habits, this workbook should give you a shortcut to writing correct English. However, it should in no way be seen as a substitute for essay writing; you learn to write well only by doing a lot of reading and composition writing. Rather, Part Three should give you the tools for writing strong and varied sentences and for editing your writing before your instructor or someone else does. When your mistakes are pointed out to you, you will better understand how to correct them.

Once you decide to embark on the journey of learning the vocabulary and rules of Standard Written English, you should naturally start at the beginning, making sure that you know all the parts of a sentence and their functions. The mechanics of English builds on itself somewhat as mathematics does. For example, you cannot be sure if subjects and verbs agree if you cannot identify verbs. And you cannot always identify verbs if you do not know that prepositional phrases and adjective clauses often separate

205

subjects and verbs. It therefore helps to know what prepositions are and how to form adjective clauses in order to identify verbs and thus avoid subject-verb errors.

Many exercises are offered in Part Three: Some are objective; others require that you compose your own sentences or even paragraphs. You can check your answers to the objective exercises in Appendix C. The review exercises at the end of each chapter will help test your knowledge of the material in that chapter.

CHAPTER 10

Parts of Speech

10.0 Introduction

In this chapter you will learn how the eight parts of speech function in a sentence. As you study the rules of grammar and punctuation, you will need to know how to identify the parts of speech, especially subjects and verbs.

Parts of Sentences

A sentence is made up of parts: clauses, phrases, and words. A sentence stands by itself as a complete unit: It has a subject and verb. A sentence may be a statement or a question:

STATEMENT

subject verb
↓   ↓
They are in a high tax bracket.

QUESTION

verb   subject
↓   ↓
Are you hungry?

A clause is one part of a sentence; a clause also has a subject and verb.

CLAUSES

subject verb   subject verb
↓   ↙   ↓   ↓
When we were young,   stamps cost fifteen cents.
   (first clause)   (second clause)

A phrase is another part of a sentence, but it does not have a subject and a verb.

PHRASES

into the house

singing in the rain

never too much

PRACTICE 1

In the following exercise, identify sentences with an *S*, clauses with a *C*, and phrases with a *P*:

1. _____ Over the most dangerous mountain range.

2. _____ While Rome burned.

3. _____ Who is on the phone?

4. _____ It is the lady from the paint company.

5. _____ Because you are ill.

6. _____ Soon it will rain.

7. _____ Climbing higher and higher into the sky.

8. _____ For the sake of humankind.

9. _____ Which is over there.

10. _____ Not in my class.

Parts of Speech

Eight parts of speech make up sentences: nouns, pronouns, verbs, prepositions, adjectives, adverbs, conjunctions, and interjections. As you study the various parts of speech in this text, remember that many words can be used as different parts of speech in different contexts; for example, the word *hate* can be used in three different ways:

I hate pain. (verb)

His expression revealed hate. (noun)

The senator received many hate letters. (noun used as an adjective)

10.1 Nouns

A *noun* is a part of speech that names a person, place, thing, or idea. Nouns are often preceded by the following groups of words:

a, an, the
this, these, that, those
my, your, his, her, its, our, their
in, of, on, by, with, to

PRACTICE 2

Underline each of the nouns in the following sentences. (The number of nouns in each sentence is given in parentheses after the sentence; there are twelve altogether. The words *they* and *you* are not nouns but pronouns.)

1. An essay on a test need not be a difficult task. (3)

2. First, students should gather their thoughts and, if time permits, write an outline. (4)

3. Next, they should write all their ideas in the most logical order. (2)

4. Be sure your sentences are clear and complete. (1)

5. If you have the time, proofread your essay. (2)

Proper Nouns

Nouns that refer to particular people, places, or things are called *proper nouns* and are capitalized. The underlined words in this sentence are proper nouns:

> Edgar Allan Poe, who lived in both England and the United States, is the author of many short stories, including "The Gold Bug" and "The Tell-Tale Heart."

PRACTICE 3

Underline the proper nouns in the following sentences:

1. In 1937, Richard Wright wrote his great book *Black Boy.*

2. It is the story of a black American growing up in the Deep South between 1905 and 1925.

3. Most of the story is set in the cities of Memphis and Jackson.

4. The book is about how Wright freed himself from the bondage of his youth.

PRACTICE 4

Underline *all* nouns in the following sentences. (The number of nouns in each sentence is given in parentheses after each sentence.)

1. Richard Wright had many obstacles to overcome. (2)

2. It was especially hard for him to obtain a good educaton because when he was young the schools for blacks were inferior to those for whites. (4)

3. His family was so poor that Wright often went to bed hungry. (3)

4. He had to buy his own clothes, books, and much of his food. (3)

5. But Wright did free himself from his hardships. (2)

6. Many things enabled him to escape: his reading, his defiance, his learning to cope, and his determination. (5)

7. He always found a way to obtain magazines and books to read. (3)

8. After the long, hard struggles of his youth, Wright entered the adult world as a free man. (5)

9. But the struggles of his youth had left him with scars. (3)

10. Most college students enjoy the book *Black Boy*. (3)

Nouns as Subjects

A noun can function as the subject of a sentence. That is, the noun is what the sentence is about. For example:

> The hurricane blew down houses, turned over cars, and destroyed most of the trees in the area.

The noun *hurricane* is a subject; it is what the sentence is about. All sentences must have subjects. Here are two more sentences in which the subject is a noun:

> My ninety-year-old *grandmother* is a spunky lady.
> The *baby* cried half the night.

PRACTICE 5

Underline the subjects of the following sentences:

1. Since the beginning of time, men have been using and abusing women.

2. Cavemen dragged, pulled, and beat women all the time.

3. Today women are striking back on behalf of their cavewomen ancestors.

4. The men in this class had better watch out.

5. Women are on the rise.

10.2 Verbs

A *verb* is a part of speech that says what a subject is (was, will be) or does (did, will do). Here is an example of a verb that says what a subject is:

subject verb

↓   ↓

My <u>grandmother</u> <u>is</u> ninety years old.

Below is a verb that says what a subject does:

subject verb

↓ ↓

The <u>deer</u> <u>leaps</u> over the fence escaping the hunters.

PRACTICE 6

Write sentences (thoughts that will stand on their own) using the following subjects and verbs:

1. (criminals, lead) _____

_____

2. (president, takes) _____

_____

3. (looks, tell) _____

_____

4. (architect, designed) _____

_____

5. (tests, measure) _____

_____

6. (smoking, causes) _____

_____

7. (high school bands, _____) _____
(supply verb)

_____

8. (police officers, _____) _____
(supply verb)

_____

9. (_____, swam) _____
(supply subject)

_____

10. (_____, kissed) _____
(supply subject)

_____

Simple Verbs and Verb Phrases

A verb that is just one word is called a *simple verb*. A verb that is made up of more than one word is called a *verb phrase*. The words that go along with a main verb to make up a verb phrase are called *helping verbs*.

SIMPLE VERB

love

VERB PHRASES

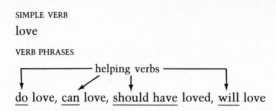

do love, can love, should have loved, will love

PRACTICE 7

Underline the subjects once and the verbs twice in the following sentences. Be sure to underline the helping verbs as well as the main verbs.

1. I do believe the testimony.

2. The testimony could hurt the defendant.

3. The troop should go on more hikes.

4. The extra five minutes should have made the difference.

5. The Marines want a few good people.

6. David should have been chosen.

PRACTICE 8

Write sentences using the following verb phrases:

1. (can understand) _____

2. (should know) _____

3. (must wait) _____

4. (can eat) _____

5. (will be seated) _____

Linking Verbs

Linking verbs tell what a subject is, was, or will be. Thus, they can be any form of the verb *to be*, such as *am, is, are, was, were, has been*, or *will be*. Other linking verbs are *become, feel, seem, look*, and *appear*. For example:

My ninety-year-old grandmother is a spunky lady.

Grandmother is the subject of the sentence, or what it is about. *Lady* is a *predicate nominative:* It renames the subject and is linked to the subject by the verb *is*. Think of the linking verb as an equal sign in an equation:

    grandmother = lady

In the following two examples, the subjects and predicate nominatives are underlined once, the linking verbs twice:

Joe is the best long-distance runner on the team.

The recruits at the police academy will become officers soon.

PRACTICE 9

In the following sentences, underline the subjects and predicate nominatives once and the linking verbs twice:

1. Yesterday was the last day of the concert series.

2. Many popular movies of the early 1970s were disaster films.

3. Mr. Reynolds has been the chairman of the department for years.

4. Under the circumstances, that solution seems the best one.

5. This painting is an example of Impressionistic work.

6. Tom was the best-dressed member of the wedding party.

Subjects Placed After Verbs

Sometimes the subject comes not at the beginning of the sentence but after the verb. This may happen in a question:

    Did the instructor say that?

The sentence is about the instructor, so you know *instructor* is the subject. You can identify the verb by making the sentence into a statement:

    The instructor said that.

PRACTICE 10

Change the following questions to statements in the spaces provided. Then underline the subjects once and the verbs twice in the questions themselves. Be sure to underline the helping verbs as well as the main verbs.

1. Will the teller cash our check?

    The teller will cash our check.

2. Are Mary and Martha the sisters mentioned in the story?

    _____

3. Should the employees insist on collective bargaining?

_____

4. Is physics the most difficult freshman course?

_____

5. Should we have listened to Einstein when he warned against atomic power?

_____

   Another type of sentence in which subject and verb are reversed is one that begins with an *expletive expression* such as *there is, there are, here is, here are,* and *it is:*

   There are three possible answers to that question.

Expletives like *there* point to and introduce subjects, but are not subjects themselves. The subject in the above sentence is *answers*; the verb is *are*.

PRACTICE 11

   In the following sentences underline the subjects once and the verbs twice, and draw an arrow from the expletive expression to the subject.

   1. There is a bug in my Coke.

   2. There are five volunteers for the job.

   3. Here is all my change.

   4. Here are four examples of prejudice in our newspaper.

   5. There is still one of us left.

   6. There are still three of us left.

   7. It was a bad day at Black Rock.

PRACTICE 12

   Underline the subjects once and the verbs twice in the sentences below. Be sure to underline helping verbs as well as main verbs.

   1. Will television ever replace classrooms and teachers?

   2. Many children watch "Sesame Street" and other educational programs.

   3. Perhaps such programs will occupy more and more of our children's time in the future.

   4. What did Neil Armstrong say when he set foot on the moon?

5. There are two main advantages to such a computerized system.

6. Students learn best in a nonthreatening environment.

7. In her class, no one feels embarrassed by their mistakes.

8. Second, a person can progress at his or her own speed.

9. One drawback, however, is the isolation of television viewing.

10. Will the space program survive the budget cutbacks?

11. There are no opportunities for a person to relate to others.

12. The team should have chosen her as captain.

13. A young couple often has difficulty establishing credit.

14. Teaching techniques should combine both traditional and innovative approaches.

10.3 Objects and Prepositions

Direct Objects

A *direct object* is a noun that receives the action of a verb. Here are two examples:

John threw the javelin.

Javelin is the direct object of the action verb *threw*. You can check this by asking the question, "John threw *what?*"

Mark invited his girlfriend.

Girlfriend is the direct object of the action verb *invited*. You can check by asking, "Mark invited *whom?*"

PRACTICE 13

In the sentences that follow, underline the subject once and the verb twice, and circle the direct object. Say whether the object tells *what* or *whom*.

1. We watched (television) on Thursday evening. *tells what*

2. The girls baked peanut butter cookies.

3. Andy asked Melissa for a date.

4. Andy ate two dozen cookies and drank a quart of apple cider.

5. Andy had a stomach ache on Friday.

6. The math instructor returned the tests.

7. Karen defeated Janice in the tennis tournament.

8. She finished the problems in an hour.

9. On the next day of class she easily passed the test.

10. The teacher wrote a helpful comment on the paper.

Objects of Prepositions

A noun may also serve as the *object of a preposition*. A preposition, which is usually a short word, connects a noun to the rest of the sentence. For example:

It is a difficult job even <u>for</u> a hard-working person.

For is the preposition, and it connects *hard-working person* to the rest of the sentence. *Person* is the object of the preposition and *hard-working* is the modifier of the object.

Below are some of the most common prepositions. The underlined words are examples of objects of the prepositions.

above (above the <u>city</u>)	from (from <u>John</u> and <u>Polly</u>)
across (across the <u>river</u>)	in (in those <u>days</u>)
after (after his <u>death</u>)	into (into the <u>unknown</u>)
among (among his <u>strengths</u>)	like (like <u>King Kong</u>)
at (at the <u>crossroads</u>)	of (of human <u>bondage</u>)
before (before <u>breakfast</u>)	on (on the <u>mountain</u>)
behind (behind the <u>door</u>)	onto (onto the <u>roof</u>)
below (below <u>sea level</u>)	over (over <u>hill</u> and <u>dale</u>)
between (between <u>you</u> and <u>me</u>)	through (through the <u>woods</u>)
by (by <u>train</u>)	to (to his <u>house</u>)
down (down the <u>street</u>	up (up the <u>stairs</u>)
during (during <u>class</u>)	upon (upon this <u>rock</u>)
for (for <u>whom</u>)	with (with your <u>personality</u>)
	without (without <u>me</u>)

PRACTICE 14

Write your own prepositional phrases for each of the twenty-seven prepositions listed above. Then use ten of these phrases in sentences, underlining the objects of the prepositions. For example, you might write this prepositional phrase:

above the water

Your sentence could then be something like this:

She had a hard time keeping her head above the water.

PRACTICE 15

In the following sentences, place the prepositional phrases in parentheses and underline the objects of the prepositions. (The number of prepositional phrases in each sentence appears in parentheses after the sentence.)

1. (During the <u>sixties</u>) many people became interested (in <u>drugs.</u>) (2)

2. You could hear the names of particular drugs, such as LSD and marijuana, on the news every day. (3)

3. Experimentation with drugs increased dramatically at this time. (2)

4. With the increase in drug use came the danger of drug abuse. (3)

5. Unfortunately, drugs led to an early death for some. (2)

6. Others were not harmed by drugs. (1)

7. Some experts believe that the drug problem is getting worse in large cities. (1)

8. For some people, cocaine is the most addictive drug available on the street. (2)

9. "X," a street name for Ecstasy, is one of the most dangerous drugs to appear on the American scene. (3)

10. A psychologist at our university believes that parents who drink too much alcohol contribute greatly to the drug problem because they demonstrate their own addiction to their children. (3)

Indirect Objects

An *indirect object* is a noun that tells for whom or to whom something is done. It usually comes between an action verb and its direct object, as seen below:

> Tony gave his younger <u>sister</u> a quarter.

What Tony gave his sister was a quarter; therefore *quarter* is the direct object. The person *to whom* he gave the quarter was his sister; therefore *sister* is the indirect object.

You can identify indirect objects by seeing if they can be converted to prepositional phrases, as follows:

> The worried mother sent her *son* a care package during his first week of college.

This same thought can be expressed with a prepositional phrase:

> The worried mother sent a care package *to her* son during his first week of college.

Because *son* can be shifted to become the object of the preposition *to*, you can assume that it is an indirect object.

PRACTICE 16

Convert the following sentences with prepositional phrases to sentences with indirect objects. Underline the indirect objects.

1. Tom brought a basket of fruit to his friend.

   Tom brought his friend a basket of fruit.

2. Elizabeth gave some free advice to her instructor.

   _____

3. The news gave a shock to the family.

   _____

4. The real estate agent offered a special deal for her clients.

   _____

5. That thief sold a stolen car to my husband.

   _____

6. She made a beautiful dress for her daughter.

   _____

PRACTICE 17

Complete the following sentences using both indirect and direct objects. Underline the indirect objects and circle the direct objects.

1. The president sent *his ally a thousand (Troops)* .
2. The people gave _____ .
3. The tailor made _____ .
4. The waiter brought _____ .
5. She sold _____ .
6. The woman bought _____ .

10.4 Pronouns

A *pronoun* is a word that substitutes for a noun:

> Dr. Lawson chuckles when <u>he</u> goes to pull a tooth. (The pronoun *he* takes the place of *Dr. Lawson.*)

Representative Taylor was delighted when <u>she</u> received the award. (The pronoun *she* replaces *Representative Taylor*.)

Pronoun Case

Some pronouns change their form or *case,* according to their use in a sentence. A pronoun in the subjective case serves as the subject of a sentence:

He is the one who is guilty.

A pronoun in the possessive case shows ownership:

The birds did not make *their* nests this year.

A pronoun in the objective case can be a direct object, an indirect object, or the object of a preposition.

DIRECT OBJECT
When he caught the ball, he threw <u>it</u> back.

INDIRECT OBJECT
The pitcher threw <u>him</u> the ball.

OBJECT OF A PREPOSITION
My parents were most excited when the prize was awarded to <u>them</u>.

Study the different cases of personal pronouns listed below. (A personal pronoun usually refers to a person.)

Singular Personal Pronouns

	Subjective	*Possessive*	*Objective*
FIRST PERSON	I	my, mine	me
SECOND PERSON	you	your, yours	you
THIRD PERSON	he, she, it	his, her, hers, its	him, her, it

Plural Personal Pronouns

	Subjective	*Possessive*	*Objective*
FIRST PERSON	we	our, ours	us
SECOND PERSON	you	your, yours	you
THIRD PERSON	they	their, theirs	them

Two other pronouns change form depending on how they are used in a sentence: *who* and *whoever*. Study these forms as well.

	Subjective	*Possessive*	*Objective*
WHO	who	whose	whom
WHOEVER	whoever	———	whomever

PRACTICE 18

Using the lists above, supply the specified pronoun for each of the following sentences:

1. (third-person singular, subjective case) Kathleen is taller than

   he _____ .

2. (first-person singular, subjective case) John and _____ are studying together.

3. (first-person singular, objective case) Just between you and

   _____ , I think she is a fine instructor.

4. (first-person singular, subjective case) Clarence and _____ are the best of friends.

5. (first-person singular, objective case) The letter was addressed to your

   mother and _____ .

6. (third-person singular, possessive case) The bird built _____ nest inside the bumper of the car.

7. (first-person plural, subjective case) They are no better than

   _____ .

8. (third-person plural, objective case) Give the information to _____ before it is too late.

9. (*who*, objective case) With _____ do you play tennis?

10. (third-person plural, subjective case) "Are these _____ ?" I asked. "Yes, that's them," he replied.

11. (first-person singular, possessive case) They staked out Antonio's and

    _____ house.

The Subjective Case   The subjective case must be used in situations like the following:

> He runs as fast as I.

The pronoun *I* is used instead of *me* because the sense of the sentence is actually: "He runs as fast as I run." *I* is thus the subject of the verb *run*, which is understood.

> This is she.

She is linked to the subject, *this*, by the verb *is*, and is thus in the subjective case.

Compound Constructions Pronouns used in compound constructions should be treated as single pronouns are:

My friend and I ate cereal for breakfast.

Choose *I*, not *me*. You would not say, "Me ate cereal for breakfast."

She bought the present for Jim and me.

Choose *me*, not *I*. You would not say, "She bought the present for I."

PRACTICE 19

In the following sentences, circle the correct pronoun:

1. (I, me) took the test before John took it.
2. Rachel brought Mary and (I, me) the notes to study.
3. John saw (we, us) on the practice field.
4. David cannot type as fast as (she, her).
5. Was it really (she, her) that you saw?
6. The near-crash did not alarm Maria or (I, me).
7. The answer was apparent to both (he and I, him and me).
8. Dad gave (I, me) the stereo as a birthday present.
9. Harry and (I, me) have three children.
10. Just between you and (I, me), Mr. Norton has been acting strangely lately.
11. José does not jog as often as (I, me).
12. (Who, Whom) is your advisor?
13. (Whoever, Whomever) wants this day-old sandwich may have it.
14. Give the invitation to (whoever, whomever) you can find.
15. For (who, whom) does the bell toll?
16. This is (she, her).

Seven Kinds of Pronouns

1. *Personal Pronouns* *Personal pronouns* distinguish between the person speaking (first person), the person spoken to (second person), and the person spoken about (third person):

FIRST PERSON

I, me, we, us, my, mine, our, ours

SECOND PERSON

you, your, yours

THIRD PERSON

he, she, it, him, his, her, hers, its, they, them, their, theirs

2. *Demonstrative Pronouns* *Demonstrative pronouns* point to specific persons or things. The demonstrative pronouns are *this, that, these,* and *those.* They are often the subjects of sentences.

> <u>This</u> is my problem.
>
> <u>These</u> are the facts.
>
> <u>That</u> is your belief.
>
> <u>Those</u> should make the difference.
>
> You may do <u>this</u> but not <u>that</u>. (Here *this* and *that* are objects.)

3. Indefinite Pronouns   *Indefinite pronouns* do not identify specific individuals or things:

any	either	many	neither	some
anybody	everybody	more	nobody	somebody
anyone	everyone	most	none	someone
anything	everything	much	no one	something
each				

> <u>Somebody</u> is missing a pen.
>
> <u>Everyone</u> misses you.

Indefinite pronouns are usually singular, but they can be plural. See Chapter 13.8 for a discussion of this.

4. Intensive Pronouns   *Intensive pronouns* emphasize a particular noun or pronoun:

Singular	*Plural*
myself	ourselves
yourself	yourselves
herself	themselves
himself	themselves
itself	themselves

Note that the plural of *self* is *selves.* Also, there are no such words as *hisself* and *theirselves.*

> The players <u>themselves</u> refused to cheat.
>
> I <u>myself</u> will take the blame.

Players is emphasized in the first sentence; *I* is emphasized in the second.

5. Reflexive Pronouns   *Reflexive pronouns* show that the subject acts upon itself. They are formed like intensive pronouns.

> I hurt <u>myself</u> in the game.

You can fool other people, but you cannot fool yourself.

The person *I* hurt was *myself;* the person *you* cannot fool is *yourself.*

6. Interrogative Pronouns   *Interrogative pronouns* ask questions:

Who?	Whoever?	Which?
Whom?	Whomever?	What?
Whose?		Whatever?

Who is the best dressed?

Whose is that?

7. Relative Pronouns   *Relative pronouns* introduce dependent clauses:

who	whoever	whose	that
whom	whomever	what	which

The company makes pens that do not write.

The tree, which is outside my window, was hit by lightning.

The people who live on our block are no neighbors.

Use *who* to refer to people; *that* and *which* to refer to things. See Chapter 13.8 for a more complete discussion of how relative pronouns function in a sentence.

PRACTICE 20

The pronouns in the following paragraph are underlined. Identify each pronoun by type, using the following abbreviations: *per* (personal), *dem* (demonstrative), *ind* (indefinite), *int* (intensive), *inter* (interrogative), *reflex* (reflexive), and *rel* (relative). Note that the word *that* can be used as a demonstrative or relative pronoun.

My Aunt Birdie is a rare species of aunt who *(rel)* will soon become extinct. She *(per)* is so considerate of other people that sometimes you can actually see a halo over her head. My aunt is seventy-nine years old, five feet tall, and shaped like a loosely rolled sleeping bag. She talks to herself all the time about her old boyfriends. Her hair is snow-white, which matches her teeth that sit upon her bureau every night. She has a huge hernia that forces her to tilt to the left when she walks. Although Aunt Birdie has a hard time getting around, she will not let anyone help her. She does everything for herself. That is how she likes it.

PRACTICE 21

In this paragraph, underline the pronouns and identify them using the above abbreviations.

Aunt Birdie rises with the Mississippi sun every morning and fixes a full breakfast for Uncle Buddy and herself. This is what she likes to do most: cook for Uncle Buddy. She then goes about the business of cleaning her small, wood-frame house, which is just like the other houses in the area. What do you suppose she does next? She does what all other housewifes do: She watches her favorite soap opera. When she finishes that, she washes the clothes. Since she does not trust washing machines, she washes her clothes by hand. In the afternoon, Aunt Birdie babysits for her many grandchildren, whom she loves dearly. This is how she spends most of her days. She does everything she can for everyone, and everyone is devoted to her.

10.5 Adjectives

An *adjective* modifies or describes a noun or pronoun. Here are some examples:

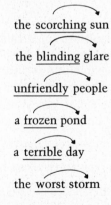

the <u>scorching</u> sun

the <u>blinding</u> glare

<u>unfriendly</u> people

a <u>frozen</u> pond

a <u>terrible</u> day

the <u>worst</u> storm

Special Types of Adjectives

ARTICLES: *A, AN, THE*

<u>a</u> house

<u>a</u> batch

<u>an</u> apple

<u>an</u> image

<u>an</u> hour

<u>the</u> truth

Note that *an* is used before words beginning with a vowel (*a, e, i, o,* or *u*) or a vowel sound (such as the *o/oh* sound in *hour* or *honest*).

PREDICATE ADJECTIVES

My canary is <u>sick</u>.

The trip seemed <u>dangerous</u> to me.

Predicate adjectives function like predicate nominatives: they follow a linking verb and refer to the subject of the sentence. In the sentences above, *sick* modifies *canary*, and *dangerous* modifies *trip*.

DEMONSTRATIVE ADJECTIVES: *THIS, THAT, THESE, THOSE*

<u>This</u> place is prettier than <u>that</u> place.

<u>These</u> places are prettier than <u>those</u> places.

Demonstrative adjectives have the same form as demonstrative pronouns. Instead of serving as subjects or objects, however, they modify nouns.

INDEFINITE ADJECTIVES: *SOME, FEW, ANY, EACH,* AND THE LIKE

<u>some</u> people

a <u>few</u> dollars

<u>any</u> approach

<u>each</u> person

PRACTICE 22

Underline the adjectives in the following sentences and draw arrows to the nouns or pronouns they modify. The number of adjectives in each sentence is in parenthesis after the sentence. (Remember that the articles *a, an,* and *the* are classified as adjectives.)

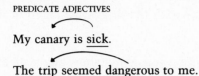

1. <u>The</u> Kool Jazz Festival is <u>a</u> mixture of <u>jazz</u> and <u>soul</u> music. (4)

2. These concerts attract different types of people. (2)

3. They bring out the rowdy ones, the dreamy lovers, the smokers, the ones who stand against the walls the whole night, and the people who use profane language. (11)

4. The rowdy ones are young. (3)

5. They dance, scream, push, and blow those loud whistles. (2)

6. The dreamy lovers sit through the whole concert watching one another with moony eyes. (5)

7. The smokers fill the air with the disgusting smell of marijuana. (4)

8. The wall-standers are unfriendly to everyone, even to one another. (2)

9. The cursers sit everywhere and do not show any respect for anyone, not even for the older people. (4)

10. Still, the Kool Jazz Festival is terrific; I never miss it. (2)

PRACTICE 23

Use the following adjectives in sentences. (Consult a dictionary for any meanings you do not know.) Draw arrows to the nouns or pronouns they modify.

1. (gleaming) *His gleaming eyes met mine.*

2. (ferocious) _____

3. (malignant) _____

4. (superior) _____

5. (pernicious) _____

6. (magnanimous) _____

7. (caustic) _____

8. (abundant) _____

9. (patronizing) _____

10. (detailed) _____

Comparative and Superlative Adjectives

Many adjectives change in form when the nouns they modify are compared and contrasted with other nouns. You may describe a farm scene as *lovely*, but if you think it is prettier than another farm scene, you say that it is *lovelier* than the other one, and if you think it is the prettiest farm scene anywhere, you say that it is the *loveliest* of them all. In comparing two nouns, use *comparative adjectives*; in comparing three or more nouns, use *superlative adjectives*.

COMPARATIVE ADJECTIVES

The work is <u>harder</u> than it was before. (Here you are comparing present work with previous work.)

The grass is not greener in California. (Here you are comparing grass in California with grass elsewhere.)

The work is more fulfilling than before. (If an adjective has three or more syllables, use *more* before the adjective instead of changing the ending.)

SUPERLATIVE ADJECTIVES

My cat is the smartest in the neighborhood. (Here the cat is compared with all the cats in the neighborhood.)

My cat is the most unpredictable cat in the neighborhood. (Use *most* before superlative adjectives of three or more syllables.)

Irregular Forms   A few adjectives change in form completely when used as comparative or superlative adjectives:

Basic Form	Comparative Form	Superlative Form
bad	worse	worst
good	better	best
far	farther	farthest
little	less	least
much	more	most

PRACTICE 24

Supply comparative and superlative forms of appropriate adjectives in the sentences below:

1. Halloween is a pretty cat, but Full Moon is _*prettier*_. They are the _*prettiest*_ cats on the block.

2. She is difficult, but her husband is even _____. As a couple, they are the _____ people I know.

3. Yesterday was cold, but today is _____. This is the _____ winter we have had in some time.

4. She has a bad attitude, but Molly's attitude is _____. And Emily's is the _____ of all.

5. Uncle Ed eats only a little at night, but Aunt Buzzy eats _____. And their daughter eats the _____ of all.

6. That essay was pretty good, but you have done _____. I have yet to see your _____ work.

7. The dessert was tasty, but the chicken pie was _____. In fact, it was the _____ chicken pie I have ever eaten.

8. My cold was bad, but then it got _____. It is the _____ cold I have ever had.

9. It is a little traveled road. It is _____ traveled than the other road at East Fork. It may in fact be the _____ traveled road in the entire national park.

10. My work is already fulfilling, but I would like it to be even _____. I have always wanted to find the _____ work possible.

PRACTICE 25

Use the following adjectives in their basic, comparative, and superlative forms in one or more sentences:

1. (rainy) *It is a rainy spring this year, certainly rainier than last year. It may be the rainiest spring this decade.*

2. (distinguished) _____

_____

3. (green) _____

_____

4. (happy) _____

_____

5. (good) _____

_____

6. (little) _____

_____

7. (bad) _____

_____

10.6 Adverbs

An *adverb* modifies or describes a verb, adjective, or other adverb:

He drove <u>wildly</u>.

The child wept <u>quietly</u>.

The adverbs above tell how he *drove* and how the child *wept:* They modify verbs.

The very large man is my father.

She is extremely wet.

These adverbs tell just how *large* the man is and just how *wet* she is: They modify adjectives.

He was running so rapidly that no one could keep up with him.

The car was going quite slowly on the interstate.

These adverbs tell just how *rapidly* he was running and just how *slowly* the car was going: They modify other adverbs.

Adverbs often end in *-ly*.

beautifully	hardly	poorly	triumphantly
cruelly	incompetently	quietly	wholly
daily	nicely	smoothly	wisely

Some adverbs do not have *-ly* endings:

almost	more	quite
always	most	too
even	never	very
fast	not	well

PRACTICE 26

Underline the adverbs in the following sentences and draw arrows to the verbs, adjectives, or other adverbs they modify. (The number of adverbs in each sentence is given in parentheses after the sentence.)

1. It was so dark that I stumbled and fell noisily over the chair. (2)

2. The flowers were so beautifully arranged that all the children noticed them. (2)

3. Although they conducted the investigation very incompetently, they did catch the thief, who had been quietly stealing from everyone. (3)

4. My neighborhood is just too noisy to enjoy. (2)

5. He generously gave his mother a most lovely home. (2)

6. The lady in the lounge has been waiting for you most impatiently. (2)

7. With his rag-tag band, he entered the city triumphantly, riding very slowly on the back of a donkey. (3)

8. It is extremely hard to work forty hours a week, attend school, raise children, and not complain. (2)

9. The Reverend Davis always begins his sermon with an unnecessarily long prayer. (2)

10. Dr. Nguyen never admits a patient who has not been carefully screened. (3)

10.7 Conjunctions

A *conjunction* joins words, phrases, or clauses in a sentence. There are three types of conjunctions: coordinating conjunctions, subordinating conjunctions, and correlative conjunctions.

Coordinating Conjunctions

A *coordinating conjunction* joins elements that are grammatically equal. There are seven coordinating conjunctions:

    and   but   for   so   yet   or   nor

Here is how they are used:

TO JOIN WORDS

the dog and his bone

TO JOIN PHRASES

not into darkness but into light

TO JOIN CLAUSES

He stayed at home, and she went to work.

See Chapter 11.2 for a more complete discussion of coordinating conjunctions.

Subordinating Conjunctions

A *subordinating conjunction* introduces a subordinate or dependent clause in a sentence. For example:

Although we were tired, we went to work anyway.

Although introduces a dependent clause (underlined) and joins this clause to the rest of the sentence. Here are other examples of dependent clauses (underlined) introduced by subordinating conjunctions:

He acts that way to his family because he hates himself.

When he went to the psychiatrist, he found out that he was bored with life.

These are some of the most common subordinating conjunctions:

after	before	so that	where
although	even though	though	wherever
as	if	till	whether
as if	in order that	unless	while
as though	since	until	
because	so	when	

See Chapter 11.4 for a more complete discussion of subordinating conjunctions.

Correlative Conjunctions

Correlative conjunctions are always used in pairs:

either/or	both/and also
neither/nor	not only/but also

Here are two examples of the use of correlative conjunctions:

Either you fix the car, or I will take it to the shop.

Not only should you listen, but you should also take notes.

See Chapter 13.7 for a discussion of the use of subjects and verbs with correlative conjunctions.

PRACTICE 27

In the sentences below, underline all conjunctions and then label them with the following abbreviations: *cc* (coordinating conjunctions), *sub* (subordinating conjunctions), and *cor* (correlative conjunctions):

1. It was both my happiest and also my saddest summer.

2. When the wind is from the south, it blows the hook in the fish's mouth.

3. Many people are walking the streets of London because, while they were playing blackjack, they drew cards whose points went over twenty-one.

4. One door closes, and another door opens.

5. If you look closely, you will discover that a good man or woman is not hard to find.

6. You will bloom where you are planted.

7. You can fool some of the people some of the time, but you cannot fool all of the people all of the time, or can you?

8. Every creature in the world either eats or is eaten.

9. Because you love, you will live.

10. He reads to his grandchildren when they ask him.

11. And he teaches them many old sayings while he has their attention.

10.8 Interjections

An *interjection* is used to express either a mild or a strong emotion. Interjections are used more commonly in speech than in writing. An expression of strong emotion is followed by an exclamation point:

Ouch!   Help!   Stop!   Wait!

An expression of mild emotion is followed by a comma and hooked to the sentence:

My, my, you certainly are clever these days.

10.9 Review Exercise

Make a list from 1 to 100 and identify each of the numbered words in the paragraphs below with one of the following abbreviations: *n* (noun), *p* (pronoun), *v* (verb), *prep* (preposition), *adj* (adjective), *adv* (adverb), *c* (conjunction), *i* (interjection), and *e* (expletive).

Once there was a pilgrim who made it his life's work to discover the highest truth
   1   2   3   4   5   6   7

that this world could teach. He heard that a certain wise man might be able to offer
8   9   10   11   12

him the most important teaching. To find the wise man, the pilgrim mounted his horse
     13   14   15   16   17

and set out on a long journey. He forded swift rivers and crossed high mountains. After
18 19   20   21   22 23   24   25   26

he had searched for months, the pilgrim finally found the great teacher sitting outside
                 27   28   29   30

of a cave. He was an old man with a long white beard. The pilgrim said to him,
31 32 33   34   35   36   37   38   39   40 41

"At last! Great teacher, I have heard that you can tell me the most important truth that
   42   43 44   45 46   47   48   49   50

this world can teach. I have been searching for you for months. Will you share your wis-
51   52   53 54   55 56   55

dom with me now?" The wise man listened attentively to the question but made no
                                57   58   59   60

response. The seeker of the truth waited and waited. Hours passed. Finally, after hours
            61   62   63   64   65   66   67

of silence, the wise man looked at the horse the pilgrim was riding and asked him why
                    68   69   70   71

he was not looking for a horse instead of enlightenment. The pilgrim responded that
       72   73   74   75

obviously he already had a horse. The wise man smiled and retreated to his cave.
76   77   78   79   80   81   82

The pilgrim thought about this experience for a long time and finally figured out
                   83   84   85   86   87   88 89   90   91

what the wise man was telling him. What do you think the message was? Do you
92   93   94   95 96   96   97   98   99

agree with the wise man?
100

CHAPTER 11

Writing Effective Sentences

11.0 Introduction

In this chapter you will learn different ways of expressing yourself in sentences. As you study simple, compound, and complex sentences, you will learn how to give variety to your writing. You will also learn several ways to use commas.

A sentence is a group of words expressing a thought that can stand on its own. Most everything that you write in a freshman English course should be in sentence form. Exceptions are titles of essays and sometimes quotations from conversations. Here are two tests that will help you determine whether a statement is a sentence:

1. If you made the statement to someone, would it make sense? If someone wrote only the statement on a note to you, would it make sense?
2. Does the statement have a subject (at least understood) and a verb?

Writing in complete sentences is a natural process because we usually talk in sentence form. To write consistently in complete sentences, the most important thing to remember is to *listen* to what you are writing. Read your writing aloud, sentence by sentence, and ask if each sentence can stand alone.

PRACTICE 1

Remain silent for ten seconds and then write down exactly what you are thinking:

_____

_____

_____

Did you write in whole sentences? What are the subjects and verbs? Your instructor may ask several people to read aloud what they wrote down to see if most of the class expressed themselves in whole sentences.

PRACTICE 2

Identify which statements on the list below are sentences (mark these *S*) and which are not sentences (mark these *N*). Apply this test: If you made the statement to someone, would it make sense? Would it make sense if you received it by itself in a note? Remember that whole sentences can begin with pronoun subjects.

1. __*S*__   Shut the door.

2. _____   Will you help me with my homework?

3. _____   Because they live on Park Place.

4. _____   When I leave home at seven to catch the 7:15 bus.

5. _____   The novel about the best of times and the worst of times.

6. _____   The time I went to see Aunt Nancy in Philadelphia.

7. _____   Which is a most controversial law.

8. _____   You should know what to do.

9. _____   To dress up my walls with brightly colored paintings.

10. _____   First, how my pet and I are alike.

PRACTICE 3

Choose ten people that you know and write one complete sentence about each. You may want to write about their work, their personality, or what they were doing the last time you saw them. Apply the sentence test: Does your statement make sense by itself? Underline the subject once and the verb twice. For example:

> Charles Tubman was trying to sell me his 1970 Cadillac when I saw him yesterday.

11.1 The Simple Sentence

A *simple sentence* consists of only one independent clause. Clauses can be dependent (those that cannot stand alone) or independent (those that can stand alone). The following are dependent clauses:

> because they are our neighbors

when the <u>test</u> <u>is administered</u>

which <u>she</u> <u>gave</u> us

as the <u>president</u> <u>says</u>

Each clause has a subject (underlined once) and verb (underlined twice), but none can stand alone; thus, they are called dependent. (If written by themselves, they would be fragments.)

The following clauses, however, are independent:

they are our neighbors

the test is administered each Friday

she gave us a dictionary

the president said it

Each could be written as a simple sentence, as follows:

They are our neighbors.

The test is administered each Friday.

She gave us a dictionary.

The president said it.

They are sentences because each has a subject and verb and can stand alone; they are simple sentences because each consists of one independent clause. Notice that, as sentences, each begins with a capital letter and ends with a period.

A simple sentence often has two or more subjects (called compound subjects) or two or more verbs (called compound verbs):

<u>Anthony</u> and <u>Alice</u> made A's. (compound subjects)

They <u>walked</u> and <u>jogged</u> for three hours. (compound verbs)

PRACTICE 4

Write simple sentences using the designated words as subjects. Underline the subjects once and the verbs twice.

1. (Charlie Brown) _____

_____

2. (the catcher) _____

_____

3. (Ronald Reagan) _____

_____

4. (tennis and swimming) _____

_____

5. (Jackie and Susan) _____

_____

PRACTICE 5

Write simple sentences using the designated words as verbs. Underline the subjects once and the verbs twice.

1. (strutted) _____

_____

2. (teased and flirted) _____

_____

3. (loves) _____

_____

4. (comes and goes) _____

_____

5. (devoured) _____

_____

PRACTICE 6

Underline the four simple sentences in the paragraph below:

This story began in 1943, when my mother was a little girl. One day she was running and playing in the corn field. A crow flew around the field and suddenly lit on my mother's shoulder, and she gave him an ear of corn. Every day from then on the crow and my mother would meet in the corn field. Mother would feed the crow, and the crow would perch on her shoulder. They walked together that way all over the field. One day, Mother went to the field to play, and the crow was lying in the dirt, dead. She told her mother, who said, "Baby, the dead crow means that someone very close to you is going to die." That night her uncle, Al Reynolds, died of a heart attack.

11.2 The Compound Sentence

A *compound sentence* consists of two or more independent clauses, each of which has its own subject and verb and is able to stand alone. For example:

The slender girl pushed the big car, and her father gave her encouragement.

Both underlined clauses are independent: They could be written as simple sentences. The joining word *and* is called a coordinating conjunction because it joins two clauses. There are seven coordinating conjunctions. Memorize them.

and   but   for   or   nor   yet   so

Here are three more compound sentences with coordinating conjunctions:

He really did not mean to do it, but he could not help himself.

The faces of the jurors were tense, for they were about to sentence a man to die.

He could rush into battle and be killed, or he could desert and be executed.

Notice that a comma is used before each coordinating conjunction above.

PRACTICE 7

In the paragraph below, underline the compound sentences and insert the necessary commas before the coordinating conjunctions:

This past Tuesday night, my husband and I were shopping at Maison Blanche and we were about to call it a night. Just before we left, we met Ed, an old friend from high school days. I asked the usual question about how his family was. To our shock, we discovered that Ed and his wife had been divorced. I have come across this unhappy situation many times but each time it shocks and saddens me. The rising divorce rate is especially distressing for many of the marriages could have been saved. Since Tuesday night I have been depressed and have been wondering how secure my own marriage is.

Using Coordinating Conjunctions

As pointed out above, compound sentences consist of two or more independent clauses. If you leave out the coordinating conjunction, each clause can function as a simple sentence. For example:

Our club sponsored a car wash on Saturday, and we were quite successful.

I like strawberry ice cream, but Sal prefers chocolate chip.

If you left out *and* in the first sentence, you would have two separate sentences. By using *and*, however, you show a close relationship between two ideas. In the second sentence *but* shows a contrast between two ideas. Each of the seven coordinating conjunctions has a special function:

1. *And* means addition:

   The Bernados sisters are having a big party Saturday night, <u>and</u> everyone is invited.

2. *But* means contrast:

   The Bernados sisters are having a big party Saturday night, <u>but</u> their parents do not know it.

3. *For* shows reason and thus means roughly the same as *because:*

   The Bernados sisters are having a big party Saturday night, <u>for</u> it is the only time everyone can come.

4. *Or* shows choice:

   The Bernados sisters may have a party Saturday night, <u>or</u> they may choose to have it Friday night instead.

5. *Nor* (like *or*) shows choice, but *nor* shows negative choice:

   Tony does not plan to come, <u>nor</u> will he encourage his friends to come.

   Notice that when *nor* joins clauses, the order of the second clause is inverted as in a question.

6. *Yet* (like *but*) shows contrast:

   Tony does not plan to attend the party, <u>yet</u> he admits it will probably be fun.

7. *So* shows results and thus means roughly the same as *therefore:*

   Tony does not plan to attend the party, <u>so</u> he will be free on Saturday night.

PRACTICE 8

Combine the following pairs of sentences using *and, but, for,* and *or* at least once:

1. It is best not to thrash around in shark-infested waters. The movement and the sound might attract the sharks.

2. My family is planning to leave town on the tenth. We will be gone about two weeks.

3. Our house is small and dark. I like it.

4. You need to make a decision quickly. Time is running out.

5. We may go to a movie tonight. We may stay home and watch TV.

6. I am usually in bed by 10:00 P.M. My roommate is a night owl.

7. Our tennis match is scheduled for late afternoon. We plan to have dinner afterward.

8. I may decide to continue my subscription to *Time* for another year. I may cancel it now.

Did you insert commas before the coordinating conjunctions?

PRACTICE 9

Combine the pairs of sentences below using *nor, yet,* and *so* at least once. (Remember: You must change the order of the wording of the sentence when you use *nor.*)

1. My sister is not fond of raw oysters. She does not like any other shellfish.

2. This movie is rated PG. We probably should not take your four-year-old niece.

3. Julio is rather an odd-looking character. Many women find him attractive.

4. Amy will enter an ice-skating competition next month. She practices several hours a day.

5. In buying his clothes, George does not listen to his friends' advice. He does not pay attention to current fashion either.

6. Marcus Duffy is in his sixties. He still jogs several miles a day.

Did you insert commas before the coordinating conjunctions?

PRACTICE 10

Complete the following compound sentences. Be sure that each has two independent clauses.

1. When summer comes, I will _____, and then I will _____.

2. Most people believe _____, but I think that _____.

3. I must _____, for it _____.

4. I know I _____, yet _____.

5. I _____, so I should be able to _____.

6. I will neither _____, nor will I _____.

7. I may become a _____, or I _____.

PRACTICE 11

Compose seven compound sentences using each of the coordinating conjunctions. Be sure that each sentence has two independent clauses.

11.3 The Compound Sentence with a Conjunctive Adverb

One way to join two independent clauses is with a *conjunctive adverb.* Conjunctive adverbs include *then, moreover, consequently, however,* and *for example.* Sometimes the conjunctive adverbs are preceded by the conjunction *and,* as follows:

First, they held up the store, <u>and</u> <u>then</u> they shot the owner.

More often, conjunctive adverbs are preceded by a semicolon (;):

It is a good day for catching pompano; <u>however</u>, with my luck we will probably catch toad fish instead.

Here are some of the most common conjunctive adverbs, organized by function:

1. Time: *then, next*

First, we visited the Washington Monument, and <u>then</u> we toured the White House.

2. Addition: *also, moreover, furthermore*

We saw Saint John's Church, and <u>also</u> we toured some of the exhibits in the Smithsonian.

We saw Saint John's Church; <u>moreover</u>, we toured some of the exhibits in the Smithsonian as well.

3. Results: *consequently, thus, therefore*

Summer vacation begins on the first of June; <u>consequently</u>, I cannot begin to work until then.

4. Contrast: *however, nevertheless, on the other hand*

Rudolfo originally planned to join us; <u>however</u>, he later changed his mind.

5. Illustration: *for example, for instance*

We have many privileges in this country that we take for granted; <u>for example</u>, almost everyone has easy access to a public library.

Note that a comma follows most conjunctive adverbs, as shown in four of the examples above. However, a comma does not usually follow *then* or *also.*

PRACTICE 12

Using the above examples as models, write five of your own compound sentences using a conjunctive adverb from each group. Be sure to use commas and semicolons correctly. You might write something like:

First, I will finish college, and then I will go to law school.

PRACTICE 13

Combine the following pairs of sentences with *and* and a conjunctive adverb or with a semicolon and a conjunctive adverb. Use at least one conjunctive adverb from each of the five groups above. Supply commas as needed.

1. I must study first, ~~After that~~ *and then* I may go to the movies with you.

2. I was not sick after eating the pizza and marshmallows, *;however,* Helen and Tom missed two days of school because of their indulgence.

3. We had many things to talk about. The time passed quickly.

4. The poet Keats died in his mid-twenties. His poetry is more valued than that of many a writer who lived to a ripe old age.

5. The barbeque restaurant will probably be more successful now that it is in a better location. Its new management is first-rate.

6. Paula knows how to fix anything. She even fixed her grandfather's cuckoo clock.

7. It was only a small, inexpensive gift. It was a well-chosen one.

8. I enjoy working in the early morning because I feel rested then. It is the only time the house is quiet.

9. Every day Mrs. Carr picks whatever is ripe. After that she feeds the chickens.

10. Christy Brown was an Irish writer who was severely brain damaged from birth. He published several extraordinary books in his lifetime.

11. The day was clear and sunny. We decided to move the party out of doors.

12. Thousands of people greet each other every day in the Los Angeles airport. It is not the place to form a lasting relationship.

11.4 The Complex Sentence with a Subordinating Conjunction

A *complex sentence* consists of an independent clause and one or more dependent clauses. Here are two ways to write the same sentence:

dependent clause   independent clause
        ↓   ↓
Because I was sick, I stayed home.

independent clause dependent clause
↓   ↓
I stayed home   because I was sick.

Notice that a comma comes after the dependent clause when it begins a sentence but that it does not come before the dependent clause when it ends the sentence. You can usually recognize dependent clauses in complex sentences by the words that introduce them. There are two classes of these words: *subordinating conjunctions* (such as *when, while, because, if, before,* and *unless*) and *relative pronouns* (such as *who, whom, which,* and *that*).

Here are some of the most common subordinating conjunctions, arranged by function:

1. To show time: *as* (at the same time), *after, before, when, while*

   _____As_____ I ate (was eating) my supper, the disk jockey called.

2. To show cause or reason: *as, because, since, in order that, so that*

   He will do anything for you _____because_____ you are his best friend.

   She married a man she hardly knew _____so that_____ she would not be alone.

3. To show condition: *if, in the event that, till, until, unless*

   _____If_____ the two countries go to war, we will have to take sides.

   I cannot tell you how you are doing _____until_____ you turn in your essays.

4. To show a contrasting thought: *although, even though, even if, though, whether, while*

   I am still going fishing, _____even though_____ it is raining.

   I am still going fishing, _____whether_____ it is raining or not.

   Shopping with money is frustrating, _____while_____ shopping without money is fun.

Note that commas are usually inserted before contrasting-thought clauses.

5. To show place: *where, wherever*

   _____Wherever_____ Naomi goes, Ruth will go.

6. To show the manner in which or how: *as if, as though*

   We felt _____as if_____ we would never make the last mile.

PRACTICE 14

Using the above examples as models, write six complex sentences using a subordinating conjunction from each group. Be sure to place a comma after the dependent clause when it begins a sentence. You might write something like:

Before I finish college, I want to take a course in astronomy.

PRACTICE 15

In the selection below, underline the ten dependent clauses that begin with subordinate conjunctions and supply the four missing commas:

As I walked up the gravel road I looked up at the morning sky. It was beginning to turn dark blue in places. Everything was still the same, including the tall pine trees, the wire fences, the houses, and even the "you-keep-out" sign posted to a tree. The leaves on the trees were trembling because the wind was blowing slightly. Dew was falling to the ground from the trees. Some even fell on me.

I continued walking until I saw a small child with light brown hair. She wore a little rust-and-blue-plaid dress. Barefoot, she was playing in a pile of sand and gravel. She acted as though she did not have a care in the world. I walked closer to the girl, and I noticed her blue eyes. They were the same color as my eyes when I was young. Then I noticed the dress. It looked like the dress my parents bought for me years ago.

As she looked up she asked what I was doing there. When she spoke I realized I was seeing myself when I was young. I was stunned. Then, without allowing me to answer, she asked me to sit down and play with her. But I told her that I did not have the time. While I was turning to leave I changed my mind. But she was gone, just as the past has been gone from my memory, until now.

PRACTICE 16

Write complex sentences using the following dependent clauses. Circle the subordinating conjunction, and at the end of the sentence indicate which of the six functions explained above it serves.

1. (When) the moon comes over the mountain, *the witches come out to dance. #1 - time*

2. Although candy is dandy _____

_____

3. While Mrs. Toodle was looking out of the window _____

_____

4. If you mail in one Fritzie box top and two dollars _____

_____

5. Because Mary talks to her plants _____

_____

6. Unless I pass this math test _____

_____

If you did not put a comma after each introductory dependent clause, do so now.

PRACTICE 17

Write complex sentences using the following dependent clauses. Circle the subordinating conjunction, and indicate which of the six functions explained above it serves.

1. _____ after you went home.

2. _____ because it is stormy.

3. _____ while we were watching the Saturday night special.

4. _____ before I get really mad.

5. _____ unless you really want me to.

If you put in any commas, go back and take them out.

PRACTICE 18

Write complex sentences using the following subordinating conjunctions to introduce dependent clauses:

1. *You should always check your oil* _____ before *you leave on a long trip.* _____

2. _____ because

_____

3. _____ since

_____

4. _____ unless

_____

5. _____ while

_____

6. _____ if

_____

PRACTICE 19

Now reverse the independent and dependent clauses you wrote for Practice 18 (as shown in the diagram on page 243) and supply commas where needed. You might write something like:

1. *Before you leave on a long trip, you should always check your oil.*

2. _____

_____

3. _____

_____

4. _____

_____

5. _____

_____

6. _____

_____

Combining Sentences

If you are going to say what you want to say in your writing, you will write many complex sentences. There is nothing wrong with using simple sentences—they can be strong and will give your writing variety—but if you write only simple sentences, your writing will sound flat and unnatural. The following choppy simple sentences can be combined as indicated. (The dependent clauses are underlined.)

CHOPPY
The show was over. The last person had left. We finally went home.

COMBINED
When the show was over and the last person had left, we finally went home.
(Note that a comma follows the dependent clause.)

CHOPPY

I was sweeping the rug. I saw a little mouse staring at me.

COMBINED

While I was sweeping the rug, I saw a little mouse staring at me. (Note that a comma follows the dependent clause.)

CHOPPY

I know you will not change your mind. You have shown courage in the past.

COMBINED

I know you will not change your mind because you have shown courage in the past. (Note that there is no comma before a dependent clause at the end of a sentence.)

PRACTICE 20

Combine the following sentences by using the subordinating conjunctions *although, because,* or *when.* If the dependent clause comes at the beginning of the sentence, put a comma after it.

1. The president stood by what he said. ~~He~~ *because he* was a man of great conviction.

2. I am leaving. I am afraid I will get caught in the rain.

3. It is easy to see a glass as half-empty. It is better to see it as half-full.

4. The terrorists attacked the embassy. Two people were killed.

5. Eighteen-year-olds should be able to buy alcohol. They are old enough to fight and old enough to vote.

6. Eighteen-year-olds are old enough to fight and vote. They should still not be able to buy alcohol.

PRACTICE 21

Combine the sentences below by using each of the following subordinating conjunctions at least once: *when, while, since, because,* and *although.* (You will need to change some of the wording.)

1. We moved to a new town. At that time I was five years old.

   We moved to a new town when I was five years old.

2. Josh does not have enough money to live comfortably. For that reason he is looking for a new job.

   Because Josh does not have enough money to live comfortably, he is looking for a new job.

Copyright © 1987 Houghton Mifflin Company

3. I moved to Jefferson City about five years ago. At that time I was puzzled by certain words I heard people use.

———————————————————————————————————

———————————————————————————————————

4. Some words were very hard to understand. The reason was that people pronounced them in a funny way.

———————————————————————————————————

———————————————————————————————————

5. I frequently had to ask people to repeat themselves. I could not understand what they were saying.

———————————————————————————————————

———————————————————————————————————

6. Some words, like *yat,* were clearly pronounced. All the same they were so odd that they sounded foreign.

———————————————————————————————————

———————————————————————————————————

7. I finally asked someone what *yat* meant. I was told that *yat* comes from the greeting *whereya at.*

———————————————————————————————————

———————————————————————————————————

8. Some people in the city use *yat* all the time. For that reason they are called *yats.*

———————————————————————————————————

———————————————————————————————————

9. Many *yat* mothers call their children by names such as Precious, Sweetheart, and Dawlin'. Angry *yat* mothers call their children Noodlebrain.

———————————————————————————————————

———————————————————————————————————

11.5 The Complex Sentence with an Adjective Clause

Dependent clauses within complex sentences often function as adjectives; that is, they describe nouns or pronouns. *Adjective clauses* usually begin with one of the following relative pronouns:

who, whose, whom
whoever, whomever
that, which, what
whichever, whatever

For example:

Marcia, who is quite talented as a musician, is coming for a visit.

The dependent clause *who is quite talented as a musician* describes the proper noun *Marcia.*

Sometimes the relative pronoun in an adjective clause is omitted but nevertheless understood:

Kurt Vonnegut is a writer I admire.

The relative pronoun *whom* has been omitted.

Kurt Vonnegut is a writer whom I admire.

The dependent adjective clause may begin with *where* or *when*. For example:

I am planning to make a trip to Israel, where three of the world's great religions were born.

PRACTICE 22

Underline the adjective clauses in the following sentences. Draw arrows to the nouns or pronouns they describe.

1. Everybody wants a life that is filled with good friends and good times.

2. Joe, who is usually the last to leave a party, did not tire until almost dawn.

3. My car, which has not been washed in two years, looks like a piece of junk.

4. The town where I grew up has changed dramatically in the last few years.

5. Anita, who was very tall for her age, took a lot of teasing from her friends.

6. I gave my bike to Karen, who did not have a way to get to school.

7. He is the one I would like to see run for office.

8. The year 1963, when President Kennedy was assassinated, was a turning point in my life.

Using Commas with Adjective Clauses

You probably noticed that some adjective clauses in the sentences above were set off by commas whereas others were not. If the adjective clause is essential to the meaning of the sentence, do *not* use commas. For example:

> People who need people are the luckiest people in the world. (If you omitted *who need people,* the sentence would not make sense. Therefore, you do not use a comma.)

If, however, the adjective clause is not essential to the meaning of the sentence, you set it off with a comma or commas. For example:

> Mother, who is nearly eighty, is still in excellent health. (If you omitted *who is nearly eighty,* the sentence would still make sense. Therefore, you need commas.)

PRACTICE 23

Underline the adjective clauses in the following sentences. Then decide whether commas are needed to set off the clauses. (*Hint:* Clauses beginning with *which* are usually set off by commas; clauses beginning with *that* are usually not set off by commas.)

1. Jennifer, <u>who is a very neurotic person</u>, still sleeps with a teddy bear.

2. Rafting down the Colorado River is the one experience that he will never forget.

3. The plan that we finally decided upon was our best alternative.

4. My typewriter which has not been cleaned in eight years is in poor condition.

5. Everybody rushed to meet the celebrity who was doing his best to avoid the crowd.

6. The film that Altman directed was the best.

7. Friends who talk behind your back are no friends.

8. I moved to California where the grass was not greener but brown.

PRACTICE 24

Make complete sentences with the following clauses, using commas as necessary. Use the clauses in the middle or at the end of sentences.

1. (which is something I have always wanted to do) *Skiing, which is something I've always wanted to do, is quite expensive.*

2. (who are the nicest people you will ever meet) _____

_____

3. (where I plan to live) _____

_____

4. (which is a dangerous sport) _____

_____

5. (that killed him) _____

_____

6. (who killed him) _____

_____

Using *Who, Whose, Whom, That,* and *Which* with Adjective Clauses

Use *who, whose,* and *whom* to refer to people. For example:

The person <u>who does the work</u> will be the one to succeed.

He is the player <u>whom we talked about earlier.</u>

Use *that* or *which* to refer to things. For example:

The car, <u>which I bought with my own money,</u> is a beauty.

The things <u>that we enjoy most</u> are free.

Ordinarily *which* clauses are set off by commas; *that* clauses are not.

PRACTICE 25

Write complete sentences with adjective clauses modifying the following subjects:

1. The space program, *which suffered a great tragedy in 1986, lost some support.*

2. My mother, who _____

_____

3. Cigarettes, which _____

_____

4. Laws that _____

_____

5. Friends who _____

_____

6. The house where _____

_____

7. Parents whose _____

_____

Check to see if you used commas correctly.

PRACTICE 26

Again write complete sentences with adjective clauses modifying the following subjects. However, this time you must also supply the appropriate relative pronoun or *when* or *where*.

1. John Wayne _____

_____

2. A person _____

_____

3. Terrorists _____

_____

4. A friend _____

_____

5. My closest friend _____

_____

6. My home town _____

_____

7. Car keys _____

_____

8. The best thing _____

_____

9. Labor Day _____

_____

10. Children _____

_____

Check to see if you used commas correctly.

Combining Sentences

By using adjective clauses, you can avoid writing too many simple sentences and thus give variety to your compositions. Notice how these simple sentences can be combined by making one of them an adjective clause.

> SIMPLE
>
> The car trip was an unforgettable experience. I took the trip with my brother Tom.
>
> COMBINED
>
> The car trip that I took with my brother Tom was an unforgettable experience.
>
> SIMPLE
>
> Tom and I had been looking forward to the trip for a long time. We both like the out-of-doors.
>
> COMBINED
>
> Tom and I, who both like the out-of-doors, had been looking forward to the trip for a long time.

PRACTICE 27

Combine the following pairs of sentences by using *who, which,* or *that* to make one sentence an adjective clause:

1. The hillsides were covered with trees of fiery red and orange. They extended as far as the eye could see.

   _____

   _____

2. My parents would love to see a mountainside with trees turning red and gold. They have never been to New England.

   _____

   _____

3. Our decrepit Volkswagen did its best on the mountain roads. It was loaded down with luggage.

   _____

   _____

4. We finally arrived at the ski lodge. It was to be our home for the next few weeks.

   _____

   _____

5. The owner of the lodge helped us unload. He looked like an aging Woody Allen.

   _____

   _____

6. I remember watching the first snowfall. It was a sight worth traveling four days to see.

   _____

   _____

7. The local people probably would not share my enthusiasm over snow. They have experienced icy roads and snow-shoveling all their lives.

   _____

   _____

11.6 The Sentence with an Appositive

An *appositive* is a word, phrase, or clause that gives more information about a noun, a noun phrase, or a pronoun. Here are several examples of appositives:

> This is Tom, <u>my brother</u>. (The word *brother* further identifies the proper noun *Tom*.)
>
> She is going to Texas, <u>the second largest state</u>, and then to California. (The phrase *the second largest state* further identifies the proper noun *Texas*.)
>
> Al found a cushion, <u>the only thing left to sit on</u>. (The phrase *the only thing left to sit on* further identifies the noun *cushion*.)

Notice that the above appositives are set off by commas.

Use appositives frequently in your writing. They will help your writing sound smooth and give it variety. These two sentences are choppy:

> John watches television twelve hours a day. He is a nearsighted person.

To combine them, take the "meat," or substance, of the second sentence and place it next to *John:*

> John, a nearsighted person, watches television twelve hours a day.

Here is another example:

> He will sell you almost anything. For example, he will sell you jewelry, an old bicycle, a new pocketbook, and yesterday's newspaper.

There is no need to repeat *he will sell you*. Simply write:

> He will sell you almost anything, for example, jewelry, an old bicycle, a new pocketbook, and yesterday's newspaper.

PRACTICE 28

Complete the appositives in the following sentences:

1. She plays four sports, tennis, *basketball*, *soccer*, and *golf*.

2. The United States, a nation of _____, is the home of 225 million people.

3. *ET* (or supply your own title _____), a movie about _____, was a huge success.

4. The Bears are happy about their new quarterback, a man who _____.

5. Sabrina, a _____, gives me a ride to school every day.

PRACTICE 29

Using the above sentences as models, combine the following pairs of sentences so that one becomes an appositive. Insert commas as necessary.

1. The puppy chewed up everything in sight. He chewed up shoes, news-papers, and even the corner of the couch.

   The puppy chewed up everything in sight, for example, shoes, newspapers, and even the corner of the couch.

2. Greece is a popular vacation spot for Europeans. It is a land of blue skies and whitewashed houses.

   _____

   _____

3. Updike's latest novel is supposedly his best. It is a book about failing relationships.

   _____

   _____

4. The defensive-driving coach was a little nervous about his new pupil. His pupil was a man convicted three times of driving while intoxicated.

   _____

   _____

5. Maria decided not to join the neighborhood softball team. It is a team well-known for its fierce competitive spirit.

   _____

   _____

PRACTICE 30

Complete the appositives in the following sentences:

1. Sharon, _____, is endangering her health by eating only raisins, nuts, and lettuce leaves.

2. Many courses at our college are difficult, especially _____,

   _____, and _____.

3. She bought everything in sight, everything from _____ to

   _____.

4. I have three favorite movie stars, _____, _____, and

   _____.

5. We have discussed several controversial issues in class, for example,

   _____, _____, and _____.

6. And then I took Algebra 102, a course _____.

PRACTICE 31

Using the sentences above as models, combine the following pairs of sentences so that one becomes an appositive. Insert commas as necessary.

1. Paco brought everything he thought he might need for a weekend visit. He brought everything from five outfits to a videotape recorder.

   _____

   _____

2. I have three favorite politicians. They are Ted Kennedy, George Bush, and Clint Eastwood.

   _____

   _____

3. Movies rated *R* may include controversial material. There may be both sex and violence.

_____

_____

4. Choon Jai likes horror films. He especially likes the old-fashioned ghost stories with creaking doors and rattling chains.

_____

_____

5. Joan gave me a Christmas present that I really needed. It was a heavy wool sweater.

_____

_____

6. He reads magazines every chance he gets. He reads everything from *The Reader's Digest* to *Sports Illustrated*.

_____

_____

PRACTICE 32

Compose your own sentences with appositives using the following subjects:

1. John Kennedy, the *youngest man ever elected president, was loved and hated.*

2. New York City, a _____

_____

3. Tina Turner, a _____

_____

4. The Vietnam War, a _____

_____

5. Baseball, the _____

_____

6. February, the _____

_____

7. AIDS, a _____

_____

8. The library, a _____

_____

9. Ronald Reagan, our _____

_____

Be sure that you have used commas correctly.

11.7 Review Exercises

Your writing will be more effective if you use different kinds of sentences. In this chapter the following kinds of sentences have been discussed:

1. The simple sentence: She pushed the car.
2. The compound sentence: The skinny girl pushed the car, and her father watched.
3. The compound sentence with a conjunctive adverb: She pushed the car; however, her father just watched.
4. The complex sentence with a subordinate conjunction: She pushed the car while her father watched. Or: While her father watched, she pushed the car.
5. The complex sentence with an adjective clause: The skinny girl, who was not yet sixteen, pushed the car.
6. The sentence with an appositive: The skinny girl, about sixteen years old, pushed the car.

As you write, try to use different kinds of sentences. You do not speak in sentences that are only simple or compound in structure. You do not need to write that way either. This does not mean that you should avoid all simple or compound sentences, but merely that you should try to make your sentences sound natural and to give them variety.

REVIEW EXERCISE 1

Complete the following by constructing the designated type of sentence:

1. (a simple sentence) Soap operas *offer entertainment to many*.

2. (a compound sentence) Soap operas are _____, but _____.

3. (a compound sentence with a conjunctive adverb) Soap operas _____ _____; _____, _____.

4. (a complex sentence with a subordinate conjunction) Soap operas _____ _____ while _____.

5. (a complex sentence with an adjective clause) Soap operas, which _____, _____.

6. (a sentence with an appositive) Soap operas, _____, _____.

REVIEW EXERCISE 2

Construct the six kinds of sentences named above for two of the following subjects:

cats
sex
writing
grades
marriage

REVIEW EXERCISE 3

The following essay has been written in mostly simple sentences. Now rewrite it again, this time using as many of the six types of sentences listed above as seem appropriate. Remember that it is usually good to use some simple sentences. Be sure to use commas and semicolons correctly. (*Note:* The student said she wrote this essay in response to television commercials that make people who are a bit overweight, like herself, feel that something is terribly wrong with them.)

Tons of Fun

One of America's most widespread problems is obesity. More than a fourth of our population has this problem. Millions of people are trying to lose weight. But we forget. Being fat has many good points as well.

Let's say you have a weight problem. You finally accept the fact that you are fat and likely to remain so. The fun begins. After this point you do not have to worry about starving yourself with all those new diets. You can live by the old saying. The old saying is "Eat, drink, and be merry." At night you can sit back and enjoy television. You do not have to worry about all the calories you consumed during the day.

You can learn to live with yourself and your size. You can also start putting a little more money toward your food bill. Now you do not have to worry about what clothing is in style. The reason for this is you cannot fit into most of the modern clothes anyway. You do not have to pay forty dollars or more for a pair of tight jeans. The reason for this is that all of your jeans are tight. Being fat will even help you learn an important skill. Not many clothes in the store will fit you. You will most probably have to learn to sew.

One day love enters your heart. Ms. Right or Mr. Handsome enters your life. You will not have to answer the questions: Why did she go out with me? Why did he ask me to marry him? You will know the answer. It was not because of your body.

One last point. The government will be very proud of you. You will be well insulated. You will not need to turn the heater so high and contribute to the energy crisis. Obesity may be bad for your health. If you find that you cannot lose weight, cheer up. You will discover that fat can be fun.

REVIEW EXERCISE 4

Write a three-paragraph paper about someone you know well. In the first paragraph, describe the person's family life. In the second, describe the person's work either in the home or outside. In the third, describe the person's special interests (what he or she enjoys most). Label each sentence as either simple, compound, complex, or compound-complex (if it consists of two or more independent clauses and at least one dependent clause). Be sure that you have at least:

three simple sentences
three compound sentences (joined by words like *and* and *but* or words like *however* preceded by a semicolon)
eight complex sentences (with dependent clauses introduced by subordinate conjunctions such as *when* and *because* or words like *who, that,* and *which*)

You may want to begin your paper something like this:

My friend Ben Smith has two families. One is back home in Chicago, and the other
(simple)   (compound)

is here in Colorado Springs. In Chicago, Ben has a mother and stepfather and several
(complex)

brothers and sisters, who write him all the time. In Colorado Springs, he has a girlfriend
(complex)

named Tammy, who goes everywhere with him when he is off duty. Tammy works as a

secretary for a lawyer named Marilyn Spenser.
(simple)

Ben is a corporal at Fort Carson, and he works on light motor vehicles. Although he
(compound)

likes his work, he says that he is bored much of the time. . . .
(complex)

CHAPTER 12

Preventing Sentence Errors

12.0 Introduction

In this chapter you will learn how to avoid the following sentence errors:

fragments
run-on sentences
adjective and adverb confusion
dangling modifiers
misplaced modifiers
faulty parallelism

12.1 Preventing Fragments

Be sure that you write consistently, in whole sentences. As pointed out in the last chapter, you can tell whether a statement is a sentence if it meets these two tests:

1. If you made the statement to someone, would it make sense? If someone wrote the statement on a note to you with nothing else on the note, would it make sense?
2. Does the statement have a subject (at least understood) and a verb?

A group of words that is not a complete thought (and thus not a sentence) is called a *fragment*.

PRACTICE 1

Applying the two tests given above, mark the following either *S* for whole sentences or *F* for fragments:

_____*F*_____   1. Which is what I have been thinking.

_____   2. Which one of you is going?

_____   3. Because of the great danger of nuclear fallout.

_____   4. He made the decision because he had to.

_____   5. First, the dangers of the space program.

_____   6. One that anybody who has had basic math should be able to do.

_____   7. Knowing that she would never be alone again.

_____   8. Just knowing her makes me feel good.

_____   9. Although it was against the law.

_____   10. Not the best choice she could have made.

_____   11. It was not I who did it.

Types of Fragments

If you read each sentence you write separately, you will avoid most of these common types of fragments:

1. The dependent clause fragment:

ERROR

Which is what we should have done in the first place. (Never start a sentence with *which* unless you are asking a question.)

CORRECTION

We finally drove to Oregon, which is what we should have done in the first place.

ERROR

Because it is too late. (A clause that begins with *because* must be accompanied by an independent clause.)

CORRECTION

We will have to live with the consequences because it is too late.

2. The fragment in which either subject or verb is omitted:

ERROR

First, sex education, a way to prevent early pregnancies. (When you introduce a new topic in a paper, you must write a complete sentence. Here the verb is missing.)

CORRECTION

First, sex education is a way to prevent early pregnancies.

ERROR

There many points of view on the subject. (The verb has been omitted.)

CORRECTION

There are many points of view on the subject.

3. The appositive fragment:

ERROR

One that the men on board ship are still complaining about. (Join an appositive fragment to the preceding sentence with a comma.)

CORRECTION

The chief made an unpopular decision, one that the men on board ship are still complaining about.

ERROR

Particularly, Ensign Tomlinson and Lieutenant Dombroski.

CORRECTION

The officers became more seasick than the enlisted personnel, particularly, Ensign Tomlinson and Lieutenant Dombroski.

4. The participle fragment:

ERROR

Knowing that the end was near. (Participle phrases written without independent clauses are fragments. You can identify the participles because they are verb forms ending in *-ing*: here, for example, *know* + *-ing*.)

CORRECTION

She called her children to her bedside, knowing that the end was near.

5. Fragments beginning with *not*:

ERROR

Not "Holligans," as they are called by the Navy. (Rarely is it correct to begin a sentence with *not*. Join fragments beginning with *not* to the preceding sentence with a comma.)

CORRECTION

Coast Guard officers and enlisted personnel are the best, not "Holligans," as they are called by the Navy.

6. Fragments beginning with a contrasting word:

ERROR

Although we did not get out to sea very much. (Statements beginning with words like *although*, *even though*, and *unless* are sometimes afterthoughts that are written as fragments. Correct them by joining them to the previous sentence with a comma.)

CORRECTION

The *Chilula* was a fine ship to serve on, although we did not get out to sea very much.

Copyright © 1987 Houghton Mifflin Company

PRACTICE 2

Using the above corrected sentences as models, make whole sentences out of the following fragments:

1. (which was our policy) *Allowing customers to return merchandise, which was our policy, helped improve our business.*

2. (because they supported terrorists) _____

_____

3. (second, the high cost of the space program) _____

_____

4. (one that you will never forget) _____

_____

5. (helping us whenever she could) _____

_____

6. (not what you think I am) _____

_____

7. (although we did have to break the law to do it) _____

_____

PRACTICE 3

Correct the three fragments in this paragraph:

A salesman must have the ability to handle customers in the right manner. Even if they are hard to handle. I work as a salesman at Danny's Men's Store. Some of the wildest people in the world shop at Danny's. Men do not know what they want to buy, and women do not know what size their husbands wear. A salesman has to try to fit a certain type of garment to a certain type of person. Whether that person is a sportsman, a swinger, or a conservative. I have been working at Danny's for three years and still have not learned how to deal with all the customers. Because some of them are crazy. It is especially hard to serve the ones who come in barefooted.

PRACTICE 4

Correct the three fragments in this paragraph:

I too feel sad for the young man in the poem. He was so much an individual and so creative, but he could not share himself. There was no one to see his picture, no one to react. No one to care. He had only himself to hold onto, but that got very lonely. He threw away his picture, gave up his old self, and put on a tie. When he could take it no longer. He was the flower trying to grow in the crack in the sidewalk of society. The sun still shone. The rain still fell, but there was no one to support him, so he gave up. And lost himself and was dead before he died.

PRACTICE 5

Correct the three fragments in the paragraphs below:

As you go through the front door of my dream house, you first enter the living room. The room has a huge picture window opening on a garden. There two distinct areas within this room. One area contains an overstuffed, floppy sofa with three pieces that join together. The other area, a sixty-inch television screen and all the component parts of the latest stereo equipment.

As you move through the living room, you come to the dining room and kitchen on the right. There you see the latest appliances, such as a refrigerator-freezer with a drinking fountain, a dishwasher, a microwave oven, a conventional oven, and a garbage disposal. There is a small room to the side of the kitchen. Contains shelves to store food that does not need to be refrigerated.

PRACTICE 6

Correct the three fragments in this paragraph:

Americans take pride in the wide variety of goods that are available to the public. Thousands of companies, factories, and stores supply us with millions of different products very neatly packaged in colorful, "easy to open" boxes. All tagged with labels saying "new and improved." Many show glossy photos of happy folk enjoying the product. They suggest the image of an ideal, simple way of life. While in reality our lives are growing more complicated all the time. An overabundance of material goods creates many problems. Such as how to operate self-propelled lawn mowers, sensor-touch ovens and ribbonless typewriters. I ask you, is this progress?

PRACTICE 7

Correct the five fragments in the following paragraph:

Television has been around for almost half a century. It was first introduced to the public at the World's Fair in 1939. But did not achieve widespread popularity until the 1950s. Which was considered television's golden era. A time of continual experiments, all of which were done live. Entertainment shows such as "I Love Lucy" and "The Life of Riley" made their appearance. There were also quite a few excellent children's shows. "Howdy Doody," "Lassie," "The Wonderful World of Disney," to name only a few. Through the years, television has expanded its scope. And added bigger and better variety shows along with dramas and soap operas. People will always turn to television as a source of entertainment and relaxation.

PRACTICE 8

Correct the seven fragments in this paragraph:

Registration day totally changed my views about college life. I had thought college would be a well-ordered, calm, and relaxing place. I had my schedule all prepared, and everything seemed perfect. The hours and instructors I wanted and the classes I needed. Everything was arranged in the proper order. I was even early that day. Because I knew registration would be crowded. However, I was not prepared for the sight before me when I walked into the University Center. People running around like chickens with their heads cut off. Frantically searching for answers. Some lying on the floor in a daze, others leaning against walls to write in changes on their schedule cards. A few even seemed near tears. For a moment I thought about forgetting college and going back to work at McDonald's. However, I eventually pulled myself together and sprinted across the floor. An area littered with bodies and schedule cards. After thirty minutes of grabbing, kicking, and running, I was a registered college student. Not a happy one, but registered, nevertheless.

12.2 Preventing Run-on Sentences

Run-on sentences consist of two sentences run together with either no punctuation or only a comma. A run-on sentence with no punctuation is called a *fused sentence;* a run-on sentence with a comma is called a *comma splice.* Here are two examples of run-on sentences:

Capital punishment is ethically unacceptable it is against the morals of civilized societies.

(This is a fused sentence. One sentence should end and the other begin after *unacceptable*.)

Capital punishment is ethically unacceptable, it is against the morals of civilized societies.

(This is a comma splice, in which two sentences are incorrectly joined, or spliced, with a comma.)

When you edit your papers, read your sentences one at a time to determine if you have run any sentences together. Here are two more examples of run-on sentences:

The work was harder than I thought it was going to be, it almost killed me. (The first independent clause can function alone as a complete sentence because it has a subject, *work*, and a verb, *was going*. The second independent clause can also function by itself as a complete sentence: It has a subject, *it*, and a verb, *killed*.)

The Saints lost game after game, however, they did not give up. (The first independent clause ends with *game*. It can function alone as a complete sentence because it has a subject, *Saints*, and a verb, *lost*. The second independent clause begins with *however*. It can also function by itself: It has a subject, *they*, and a verb, *did give*. Note that you can begin sentences with *however*.)

Once you have identified a run-on sentence, you can correct it by several methods. Four ways to correct the run-on sentence, *I came to the open field, it was not like the one I remember*, are listed below:

1. Make two sentences:

   I came to the open field. It was not like the one I remember.

2. Insert one of the seven coordinating conjunctions (*and, but, for, yet, so, or,* and *nor*) with a comma:

   I came to the open field, but it was not like the one I remember.

3. Insert a semicolon and a conjunctive adverb such as *then, for example, on the other hand, also, however, moreover, consequently,* and *therefore*:

   I came to the open field; however, it was not like the one I remember.

4. Make one of the independent clauses into a dependent clause, changing the wording as necessary. (Some dependent clauses begin with subordinating conjunctions such as *while, when, as, because,* and *although*; others begin with relative pronouns such as *which, who,* and *that*.)

   When I came to the open field, I realized that it was not like the one I remember.

   I came to the open field, although it was not like the one I remember.

   I came to the open field, which was not like the one I remember.

PRACTICE 9

Correct the following run-on sentences by making them into two sentences:

1. Today many people are completely dependent on their watches. *They* they would be nervous wrecks without them.

2. Go ahead and check the water it looks good to me.

3. Shut the door it is cold in there.

4. It does not make a lot of difference which one you take both roads will get you there.

5. You are a changed woman your past does not matter to me now.

6. It was not my imagination, it was a little girl.

7. Look at all of those people someone will surely help us.

8. Where I live is only about five blocks from the university, the blocks are not long, and each has only four or five houses.

9. Take me, for instance, I am not your average success story.

PRACTICE 10

Correct the following run-on sentences by inserting the designated coordinating conjunction (with a comma) between the two independent clauses:

1. (and) I just bought a new dress *, and,* I know you will like it.

2. (but) He enjoyed the camp last summer he is not going again.

3. (for) There is no need to worry we will get there on time.

4. (yet) I did not like what she was telling me, I knew she was right.

5. (so)   It began to rain we had to call off our picnic.

6. (or)   I am driving to Seattle, I am not going anywhere.

7. (nor) He will not go to school, he will not look for a job. (When you use *nor* you have to change the wording of the sentence, for example: *He is not too young, he is not too old* becomes *He is not too young, nor is he too old.*)

PRACTICE 11

Using each of the seven coordinating conjunctions at least once, correct the following run-on sentences. Insert commas as necessary.

1. The cabin was cold *, and* there was no more firewood.

2. He was a strange young man, I liked him.

3. She gave me a big shove I fell in the fish pond.

4. Dorm life is unpleasant sometimes, it has been all right on the whole.

5. Cynthia said, "Marry me, I will not see you again."

6. My cat is fed well she is still skinny.

7. Let me go I have to be in class in two minutes.

8. He brought this date home she had not met his parents.

9. I finished high school at Saint Joseph's Academy, now here I am at the university.

10. He will not sleep, he will not eat.

PRACTICE 12

Correct the following run-on sentences by inserting a semicolon before the conjunctive adverbs:

1. He ruined his health ; then he ruined his marriage.

2. She is not the most considerate person, however, she is the most intelligent.

3. A few things are still inexpensive, for example, you can still buy water for almost nothing.

4. High school was strict, however, college is not strict enough.

5. You first make a cream sauce, then you brown the shrimp in another pan.

6. The whale turned over on its back as though it were dead, then it started breathing again.

7. If sex education were taught in high school, the number of teen-age pregnancies would decline, moreover, young people would protect themselves more effectively against venereal disease.

8. Invasion was not our goal, however, it did seem necessary.

9. The surgeon general issued a stern warning against cigarette smoking, consequently, 30 percent of the nation's smokers have quit the habit.

PRACTICE 13

Correct the following run-on sentences by using one of the following subordinating conjunctions—*if, when, since, although, while,* or *because*—to introduce the first or second clause. Insert commas as necessary.

1. I hate to go shopping with Joyce *because* she takes so long.

2. He graduates this May, I am going to miss him.

3. You study in our room, I will study in the library.

4. The states of our nation are different in most ways, they do have one thing in common.

5. The Equal Rights Amendment will be proposed again and will eventually pass, it will take many years.

6. Kids are playful, joyful, and bright that is why I decided to write about my little sister.

PRACTICE 14

Correct the following run-on sentences by using any of the four methods described on page 271. (Two sentences are correct.) Remember to use a semicolon or a coordinating conjunction before a conjunctive adverb.

1. I could not believe my eyes the car was just what I needed.

2. Shut the door, let's keep as warm as possible.

3. The rock hit him beneath his eye it taught him a lesson.

4. Our youth are not the problem, however, they do have a lot to learn.

5. I need those notes, please give them to me.

6. Give me your tired and your poor I will make them into a great nation.

7. The students at this university are not very friendly, in fact they are sometimes hostile.

8. I started college in the fall of 1981 in so doing, I jumped from the frying pan into the fire.

9. Russell is 6'5" he weighs 175 pounds.

10. Usually, I work eight to five, but sometimes I must work many overtime hours.

11. I really enjoy going out with college men, I know they will not be jerks.

12. She had a demanding style of teaching, moreover, she expected perfection.

13. "Try harder," you say to yourself there is one more ball left to play.

14. The noise has stopped, and the lights are out, all except the one that says "tilt."

15. That is how the machine really wins it eats your money.

16. Young drug abusers are responsible for their own actions, however, adults do contribute to the problem by their own addictive behavior.

17. Run-on sentences are often hard to detect, sometimes they flow together very smoothly.

18. We have lost our sense of purpose as a nation, moreover, we seem not to care.

19. The space program will never be what it once was, it has lost much popular support.

20. That country's leader may be our enemy, however, its people are probably very much like ourselves.

PRACTICE 15

Correct the run-on sentences in the following student essay by using one of the four methods described on page 271:

A Sunday Morning Revelation

It was a calm, peaceful morning as I walked down the main street of Atlanta. Everything was so quiet because it was Sunday, people were still in church. When I arrived at Main and Broad, near the Liberty Monument, I saw seventy-five Knights of the Ku Klux Klan marching up Broad to Main Street. They were in their usual attire, however, the faces of their hoods were open. (2 run-on sentences)

My name is Tyronne Pellisier, and I am the president of the Atlanta NAACP Youth Council. I had gone downtown on this particular Sunday morning because I had never seen the Klan before, I wanted to see what many black folks fear most in the world. The Klan members were not at all what I expected. As they approached Main Street, they were shouting, "White power," it struck me funny to see white people hollering about white power in a city that is owned mostly by whites. (2 run-on sentences)

The group was composed of people who were too young to know what hate is and others who were too old to do anything about it. They stopped their march in front of the Liberty Monument, their leader got everyone's attention and began to make a noisy speech. "We must organize and unify ourselves. Next year will be too late," he said. "Huh, too late for what?" I asked myself. I got up close so that they could see my NAACP button, every now and then I shouted out, "Black power." But they did not seem to mind. (2 run-on sentences)

I came to the conclusion that the Klan simply was not as powerful and violent as it used to be. I had thought we would lead a protest against them, however, after seeing what I saw, I do not think it would be worth the time. Do not get me wrong though, I have not let them off the hook. It is just that I do not see them as such a threat. I hope that some day the Klan and its silent followers will see the light and realize that poor people of all colors need to band together. (2 run-on sentences)

Common Types of Run-on Sentences

The following types of run-on sentences are common:

1. Run-on sentences with pronoun subjects in the second clause:

   ERROR

   Boot camp was just what I had expected, it was terrible. (It is very easy to run these two independent clauses together when writing them because when you say them, you say them in one breath. However, the comma before the pronoun *it* does not correct the run-on. What noun in the first clause does *it* stand for?)

   CORRECTION

   Boot camp was just what I had expected. It was terrible.

   ERROR

   My drill instructor at Parris Island surprised me, he was actually quite nice. (The comma before *he* does not correct the run-on. What noun in the first clause does *he* stand for?)

   CORRECTION

   My drill instructor at Parris Island surprised me because he was actually quite nice.

2. Run-on sentences with *then:*

   ERROR

   First you knead the dough, then you smooth it out with a rolling pin. (You cannot join two independent clauses with *then* unless you place a semicolon or *and* or *but* before it.)

   CORRECTION

   First you knead the dough; then you smooth it out with a rolling pin.

   Or,

   First you knead the dough, and then you smooth it out with a rolling pin.

3. Run-on sentences with other conjunctive adverbs such as *however, moreover, therefore,* and *consequently:*

ERROR

Bake the cookies for about half an hour, however, if you have a slow oven, bake them a little longer. (When a conjunctive adverb introduces an independent clause, either use a semicolon before it or make two sentences.)

CORRECTION

Bake the cookies for about half an hour; however, if you have a slow oven, bake them a little longer.

Or,

Bake the cookies for about half an hour. However, if you have a slow oven, bake them a little longer.

4. Run-on sentences in narratives:

ERROR

I looked across the field and saw a little boy, the child reminded me of someone I knew. (In telling stories aloud, you probably run sentences together, but in writing you must write them separately or join them correctly.)

CORRECTION

I looked across the field and saw a little boy. The child reminded me of someone I knew.

5. Run-on sentences in quoted speech:

ERROR

The drill sergeant made me say, "This is my rifle, you do not call this weapon a gun." (Make run-on sentences in quotations into two sentences.)

CORRECTION

The drill sergeant made me say, "This is my rifle. You do not call this weapon a gun."

PRACTICE 16

Using the above corrected sentences as models, correct the following run-on sentences:

1. Heart disease is an extremely dangerous illness, it is the number one killer disease in this country.

2. The president was on the defensive, he could not explain why he had made such a statement.

3. Both houses of Congress must agree on the bill, then it must go to the president for his signature.

4. First you gather the information, then you analyze it.

5. Our dog Lucifer looks ferocious, however, he is as gentle as any dog I know.

6. Eighteen-year-olds can vote and fight for our country, therefore, they should be able to buy alcohol.

7. We began climbing to the top, the wind was so strong that we could not stand up straight.

8. It was too dark to go any further, we turned around and went home.

9. She turned to me and said, "Will you just listen to me, I have something to say that will surprise you."

10. I answered, "What do you want from me, I can no longer help you."

PRACTICE 17

Correct the following run-on sentences using one of the four methods.

1. My sister Marie enlisted in the air force two years ago, *and* she is stationed in England now.

2. She took a special liking to one elderly couple they accepted her as a member of the family.

3. They gave Marie a standing invitation to stop by on holidays she had only to give them a phone call.

4. Marie was also invited to several dart tournaments darts is a game the British especially love.

5. The beautiful English countryside impressed her as much as the warmth of the people it is a land whose rolling hills remain green all year.

6. Many of these hills are dotted with small farms, one can often see small herds of sheep grazing leisurely on them.

7. Marie also visited France and Italy, she loved the beautiful beaches in the south.

8. She found the French people very friendly, too, they are especially hospitable to those who make an effort to speak their language.

9. However, her favorite European country is Switzerland, it has breathtaking scenery and a brisk, cool climate.

10. The city of Geneva is especially lovely, it is located on a clear, blue lake.

11. On one occasion she went mountain climbing in the Alps, however, the snow forced her to turn back before she reached the top of the Matterhorn.

12. They rode the lift to the lodge, then they set out on foot across a sky-high glacier.

13. The snow was fresh on the glacier, the sun was blinding.

14. She and her party were tied together by ropes, however, no one slipped.

PRACTICE 18

Correct the run-on sentences in the following student essay by using one of the four methods.

The Weekend Camper

If anyone had told me three years ago that I would be spending most of my weekends camping, I would have laughed heartily. Campers, in my eyes, were nothing but masochists who enjoyed insect bites, ill-cooked meals, and damp sleeping bags, they had nothing in common with me. I was to learn a lot about camping since then, however. (1 run-on sentence)

The friends who introduced me to camping thought that it meant being a pioneer. The first trip they took me on, we roughed it, we slept in a tent, cooked over an open fire, and hiked to the shower and bathroom facilities. This brief visit with Mother Nature cost me two days off from work, recovering from a bad case of sunburn. There was no shade, the tallest tree on our campsite was three feet tall. Another memento from the trip was the doctor's bill for my son's poison ivy. (2 run-on sentences)

I was, nevertheless, talked into going on another fun-filled holiday in the wilderness, this time we camped with friends who believed that Daniel Boone would have been proud to use the light bulb if he had known about it. There was no tent, we had a pop-up camper with comfortable beds and an air conditioner. These nature lovers had remembered to bring all the necessities of life they brought lounge chairs, a screened porch, the TV, and even a blender. I can still taste those piña coladas. (3 run-on sentences)

After that trip, my husband and I became quite interested in camping, we have done a lot of it since. Recently, we purchased a twenty-eight-foot travel trailer complete with bathroom and built-in TV antenna. There is a separate bedroom, a modern kitchen with refrigerator and roll-out pantry, the trailer even has matching carpet and draperies. (2 run-on sentences)

I must say that I have certainly come to enjoy camping. It must be true that, sooner or later, everyone finds his or her way back to nature, I recommend that you find your way in style. (1 run-on sentence)

12.3 Preventing Adjective and Adverb Confusion

It is easy to confuse adjectives and adverbs. Remember that adjectives must modify nouns or pronouns; adverbs must modify verbs, adjectives, or other adverbs. The following sentence, for example, is incorrect:

I did good at that high school.

If you look up *good* in a dictionary, you will see that it cannot be used as it is here: as an adverb modifying the verb *did*. The adverb *well* should be substituted instead:

I did well at that high school.

Likewise, this sentence is incorrect:

He arrived as quick as he could.

Quick is an adjective; however, the adverb *quickly* must be used to modify the verb *arrived:*

She arrived as quickly as she could.

Sometimes adjectives follow linking verbs such as *is, are, seem,* and *appear.* They do not modify these verbs, however, but rather the subjects of the verbs. For example:

He seems lazy to me.

Lazy, the adjective, modifies the subject *he; lazily,* the adverb, would be incorrect.

PRACTICE 19

Two of the following sentences require adjectives, which follow linking verbs. The rest require adverbs. Choose the correct word and draw an arrow to the word it modifies:

1. Carry those dishes just as (careful, carefully) as you can.

2. The librarian looked at me very (curious, curiously).

3. He has fixed up the room very (nice, nicely) for the children.

4. Her fingers were moving across the keys (rapid, rapidly).

5. She looks (beautiful, beautifully) in her wedding gown.

6. These dogs bark so (loud, loudly) that they wake the whole neighborhood.

7. You did (good, well).

8. The WILD jazz band plays (good, well).

9. With her new hair style, she certainly looks (good, well).

10. The waiter frowns at me (frequent, frequently).

11. They have been carrying on (crazy, crazily) lately.

PRACTICE 20

Using the above sentences in Practice 19 as models, complete the following exercises in whole sentences:

1. Use *well* to describe something that you are not good at doing.

   I do not type well.

2. Use *quietly* to describe something a cat does that hardly anyone notices.

   _____

3. Use *nicely* to describe how someone always greets you.

   _____

4. Use *well* to describe the skill with which a good quarterback throws the ball.

   _____

5. Use *good* after the verb *looks*.

   _____

12.4 Preventing Dangling Modifiers

What is wrong with the following sentences?

> While sailing, a shark broke close to our boat.
>
> Having eaten a large meal, it was time to go home.
>
> To do well, determination is necessary.

Each sentence has the same problem: The subject is not clear. In the first sentence, the shark seems to be the subject, but sharks are not known for sailing. In the second, the reader is not told who ate the large meal; it certainly was not *it*. In the third example it is not clear who is trying to do well.

In the above sentences, *while sailing, having eaten a large meal,* and *to do well* are called *dangling modifiers.* They are supposed to describe subjects in these sentences, but since the subjects are not clear, the modifiers do not connect—they dangle.

The above sentences can be corrected as follows:

While sailing, we saw a shark that broke close to our boat.

Having eaten a large meal, we realized that it was time to go home.

To do well, one must have determination.

To correct dangling modifiers, first place the subject that you want your modifier to describe immediately after the modifier; then complete the sentence. In the first sentence, *we* were sailing, so the subject is *we.* In the second, *we* ate the meal, so again the subject is *we.* The goal of doing well applies to anyone, so the subject in the last example is. the indefinite pronoun *one*; it could also be *you.*

PRACTICE 21

Complete the following sentences with appropriate subjects for the modifiers:

1. Having breathed her last, *she rolled over and died* .

2. Running from the police, _____.

3. To stop crime, _____.

4. Having witnessed the great event of the century, _____.

5. Watching the deliberations in Congress, _____.

6. Determined to succeed, _____.

7. To love your neighbor, _____.

8. Having been discovered, _____.

9. To succeed in the business world, _____.

10. Spending his money carelessly, _____.

11. Intending to do a good thing, _____.

PRACTICE 22

Correct these sentences by writing an appropriate subject after the dangling modifier. Change the wording as necessary to convey the intended meaning of the sentence.

1. Having spent all their money, *they headed home.* ~~it was time to go home.~~

2. Built on a rock foundation, there is no problem with a house falling down.

3. To be a good father, it is necessary to spend a lot of time with the children.

4. While swimming in the river, a bad thunderstorm scared us.

5. To do your best, it is important to stay in good shape.

6. While eating his supper, the squirrel ran across the hunter's plate.

7. Convicted of a third felony, the judge sent the man to prison for life.

8. Having awoken early, no one could find them.

9. To bloom where one is planted, it is necessary to make the best of the situation.

12.5 Preventing Misplaced Modifiers

What is wrong with the following sentences?

He left his car to be sold with the dealer.

The president spoke to the terrorists who survived with tough language.

The farmers in our county almost earned ten million dollars.

In each sentence a modifier is out of place. In the first example, it sounds as if the car and the dealer are to be sold together. In the second sentence, it sounds as though the tough language of the terrorists had enabled them to survive. Finally, in the last sentence, it seems as though the farmers, instead of earning an amount close to ten million dollars, did not earn a cent.

In the above sentences, *with the dealer, with tough language,* and *almost* are misplaced modifiers. They are intended to describe certain words in the sentences, but because they are misplaced, they modify the wrong words.

The above sentences can be corrected as follows:

He left his car <u>with the dealer</u> to be sold.

The president spoke <u>with tough language</u> to the terrorists who survived.

The farmers in our county earned <u>almost</u> ten million dollars.

To correct misplaced modifiers, identify the words that you want your modifiers to describe and place the modifiers as close to those words as you can. Sometimes you will need to rewrite the sentences. In the first sentence above, *with the dealer* tells where he left the car, so you should move this phrase as close as possible to the verb *left.* In the second, *with tough language* tells how the president spoke, so you should move this phrase next to the verb *spoke*. In the last example, *almost* describes an amount of money that is not quite ten million dollars, so you should move *almost* next to *ten million dollars*.

PRACTICE 23

Rewrite the following sentences, moving the modifiers to their intended places. Then draw an arrow from the modifiers to the words they are intended to modify. Change the wording as necessary.

1. My aunt was rushed to the emergency room at the hospital with a failing heart.

   My aunt, with a failing heart, was rushed to the emergency room at the hospital.

2. The interns on duty were able to save her life in the emergency room.

   _____

   _____

3. Her stay in the hospital almost cost her three hundred dollars a day.

   _____

   _____

4. Dr. Regina Watts testified before the House Welfare Committee on behalf of neglected children.

   _____

   _____

5. The committee members listened to her appeal on behalf of the children with great interest.

   _____

   _____

6. Later the legislature passed the bill almost to appropriate one hundred thousand dollars. I believe the exact amount they approved was ninety-seven thousand dollars.

   _____

   _____

7. The children will now be helped by the state representatives who have been neglected.

   _____

   _____

8. Dr. Watts and the other members of Agenda for Children have made an important contribution to the children of this state with their determined leadership.

_____

_____

9. Dr. Watts has nearly recruited three hundred members for Agenda for Children.

_____

_____

10. The members argue for various priorities they have established convincingly.

_____

_____

11. The legislative victory shows what one person can do to change things with a dream.

_____

_____

12.6 Preventing Faulty Parallelism

What is wrong with these sentences?

I like swimming, hiking, and to collect things.

Capital punishment deters crime, eliminates dangerous criminals, and finally society has a right to demand retribution.

You will need to gather ahead of time the eggs, the flour, baking powder, honey, and the shortening.

Each sentence has the same problem: *faulty parallelism.* When you write words as items in a series, they should have a parallel grammatical structure. In the first sentence, *swimming* and *hiking* are gerunds (verbs made into nouns by adding *-ing*), but *to collect things* is not similar in structure. In the second example, the first two arguments for capital punishment are written as verbs with objects, but the third argument includes a subject (*society*) as well. Thus, it is not parallel to the first two arguments. In the third sentence, *the* is included before three items in the series but not before the other two. You can make these items parallel by using *the* only once, before *eggs*, or by using *the* before all five items.

The above sentences can be corrected as follows:

I like swimming, hiking, and collecting things.

Capital punishment deters crime, eliminates dangerous criminals, and satisfies society's need for retribution.

You will need to gather ahead of time the eggs, flour, baking powder, honey, and shortening.

PRACTICE 24

One item in each sentence below is not parallel to the others. Rewrite that item so that it is parallel.

1. The various neighbors on my block could be classified as friendly, indifferent, and ~~some are just plain mean.~~ *just plain mean.*

2. In my view capital punishment does not deter crime, is used only against the poor, and people should not be subject to such cruel and unusual punishment.

3. He enjoys his nap in the afternoon, his bike ride in the early evening, and to read novels at night.

4. Manning watches the soap operas in the morning, the news programs in the late afternoon, and television movies at night.

5. Her responsibilities are to make the customers feel welcome, to show them to a table, and finding them a waiter.

6. When I graduate from this university, I am going to save some money, then open my own business, and finally sitting back and getting rich.

12.7 Review Exercises

REVIEW EXERCISE 1

Correct the following fragments and run-on sentences, changing the wording as necessary:

1. And finally, ~~the~~ *my neighborhood is filled with* unique sounds ~~in my neighborhood.~~

2. The Reverend Winn did not want to talk about her illness*. Instead,* instead she wanted to talk about what we were doing.

3. There very few young people in this neighborhood who go to high school.

4. Because she wanted the room to be just the way it was when her parents died.

5. First you make a roux of white flour and fat, then you add chopped vegetables.

6. She never answers a question with a short answer. While Melvin never answers a question with anything but a grunt or a groan.

7. My instructor gave me a little speech, she said that the time was now or never.

8. This university is not what I had expected, it is not very friendly.

9. Send me the bill, however, I cannot pay everything right now.

10. A person for whom I have the highest respect.

11. My grandmother said, "You have your boyfriend, why can't I have mine?"

12. We have not raised the necessary revenue to fund Social Security, consequently, the money will soon be gone.

REVIEW EXERCISE 2

Edit the following student essay, changing the wording as necessary. It now contains eight fragments and seven run-on sentences.

An Experience I Would Like to Forget

One afternoon, my brother Kenneth and I played football for several hours until we were worn out. We then decided to go to the drugstore on the corner of Clairborne and Upperline. A place where we could cool off and buy a cola. I walked down the wide aisle toward the soft drink machine, I passed some cherry candy that I suddenly wanted, but I only had money for a Coke. I took two packs of candy. While a middle-aged woman was serving my brother.

We left the store and went around the corner, I showed Kenneth what I had done. He said, "Why did you do that, you better hope Paw doesn't find out." I began to worry that Kenneth would tell John, our older brother.

A little bit later several of us were sitting on a neighbor's porch and talking. When Kenneth came up and said, "Richard, Daddy wants you." I noticed that Kenneth had a funny smile on his face, so I asked him, "What are you smiling about?" "Nothin'," he replied.

When I got home, my mother and father were waiting for me in the living room. Sitting on the sofa. My brother John on a chair next to them. My father said in an angry tone, "Richard, why did you steal that candy?" I knew then that John had told them what I had done. Not that I had done that much that was wrong.

I answered my father in a scared and trembling voice, "I don't know why I took it, Dad." My mother looked at me as though I had robbed a bank, then she said she was very disappointed in me. I looked at my father. Knowing what he was going to say. His voice got stronger and stronger, however, there was nothing I could do. Finally, he said, "You know what's next?" I knew, but I acted as if I did not.

He then said, "Let's go in the back and discuss the matter, I think you'll learn about stealing in the future." I started crying for Mom to help me. Because now I was really scared. But she just turned her back, my father closed the door.

REVIEW EXERCISE 3

Each of these sentences contains one of the following errors:

a misused adjective or adverb
a dangling modifier
a misplaced modifier
a faulty parallel construction

Correct the errors, changing the wording as necessary:

1. When I saw my doctor, she spoke ~~nice~~ *nicely* to me, as she always does.

2. Having seen the worst effects of the bombing, it was time to go home.

3. Dr. Lofton told him to stop smoking in an angry voice.

4. They did good in their competition with State.

5. We almost spent ten thousand dollars on that car.

6. Gather information, analyze the information, and then you should write your purpose statement.

7. I never have danced very good.

8. Wading in the inlet, a four-foot shark swam right by me.

9. She likes to work hard, play hard, and sleeping hard.

10. The police officer spoke gentle to the people involved in the accident.

11. The victory shows what a team can do to opponents determined to win.

CHAPTER 13

Subject-Verb Agreement

13.0 Introduction

In this chapter you will study how to make verbs agree with their subjects. When you should add an -s to a verb can sometimes be most confusing. When you should choose *is* or *are* or *was* or *were* can also be confusing. This chapter gives the rules for subject-verb agreement and contains many practice exercises.

In standard English, the verb and the subject of a sentence must agree with each other. If the subject is one person, place, or thing, then the verb must also be singular. Here are examples of singular subjects with singular verbs:

The train stops at every station.

Gasoline costs a lot these days.

Roberta cries over the lost children.

Each subject is one: one train, one kind of fuel (gasoline), and one person (Roberta). The -s added to the verbs indicates that each verb is also singular. Because the subjects and the verbs are both singular, they are said to agree with each other.

Here are examples of plural (more than one) subjects and verbs:

The trains stop at every station.

Every day their colds get worse.

Rudy and Mary plan everything together.

Each of these subjects is more than one: more than one train, more than one cold, and two people named Rudy and Mary. The fact that the verbs do not end with -s indicates that they are plural.

The great confusion over subject-verb agreement arises from the fact that you add an -s to form the plural of most nouns but omit the -s to form the plural of verbs. For example, *one cabin* becomes *two cabins*, but *she lives* becomes *they live*. *Cabin* is a singular noun. To make the word plural, you add an *-s. Lives* is a singular verb. To make it plural, you omit the *s*.

PRACTICE 1

Make plural nouns and plural verbs for the following examples:

1. *A boy* becomes *two* ___*boys*___, but *Mia sews* becomes *they* ___*sew*___

2. *A sister* becomes *two* _____, but *Chris runs* becomes *they* _____

3. *One fist* becomes *two* _____, but *she asks* becomes *they* _____

4. *A risk* becomes *two* _____, but *Tom risks* becomes *they* _____

5. *A play* becomes *two* _____, but *Sue plays* becomes *they* _____

6. *One dream* becomes *two* _____, but *Gina dreams* becomes *they* _____

PRACTICE 2

Make singular nouns and singular verbs for the following examples:

1. *Two cats* becomes *one* ___*cat*___, but *they hit* becomes *he* ___*hits*___

2. *Two boxes* becomes *one* _____, but *they cost* becomes *it*

3. *Two buses* becomes *one* _____, but *they love* becomes *she*

4. *Two bills* becomes *one* _____, but *they bill* becomes *he*

5. *Two dances* becomes *one* _____, but *they dance* becomes *she*

6. *Two types* becomes *one* _____, but *they type* becomes *he*

PRACTICE 3

Make complete sentences out of the following, showing present-time (on-going) action. (Do not use *is, are, was,* or *were.*) Write *S* over each singular subject and singular verb. Write *P* over each plural subject and plural verb.

1. *Our instructor* always involves *us in her class*.
2. Musicians always *play at the club*.
3. Every day the sisters _____.
4. The new dances always _____.
5. _____ always dances _____.
6. _____ whacks _____.
7. Every day the sports fans _____.
8. _____ always fans _____.
9. Every year the dresses _____.
10. _____ usually dresses _____.
11. _____ seems _____.
12. _____ robs _____.

13.1 Verb Conjugation

To discuss the different verb forms, it is helpful to illustrate them. Here is an illustration for the verb *decide* in the present tense (showing action going on now):

	Singular	*Plural*
FIRST PERSON	I decide	we decide
SECOND PERSON	you decide	you decide
THIRD PERSON	he, she, or it decides (or Bill, Mary, or the dog decides)	they decide (or the people decide)

Such illustrations are called *conjugations.*

First person is *I* for singular and *we* for plural; second person is *you* for both singular and plural; third person is *he, she,* or *it* for singular or *they* for plural, or noun subjects such as Bill, Mary, the dog, or the people. As shown above, the first-person plural of the verb *decide* is *we decide;* the third-person singular is *he, she,* or *it decides;* and the third-person plural is *they decide.*

You can see from the above conjugation of *decide* that only the third-person singular of a present-tense verb takes an -*s* at the end. If your subject is one of the pronouns *he*, *she*, or *it*, you know immediately to add the -*s*. If your subject is *they*, you know to omit the -*s*. If your subject is a singular noun, add the -*s* ending; if the noun is plural omit it.

Look at these sentences:

(he)
John plays the stock market.

(she)
Mary seems to be understanding.

(it)
The ship sails around the world.

Because you can substitute *he* for *John*, *she* for *Mary*, and *it* for *ship*, each subject is singular and each verb must be singular (with the -*s* ending).

Now look at these examples:

(they)
John and Carlos play the stock market.

(they)
Mary and Martha seem to be understanding.

(they)
The ships sail around the world.

Because you can substitute *they* for each of these subjects, you must use a third-person plural verb for each, that is, a verb that does not end in -*s*.

PRACTICE 4

Write the pronoun that you would substitute for each of the following noun subjects above the subject, and then choose the correct verb. Finally, complete the sentences.

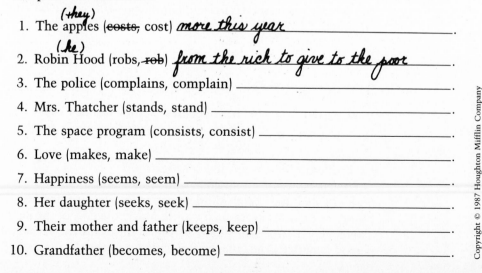

1. *(they)* The apples (~~costs,~~ cost) *more this year* _____.

2. *(he)* Robin Hood (robs, ~~rob~~) *from the rich to give to the poor* _____.

3. The police (complains, complain) _____.

4. Mrs. Thatcher (stands, stand) _____.

5. The space program (consists, consist) _____.

6. Love (makes, make) _____.

7. Happiness (seems, seem) _____.

8. Her daughter (seeks, seek) _____.

9. Their mother and father (keeps, keep) _____.

10. Grandfather (becomes, become) _____.

PRACTICE 5

Compose sentences using the following verbs in the present tense and in the person indicated:

1. (*hope*: first-person plural) *We hope this year will be a year of peace.*

2. (*involve*: third-person singular) *Our mayor involves the citizens in city government.*

3. (*practice*: second-person singular) _____

4. (*spend*: second-person plural) _____

5. (*sew*: third-person plural) _____

6. (*consist*: third-person singular) _____

7. (*give*: first-person singular) _____

8. (*become*: third-person singular) _____

9. (*say*: third-person plural) _____

10. (*use*: third-person plural) _____

11. (*seem*: third-person singular) _____

12. (*seem*: third-person plural) _____

13.2 Irregular Noun Subjects

When used as third-person subjects, the following types of nouns are irregular and thus deserve special attention:

1. Most collective nouns (such as *family, class, team, union,* and *political party*) take singular verbs (those with the *-s* ending):

    Her <u>family</u> <u>meets</u> all her needs. (*One family* meets her needs.)

    The <u>class</u> <u>seems</u> to like the new instructor.

    Our <u>team</u> <u>plays</u> best under pressure.

    The <u>union</u> often <u>threatens</u> to go on strike.

    The <u>Democratic Party</u> <u>supports</u> the minimum wage.

    But note these exceptions:

    The <u>police</u> <u>appreciate</u> law-abiding citizens.

    The <u>Dallas Cowboys</u> <u>win</u> many more games than they lose.

2. Some collective nouns, such as *jury,* can take either a singular or plural verb depending on the meaning of the sentence:

    The <u>jury</u> <u>seems</u> deadlocked. (Here *jury* is considered as one unit.)

    The <u>jury</u> <u>disagree</u> and cannot reach a verdict. (Here *jury* is considered as a group of individuals.)

3. If the word *people* is understood—but not written—as part of a subject, the subject takes a plural verb:

    The <u>rich</u> <u>get</u> richer, and the <u>poor</u> <u>get</u> poorer. (The writer is saying that the *rich people* get richer and the *poor people* get poorer.)

    The <u>courageous</u> <u>die</u>, but the cowards live. (The writer is speaking of *courageous people.*)

4. A noun that is plural in form (with an *-s* ending) but singular in meaning usually takes a singular verb:

    The <u>United States</u> <u>gives</u> some of its money to third world countries. (The *United States* is one nation.)

    Some think that <u>politics</u> <u>corrupts</u>. (*Politics* is one activity.)

    But note these exceptions:

    The <u>scissors</u> <u>turn</u> up each time I lose them.

    My son's <u>pants</u> <u>tear</u> each time he goes fishing.

PRACTICE 6

Choose the correct verb in each sentence below:

1. The police (raids, (raid)) a different bar every night.

2. The United States (experiences, experience) hard times as well as prosperous times.

3. The jury (eats, eat) fine meals at the government's expense.

4. The poor (pays, pay) the taxes, and the rich (pays, pay) the tax lawyers.

5. Each graduating class (gives, give) the school a nice present.

6. The family (acts, act) as one unit.

7. Politics (makes, make) the world go round.

8. Even the experienced (makes, make) mistakes when they are not careful.

9. The people of the world (needs, need) to unite against nuclear destruction.

10. His pants (shows, show) a lot of wear.

11. The handicapped (demands, demand) equal access to public facilities.

12. The jury (argues, argue) among themselves.

13. The police (supports, support) gun control.

14. The U.S.S.R. (wants, want) to be first militarily.

15. The New Orleans Saints never (quits, quit).

16. The Republican Party usually (supports, support) business interests.

17. The United States (gives, give) away a lot of money.

18. The powerful (controls, control) all business in that country.

13.3 Verb Endings

For verbs that end in *-ch*, *-sh*, *-ss*, *-x*, *-z*, or *-o*, add *-es* in the third-person singular of the present tense:

I, you, we, and they reach, but he reaches
I, you, we and they boss, but she bosses
I, you, we and they push, but she pushes
I, you, we, and they box, but Ali boxes

You add *-es* to these verbs simply because they would be hard to pronounce if you added only an *-s*. The *-es* adds an extra syllable to the words and makes pronunciation easier. Note, however, that *ask* and *cost* take an *-s*, not an *-es*, ending: *she asks, it costs*.

PRACTICE 7

Write sentences using the designated verbs in the present tense and in the person indicated:

1. (*preach*: third-person singular) *My wife preaches to me all the time about my rumpled shirts.*

2. (*pinch*: third-person singular) _____

_____

3. (*fuss*: third-person singular) _____

_____

4. (*cost*: third-person singular) _____

_____

5. (*cost*: third-person plural) _____

_____

6. (*rush*: third-person plural) _____

_____

7. (*crush*: third-person plural) _____

_____

8. (*ask*: third-person singular) _____

_____

9. (*bless*: third-person singular) _____

_____

Do and *Go*

Forms of *do* and *go* are particularly troublesome to some students. Note the following conjugations:

I, you, we and they do, but it does
I, you, we and they go, but he goes

To make *do* or *does* negative, you add the adverb *not* or, in a contraction, the suffix *-n't*. (A *suffix* is a letter or letters that are added to the end of a word.)

I do not (or I don't)
It does not (or it doesn't)

Note: The more formal the writing, the less you should use contractions.

PRACTICE 8

Use *do, does, don't,* or *doesn't* in the following sentences:

1. Dr. Greenway __*doesn't*__ want to be bothered by his children.

2. Our instructor _____ care about her students.

3. This city _____ not have many dry days.

4. Only on the weekends _____ the noise become unbearable.

5. Why make a young woman keep a man she _____ want?

6. They _____ have a lot of money; in fact, you could call them rich.

7. I had to tell her that Santa _____ come to our neighborhood.

8. It _____ hurt anymore; all my tears are shed.

9. The English _____ seem to cherish the queen.

10. She, in turn, _____ care about her people.

11. _____ it seem strange that our allies go to war with each other?

Verbs That End in -y

If a verb ends in -y and is preceded by a consonant, change the -y to -i and add -es to form the third-person singular in the present tense. (A *consonant* is any letter other than one of the five *vowels*: a, e, i, o, u.) *I cry* thus becomes *she cries* because the -y is preceded by the consonant r.

> I, you, we, and they spy, but she spies
> I, you, we and they carry, but it carries
> I, you, we and they bury, but he buries
> I, you, we, and they dry, but she dries

If, however, a verb ends in -y and is preceded by a vowel, simply add an -s to the verb. *They enjoy* thus becomes *he enjoys* because the -y is preceded by the vowel o.

> I, you, we and they play, but it plays
> I, you, we and they say, but she says
> I, you, we and they enjoy, but he enjoys
> I, you, we and they journey, but it journeys

Note that when you add -ing to a verb ending in -y, you do not change the -y. Thus *cry* becomes *crying*, *enjoy* becomes *enjoying*, and *journey* becomes *journeying*.

PRACTICE 9

Supply the correct verb in the present tense:

1. (carry) Mary _*carries*_

2. (defy) Ben _____

3. (try) She _____

4. (travel) Mia _____

5. (fly) A bird _____

6. (journey) The team _____

7. (bury) It _____

8. (do) It _____

9. (do + -n't) It _____

10. (go) The van _____

13.4 Have *and* Has

The verb *have* is regular except in the third-person singular, where *has* is used instead of *haves*:

	Singular	Plural
FIRST PERSON	I have	we have
SECOND PERSON	you have	you have
THIRD PERSON	he, she, or it has	they have
	(Bob has, Jill has,	(the people have)
	the cat has)	

Since *have* and *has* are frequently used as helping verbs, you should be sure that you use each form correctly. Here are examples of *have* and *has* used as helping verbs:

The <u>Dolphins</u> <u>have won</u> many games this year.

<u>Becky</u> <u>has broken</u> her arm again.

<u>She</u> <u>has loved</u> many men in her day.

PRACTICE 10

In the sentences below supply the correct form of the verb *have*:

1. The City of Detroit _____*has*_____ many industries.

2. Everyone just gathers and _____ a good time.

3. You _____ been lying to me all along.

4. China _____ more people than the United States.

5. They _____ done what they could to save her.

6. These days a soldier _____ a pretty nice life.

7. The United States _____ offered them a compromise solution.

8. The scissors _____ not cut him so far.

9. The police _____ a difficult job to do.

10. People in Latin America _____ close ties with us.

11. The class _____ elected its representative.

13.5 The Be Verbs

Be verbs are irregular. Here are the conjugations of the *be* verb in the present and past tenses:

Present Tense

	Singular	Plural
FIRST PERSON	I am	we are
SECOND PERSON	you are	you are
THIRD PERSON	he, she, or it is	they are

Past Tense

	Singular	Plural
FIRST PERSON	I was	we were
SECOND PERSON	you were	you were
THIRD PERSON	he, she, or it was	they were

Thus you would write:

PRESENT TENSE
I <u>am</u> sick.
You <u>are</u> my friend.
The police officer <u>is</u> leaving.
We <u>are</u> going.
You <u>are</u> my friends.
The police <u>are</u> leaving.

PAST TENSE
The family <u>was</u> disturbed.
The poor <u>were</u> hungry.

PRACTICE 11

Choose the correct form of each verb, and then complete the following sentences:

1. (is, are) The people *are my friends* _____

_____.

2. (was, were) My husband and brother-in-law _____

_____.

3. (is, are) The jury _____

_____.

4. (wasn't, weren't) Uncle Mac _____

_____.

5. (wasn't, weren't) They _____

_____.

6. (was, were) Congress _____

_____.

7. (isn't, aren't) The Rams _____

_____.

8. (is, are) The police _____

_____.

9. (wasn't, weren't) You _____

_____.

13.6 Subject and Verb Reversed

Questions

You reverse the order of the subject and verb when you ask a question. Note the placement of the subjects and verbs in the following questions:

Does your daughter still believe in Santa Claus?
Hasn't that plane left yet?

The verb *does believe* agrees with the subject *daughter; hasn't left* agrees with the subject *plane.*

PRACTICE 12

First turn the following statements into questions. Then underline the subjects once and the verbs twice.

1. He does need more money for the trip. *Does he need more money for the trip?*

2. She is going to the dance with you. _____

_____

3. Those children need heavier jackets. _____

_____

4. They were the ones we were looking for. _____

_____

5. The leg has healed completely. _____

_____

6. The senator doesn't deliver on his promises. _____

_____

PRACTICE 13

First write questions that begin with the following words. Then underline the subjects once and the verbs twice.

1. Does *this country want to stop illegal drugs* _____?
2. Isn't _____?
3. Aren't _____?
4. Is _____?
5. Has _____?
6. Hasn't _____?
7. Haven't _____?
8. Have _____?
9. Doesn't _____?

Expletives

You also reverse the order of the subject and verb when you use an expletive, which is an expression such as *it is, here is, there is, here are,* and *there are*. Note the placement of the subjects and verbs in the following sentences with expletives:

There is one thing you haven't told me.

There have been several occasions when he seemed crazy.

It is the house of my dreams.

Here are my plans.

The expletives in the above sentences (*there is*, *there have been*, *it is*, and *here are*) are not the subjects, but they do point to the subjects. The subjects come after the verbs but nevertheless must agree with the verbs. *Thing* agrees with *is*; *occasions* agrees with *have been*; *house* agrees with *is*; *plans* agrees with *are*.

PRACTICE 14

Underline the subject in each of the following sentences and then supply the correct verb:

1. (was, were) There _____*were*_____ deer everywhere.

2. (is, are) There _____ something I have been meaning to tell you.

3. (is, are) There _____ often street fighting on the next block.

4. (was, were) _____ there many survivors from the crash?

5. (wasn't, weren't) There _____ any use in saying it again; the dean had made up her mind.

6. (wasn't, weren't) There _____ a thing the doctors could do for him.

7. (There is, There are) _____ just two alternatives left.

8. (has, have) There _____ been more violent crime this year.

9. (hasn't, haven't) There _____ been any reason for the increase that we know about.

10. (has, have) There _____ been fewer murders, however.

11. (There has, There have) _____ been some concern in the community.

PRACTICE 15

In the following sentences underline the subject once and verbs twice. If the verb does not agree with the subject, write its correct form above.

1. There are *is* one major problem in all large cities: crime.

2. There is still hope for you if you do not miss any more classes.

3. There is no reason to suspect them of the crimes.

4. Here's the essays I've promised, written to the best of my ability.

5. There hasn't been many changes since he took over as coach.

6. There haven't been anything in my life like that experience.

7. There weren't a thing they could do about it.

8. There's several reasons for the change in policy.

9. There's just no point in trying to engage in peace talks.

10. There are, in my mind, many reasons for the talks.

11. There's some who will always disagree with the goals of peace.

13.7 Verbs with Two or More Subjects

Many of your verbs will have two or more subjects (called compound subjects). Usually they are joined by the conjunction *and*:

> Ron and Don are twin brothers. Sally and Julius study together. (Because *Ron and Don* together are the subject of the sentence and represent more than one person, they take the plural verb *are*. The same is true of *Sally* and *Julius*.)

> What I say and what I do are not always the same. (*What I say* and *what I do* each function as individual nouns, but together take the plural verb *are*.)

> Appointing officials and initiating legislation are the governor's primary responsibilities. (*Appointing officials* and *initiating legislation* each function as individual nouns, but together take the plural verb *are*.)

PRACTICE 16

In each of the following, choose the correct verb and then complete the sentence:

1. (sew, sews) Mother and I often *sew together* _____.

2. (cost, costs) Gas and oil both _____.

3. (aren't, isn't) What I want and what she wants _____.

4. (are, is) But what I want _____.

5. (give, gives) This man and this woman _____.

6. (are, is) Getting better grades _____.

7. (are, is) Getting better grades and playing more tennis _____.

8. (buy, buys) My aunt and uncle sometimes _____.

9. (seem, seems) The potatoes, corn, and spinach all _____.

10. (protect, protects) The Bill of Rights and the Constitution _____

_____.

11. (are, is) Making clothes for her children _____.

Other Ways of Joining Subjects

1. Compound subjects are sometimes connected by the conjunction *or* or the correlative conjunctions *either/or*:

   Either <u>Ron</u> or <u>Don</u> <u>is going</u> to medical school. (A singular verb is used; one of the subjects will go to medical school, not both.)

   However, if one of the subjects joined by *or* is plural, use a plural verb *when the subject closer to the verb is plural*:

   Either <u>Tina</u> or her <u>parents</u> <u>are</u> mistaken. (The verb *are* is used to agree with the plural subject *parents*.)

   But use a singular verb when the subject closer to the verb is singular:

   Either the <u>eggs</u> or the <u>bacon</u> <u>is</u> burning. (Even though *eggs* is plural, *bacon* is closer to the verb and thus determines that it is singular.)

2. The conjunction *nor* and the correlative conjunctions *neither/nor* and *not only/but also* function in the same way as *or* and *either/or*:

   Neither <u>mother</u> nor <u>father</u> <u>lets</u> me use the car.

   Not only my hotel <u>accommodations</u> but also my airplane <u>ticket</u> <u>costs</u> more this year.

   Not only my airplane <u>ticket</u> but also my hotel <u>accommodations</u> <u>cost</u> more this year.

PRACTICE 17

In each of the following, choose the correct verb and then complete the sentence:

1. (come, comes) Every day Mrs. Appleby or Mrs. St. John *comes by and brings me my supper.*

2. (are, is) Neither you nor they _____.

3. (are, is) Abraham and his son, Isaac, _____.

4. (are, is) Either Abraham or his servants _____.

5. (appear, appears) But then suddenly a ram or some other kind of animal

_____.

6. (are, is) Not only Isaac but also Abraham _____.

7. (jog, jogs) Not only the grandfather but also the children _____.

8. (jog, jogs) Not only the children but also the grandfather _____.

9. (have, has) Either Sophia or you _____.

10. (sleep, sleeps) Both the cat and the dog _____.

11. (experience, experiences) Neither Russia nor the United States _____

_____.

13.8 Verbs with Pronoun Subjects

Throughout this chapter you have been writing sentences with personal pronouns as subjects: *I, you, he, she, it, we,* and *they.* In this section you will learn the rules for verb agreement when *indefinite, interrogative,* and *relative pronouns* are used as subjects.

One type of pronoun that can cause difficulty in verb-agreement constructions is the *indefinite pronoun.* Although some are plural in meaning, the following *always* take singular verbs:

anybody	everybody	nobody	somebody
anyone	everyone	no one	someone
anything	everything	nothing	something

Thus, you would write:

Anything she wants to do is fine with us.

Everybody says that this is the hottest summer in history.

Somebody has made a mistake.

The indefinite pronoun *some* can take either a singular or plural verb. For example:

Some of the apple is rotten. (Some of *one* thing is rotten.)

Some of the apples are rotten. (Some of *several* things are rotten.)

Half, part, all, a lot, more, and *most* can also take either singular or plural verbs. You need to ask yourself if they refer to part of one thing or some of several things. For example:

A lot of your writing is clever.

A lot of the students in this class are good writers.

PRACTICE 18

In each of the following, choose the correct verb and then complete the sentence:

1. (are, is) Some of you *are still my friends* _____.

2. (cost, costs) Everything _____.

3. (are, is) Anyone _____.

4. (were, was) Some of the work _____.

5. (are, is) All of the families on the block _____.

6. (involve, involves) Everything in this life _____.

7. (tell, tells) Half of my brain _____;

   half _____.

8. (Do, Does) _____ everyone _____?

9. (have, has) Most of the prisoners _____.

10. (are, is) Much of their problem _____.

11. (Do, Does) _____ anyone _____?

Interrogative Pronouns as Subjects

A second kind of pronoun that can cause difficulty in verb-agreement constructions is the *interrogative pronoun*—a pronoun used in questions:

Who?   What?   Which?

When used as subjects these pronouns can take either singular or plural verbs, depending on the words they stand for:

What is that woman's name? (*What* refers to *one* woman's name.)

What are their names? (*What* refers to *several* people's names.)

Interrogative pronouns that do not refer to particular nouns usually take singular verbs:

What is happening?
Who is going with us?

PRACTICE 19

In each of the sentences that follow, draw an arrow from the interrogative pronoun to the noun or pronoun it refers to, and then supply the correct verb:

1. (are, is) What _____*is*_____ the best choice?

2. (were, was) What _____ their names before they got married?

3. (are, is) What _____ your agenda for the meeting?

4. (are, is) Which one of the insurance plans _____ best for your family?

5. (were, was) Who _____ the lucky winner?

6. (were, was) Who _____ the lucky winners?

Relative Pronouns as Subjects

A third kind of pronoun that can cause difficulty in verb-agreement constructions is the *relative pronoun*—a pronoun that connects an adjective clause to a main clause:

who   whose   which   that

Like interrogative pronouns, relative pronouns can take either singular or plural verbs, depending on the words they stand for.

The person who means the most to me is my husband.

The people who mean the most to me are my parents.

In the first example, *who* refers to one person and thus takes the singular verb *means*. In the second, *who* refers to more than one person and takes the plural verb *mean*.

PRACTICE 20

In each of the sentences below, underline the pronoun subject of the adjective clause, draw an arrow to the noun or pronoun it refers to, and then supply the correct verb:

1. (were, was) My friends who _____*were*_____ with me stood up for me when I was arrested.

2. (break, breaks) It is hard to remain allies with nations that _____ our treaties.

3. (mind, minds) The one who _____ his or her own business is the one who stays out of trouble.

4. (care, cares) They are the ones who _____ for you the most.

5. (turn, turns) The coins that _____ green are copper.

6. (need, needs) People who _____ others are my kind of people.

7. (believe, believes) The police who _____ in crime prevention contribute a lot to our community.

8. (talk, talks) If I have another date who _____ to me about football, I am going to scream.

9. (know, knows) Will those of you who _____ something, please leave your names?

10. (cost, costs) The gifts that _____ the most are not necessarily the best.

11. (are, is) I kept the scissors that _____ the sharpest.

PRACTICE 21

Complete these sentences by using the designated subjects with either *is* or *are*:

1. Everybody *is my friend these days*_____.
2. Anyone _____.
3. Everything _____.
4. Some of the shirts _____.
5. Half of the watermelon _____.

PRACTICE 22

Complete these sentences by supplying appropriate verbs for the relative pronouns:

1. A typewriter that *skips spaces is maddening*_____.
2. Automobiles that _____.
3. A family who _____.
4. People who _____.
5. The reasons that _____.

13.9 Present-Tense Essays

Many students have found that writing present-tense, third-person singular essays is the best practice for subject-verb agreement. In such assignments, the writer is forced to use the *-s* endings consistently. For example:

> My <u>horse</u> Pegasus <u>stands</u> taller than any other horse. His <u>coat</u> <u>shines</u> brighter than any hand-shined leather. <u>He</u> <u>holds</u> his head high, with great dignity . . . .

If you convert such a narrative to the present-tense, third-person *plural*, you of course drop the *-s* from the third-person verbs. The resulting essay may sound somewhat contrived, but it will nevertheless offer excellent practice in subject-verb agreement. For example:

> My <u>horses</u>, Pegasus I and Pegasus II, <u>stand</u> taller than any other horses. Their <u>coats</u> <u>shine</u> . . . .

The advantage of writing such third-person essays is that you naturally use your own words and sentence constructions rather than those someone has prepared for you. Consequently, what you learn by writing these essays can be more easily converted into other writing you do.

If you are having persistent difficulty in subject-verb agreement, complete the three following assignments.

PRACTICE 23

Using the present-tense, third-person singular, write a three-paragraph paper describing what your pet (real or imaginary) does each day: morning, afternoon, and evening. Include at least twenty verbs with -s or -es endings. Underline the subjects of these verbs once and the verbs themselves twice. (Use the free-writing technique explained on page 37 to develop ideas and information for your paper.) You might begin something like this:

> Every morning at six o'clock, Halloween, our cat, jumps up on the window sill
> and cries to be let out. He always wakes us up when he does this . . . .

After your instructor has checked your paper, rewrite the essay in the third-person plural, present tense, again underlining subjects and verbs. You might begin something like this:

> Every morning at six o'clock, Halloween and Full Moon, our cats, jump up on
> the window sill and cry to be let out. They always wake us up when they do
> this . . . .

PRACTICE 24

Follow the instructions for Practice 23, except this time write about the daily activities of a close friend or relative. When you rewrite the paper in the third-person plural, give your friend or relative a twin.

PRACTICE 25

Using the free-writing technique to gather ideas and information, write a present tense, third-person singular narrative that has one of the following beginnings.

Underline the subjects once and the verbs twice. (Do not worry about your verbs when you are free-writing. When you revise and rewrite, however, make sure that your subjects and verbs agree.)

> He finds himself at the age of twenty on the outskirts of Chicago with no
> money in his pockets and no relatives or friends to turn to. It is getting dark,
> and he is cold in the early fall air. He is hungry and does not know what to do,
> but he knows he must do something fast, so he . . . .

> She has always believed that somewhere in the world there lives the perfect
> mate for her. One day she finds herself at a small party feeling bored, but when
> she happens to look up toward the door, she sees him standing there alone.
> She knows as she has never known anything so definitely before, that this is
> the right person for her. She gathers her courage and she . . . .

> It is summertime. She is walking along the beach and happens to see an old
> bottle covered with barnacles. As she approaches the bottle, she sees that there
> is a piece of paper, a letter, inside the bottle. She has to break off the end of the
> bottle to get to the letter, and then she reads these words: . . . .

13.10 Review Exercises

REVIEW EXERCISE 1

In the following sentences, underline the subjects and then supply the correct verbs:

1. (is, are) There _____ *are* _____ only a few <u>soldiers</u> determined to hold out.

2. (costs, cost) The Social Security program _____ more than we can afford.

3. (is, are) The most educational programs on television _____ the news and the public broadcasting programs.

4. (wasn't, weren't) The people of your country _____ friendly to the people of our country.

5. (begins, begin) The family _____ each morning with exercises.

6. (lives, live) My friends, who _____ nearby, are always there when I need them.

7. (seems, seem) Eggs, which still _____ cheap, are one of the best foods you can buy.

8. (is, are) For the housewives and househusbands who stay home, there _____ soap operas.

9. (uses, use) A car that _____ a lot of gasoline is often cheap.

10. (has, have) I want representatives in Congress who _____ character.

11. (doesn't, don't) It _____ matter what you do.

12. (becomes, become) The police _____ angry when people are sarcastic to them.

13. (Hasn't, Haven't) _____ those things been said before?

14. (breaks, break) She _____ his serve in the third game.

15. (is, are) Either she or they _____ lying.

16. (costs, cost) Not only the hotel bills but also the flight _____ more this year.

17. (There's, There are) _____ only a few people who know what caused the nuclear disaster.

18. (helps, help) The rain bothers us but _____ the farmers.

19. (does, do) What _____ that expression mean?

20. (doesn't, don't) It _____ seem to matter what witnesses say.

21. (Doesn't, Don't) _____ your father mean anything to you?

REVIEW EXERCISE 2

Edit the following essay correcting all the verb agreement errors by writing the corrections above the line.

Uptown Versus Downtown

I presently live in Jefferson City East, which is known as the uptown area. I have been living uptown for six years and has enjoyed every moment. Before that I lived downtown and hated every moment. Mother worked hard, sometimes at two jobs, to make enough money for us to move. (1 error)

Living uptown is very pleasant. Around my neighborhood there isn't any gang fights. People are friendly and helps one another in time of trouble. I can go to the corner drugstore and not have to worry about being mugged. My mother has peace of mind knowing that neither she nor her children is going to be hurt in the streets. Mother sometimes invite people over to see the house and is not embarrassed by dirty surroundings. (4 errors)

My experience living downtown was quite different. There was gang fights every day. Sometimes in the fights people would get hurt badly or even killed. You was always scared that you would be the next to get hurt. The people in my neighborhood was not friendly at all. A nice drug store was on the corner, but we were scared of the drug addicts who gathered there. My mother was always worried about the danger in the streets; she was afraid her children would get mixed up with the wrong crowd. She was also too embarrassed to invite people to the house because of the crime in the neighborhood. This neighborhood weren't the atmosphere my mother wanted for her children. (4 errors)

These are my reasons for choosing uptown, a better place to live than downtown. I hope I can do for my children what my mother have done for us and keep them away from downtown. (1 error)

REVIEW EXERCISE 3

Using the third person, present time, write an imaginative essay about a typical day in the life of a public figure such as a politician, athlete, musician, or fictional television character. Again, use the free-writing technique to gather ideas and information. Use at least twenty verbs with *-s* or *-es* endings. Underline the subjects once and the verbs twice. You might begin something like this:

J. R. wakes up when the Texas sun shines through the crack in the heavy curtains. He thinks to himself, "Ah, what fool can I swindle today?" He laughs out loud as he thinks of all the jerks in the world . . . .

You may want to write three paragraphs, explaining what the person does in the morning, the afternoon, and the evening.

CHAPTER 14

Verb Tense

14.0 Introduction

In this chapter you will learn the different tenses, or forms, of the more common verbs. Learning the spelling rules, mastering the use of the dictionary, and practicing the irregular constructions will all help you to understand verb use.

A verb is a part of speech that says what a subject is, was, or will be or does, did, or will do. These examples show how two verbs can be used:

TO BE

My grandmother <u>is</u> ninety years old.

My grandmother <u>was</u> ninety years old.

My grandmother <u>will be</u> ninety years old.

My grandmother <u>has been</u> ninety years old for two days now.

My grandmother <u>had been</u> ninety years old for two days before she died.

TO LEAP

The deer <u>leaps</u> over the fence.

The deer <u>leaped</u> over the fence.

The deer <u>will leap</u> over the fence.

The deer <u>has leaped</u> over the fence.

The deer <u>had leaped</u> over the fence before the hunter shot him.

Each of these verb forms has a different meaning. Each refers to a different time: for the state of being, in the case of the grandmother; for the action, in the case of the deer. This distinction in time is called *verb tense*.

Each verb has four principal parts that are used to indicate different tenses. Here are the principal parts of five verbs:

Base Form	Simple Past	Past Participle	Progressive Form
love	loved	loved	loving
walk	walked	walked	walking
have	had	had	having
begin	began	begun	beginning
be	was	been	being

Of these five verbs *love* and *walk* are said to be *regular*. What makes them regular is that you add either *-d* or *-ed* to form both the simple past and the past participle. *Have, begin,* and *be,* on the other hand, are *irregular* because the simple past and the past participle are formed in other ways.

PRACTICE 1

Write the correct form of the designated verb in each of the following sentences. (*Note: drown, seem, ask,* and *plead* are all regular verbs and consequently take *-ed* endings for the simple past and past participle forms.)

1. (*begin*: past participle) I had ___*begun*___ my work before she came in.

2. (*love*: simple past) They _____ one another from the first.

3. (*begin*: progressive form) The headaches were _____ all over again.

4. (*walk*: past participle) That woman was _____ over once too often.

5. (*begin*: base form) You may _____ when you are ready.

6. (*be*: simple past) The family _____ together.

7. (*drown*: past participle) The child had _____ before they got to her.

8. (*seem*: simple past) They _____ like such nice people.

9. (*ask*: past participle) You were _____ to do your part.

10. (*plead*: simple past) They _____ with him to stay away from drugs.

11. (*have*: progressive form) I was _____ a wonderful time.

14.1 Irregular Verbs

A list of the principle parts of many irregular verbs (and a few regular verbs sometimes mistaken for irregular verbs) follows. Try to learn all of the forms as soon as possible. The underlined words remain the same except in the progressive.

Base Form	Simple Past	Past Participle	Progressive Form
arise(s)	arose	arisen	arising
awake(s)	awoke	awakened	awaking
beat(s)	beat	beaten	beating
become(s)	became	become	becoming
begin(s)	began	begun	beginning
bite(s)	bit	bitten	biting
blow(s)	blew	blown	blowing
break(s)	broke	broken	breaking
bring(s)	brought	brought	bringing
build(s)	built	built	building
buy(s)	bought	bought	buying
catch(es)	caught	caught	catching
choose(s)	chose	chosen	choosing
come(s)	came	come	coming
<u>cost(s)</u>	<u>cost</u>	<u>cost</u>	<u>costing</u>
<u>cut(s)</u>	<u>cut</u>	<u>cut</u>	<u>cutting</u>
dig(s)	dug	dug	digging
do(es)	did	done	doing
draw(s)	drew	drawn	drawing
dream(s)	dreamed	dreamed	dreaming
drink(s)	drank	drunk	drinking
drive(s)	drove	driven	driving
drown(s)	drowned	drowned	drowning
eat(s)	ate	eaten	eating
fail(s)	failed	failed	failing
fall(s)	fell	fallen	falling
feel(s)	felt	felt	feeling
fight(s)	fought	fought	fighting

Base Form	Simple Past	Past Participle	Progressive Form
find(s)	found	found	finding
fly(ies)	flew	flown	flying
forget(s)	forgot	forgotten	forgetting
forgive(s)	forgave	forgiven	forgiving
freeze(s)	froze	frozen	freezing
get(s)	got	gotten	getting
go(es)	went	gone	going
grow(s)	grew	grown	growing
hang(s)	hung	hung	hanging
have (has)	had	had	having
hear(s)	heard	heard	hearing
hide(s)	hid	hidden	hiding
<u>hit(s)</u>	<u>hit</u>	<u>hit</u>	<u>hitting</u>
<u>hurt(s)</u>	<u>hurt</u>	<u>hurt</u>	<u>hurting</u>
keep(s)	kept	kept	keeping
know(s)	knew	known	knowing
lay(s) [to put or place something]	laid	laid	laying
lead(s)	led	led	leading
leave(s)	left	left	leaving
lend(s)	lent	lent	lending
<u>let(s)</u>	<u>let</u>	<u>let</u>	<u>letting</u>
lie(s) [to recline]	lay	lain	lying
lose(s)	lost	lost	losing
make(s)	made	made	making
meet(s)	met	met	meeting
pass(es)	passed	passed	passing
pay(s)	paid	paid	paying
plead(s)	pleaded	pleaded	pleading

Base Form	Simple Past	Past Participle	Progressive Form
prove(s)	proved	proven	proving
put(s)	put	put	putting
quit(s)	quit	quit	quitting
raise(s)	raised	raised	raising
read(s)	read	read	reading
ride(s)	rode	ridden	riding
ring(s)	rang	rung	ringing
rise(s)	rose	risen	rising
run(s)	ran	run	running
say(s)	said	said	saying
see(s)	saw	seen	seeing
seem(s)	seemed	seemed	seeming
sell(s)	sold	sold	selling
send(s)	sent	sent	sending
set(s) [to put something down]	set	set	setting
shoot(s)	shot	shot	shooting
sing(s)	sang	sung	singing
sit(s)	sat	sat	sitting
speak(s)	spoke	spoken	speaking
stand(s)	stood	stood	standing
steal(s)	stole	stolen	stealing
stick(s)	stuck	stuck	sticking
swear(s)	swore	sworn	swearing
swim(s)	swam	swum	swimming
take(s)	took	taken	taking
teach(es)	taught	taught	teaching
tear(s)	tore	torn	tearing
tell(s)	told	told	telling
think(s)	thought	thought	thinking

Base Form	Simple Past	Past Participle	Progressive Form
throw(s)	threw	thrown	throwing
wake(s)	woke	wakened	waking
wear(s)	wore	worn	wearing

The Forms of *Be*

The forms of *be* deserve special attention. Here are the principal parts:

BASE FORM

be

SIMPLE PAST

was

PAST PARTICIPLE

been

PROGRESSIVE FORM

being

The present tense is conjugated as follows:

	Singular	Plural
FIRST PERSON	I am	we are
SECOND PERSON	you are	you are
THIRD PERSON	he, she, or it is	they are

The simple past tense is conjugated as follows:

	Singular	Plural
FIRST PERSON	I was	we were
SECOND PERSON	you were	you were
THIRD PERSON	he, she, or it was	they were

PRACTICE 2

Insert the indicated form of the irregular verbs in the following sentences. Check the verbs against the above list.

1. (*break*: past participle) I have __*broken*__ my hand.

2. (*lay*: simple past) Yesterday I _____ my watch on the desk.

3. (*lie*: simple past) I was so tired that I _____ down.

4. (*set*: simple past) He _____ his watch two hours fast.

5. (*lie*: past participle) They had just _____ down when the alarm sounded.

6. (*lay*: past participle) The soldier has _____ down his sword and shield.

7. (*set*: past participle) Congress has _____ us back twenty years.

8. (*drown*: simple past) The little girl almost _____ in the pool.

9. (*cost*: past participle) It has _____ us a lot to live in the city.

10. (*go*: past participle) She has _____ over that with me many times.

11. (*begin*: past participle) We have _____ to see daylight.

12. (*see*: simple past) The instructor _____ to it that we did our work.

13. (*begin*: progressive form) We are _____ a long journey.

14. (*lay*: progressive form) They are _____ their cards on the table.

15. (*hurt*: progressive form) We were always _____ one another.

16. (*break*: present tense) That country _____ its treaties whenever it wishes.

17. (*be*: progressive form) They were _____ most difficult.

18. (*be*: past participle) We had _____ soundly defeated.

19. (*be*: simple past) The bets _____ off.

20. (*be*: present tense) There _____ two remaining candidates left.

21. (*do*: past participle) She has _____ it again.

14.2 The Base Form

The base form of a verb is used in the following ways:

1. To serve as the present tense of a verb:

	Singular	Plural
FIRST PERSON	I love	we love
SECOND PERSON	you love	you love
THIRD PERSON	he, she, or it loves	they love

Note that you add an -*s* to the third-person singular form.

2. To serve as the main verb with the helping verb *do*:

I do love
she does love
they did love

3. To serve as an *infinitive* when introduced by *to:*

    I try to love   she tries to love   they tried to love

    Note: You do not add *-d* or any other ending to the base form of a verb when it is used as an infinitive.

4. To serve as the main verb when used with one of the nine helping verbs called *modals*: *will, would, shall, should, must, can, could, may,* and *might*. Modals show various degrees of possibility or probability. For example:

I will love	I shall love	I can love	I may love
I would love	I should love	I could love	I might love
	I must love		

    Note: You do not add *-d* or any other ending to the base form of a verb when it is used with a modal.

PRACTICE 3

Choose a different modal verb for each of the sentences that follow:

1. Your friends ____*can*____ come if they want to.

2. Jannie _____ ride a rodeo mule.

3. The jacket _____ dry quickly.

4. I really _____ read this text more closely.

5. We _____ adopt a child.

6. If I did not know Herb so well, I _____ think he was crazy.

7. Antonio _____ have his grades by now.

8. It _____ rain this afternoon.

9. You _____ pass this course!

Modal Verbs and Verb Tense

Ordinarily you should use *will, can,* and *may* with present-tense verbs and *would, could,* and *might* with past-tense verbs, as follows:

> You <u>know</u> you <u>will do</u> well in that class. (present tense)
>
> You <u>knew</u> you <u>would do</u> well in that class. (past tense)
>
> He <u>says</u> that I <u>can</u> go to that school. (present tense)
>
> He <u>said</u> that I <u>could</u> go to that school. (past tense)
>
> You <u>may</u> be making a mistake. (present tense)
>
> I <u>told</u> her that she <u>might be</u> making a mistake. (past tense)

Note: The modal *may* and the main verb *be* are written as two separate words, *may be. Maybe* is an adverb, as in "*Maybe* you are right."

PRACTICE 4

Choose the correct modal verb for each of the following:

1. (can, could) When I was young, you ___*could*___ buy a cola for a dime.

2. (can, could) When darkness falls out there, you _____ hear strange sounds in the woods.

3. (can, could) He thought he _____ pass the test, but unfortunately he was wrong.

4. (can, could) I hope you _____ come with us.

5. (can, could) You _____ have knocked me over with a straw.

6. (will, would) Leroy knew that he _____ win some day.

7. (will, would) If we arrive on time, we _____ get the best seats.

8. (will, would) If they had known we were coming, they _____ have hired a band.

9. (will, would) Mother said she _____ give the ring to me when I got married.

10. (will, would) The pants _____ fit when I lose weight.

11. (will, would) I thought we _____ win.

12. (may, might) The president _____ be right about inflation, but many disagree.

13. (may, might) The president _____ have been right about inflation.

14. (may, might) Regina told the dean that she _____ be thinking of another career.

15. (may, might) Students with outside jobs and children to raise _____ not find enough hours in the day to do everything.

16. (may, might) Robert said he _____ write the assigned essay, but then again he _____ not.

14.3 The Simple Past Tense

When you want to write about something that happened in the past—whether a moment ago, a year ago, or a million years ago—you will often use the *simple past tense* of the verb. To form the simple past of regular verbs, add *-d* or *-ed* to the base form:

I <u>love</u> becomes I <u>loved</u>
I <u>walk</u> becomes I <u>walked</u>

If you are in doubt about how to form the simple past for irregular verbs, check the list on pages 319–322 or consult a dictionary. Here are two simple past conjugations:

Seem (Regular)		*Begin (Irregular)*	
I seemed	we seemed	I began	we began
you seemed	you seemed	you began	you began
he, she, or it seemed	they seemed	he, she, or it began	they began

PRACTICE 5

In the first sentence of each pair below, supply the appropriate *present tense* form of the designated verb (remembering to add *-s* or *-es* when necessary); in the second sentence supply the *simple past form*. Use the list of irregular verbs above as necessary.

1. (dress) a. Carlos ___*dresses*___ "fit to kill" every day.

   b. When he was a young man, he ___*dressed*___ "fit to kill."

2. (cut) a. Lee _____ his finger when he chops onions.

   b. But yesterday, he nearly _____ his finger off.

3. (begin) a. Each time I _____ to study, someone interrupts me.

   b. The moment I _____ to study, my daughter came in for a chat.

4. (choose) a. _____ me to represent the class, please.

   b. They said that you _____ me.

5. (read) a. My husband _____ to the children every night.

   b. Last night, he _____ *Tom Sawyer.*

6. (cost) a. Gasoline _____ more each year.

   b. Ten years ago, it hardly _____ anything.

7. (drown) a. David _____ her with his love.

   b. When she rejected him, he _____ himself in tears.

8. (wake) a. When she _____ me, the cat awakes also.

   b. When she _____ me, the cat awoke also.

9. (have) a. Dr. Sanders _____ good attendance in her class.

b. Dr. Sanders _____ good attendance in her class until this semester.

10. (feel) a. I _____ you have been unfair to me.

b. I _____ you were unfair to me.

11. (get) a. Mrs. Joseph _____ up with the birds.

b. But yesterday, she _____ up before the birds.

PRACTICE 6

Applying the instructions for Practice 5 to the pairs of exercises below, supply the correct form of the designated verbs and then complete the sentences:

1. (tear) a. Marlon _____ .

b. When he _____ .

2. (lay) a. When I get ready to study, I _____ .

b. When I got ready to study, I _____ .

3. (say) a. Grandfather _____ .

b. Grandfather once _____ .

4. (ask) a. I _____ .

b. One time I _____ .

5. (use) a. They _____ .

b. In those days, my sisters _____ .

6. (look) a. Cindy _____ .

b. Two years ago Cindy _____ .

7. (quit) a. I _____ .

b. Afterwards I _____ .

8. (hit) a. Kirby _____ .

b. Kirby later _____ .

9. (begin) a. When you get older, you _____ .

b. When she got older, she _____ .

10. (plead) a. The lawyer _____ .

b. Yesterday, the lawyer _____ .

Past Tense Endings

When writing verbs in the simple past, it is often necessary to double the final letter before adding -*ed*:

<u>hum</u> becomes <u>hummed</u>

<u>refer</u> becomes <u>referred</u>

<u>stop</u> becomes <u>stopped</u>

<u>commit</u> becomes <u>committed</u>

Before doubling the final letter, make sure the verb meets the following tests:

1. The final letter is a consonant, not a vowel (*a, e, i, o,* or *u*) and not *y*. The above verbs, for example, end in *m, r, p,* and *t*.
2. The final letter is preceded by a single vowel (not a double vowel and not a consonant). This is true of all of the above examples. What are the vowels that precede the final consonants?
3. The word is either one syllable *or* the accent is on the last syllable. *Hum* and *stop* are both one-syllable words; *refer* and *commit* are both accented on the last syllable. We say:

comMIT, not COMmit

reFER, not REfer

Travel, however, is pronounced TRAvel. Thus, the simple past is *traveled*. Likewise, the simple past of *happen* is *happened*.

PRACTICE 7

Applying the three rules above, tell why you do *not* double the final letter of the following words to form the simple past:

1. help _____

2. loom _____

3. enjoy _____

4. differ _____

5. return _____

PRACTICE 8

Form the simple past of the following verbs:

1. (enjoy) Mary _____ my company those many years.

2. (prefer) Clarence said that he _____ meat and potatoes.

3. (gas) We stopped at the pump and _____ up the car.

4. (step) They ＿＿＿＿＿＿ up their passing attack in the third quarter.

5. (suppose) Chou told me that he ＿＿＿＿＿＿ he would study medicine.

6. (hum) Granny ＿＿＿＿＿＿ me to sleep every night.

7. (counsel) My advisor ＿＿＿＿＿＿ me not to take any more subjects.

Verbs That End in *-y*

To form the simple past of verbs that end in *-y preceded by a consonant*, change the *-y* to *-i* and add *-ed:*

> cry becomes cried
> apply becomes applied
> marry becomes married

For verbs that end in *-y preceded by a vowel*, just add *-ed* without changing the *-y:*

> enjoy becomes enjoyed
> journey becomes journeyed
> obey becomes obeyed
> employ becomes employed

Note: If you add *-ing* to a verb that ends in *-y*, you do not change the *-y: fry* becomes *frying.*

PRACTICE 9

Form the simple past of the following verbs:

1. (cry) She ＿＿＿＿＿＿ a river of tears over me.

2. (fry) They ＿＿＿＿＿＿ it in bacon grease.

3. (obey) Hartford always ＿＿＿＿＿＿ his mother.

4. (marry) They ＿＿＿＿＿＿ when they were much too young.

5. (bury) Kahn ＿＿＿＿＿＿ the coin in the yard.

14.4 The Past Participle

The *past participle* is the verb form that is used with the helping verbs *have, has,* and *had* to form the *perfect tenses* and with *am, are, is, was,* and *were* to form the *passive voice.*

The Past Participle with *Have, Has,* and *Had*

If a past-tense verb is written as one word, it is called the *simple past.* Other past tense constructions are formed with *have, has,* and *had.* The main verb in such constructions is called a *past participle.* To form the past participle of regular verbs, add *-d* or *-ed* to the base form:

> love becomes has loved, have loved, or had loved
>
> walk becomes has walked, have walked, or had walked

Note that the simple past and the past participle of regular verbs are formed in the same way: I *loved* and I *have loved.*

If you are in doubt about how to form a past participle for an irregular verb, check the list on pages 319–322 or consult a dictionary. Here are two sample conjugations:

Join (Regular)

PRESENT PERFECT	I have joined	we have joined
	you have joined	you have joined
	he, she, or it has joined	they have joined
PAST PERFECT	I had joined	we had joined
	you had joined	you had joined
	he, she, or it had joined	they had joined

Begin (Irregular)

PRESENT PERFECT	I have begun	we have begun
	you have begun	you have begun
	he, she, or it has begun	they have begun
PAST PERFECT	I had begun	we had begun
	you had begun	you had begun
	he, she, or it had begun	they had begun

PRACTICE 10

Supply the past participles of the designated irregular verbs in the sentences below. (If necessary, consult the list on pages 319–322.) Notice how *have* and *has* are used differently from *had.*

1. (teach) Mother had already _____**taught**_____ me how to read when I began school.

2. (rise) The sun had _____ before I arose.

3. (begin) I have _____ to develop a taste for sweets.

4. (choose) You have _____ well.

5. (sit) I have _____ in that English class one semester too many.

6. (come) It has _____ to a showdown.

7. (become) He wanted to know what had _____ of them.

8. (run) Richard had _____ completely out of money before he got that job.

9. (quit) He had _____ before he was fired.

10. (put) Tom has _____ his money where his mouth is.

11. (hit) Hurricane Gracie has _____ with all her force.

12. (lead) Debra had _____ a proper life before she met Lewis.

13. (lay) He has _____ down his sword and shield.

14. (lie) We have _____ down to rest from our labors.

15. (ring) They have not _____ that church bell for ninety years.

16. (begin) He has _____ to get a little deaf.

17. (seem) It has _____ that way to me for a long time.

18. (involve) Marcia has not _____ others in her project.

19. (go) They had _____ before we had a chance to say good-by.

20. (do) If you had _____ your project correctly the first time, you would not be in this difficulty.

21. (see) Dr. Laska has _____ me before.

When to Use *Have, Has,* and *Had*

Have and *has* are used as helping verbs to form the *present perfect tense,* which shows either of the following:

1. Action that was begun in the past but continues into the present:

    He <u>has begun</u> to get a little deaf. (The deafness came on him in the past and is still with him.)

    Georgia <u>has decided</u> to go to college. (She made her decision to go to college in the past, and the decision still stands.)

2. Action that was completed in the *recent* past:

    I <u>have spoken</u> to her about the bill. (The speaker has *just* spoken to her about the bill.)

Had is used as a helping verb to form the *past perfect tense,* which shows action that began in the past and ended in the past:

He <u>had begun</u> to get a little deaf, but <u>he</u> <u>hears</u> perfectly well now. (At some point in the past deafness came on him, but it ended in the past.)

<u>Georgia</u> <u>had decided</u> to go to college, but then <u>she</u> <u>met</u> Philip. (Georgia's decision to go to college was made in the past, but after Philip came into her life she changed her mind.)

Note: Many students overuse *had* in their writing. When you do use *had*, be sure it is necessary. The simple past will often work just as well.

PRACTICE 11

In the first sentence of each pair below, supply either *have* or *has* and the correct past participle. In the second sentence supply *had* and the correct past participle.

1. (love)   a. I **have loved** and lost many times.

   b. I _____**had**_____ _____**loved**_____ and lost many times, but then I met you.

2. (happen)   a. It _____ _____ before and will probably happen again.

   b. It _____ _____ once too often; I called the police.

3. (legalize)   a. The legislatures _____ _____ it in some states.

   b. The legislatures _____ _____ it, but then they discovered that the situation became worse.

4. (guess)   a. I _____ _____ the correct answer.

   b. I thought I _____ _____ the right answer, but, as usual, I was wrong.

5. (finish)   a. I _____ _____ my work.

   b. I thought I _____ _____ my work, but then I found out I had two more assignments.

6. (build)   a. The British _____ _____ a ship that will not sink.

   b. The British said they _____ _____ a ship that would not sink, but when it hit an iceberg it sank quickly.

PRACTICE 12

Using the sentences in Practice 11 as models, compose pairs of sentences in which you first use *have* or *has* with the past participle of the designated verb and then use *had* with the same past participle:

1. (break) a. *I have broken my finger.*
   b. *I thought I had broken my finger, but it is fine.*
2. (lift) a. _____
   b. _____
3. (begin) a. _____
   b. _____
4. (show) a. _____
   b. _____
5. (find) a. _____
   b. _____
6. (set) a. _____
   b. _____
7. (lie) a. _____
   b. _____
8. (lay) a. _____
   b. _____
9. (become) a. _____
   b. _____

Have, Has, and *Had* in Stories

When telling a story in the present tense, use *have* or *has*. When telling a story in the past tense, use *had*. For example:

He says he has lost his way. (present)
He said he had lost his way. (past)

PRACTICE 13

The following sentences are written in the present tense. Rewrite them in the past tense, changing not only *have* and *has* but other verbs as well. Remember, infinitives do not change in form when the tense changes.

1. I have *had* been shy most of my life.

2. In college I still keep to myself because I have made no friends.

3. However, I soon get to know Dr. Rosen, a drama instructor, who has taken a liking to me.

4. She has been put in charge of a school play and asks me to play an important role.

5. I can soon say that I have made many friends among the cast.

6. I have a lot to thank her for.

The Past Participle with *Am, Is, Are, Was,* and *Were*

So far you have been studying verbs in the *active voice*, that is, verbs that tell what the subject is or does in the present, past, or future:

> subj   obj
> The girl pushes the car.

Girl is the subject because she is what the sentence is about, *pushes* is the verb because it tells what the girl does, and *car* is the object because it receives the action. In the *passive voice*, however, the subject and object are reversed:

> subj   obj
> The car is pushed by the girl.

Now the subject is *car*, but instead of doing something, the car receives the action. *Girl* becomes the object of the preposition *by*.

To form the passive voice:

1. Use some form of the *be* verb as a helper, usually *am, are, is, was,* or *were*. (On occasion, *get* can take the passive voice, as in "She got married last year.")
2. Use the past participle of the main verb. For irregular forms consult the list on pages 319–322 or a dictionary.

Here are two sample conjugations in the passive voice:

Suppose (Regular)

PRESENT PASSIVE	I am supposed	we are supposed
	you are supposed	you are supposed
	he, she, or it is supposed	they are supposed
PAST PASSIVE	I was supposed	we were supposed
	you were supposed	you were supposed
	he, she, or it was supposed	they were supposed

Understand (Irregular)

PRESENT PASSIVE	I am understood	we are understood
	you are understood	you are understood
	he, she, or it is understood	they are understood

PAST PASSIVE	I was understood	we were understood
	you were understood	you were understood
	he, she, or it was understood	they were understood

PRACTICE 14

Change the following from the active to the passive voice. The object will become the subject. Either make the subject the object of a prepositional phrase beginning with *by* or, if this is awkward, omit it altogether.

1. They built the bridge to withstand hurricanes. *The bridge was built by them to withstand hurricanes.*

2. They tear my shirt every time I play football. _____

3. They tore my shirt every time I played football. _____

4. The glass split his knee wide open. _____

5. They built their house upon a rock. _____

6. The Jackson Five first sang that song. _____

When to Use the Passive Voice

Avoid overusing the passive voice in your writing. Ordinarily, your sentences are stronger when your subjects act themselves instead of being acted upon. If you want to say that Hans read the play *Julius Caesar*, write:

Hans read *Julius Caesar*.

instead of

Julius Caesar was read by Hans.

If you want to say that the bank cashes your checks, write:

The bank cashes my checks.

instead of

My checks are cashed by the bank.

However, when the receiver of the action is more important than the doer of the action, you may need to use the passive voice. For example:

She was mugged right outside the grocery store. (The writer is calling attention to the person who was mugged, not to the unknown mugger.)

Ali was finally beaten in the ring. (The writer is calling attention to the long-time boxing champion, not to the person who defeated him.)

PRACTICE 15

The passive voice is appropriately used in the following sentences. Supply the correct past participle, using the list on pages 319–322 for irregular forms.

1. (suppose) You are _*supposed*_ to spend no more than an hour on the test.

2. (write) It is _____ that you should love one another.

3. (use) They were _____ to his being late all the time.

4. (swear) I was then _____ in before the judge.

5. (hurt) My finger was _____ when I fell from the roof.

6. (say) It is _____ that I am a fine cook.

7. (drive) Alvina was _____ crazy by the gossip before she left her job.

8. (know) Nantucket is _____ as "The Gray Lady."

9. (use) But I will never get _____ to having five children.

10. (freeze) The lakes were _____ over.

11. (set) My alarm clock is _____ to go off at five.

PRACTICE 16

The passive voice is inappropriately used in the following sentences. Rewrite them in the active voice.

1. What you have done is greatly appreciated by me. _I greatly appreciate what you have done._

2. The supplies were really needed by us. _____

3. The money will be used by them to buy a car. _____

4. The doctor was called by her father. _____

5. His lecture was understood by me. _____

_____

6. The various verb forms have been carefully learned by you. _____

_____

14.5 The Progressive Form

You have studied three parts of the verb: the base form, the simple past, and the past participle. The fourth part of the verb is the *progressive form*, which is used to show continuing action either in the present or in the past. For example:

I love becomes I am loving or I was loving

I walk becomes I am walking or I was walking

The general rule for constructing the progressive form is to add *-ing* to the base form of the verb or, if the verb ends in *-e*, to drop the *-e* and add *-ing*. Here are two sample conjugations:

Walk

PRESENT PROGRESSIVE	I am walking	we are walking
	you are walking	you are walking
	he, she, or it is walking	they are walking

PAST PROGRESSIVE	I was walking	we were walking
	you were walking	you were walking
	he, she, or it was walking	they were walking

Write

PRESENT PROGRESSIVE	I am writing	we are writing
	you are writing	you are writing
	he, she, or it is writing	they are writing

PAST PROGRESSIVE	I was writing	we were writing
	you were writing	you were writing
	he, she, or it was writing	they were writing

But note the following exceptions to the general rule for constructing the progressive form:

1. Do not drop the *-e* when the verb ends in double *-e:*

see becomes seeing

flee becomes fleeing

2. Do not drop the *-e* in *singe* and *dye:*

> <u>singe</u> becomes <u>singeing</u>
>
> <u>dye</u> becomes <u>dyeing</u>

3. For verbs that end in *-ie*, drop the *-i* and the *-e*, and add *-y* + *-ing:*

> <u>lie</u> becomes <u>lying</u>
>
> <u>die</u> becomes <u>dying</u>
>
> <u>vie</u> becomes <u>vying</u>

4. For one-syllable verbs (or verbs that are accented on the last syllable) that end in a consonant preceded by a single vowel, double the final consonant before adding *-ing:*

> <u>hum</u> becomes <u>humming</u>
>
> <u>begin</u> becomes <u>beginning</u>
>
> <u>occur</u> becomes <u>occurring</u>
>
> <u>quiz</u> becomes <u>quizzing</u>

5. Do not drop the *-y* when the verb ends in *-y:*

> <u>fry</u> becomes <u>frying</u>
>
> <u>say</u> becomes <u>saying</u>

If you are in any doubt as to whether you should drop an *-e* or double a letter before adding *-ing*, consult your dictionary.

PRACTICE 17

Supply the progressive form of the designated verb below. Be sure to use the right tense. Remember, the present progressive is used with present tense verbs; the past progressive is used with past tense verbs.

1. (look) You _____*are looking*_____ very handsome these days.

2. (begin) We left because we _____*were beginning*_____ to wear out our welcome.

3. (help) She _____ me when Mrs. Malloy walked in.

4. (ask) The paper says they _____ five thousand dollars for their car.

5. (quiz) Dr. Ward _____ us on that material tomorrow.

6. (dye) I _____ my shoes when I accidentally spilled the boiling water on myself.

7. (travel) We _____ in Europe when we heard the news.

8. (lie) The old man _____ face down on the sidewalk when they found him.

9. (lay) I _____ down my sword and shield and will practice war no more.

10. (say) Now that we are in the second week of the play, she _____ her lines perfectly.

11. (hit) She became so angry that she _____ everything in sight.

12. (begin) I _____ to think I couldn't write, but then I gained confidence in myself.

14.6 Using the Dictionary for Verbs

Any time you are in doubt as to what a particular verb form is, look it up in the dictionary. A dictionary appropriate for college use will give you the parts of irregular and troublesome verbs. Suppose, for example, you look up the verb *break* (the base form). To find the various parts of the verb, first make sure you have located a verb. Verbs are designated *v* or *vb*, *vt* or *tr* (transitive verbs—those that take objects), or *vi* or *intr* (intransitive verbs—those that do not take objects). Nouns are marked *n*.

In a medium-length dictionary, you will probably see the following entry:

break (brāk) *vt.* **broke, broken, breaking**

> *break* is the base form
> (brāk) is the pronunciation
> *broke* is the simple past
> *broken* is the past participle
> *breaking* is the progressive form

In a more complete dictionary, you may see an entry like this:

break (brāk) *vt.* **broke** *or Archaic* **brake, broken, breaking, breaks**

> *brake* is an alternative for *broke* but is no longer in use
> *breaks* is the third-person singular, present-tense form

If you are given a choice of using one simple past over another, one past participle over another, or one progressive form over another, always choose the first alternative. Choose *broke*, for example, over *brake*.

In looking up a regular verb like *love* or *walk* in a medium-sized dictionary, you probably will not see any parts of the verb listed. This means that all constructions are regular: That is, you add *-d* or *-ed* to the base form for both the simple past and the past participle, and you add *-ing* to the base form for the progressive form. (If the verb ends in *-e*, you drop the *-e* and add *-ing* to construct the progressive form.)

If you look up the irregular verb *bring* in a medium-sized dictionary, you probably will see the following:

bring (brĭng) *vt.* **brought**, **bringing**

> *bring* is the base form
> *brought* is both the simple past and the past participle
> *bringing* is the progressive form

Here are two other examples of irregular verbs from a medium-sized dictionary.

hit (hit) *vt.* **hit**, **hitting**

> *hit* is the base form
> *hit* is both the simple past and past participle
> *hitting* is the progressive form

counsel (koun's'l) *vt.* **counseled** or **counselled**, **counseling** or **counselling**

> *counsel* is the base form
> *counseled* and *counselled* are two alternatives for both the simple past and the past participle (if you have a choice, use the first)
> *counseling* and *counselling* are two alternatives for the progressive form (if you have a choice, use the first)

PRACTICE 18

Find the base form of the following verbs in a dictionary and write the other three parts of the verb in the designated blanks.

Base Form	Simple Past	Past Participle	Progressive Form
1. creep	*crept*	*crept*	*creeping*
2. weave			
3. mow			
4. bend			
5. shine (to give light)			

6. forbid _____ _____ _____

7. shoulder _____ _____ _____

8. hang (to execute) _____ _____ _____

9. harken _____ _____ _____

10. happen _____ _____ _____

11. spay _____ _____ _____

14.7 Avoiding Tense Shifts

Ordinarily you write in either the present tense or the past tense, but not in both. For example, you write:

> She says she pushes the car while her father watches.

or

> She said she pushed the car while her father watched.

but not

> She says she pushed the car while her father watches.

Note: Will and *can* are ordinarily used with present-tense verbs, while *could* and *would* are ordinarily used with past-tense verbs. For example:

> The president is going to veto the budget so that he can get more money for defense. (present tense)
>
> The president vetoed the budget so that he could get more money for defense. (past tense)
>
> He says he can eventually get the appropriation. (present tense)
>
> He said he could get the appropriation, but it failed. (past tense)

PRACTICE 19

In the following sentences, some of the verbs are in the present, some in the simple past. Write them all in the simple past.

1. They ~~surprise~~ *surprised* us when they came to our school.

2. When I was young, I use to tear the heads off my sister's paper dolls.

3. She got so mad that she turns red.

4. They always dress up when they went out to eat.

5. We work, we work, and we work, but we got nowhere.

6. When we return, we freed the prisoners.

7. My wife said you advertise a car in the morning paper.

8. They acted as if they have never seen a young lady before.

9. Maria said that she will study harder this semester.

10. The president told the nation that he can balance the budget.

11. We come home after the war, just as we said we will.

PRACTICE 20

The following student narrative is written in the present tense. Rewrite it in the past tense. Don't change verbs inside the direct quotation, and don't change infinitives (phrases like *to have* and *to see*).

A Christmas to Remember

It is a cold, rainy Christmas morning The year is 1977. For some reason, I know once I get out of bed that this Christmas is going to change my life.
[handwritten corrections above the line: "was" over "is"; "was" over "is"; "knew" over "know"; "got" over "get"; "was" over "is"]

The morning goes by slowly because everybody is complaining about everything. But the fussing really starts when a strange man I have never seen before comes by to see me. I am puzzled, but my mother knows him. Everybody thinks he is one of my boyfriends, although he is twice as old as I am. My mother doesn't say a word.

When I go into the kitchen to get away from everyone, my father, Sidney, follows and starts telling me that the man is entirely too old for me and that I should find a boyfriend my own age. That is the last straw. We throw harsh words at each other. I tell him that he is as crazy as he looks, and he tells me that I am headed for trouble. I become very upset.

When I go back in the living room, Momma and the man are just sitting there looking at each other. Tears roll down my mother's face as she looks at tears rolling down my face. One reason that I am so upset is that this strange man and Momma keep looking at every move I make. Finally, I can take it no longer, and I turn to the strange man and ask who in the world he is. The man, whom my mother calls Robert, turns toward me, gets up slowly, and tells me that he is my real father. The whole family begins to laugh.

I am very shocked and can't say a word. My mother cries some more and says, "Don't laugh, because it is true. Robert is Roberta's father." I will never forget that face and those words. I run out of the house and into the carport and weep. My mother then comes out to talk to me, but I have nothing to say to her because I am ashamed and hurt. I can't bring myself to face my brothers and sisters, and I certainly can't bring myself to face Sidney. I love him so much.

But things work out just fine after that day. We go on with our lives, although I feel funny for a long time. I tell my mother and Sidney that I never want to see that man again, that Sidney is my father, not Robert.

PRACTICE 21

The student essay on page 43 entitled "The Road of My Life" is written in the present tense. Rewrite it in the past tense.

PRACTICE 22

Write a three-paragraph paper (in the past tense) telling what you did in the morning, afternoon, and evening of one particular day. You may choose either a typical day or an unusual day. Proofread carefully to make sure the past tense is used correctly. You might begin your paper something like this:

> One morning during my senior year in high school, I woke up while it was still dark. I heard the sound of someone walking through the house. I got up and . . .

PRACTICE 23

Complete one of the free-writing assignments on page 45. Do not worry about using your tenses correctly while you are free writing. But as you revise and rewrite, make sure your verbs are in the past tense. (If you have already written one of these assignments in the present tense, simply rewrite it in the past tense.)

14.8 Verbals: Infinitives, Participles, and Gerunds

Verbals are words that come from verbs but are used as adjectives, adverbs, and nouns. There are three kinds of verbals: infinitives, participles, and gerunds. Like verbs, verbals sometimes take objects.

Infinitives

The *infinitive*, which is introduced by *to*, is the same as the base form of the verb. It can be used as a noun, adjective, or adverb:

To live is to grow. (These two infinitives are used as nouns, the first as a subject, the other as a predicate nominative.)

There must be another way to solve that problem. (This infinitive phrase is used as an adjective modifying *way*. Within the infinitive phrase, *problem* is the object of *to solve*.)

Sandra came out to say good-by. (This infinitive phrase is used as an adverb modifying *came out*. Within the infinitive phrase, *good-by* is the object of *to say*.)

Keep the following in mind when using infinitives:

1. The form of the infinitive does not change when the tenses change. Even when writing in the past tense, you do not add a *-d* or *-ed* to the infinitive:

   I did not like to walk those long distances when I was in the army.

2. When an infinitive or an infinitive phrase is the subject in present-tense constructions, use the third-person singular verb:

   To jog the entire distance requires months of training.

   Of course, if you use two or more infinitives as subjects, you need to use a plural verb:

   To live and to love were the two things he asked.

3. As a general rule, do not split infinitives. Choose:

   It is not always easy to like the one you love.

   instead of

   It is not easy to always like the one you love.

PRACTICE 24

Compose sentences using the following infinitives as subjects:

1. (to love) *To love others does not come easy to our friend.*

2. (to succeed) _____

   _____

3. (to read and to fish) _____

   _____

4. (*to spend*) _____

_____

5. (*to understand the Russians*) _____

_____

6. (*to make me happy*) _____

_____

7. (*to have seen*) _____

_____

Participles

The *present participle* is the same as the progressive form of the main verb and is constructed with an *-ing* ending. The *past participle* used as a verbal is the same past participle you have been studying. It often ends in *-ed*.

Present Participle	*Past Participle*
seeing	seen
beginning	begun
loving	loved
prejudicing	prejudiced
handicapping	handicapped
shocking	shocked

Both the present and past participles can be used as adjectives:

It was a <u>disturbing</u> day at the bank. (The present participle modifies the noun *day*.)

<u>Seeing what happened</u>, the boy pulled out his cap pistol. (The present-participle phrase modifies the subject *boy*. *What happened* is the object of the participle *seeing*.)

<u>Shocked</u>, the robber handed over the money to the boy. (The past participle modifies the subject *robber*.)

<u>Satisfied</u>, the boy put his pistol back in his pocket. (The past participle modifies the subject *boy*.)

PRACTICE 25

Supply the correct participle of the designated verb in each of the following sentences:

1. (see) *Seeing* Sandra ahead, he walked as fast as he could to catch up with her.

2. (love) Although _____ by her parents, the child still had severe emotional problems.

3. (begin) Having _____ the climb to Long's Peak, we were determined to finish.

4. (shock) _____ at the news, his parents broke down in tears.

5. (begin) _____ again, we picked up our packs and moved on.

PRACTICE 26

Using the sentences in Practice 25 as models, compose sentences using the following participles:

1. (determined to win) *Determined to win, the Saints made two touchdowns in the final quarter.*

2. (prejudiced by their ignorance) _____

3. (finally beaten) _____

4. (having begun) _____

5. (shocked by the news) _____

6. (singing to herself) _____

7. (believing in herself) _____

8. (praised by all) _____

9. (crawling the last mile) _____

Gerunds

The *gerund* is formed like a present participle, but it is always used as a noun:

Copyright © 1987 Houghton Mifflin Company

subj   pred nom

<u>Seeing</u> is not always <u>believing</u>. (The first gerund is the subject; the second is a predicate nominative.)

subj

<u>Living the good life</u> was no longer possible for him. (The gerund phrase is the subject of *was*. *Life* is the object of the gerund *living*.)

obj

To my way of <u>thinking</u>, he is a fool! (The gerund is the object of the preposition *of*.)

subj   subj

Are <u>fishing</u> and <u>hunting</u> what you enjoy most? (Since two gerunds serve as the subject, a plural verb is necessary.)

PRACTICE 27

Supply the correct gerunds of the designated verbs in the following sentences:

1. (shock) Dr. Khan enjoys __*shocking*__ everyone in her biology class.

2. (begin) In the _____, God created the heavens and the earth.

3. (do, be) _____ is _____.

4. (give) We reached an agreement without our _____ in.

5. (wait) They like _____ on us.

PRACTICE 28

First underline the subject or subjects in each sentence below, and then choose the correct verb:

1. (make, makes) <u>Facing all those dishes</u> __*makes*__ A. J. wish he was not so liberated.

2. (are, is) Seeing the sun rise over the Cumberland Hills _____ something that has great meaning for me.

3. (are, is) To work hard, to play hard, and to have a cooperative family _____ what I want most in life.

4. (are, is) To be or not to be _____ the question.

5. (are, is) Skating, fishing, and playing tennis _____ my favorite sports.

6. (prepare, prepares) Working hard in English and math _____ you for college.

14.9 Review Exercises

REVIEW EXERCISE 1

The following sentences are written in the present tense. Rewrite them in the simple past. Some sentences will require two or more changes in tense.

1. Florence minds the children while John travels to Europe.
   minded ... *traveled*
2. The wise men journey on their way.
3. They fry the fish as soon as they catch them.
4. She tries to do everything her father asks her to do.
5. Johnson visits me when I am sick.
6. He says that one person can make a difference.
7. After they walk away, they just vanish from my life.
8. What I like best about the play is the scenery.
9. They bus the children to school from the next county.
10. They train for months before the season starts.
11. He lies to me about this and that.
12. Mrs. Sanchez snaps at us when we are misbehaving.
13. For the first time in his life, he breaks down and cries when he hears the news.
14. They prefer to fly rather than to drive.
15. We forget that communist countries might differ a lot from each other.
16. They cherish their children and tend to them gently.
17. The preacher says that God caused Scripture to be written.
18. I apply for that job at least once a year.
19. Joe finishes shaving and combs his hair.
20. It suddenly occurs to the senator that he is mistaken.
21. They never fly if they can avoid it.

REVIEW EXERCISE 2

Correct the verb errors and the shifts in tense in the following student essay.

Two Children—Two People

I am the mother of two fine children. I have been bless with a child of each sex. My daughter, Corinne, is seventeen years old and thinks she is a woman of the world. Will, my son, is fourteen. He has suddenly discover a light brown mustache, deep voice, and girls! Although I love my children dearly, I sometimes wonder how they can be brother and sister; they are so different. (2 verb errors)

Attitudes about the value of money in our home are most interesting. Will is very concern about cash at all times. He keeps both his hard-earned money and his birthday money locked in the top drawer of his dresser. He is know in our home as one who is "tight with a buck." When you ask him for a loan of perhaps one dollar, he may or may not give it to you. We are wondering when he will start charging us interest on each dollar we borrow. Corinne, on the other hand, still has uncashed checks earned from her job at Walgreen's dating back to July, 1983. She does not realize that she has not cash them. When one walks through Corinne's bedroom, one sees nickles, dimes, and quarters that are spreaded all over the dresser, desk, and night table. One thing is true about Corinne, though: She cheerfully lends you money and is anything but a miser. (4 verb errors)

Entering Will's bedroom is a pleasure. Everything has a place. Books are pile neatly on the desk; the bed is rarely unmade. The closet is always very well organize, with clothes hung up and shoes lined up in a neat row. Will is a systematic and methodical young man, and his room speaks for his neatness. Corinne's room, on the other hand, is mass confusion. Shoes are everywhere. Clothes are hung over chairs and laying on the bed, which, by the way, is hardly ever made. It would not surprise me to find an old apple core under the bed. That's Corinne for you; she is disorganized but very relaxed. (3 verb errors)

Will's and Corinne's personalities are like the sun and the moon. Will is extremely quiet and basically a loner, with only one or two close friends. Corinne was just the opposite. She always has had an effervescent personality. She felt immediately at ease with strangers and has had many friends. Despite their differences, however, my two children have one important thing in common: They really care deeply for each other.

It is my hope that they will continue to care for one another for the rest of their lives. (2 shifts in tense)

REVIEW EXERCISE 3

Write an imaginative essay describing what a typical day (or a special day) in your life would be like if you were a public figure such as a politician, a great musician, a well-known athlete, or a fictional television character. Write the essay in the past tense. When you finish, underline the subjects once and verbs twice. Be sure that you have used all verbs correctly. You may want to write three paragraphs explaining what you did in the morning, the afternoon, and the evening. You could begin something like this:

My wife Nancy called to me from the shower, "Ronald, you have slept too long." I stumbled out of bed, opened the curtains, and saw that the sun had just begun to rise the capitol. I hollered back to Nancy, "It sure is hard to run a country!" I would have slept until twelve if Nancy had not wakened me. As I dressed, I thought about the Russians and how I hoped they would not bother us today because today was going to be a special day. . . .

CHAPTER 15

More Practice Using Verbs

15.0 Introduction

This chapter contains additional explanations and practice for correcting subject-verb agreement and verb-tense errors.

Standard and Nonstandard Verbs

If you are still having difficulty with verbs, do not despair. Many students have great trouble mastering standard verbs. Usually the problem arises because these students are used to hearing and speaking nonstandard verb forms. When they are asked to write standard forms, they have to use verbs that do not sound right to them. Then they start overcorrecting and making errors they did not make before. If you have this problem, you *can* master standard verb forms, but you will probably need a lot of practice. This chapter is designed to give you that practice with subject-verb agreement and verb tense.

15.1 Subject-Verb Agreement

If you are confused about when to add the final -*s* to a verb and when to leave it off, be sure that you first know the easier subject-verb constructions. Review the conjugations of the regular verbs *love* and *carry*:

	Singular	*Plural*
FIRST PERSON	I love	we love
SECOND PERSON	you love	you love
THIRD PERSON	he, she, or it loves	they love

	Singular	*Plural*
FIRST PERSON	I carry	we carry
SECOND PERSON	you carry	you carry
THIRD PERSON	he, she, or it carries	they carry

You can see immediately that if your subject is *I, you, we,* or *they,* you form the verb without the *-s.* Of course, you must first be able to identify the verb. To do this, ask what your subject *is* or *does.*

Now review the conjugation of *have:*

	Singular	*Plural*
FIRST PERSON	I have	we have
SECOND PERSON	you have	you have
THIRD PERSON	he, she, or it has	they have

Notice that the verb *have* is regular, like the other two shown above. The only difference is that the third-person singular of *have* is *has,* not *haves.* But for *I, you, we,* and *they,* the correct form is always *have.*

Finally, review the conjugation of *do:*

	Singular	*Plural*
FIRST PERSON	I do (don't)	we do (don't)
SECOND PERSON	you do (don't)	you do (don't)
THIRD PERSON	he, she, or it does (doesn't)	they do (don't)

The verb *do* is also regular, except for the third-person singular which is *does* (or *doesn't*).

PRACTICE 1

In the following sentences underline the subjects once and the verbs twice. Using the four conjugations above as models, determine whether the subjects and verbs agree. If they do not agree, change the verbs to correct the sentence.

1. We refuse their money and we ~~keeps~~ keep our pride.

2. You say you love your country, but you acts in a different way.

3. I says to myself, "Bingo, you're in trouble again."

4. They like our country, but they just loves our tourists.

5. We in the dancing troupe does our best.

6. I don't care what we do, I don't care what you do, and I don't care what they do, but I do care about what He (God) do.

7. They, in their own way, loves their children.

8. They seems to know what they believe.

9. We carries a heavy burden, but we don't complain.

10. As for shoes, they costs more each year.

11. Haven't they had enough trouble for a while?

12. You and your family has to pay attention.

13. Hasn't those summer days been beautiful?

14. You have my trust, and I have your trust.

15. We surely has a lot to be thankful for.

16. We asks and we do receive.

15.2 Third-Person Endings

Making verbs agree with subjects is more complicated when the subjects are in the third person. For example, which of the following forms do you use?

loves *or* love carries *or* carry does *or* do (doesn't *or* don't)
has *or* have

If the pronoun subject is *he*, *she*, or *it*, you always use the form with the *-s* ending:

he loves	he carries	he does (doesn't)	he has
she loves	she carries	she does (doesn't)	she has
it loves	it carries	it does (doesn't)	it has

If the pronoun subject is *they*, you always use the form without the *-s* ending:

they love they carry they do (don't) they have

But what form do you use when the subject is not a pronoun (that is, not *he*, *she*, *it*, or *they*) but a noun? Which of the following is standard?

Robin Hood robs	or	Robin Hood rob
the house costs	or	the house cost
the cat doesn't	or	the cat don't
the people lives	or	the people live
Mary and Will sees	or	Mary and Will see

To decide which verb form to use, all you need to do is to ask yourself if the subject is one or more than one. If the subject is one, use the verb with the *-s* ending. If the subject is more than one, use the verb without the *-s* ending, as follows:

Robin Hood (one) robs
the house (one) costs
the cat (one) doesn't
the people (more than one) live
Mary and Will (more than one) see

PRACTICE 2

Read each of the following sentences carefully. If the subject is singular, write *S* above it. If the subject is plural, write *P* above it. Change the verbs to agree with the subjects. (One sentence is correct.)

1. The police ~~asks~~ him for his license, and he ~~give~~ it to them.
2. Mary don't like to discipline her mischievous little boy.
3. Her husband try out the merchandise before he buys it.
4. What interest me most about New York is Central Park.
5. She clean her house while her daughters just sits around.
6. It don't cost as much this year.
7. Mia fix her van just as good as new.
8. Let me tell you about all the things she do for me.
9. The government employs a lot of people at the navy yard.
10. If Stan push me again, he is going to regret it.
11. In the summer Ferdinand sleeps, eats, and watch a lot of television.
12. Each time the class sings, the music teacher ask me please not to sing.
13. The people comes running and climb down the bank toward me.
14. Mama Linda is very loving and care a lot for lonely children.
15. If the recipe don't come out the way it should, try, try again.
16. It seem that we have a war on our hands.
17. The comet don't appear again in this century.

15.3 The Be Verbs

Review these conjugations for the *be* verbs:

Present Tense

	Singular	*Plural*
FIRST PERSON	I am	we are
SECOND PERSON	you are	you are
THIRD PERSON	he, she, or it is	they are

Past Tense

	Singular	*Plural*
FIRST PERSON	I was	we were
SECOND PERSON	you were	you were
THIRD PERSON	he, she, or it was	they were

If the subject is *I*, always use *am* in the present tense and *was* in the past tense.

If the subject is *you*, *we*, or *they*, always use *are* in the present tense and *were* in the past tense.

If the subject is *he*, *she*, or *it*, always use *is* in the present tense and *was* in the past tense.

If, on the other hand, the subject is a noun, ask if it is one or more than one. If it is one, use *is* or *was*. If it is more than one, use *are* or *were*. For example:

John (one) is going

Gina (one) is my sister

the family (one) was together

the dog (one) was sleeping

the police (more than one) are coming

the sisters (more than one) are together

the families (more than one) were together

Tom and Gina (more than one) were seen

PRACTICE 3

Choose the correct verb for each of the following sentences:

1. They said that we (was, were) not chosen.
2. I am what I (am, are), you are what you (is, are), and we are what we (is, are), so let's live and let live.
3. We (was, were) the last survivors to return.
4. (Weren't, Wasn't) they the winners?
5. (Isn't, Aren't) that the truth!

PRACTICE 4

Underline the noun subjects of the following sentences. If the subject is singular, write *S* above. If the subject is plural, write *P* above. When necessary, change the verbs to agree with the subjects. (Some verbs are correct.)

1. The governments of those countries wasn't at all cooperative. *[P above "governments"; "wasn't" crossed out, "weren't" written above]*

2. Those fish was delicious.

3. The soldiers wasn't so sure of their position.

4. There was some students still in doubt.

5. There isn't a chance of your going.

6. It is surprising that there isn't more of them going.

7. The so-called boat people either died or were brought to this country.

8. The nations who was gathering their armies for battle met one last time.

9. Weren't the police called to the scene of the accident?

10. Isn't the United States trying to mediate that controversy?

11. Neither Red nor his parents was responsible.

PRACTICE 5

Use *is* or *are*, or *was* or *were* to complete the following sentences:

1. Yesterday, the Dallas Cowboys *were at their best* _____.

2. Today, the family who _____.

3. Either the House or the Senate _____.

4. There _____ some of the dinner left.

5. Neither you nor we _____.

6. People who _____.

15.4 Subjects with Two or More Verbs

When you use two or more verbs with one subject, be sure that all verbs agree with the subject. For example:

> Ron and Don are twin brothers and look exactly alike.
>
> Every night, Julius studies his notes and reads the assigned chapters but seems to get nowhere.

In the first sentence the plural subject *Ron* and *Don* takes the plural verbs *are* and *look*. In the second sentence the singular subject *Julius* takes the singular verbs *studies*, *reads*, and *seems*.

PRACTICE 6

Underline the subjects of the following sentences, and supply appropriate present-tense verbs:

1. <u>She</u> gives her check to her parents and ____*does*____ most of the housework as well.

2. I clean the dishes, scrub the floors, work in the yard, and much of the time _____ like Cinderella.

3. She is selfish with her possessions and also _____ a bad temper.

4. The radio and television are on all the time and _____ so much noise that I cannot think.

5. The people on my street sometimes yell at their children and _____ things I do not want to repeat.

6. My husband does not drive himself but _____ everyone else how to drive.

PRACTICE 7

Write a sentence using each pair of verbs below *with the same subject:*

1. (loves, hates) *Our dog loves winter but hates summer.* _____

   _____

2. (sings, dances) _____

   _____

3. (defends, accuses) _____

   _____

4. (lives, dies) _____

   _____

5. (is, is not) _____

   _____

6. (does, does not) _____

   _____

7. (has, hasn't) _____

_____

PRACTICE 8

In the following sentences, rewrite the nonstandard verbs in standard English. (Some sentences are correct.)

1. She and I ~~was~~ *were* the smartest students in the kindergarten.

2. I hope this paper gives you some ideas about what to do on a rainy weekend and help make your rainy weekends more pleasant.

3. When we arrived, they had stopped serving dinner and was now serving breakfast.

4. A good newspaper reporter goes out and face the world directly to get a story.

5. On weekends, she usually goes to parties or attends school events.

6. Every evening about six o'clock, she sits on the front porch and gossips with the neighbors.

7. Sometimes he catch himself before things become too rough and makes a joke out of what has been happening.

8. I think the way I was brought up and the schools I attended have a lot to do with the problems I am having now.

9. April drives in the car pool five days a week and take the children to swimming class twice a week.

10. When night falls, the young people in the neighborhood come out and play their radios.

11. They love each other and plans to get married soon.

15.5 Subjects and Verbs Separated

Many times in your writing, your verbs will not come immediately after your subjects but instead will be separated by words, phrases, and clauses. These constructions sometimes cause verb-agreement difficulty. The following samples are correct:

I always <u>take</u> the easy way out.

The <u>programs</u> that I have mentioned <u>teach</u> children quite a lot.

Subjects Separated from Verbs by Prepositional Phrases

Prepositional phrases often separate subjects from verbs, as in these examples:

One of us is crazy.

The people in my neighborhood are nice.

In the first example the prepositional phrase *of us* separates the subject *one* from the verb *is*. In the second the prepositional phrase *in my neighborhood* separates the subject *people* from the verb *are*. Many prepositional phrases that separate subjects from verbs begin with *of, on,* and *in*.

PRACTICE 9

In the following sentences, underline the subjects once and the verbs twice, and put parentheses around the prepositional phrases. Change the verbs to agree with the subjects where necessary.

1. The sounds (of my neighborhood) *change* changes from hour to hour.

2. All the houses on my block are brick.

3. Everybody in my classes are working very hard.

4. My first few years of school was my most difficult ones.

5. The sounds in my neighborhood is so loud that they disturb the dogs.

6. My great-grandmother, in most people's eyes, seem to be just a mean old woman.

7. Just the thought of her children are quite satisfying to Mother.

8. The construction work on the houses begin next month.

9. One of us is able to do the job alone.

10. Harold Muskie of Chase Metropolitan Bank recommends the *Wall Street Journal*.

11. Their dreams for a better life was fulfilled that day.

Subjects Separated from Verbs by Adjective Clauses

Sometimes subjects and verbs are separated by adjective clauses, as follows:

My friends, who saw me get up out of that muddy water and then fall back in again, were laughing at me.

The attempts that she makes to help others sometimes fail.

The book she was reading was stolen from her desk.

Note that in the last sentence the relative pronoun *that* is omitted but understood.

PRACTICE 10

In the following sentences, underline the subjects once and the verbs twice, and put parentheses around the adjective clauses. Change the verbs to agree with the subjects where necessary.

1. Small <u>children</u> (who are not in school) <u>has</u> *have* more time to play.

2. Those who don't have the money gets the long sentences.

3. The things she has left behind means so much to her family.

4. The children who live in my neighborhood play baseball every afternoon.

5. The school where my mother taught for the last seven years is closing.

6. The gifts he brings to my son comes from his heart.

PRACTICE 11

Write sentences with the following phrases and clauses. Place them between the subjects and verbs, and keep the verbs in the present tense.

1. (who wears her hair down to her shoulders) *Geraldine, who wears her hair down to her shoulders, washes it every night.*

2. (which is my most difficult course) _____

_____

_____

3. (which are the best cars on the market) _____

_____

_____

4. (of the people I will write about) _____

_____

_____

5. (who is hard to control) _____

_____

_____

6. (who eat too much ice cream) _____

_____

_____

15.6 Verb Tense

As you have learned, each verb has four parts:

	Base Form	Simple Past	Past Participle	Progressive Form
REGULAR	I love	I loved	I have loved	I am loving
IRREGULAR	I begin	I began	I have begun	I am beginning

Verbs are regular if you add -d or -ed at the end to form both the simple past and the past participle. Thus, the verb *love* is regular. Verbs are irregular if the simple past or the past participle is formed in any other way. Study the following conjugation of *love* carefully and notice how the principal parts of the verb are used either alone or with helping verbs. If you need to know a particular form of an irregular verb, simply substitute the irregular verb in the *love* construction. For example, you can see that *I had loved* is the past perfect of *love* and that this construction takes a past participle. Therefore, you must use a past participle with *begin* to express the past perfect: *I had begun*.

	Singular	Plural

Present Tense

FIRST PERSON	I love	we love
SECOND PERSON	you love	you love
THIRD PERSON	he, she, or it loves	they love

Simple Past Tense

FIRST PERSON	I loved	we loved
SECOND PERSON	you loved	you loved
THIRD PERSON	he, she, or it loved	they loved

Perfect Tense with Have or Has

FIRST PERSON	I have loved	we have loved
SECOND PERSON	you have loved	you have loved
THIRD PERSON	he, she, or it has loved	they have loved

Perfect Tense *with* Had

FIRST PERSON	I had loved	we had loved
SECOND PERSON	you had loved	you had loved
THIRD PERSON	he, she, or it had loved	they had loved

Passive Voice *with* Am, Is, *or* Are

FIRST PERSON	I am loved	we are loved
SECOND PERSON	you are loved	you are loved
THIRD PERSON	he, she, or it is loved	they are loved

Passive Voice *with* Was *or* Were

FIRST PERSON	I was loved	we were loved
SECOND PERSON	you were loved	you were loved
THIRD PERSON	he, she, or it was loved	they were loved

Progressive Tense *with* Am, Is, *or* Are

FIRST PERSON	I am loving	we are loving
SECOND PERSON	you are loving	you are loving
THIRD PERSON	he, she, or it is loving	they are loving

Progressive Tense *with* Was *or* Were

FIRST PERSON	I was loving	we were loving
SECOND PERSON	you were loving	you were loving
THIRD PERSON	he, she, or it was loving	they were loving

Now turn to page 319 and memorize all the principal parts of each verb.

PRACTICE 12

Write sentences using the following regular and irregular verbs. Refer to the above conjugation of the verb *love* as necessary, but try to write the irregular forms without looking at the list on page 319.

1. (*love:* progressive form) *I am loving my work these days.*

2. (*love:* passive voice) _____

   _____

3. (*love:* perfect tense with *had*) _____

   _____

4. (*drown*: passive voice) _____

_____

5. (*find*: perfect tense with *have*) _____

_____

6. (*fly*: present tense, third-person singular) _____

_____

7. (*freeze*: passive voice) _____

_____

8. (*go*: perfect tense with *had*) _____

_____

9. (*happen*: progressive form) _____

_____

10. (*lay*: simple past) _____

_____

11. (*lead*: simple past) _____

_____

12. (*lie*: progressive form) _____

_____

13. (*lose*: base form with *do*, *does*, or *did*) _____

_____

14. (*pay*: perfect tense with *had*) _____

_____

15. (*see*: simple past) _____

_____

16. (*set*: progressive form) _____

_____

17. (*sing*: simple past) _____

_____

18. (*steal*: passive voice) _____

_____

19. (*take*: passive voice) _____

_____

20. (*teach*: simple past) _____

_____

21. (*throw*: perfect tense with *has*) _____

_____

Now check your irregular verbs against the list on page 319.

PRACTICE 13

Correct the verbs in the following sentences. (Two of the sentences are correct.)

1. Richard Wright's mother almost be̶a̶t̶ed *beat* him to death when he was four years old.

2. In his youth he lied, stolen, and struggled to contain his seething anger.

3. And there was the time that he prove to his family that he was his own boss.

4. He went to all the bars, stayed out late at night, and try to impress his friends.

5. As he stood there and watch Shorty being kicked, he felt pity and disgrace.

6. He wrote what he felt and what he want to express.

7. Richard did not have any money, so he lied and say he was not hungry.

8. He was talking to the woman who hire him for his first job.

9. Richard had struggle and worked to get ahead.

10. He went home when he had finish.

11. When he was young, he use to sell newspapers on Saturday.

12. He had gave the speech that the principal write.

13. There were many things that enable him to break free.

14. His stubbornness did help him in some ways, but it hurt him in other ways.

15. Another obstacle he have to overcome was that he could not earn enough money.

16. As time went on, he manage to free himself from his bondage.

17. He slipped into Ella's room and took the book from her shelf.

18. He had hided the books to read, and he learn many things from them.

19. He then took the book and run home to his mother.

20. In the end he went north and escape his bondage.

21. The conditions begun to change after he left.

15.7 Tense Shifts

Ordinarily, you must keep the tenses of your verbs consistent. If a sentence has one verb in the present tense, for example, the other verbs in the sentence should usually be in the present as well. The verb tenses in these two sentences are consistent:

When the wind <u>is</u> from the south, it <u>blows</u> the hook into the fish's mouth.

When the wind <u>was</u> from the south, it <u>blew</u> the hook into the fish's mouth.

But the tenses in this sentence shift:

When the wind <u>was</u> from the south, it <u>blows</u> the hook into the fish's mouth.

The suggestions below should help you avoid tense shifts when you write in the past tense:

1. It is hard to hear the *-d* or *-ed* endings of some verbs. If you cannot hear the endings, follow the rules for forming past-tense endings:

   INCORRECT
   She is <u>suppose</u> to know.

   CORRECT
   She is <u>supposed</u> to know.

   INCORRECT
   I <u>use</u> to go fishing.

   CORRECT
   I <u>used</u> to go fishing.

   INCORRECT
   He <u>ask</u> me to sing.

   CORRECT
   He <u>asked</u> me to sing.

   INCORRECT
   It <u>seem</u> to be raining.

   CORRECT
   It <u>seemed</u> to be raining.

2. Ordinarily, use *will, can,* and *may* with present-tense verbs and *would, could,* and *might* with past-tense verbs:

   > I <u>will</u> believe her if she <u>tells</u> me she is innocent.

   > I <u>would</u> believe her if she <u>told</u> me she was innocent.

   Also, as a general rule use *have* or *has* with present-tense verbs and *had* with past-tense verbs:

   > The council <u>says</u> we <u>have</u> spent too much money.

   > The council <u>said</u> we <u>had</u> spent too much money.

3. Sometimes when you are writing in the past tense, you will want to make a comment in the present. In this case be sure to write that comment in the present tense:

   >   past   present
   > . . . So those <u>were</u> the good old days. I <u>wish</u> I could be eleven again.

PRACTICE 14

Correct the tense shifts and other verb errors in the following sentences:

1. When the birds begin to sing, it m̶e̶a̶n̶t *means* spring has come.

2. When the passengers got off the plane, they seem terrified.

3. The woman at the bank ask me how much insurance I wanted.

4. Representative Taylor said she will vote her conscience.

5. Uncle Charlie always sang that corny old song about how he love to go "swimmin' with the women."

6. When we were young, we use to help milk the cows.

7. When the tomatoes ripened, we have to stop what we were doing so that we can help harvest them.

8. Neddie come in the barn and started throwing tomatoes at me.

9. My grandfather say he had never seen two boys who could get into so much trouble.

10. We use to help him grind the corn for golden grits.

11. He ask us to see if the chickens were "a sittin' or a settin'."

PRACTICE 15

Correct the tense shifts and other verb errors in the following student essay:

Lynette's Baby

told

On September 20, 1978, my sister Lynette began having light cramps. She t~~ells~~ my mother how she had suffered the night before and how my father had stayed up with her all night and rub her stomach during the pains. My mother tells her to get dressed so that we could leave for the hospital. (3 errors)

As soon as we left the house, the pains begin to hit Lynette every five minutes. Mother had call the doctor from the house next door, and he was waiting for us when we arrive at the hospital. After the doctor examine Lynette, he said, "It's the real thing. You will have that baby today." (4 errors)

Lynette screamed, and I start shaking. I tell my mother that I was going to the cafeteria. She said, "No, you're not. You stay here. This should teach you not to get serious with any boy unless you are married." I stood there biting my nails and making funny noises every time Lynette has a pain. The doctor left the room and tells my mother to come with him. He ask me to stay there and to wait for her water bag to break, so I just stand there trying to figure out what a water bag was. I did not know what I was suppose to do. (7 errors)

When my mother and the doctor came back in, they told me that they will have to do a "section." At the time I didn't know what a section was either. A section of what? But then they changed their minds and take Lynette to the delivery room. She was in a lot of pain. The doctor would say, "Push, push, push hard, Lynette, push, or you'll smother yourself and the baby." When I heard this I say to myself, "Jesus, please don't ever let me get pregnant, even when I get married." (3 errors)

I finally told my mother that it was just too much for me, and I leave to sit in the waiting room. A little bit later she join me. Then the doctor come out and told my mother, "Lady, your daughter is something else. She is quite a fighter. It's a girl." (3 errors)

Lynette asked me to name the baby, so I name her Theresa, after our aunt. Since that time Lynette has had another baby, and I name that one too. The second time Mother took our younger sister, Gina, to the hospital to watch the delivery. So we have all learn how hard it is to have a baby. (3 errors)

15.8 Review Exercises

REVIEW EXERCISE 1

Underline the subjects in the following sentences, and then change the verbs to agree with these subjects. (Some verbs are correct.)

1. A child believe what she sees.

2. If a child watch certain television programs, he or she learns many useful things.

3. My Aunt Kathleen always say she is going to live forever.

4. Best of all, television informs its viewers of the local and national news.

5. As far as snacks is concerned, no one needs them.

6. It seems to me that the president try to do the right thing.

7. When the sauce starts to boil, reduce the heat and simmer it for ten minutes.

8. If Mrs. Frances ask me to stop, I do what she ask.

9. Sal knows better than to call me that name again.

10. Marlene always hurt the man she love.

REVIEW EXERCISE 2

Underline the subjects in the following sentences, and then change the verbs to agree with the subjects. (Some verbs are correct.)

1. Uncle Sam have a good job waiting for you.

2. Those teen-agers are the ones who has been causing the problem.

3. There hasn't been any more problems since you spoke to her.

4. The drunkards on the corner is called "the birds" because they are on the corner before the birds gets up.

5. Junkyard Sam is nicest man in the entire downtown.

6. The people in Little Rock is the nicest people you will meet anywhere.

7. There weren't anyone left that I could trust.

8. Beatrice don't mean what she says.

9. Was they listening to what I said?

10. Doesn't it make sense to look at all the possibilities?

11. No, it don't.

12. New Orleans have many streets with French and Italian names.

13. The victim who have complained is the one they are watching.

14. Hasn't someone claimed the victory?

15. The people who live in darkness has seen a great light.

REVIEW EXERCISE 3

Correct the errors in subject-verb agreement in the following student essay. (Do not change any verbs inside quotation marks.)

Sweet Albert Dee

There is only one Sweet Albert Dee, and he's my uncle. Sweet Albert is about 5'2" tall and look like a child, even though he is in his fifties. He have a head shaped like an apple. Albert Dee "smokes" old cigar butts although he never light them because, he say, "Smokin' is not good for you." (4 errors)

Albert is an unusual person and never do anything he don't feel like doing. If he don't feel like talking, he don't. His reasoning is a little strange on subjects such as bathing and working. I remember once I asked, "Uncle, why don't you like to take baths?" He replied, "Mary, just 'cause God made a lot of water, that don't mean he want you to use it all up." When my mother asked him why he didn't get a job, he answered, "As long as I can eat free, I don't need a job." Albert Dee think it is enough to enjoy life. (5 errors)

Unfortunately, my uncle is a very heavy drinker. He drink anything from moonshine to what he call "mad dog." And he say he don't care if the alcohol destroy his liver because he believe he can always get another one. Poor Albert Dee won't live too long. Besides drinking and not taking baths, he love to sing silly songs. When he drink too much, he always sing what he call a "lover's chant." It go something like this: "Ooh-ya-ya-ya-haya-ha-ha." He repeats this over and over until he fall asleep. (12 errors)

Sweet Albert Dee isn't a bad person. He just have his own philosophy about life and how to live it; that's all. Albert is really a nice old man who happen to be a little weird and to have a drinking problem. Sometimes I thinks that maybe everyone should be a little weird, and then maybe the world could be as happy as Sweet Albert Dee. (3 errors)

REVIEW EXERCISE 4

Correct the verb-tense errors in the following student paper. Remember:

1. Keep your verb tenses consistent. If a sentence has one verb written in the present (or past) tense, ordinarily the other verbs should be written in the present (or past) tense. When changing from the present tense to the past tense, *will* usually changes to *would*, *can* to *could*, and *may* to *might*.
2. Look closely at your verb endings. Have you added the appropriate ending such as *-d* or *-ed*? Have you used the correct form of irregular verbs?

The Good Old Days

When I think of the good old days, I think most of all of sports, especially fishing, football, and what my friends and I use to call "roller-ball." Fishing was always the most important thing in my life because I was raised on Grand Isle, an island off the coast of Louisiana. From the age of two, I fish every chance I had. I really like going out on my father's boat to the oil rigs in the Gulf of Mexico, where we tied up the boat. We catched many kinds of fish, including bull reds, tuna, sharks, and wahoo. (4 errors)

Once when I was about ten years old, I hook a large fish in Crystal Bay. I fought him for about forty-five minutes before he surface, and then my father takes over for another half-hour. When that 185-pound marlin, which is now mounted over my bed, was finally brought in, I nearly lose my eyes. That was just one of my favorite fishing trips. (4 errors)

After a long day of fishing, with my friends Mike, Tommy, and Bean, I often play football. Sometimes, if we were feeling tough, we will challenge the boys from the other neighborhoods. One afternoon, we played for two hours with neither side scoring. "I'll put an end to this," Mike said. When the ball come to him, he run almost all the way for the touchdown, but then he was hit by Jim Fontenot of the other team. As Mike fell to the ground, he hitted his head on my knee and received a concussion and a broken nose. Despite his injuries he said, "Don't you worry about me. I'll be all right." And he was. (5 errors)

Roller-ball was the funniest game we ever play. We use a large rubber ball and a broomstick. The object of the game was to hit the ball and roll—not run—to the base. Passers-by in cars use to stop and look at us rolling in the grass. (3 errors)

Those games were special to me then and they still are. When Mike, Tommy, Bean, and I are together with our girlfriends, we spent the whole evening talking about the good old days. Sometimes we have ask the girls to sit down while we acted out a few of our old memories. (3 errors)

CHAPTER 16

Using Pronouns Correctly

16.0 Introduction

Pronouns can be misused in many ways. In this chapter, you will learn how to avoid various types of pronoun errors. Before beginning, review the introduction to pronouns in Chapter 10.4.

16.1 Avoiding Errors in Pronoun Case

The way a pronoun is used in a sentence is called the *case*. The following are typical errors in case:

INCORRECT

Marcus and me were always getting into trouble. (*Marcus and me* is the subject, but the subjective case of *me* is *I*.)

CORRECT

Marcus and I were always getting into trouble.

INCORRECT

To who should I address this letter? (The preposition *to* takes the objective case, which is *whom*, not *who*.)

CORRECT

To whom should I address this letter?

INCORRECT

Are those them? (The personal pronoun is used as a predicate nominative. Thus, the subjective case, which is *they*, is necessary.)

CORRECT

Are those they?

INCORRECT

The apartment is just right for you and I. (The preposition *for* takes the objective case, which is *me*, not *I*.)

CORRECT

The apartment is just right for <u>you and me</u>.

INCORRECT

Carlos is older than <u>her</u>. (The sentence is saying that "Carlos is older than *she is*." Thus, the subjective case, *she*, is needed for the pronoun.)

CORRECT

Carlos is older than <u>she</u>.

PRACTICE 1

Correct the errors in pronoun case. (One sentence is correct.)

1. Mark was very hurt and began spreading many lies about Troy and ~~I~~ *me*.

2. Because he was older than me, he graduated before me and went away to college.

3. When me and Michael broke up, Mother knew just how hurt I was.

4. Now I realize that the little girl and I are closer than ever.

5. Just between you and I, that man is crazy.

6. It was her who finally spoke up.

PRACTICE 2

Correct the errors in pronoun case in the following student paper, and be able to explain why you made the changes.

My Summer at Nantucket

Students who work at resorts in the summer often have unusual experiences. Last summer, my friend Regina and me traveled a thousand miles to work at Nantucket, which is a resort island twenty miles from the Massachusetts shore. We arrived with very little money in our pockets, and it was still quite cold. We didn't bring enough clothes and were nearly freezing. Someone told Regina and I to go to the local thrift shop, where we could buy cheap coats. Regina bought a fine old overcoat for three dollars, but I didn't have as much luck as her, so I had to huddle up in my blanket to keep warm. (3 errors)

Besides being cold, we were also hungry. Our friend Randy from Penn State was working as a dishwasher and brought Regina and I scraps of food every night. Regina and me did not have any regular place to live so we stayed with various friends in rooms they had rented, sleeping on the floor. We looked and looked for jobs, but no one wanted to give either she or me employment. (3 errors)

At this point I was getting desperate. I did not know to who I could turn for help. I was determined not to ask my parents for money. Just between you and I, they were furious with me for leaving home to go to Nantucket. "Whom do you girls think you are," my dad said, "traveling a thousand miles to work at some funny resort island?" But us "girls" (I am nineteen and Regina is twenty) went anyway. (4 errors)

Just before starvation set in, I got a job as a janitor at a hotel, and Regina got a job as a "bag boy" in a supermarket. When I wrote my father and told him about our jobs, he thought that Regina and me were completely crazy. "You mean you traveled a thousand miles to mop floors?" he wrote back. My summer in Nantucket was an unusual experience, and it was also the most fun Regina and me ever had. Whomever said that parents are always right? (3 errors)

16.2 Avoiding Pronouns with Unclear Antecedents

The noun or pronoun for which a pronoun stands is called its *antecedent* (meaning it goes *before* the pronoun). When you use a pronoun, make sure the antecedent is clear.

> April is the worst month of the year. It is the time when they make you pay your taxes.

The antecedent of *It* is clearly *April*, so there is no problem. But what is the antecedent of *they*? The writer assumes you will think of the federal government, but such an assumption is not enough. Follow this important rule: *If there is no clear antecedent for a pronoun, replace the pronoun with an appropriate noun.* The two sentences could read:

> April is the worst month of the year. It is the time when the federal government makes you pay your taxes.

PRACTICE 3

In the following sentences the antecedents of the underlined pronouns are unclear. Replace them with appropriate nouns or pronouns. Also, change verbs as necessary.

1. Sex education should be taught in high school because parents are either too scared or too busy to teach the facts of life to ~~them.~~ *their children*

2. In the final game I was playing defense and went to make a tackle. When I hit <u>him</u>, he fell on his side and on my finger.

3. When I was in the service, <u>they</u> would not let me grow my hair longer than an inch.

4. One thing I don't like about that restaurant is that <u>they</u> are always trying to rush you.

5. No one likes living on the brink of nuclear war. There have been many attempts to change <u>this</u>, but so far none has succeeded.

6. I took my automobile to the dealer to be fixed, but <u>they</u> wanted to charge far too much for the repairs.

7. My son would like to major in business, but <u>they</u> are a bit too demanding for him.

8. Our unemployment rate continues to rise. I don't know what the president should do about <u>this</u>, but he should do something.

9. My typewriter is broken, but <u>he</u> said that he would fix it for almost nothing.

10. I hope to be out of my apartment soon; <u>they</u> are charging too much rent and do not want to make any repairs.

11. When I was in the hospital, <u>they</u> took very good care of me.

16.3 Avoiding Errors in Pronoun Agreement

Personal pronouns (*I, you, she, they,* and the like) must agree with the nouns they replace in both *number* and *person.* (The nouns they replace are their antecedents.)

> Popular music is an art form, and <u>it</u> is the principal art form for many young people.

Instead of repeating the word *music,* you naturally substitute the pronoun *it;* otherwise, the sentence would be awkward:

> Popular music is an art form, and popular music is the principle art form for many young people.

Thus, it is appropriate to use a pronoun to replace *music* the second time it is used, but the pronoun must agree with its antecedent in number and person.

The following list of personal pronouns in the subjective case shows why *it* appropriately replaces *music* in the above example:

	Singular	*Plural*
FIRST PERSON	I	we
SECOND PERSON	you	you
THIRD PERSON	he, she, or it	they

Agreement in number means that singular pronouns must be used to replace singular antecedents and plural pronouns must be used to replace plural antecedents. In the sentence above, it is therefore appropriate to use *it* instead of *they* because *music* is singular.

Agreement in person means that first-person pronouns must be used to replace first-person antecedents, second-person pronouns to replace second-person antecedents, and third-person pronouns to replace third-person antecedents. It is therefore appropriate to use the third-person pronoun *it* to replace *music* because *music*, as a noun, is in the third person.

Pronouns used as objects or to show possession should be written in the objective or possessive case. For example:

Francine was so nice to me that I will never forget her.

Her is in agreement with *Francine* and is the object of the verb *forget*.

PRACTICE 4

Substitute the correct personal pronoun (subjective case) for each of the following antecedents:

1. Charles and I ____we____   6. You and he _____

2. the cat (sex unknown) _____   7. the police _____

3. the government _____   8. Geraldine _____

4. the police force _____   9. Mary and Martha _____

5. The Ricos and I _____   10. the people _____

Now list the personal pronoun in the objective case that you would substitute for each of the above antecedents:

1. _____   2. _____   3. _____   4. _____   5. _____

6. _____   7. _____   8. _____   9. _____   10. _____

PRACTICE 5

Choose the correct pronoun in each of the following, and draw an arrow to the noun or pronoun (the antecedent) that it replaces. In two sentences, you will have to choose the correct verb as well.

1. Movies rated X are for adults only because (it, they) often (contains, contain) explicit sex and violence.

2. The world would have more crime than (it, they) could handle if everyone saw X-rated movies.

3. Ticket clerks at theaters that show X-rated films often take advantage of my son by selling (him, them) a ticket without asking for proper identification.

4. Hawaii is known for the many beautiful islands (it, they) (has, have).

5. When I go downtown and see an old lady begging with a cup, I feel sorry for (her, them).

6. *King Tut* is an exciting book; it keeps the reader on (his or her, their) toes all the time.

7. Most mystery stories do not end the way you expect (it, them) to.

8. The government is the worst offender; (it, they) (waste, wastes) more money than anyone else.

9. When Mexico suffered a great earthquake, (it, they) asked other nations for assistance.

10. A considerate doctor explains things to a patient so that the patient will understand (his or her, their) illness.

11. A person who gives has much given back to (him or her, them).

PRACTICE 6

In the first part of each exercise below, use the designated noun in a sentence. In the second part, write another sentence in which an appropriate pronoun replaces the noun.

1. (bird) a. *Each morning a bird sits outside my window.*
   b. *I am going to feed it today.*

2. (music) a. _____
   b. _____

3. (a car) a. _____
   b. _____

4. (person) a. _____
   b. _____

5. (Russia) a. _____
   b. _____

6. (woman) a. _____
   b. _____

7. (people) a. _____

b. _____

PRACTICE 7

In the sentences that follow, change the pronouns to agree with their antecedents. Change other words as necessary. (One sentence is correct.)

1. My glasses are very important to me because without ~~it~~ *them* I could not function.

2. Because the United States uses more oil than they can produce, they have to import great quantities from other countries.

3. In conclusion, each state is unique in their own culture, industry, and natural environment.

4. Marge was determined to help her father and brother because she loved him.

5. I have had three jobs since I began working, and each has been rewarding in its own way.

6. My husband gets furious at neighbors who borrow things and never think to return it.

7. When people first met my grandfather, he found him charming.

8. As they got to know my grandfather, however, you found him less charming and more cantankerous.

9. The United States was in an oil crisis; they imported too much of their oil.

10. These working mothers have more responsibility than they can handle. She needs a lot more help from her husband.

11. When one joins a car pool to get to work, they help save oil.

16.4 Avoiding Pronoun Gender Confusion

When a pronoun refers to a male, use *he*, *him*, or *his*:

Dr. Carl Regaldo asked me to come see him.

When a pronoun refers to a female, use *she*, *her*, or *hers*:

Prime Minister Thatcher asked her people to trust her new program.

But what do you do when the antecedent is a person whose gender is unknown, or if it is a word like *lawyer*, *teacher*, *parent*, or *someone*, which could refer to both men and women? You could say:

A lawyer has to work hard to build <u>his</u> practice.

But many women, as well as men, are lawyers. Thus you could say:

A lawyer has to work hard to build <u>her</u> practice.

But many men, as well as women, are lawyers. Therefore you *might* say:

A lawyer has to work hard to build <u>their</u> practice.

However, the pronoun *their* is clearly wrong because its antecedent is the singular word *lawyer*.

Up until fairly recently most English texts instructed students to use the male pronoun if the antecedent was not clearly female. Thus, they taught that you should say, "A lawyer has to work hard to build <u>his</u> practice." Although this use of the masculine pronoun is still correct, more and more textbooks and teachers are turning away from it and suggesting the following alternatives:

To avoid such gender confusion, avoid the pronoun altogether whenever possible. Simply say:

A lawyer has to work hard to build a practice.

Or make the *antecedent* plural:

<u>Lawyers</u> have to work hard to build <u>their</u> practices.

If it is not possible to avoid using the pronoun or to make the antecedent plural, use the double pronouns *he or she*, *him or her*, or *his or her*. If you were announcing to a group of men and women that a car parked outside had its lights on, you could say:

<u>Someone</u> has left <u>his or her</u> car lights on.

If you do use an expression like *he or she* (or *him or her*), try not to do so more than once in a paragraph, and never use it more than once in a sentence. Never write:

<u>He or she</u> left <u>his or her</u> umbrella in the auditorium.

PRACTICE 8

In the following sentences either omit the male or female pronouns or make the antecedents and their verbs plural to avoid the problem of gender confusion. You will have to change some other words as well.

1. These days a good teacher has a hard time keeping his job.

   These days a good teacher has a hard time keeping a job.

2. A doctor must be available to his patients all of the time.

   Doctors must be available to their patients all of the time.

3. This type of nurse is always ready to help a patient with any problem he may have. _____

_____

4. Then, there is the nurse who is concerned about her work only when someone is watching her. _____

_____

5. This person is at the bottom; he lives in poverty. _____

_____

6. Each of my parents helps me in his own way, and I am grateful for what each has done. _____

_____

7. It is difficult for a parent to relate to his child these days. _____

_____

8. A person with a problem should make sure that she sees somebody trained to help. _____

_____

9. A teacher should be completely fair to his students. _____

_____

10. In addition, a teacher should plan all her classes carefully. _____

_____

Indefinite Pronouns and Gender Agreement

A special problem arises in gender agreement when you use a personal pronoun to replace an indefinite pronoun like *each*, *anyone*, *someone*, *everyone*, *no one*, and so on. (See page 222 for a more complete list.) Most indefinite pronouns are singular, which means that you probably will need to use *he or she*, *him or her*, or *his or her* for agreement. For example:

Anyone may submit his or her application now.

No one should go on such a strict diet without his or her doctor's permission.

You can bet that someone will not do his or her share.

As pointed out above, however, try to limit the use of the double pronoun to once in a paragraph.

On occasion, when the indefinite pronoun *clearly* refers to a group of people, it is appropriate to use it with a plural pronoun—*they, them,* or *their.* For example:

Everyone was clapping <u>their</u> hands.
Everybody worked as hard as <u>they</u> could.

PRACTICE 9

Write sentences in which the indefinite pronouns shown below are the subjects. Use the designated possessive pronouns to refer to them.

1. (anyone, his or her) *Anyone who wants his or her paper should see me after class.*

2. (someone, his or her) _____

_____

3. (anybody, his or her) _____

_____

4. (no one, his or her) _____

_____

5. (each one, his or her) _____

_____

6. (everybody, their) _____

_____

16.5 Avoiding Pronoun Person Shifts

A fairly common pronoun-agreement problem is a shift in person within the same sentence. For example:

I came to realize that because <u>you</u> are on earth for only a short time, <u>one</u> should do the things <u>one</u> wants.

The writer began with the second person *you* and shifted to the third person *one.* Here are two ways to correct the error:

I came to realize that because <u>you</u> are on earth for only a short time, <u>you</u> should do the things <u>you</u> want.

I came to realize that because <u>one</u> is on earth for only a short time, <u>one</u> should do the things <u>one</u> wants.

PRACTICE 10

Correct the shifts in pronoun person in the sentences below. (One sentence is correct.)

1. If you have ever lived as a "Navy brat" you know that such a life can be frustrating, especially if ~~one has~~ *you have* moved around as much as I have.

2. When one goes to see her, you should plan on spending the whole day because she always has to bake something for you to eat.

3. Mrs. Lewis passes everyone in her class whether you have good grades or not.

4. One's social class has more to do with your personality than you think.

5. They were always there when I needed them and would always talk to you in a nice tone of voice.

6. Someone has stolen your bicycle.

7. This statement is very strong because it tells me that you should forgive people who have sinned against me.

8. When one sees the view of that salt water marsh, you are moved by its beauty.

9. Parents' great fear is that their children will use drugs that are dangerous to you.

10. We should be careful before believing what they tell you.

11. One should not listen to all you hear.

16.6 Avoiding Other Pronoun Errors

Other pronoun errors include the following:

1. Reversing the order of pronouns:

   INCORRECT
   She took <u>me</u> and Robert for a ride.

   CORRECT
   She took Robert and <u>me</u> for a ride.

   Always put yourself last.

2. Using the wrong personal pronoun with a gerund:

   INCORRECT
   She was driven crazy by <u>him</u> nagging.

CORRECT

She was driven crazy by <u>his</u> nagging.

Use the possessive form of the personal pronoun with a gerund.

3. Using the incorrect relative pronoun:

INCORRECT

The woman <u>which</u> lived next door was an alcoholic.

CORRECT

The woman <u>who</u> lived next door was an alcoholic.

Use *who* and *whose* with people and *which* and *that* with things.

16.7 Summary of Common Pronoun Errors

The following are typical pronoun errors or awkward constructions:

1. Errors in case:

INCORRECT

<u>Sal and me</u> drove to Minneapolis

CORRECT

<u>Sal and I</u> drove to Minneapolis

INCORRECT

Just between <u>you and I</u>, the trip was terrible.

CORRECT

Just between <u>you and me</u>, the trip was terrible.

2. Unclear antecedents:

INCORRECT

When my mother was in the hospital, <u>they</u> treated her well.

CORRECT

When my mother was in the hospital, <u>the staff</u> treated her well.

3. Pronouns that do not agree with their antecedents:

INCORRECT

<u>Anyone</u> who wants to join should see <u>their</u> counselor.

CORRECT

<u>Anyone</u> who wants to join should see <u>his or her</u> counselor.

CORRECT

If <u>you</u> want to join, see <u>your</u> counselor.

Copyright © 1987 Houghton Mifflin Company

INCORRECT

<u>Washington</u> is known for <u>their</u> outdoor concerts.

CORRECT

<u>Washington</u> is known for <u>its</u> outdoor concerts.

Note: Do not overuse *his or her* constructions.

4. Awkward gender use:

AWKWARD

If a <u>person</u> wants to succeed in nursing, <u>she</u> must study hard.

BETTER

If <u>one</u> wants to succeed in nursing, <u>one</u> must study hard.

AWKWARD

Each <u>parent</u> should give <u>his</u> child love.

BETTER

<u>All parents</u> should give <u>their</u> children love.

5. Pronoun-person shifts:

INCORRECT

The way <u>one</u> dresses will have much to do with <u>your</u> success.

CORRECT

The way <u>you</u> dress will have much to do with <u>your</u> success.

6. Pronouns out of order:

INCORRECT

They showed <u>me and Robert</u> a good time.

CORRECT

They showed <u>Robert and me</u> a good time.

7. Incorrect relative pronouns:

INCORRECT

The <u>people which</u> you befriend will not forget you.

CORRECT

The <u>people whom</u> you befriend will not forget you.

INCORRECT

The <u>people which</u> befriend you are the ones you will not forget.

CORRECT

The <u>people who</u> befriend you are the ones you will not forget.

16.8 Review Exercise

Correct all pronoun errors and awkward construction in the following sentences, rewriting as necessary. (Three sentences are correct.)

1. You can test the loaves by tapping them with your finger; it should sound hollow.

   _____

2. When the bread is thoroughly cooled, wrap them securely with foil.

   _____

3. Mrs. Williams does not mind paying high taxes because she feels they may be benefiting someone who really needs it.

   _____

4. The people you think are carefree are often the very ones who take life most seriously.

   _____

5. I think a child's interest in reading depends on the material he or she is given in his or her early years of schooling.

   _____

6. It was a first for Mary and I.

   _____

7. The old lady took the drug because the doctors prescribed them for her.

   _____

8. If you drive Manuel and I to work every day, we will pay you well.

   _____

9. Just because you are older than I, that does not give you the right to boss me around.

   _____

10. Our parents gave me and Mary a good home.

    _____

11. When one takes Spanish from Dr. Fernandez, you should plan on having a lot of work.

    _____

12. To who is the letter addressed?

    _____

13. Anyone turning in their paper late will lose a letter grade.

_____

14. I came to realize that he and I would never work out our problems unless we got help.

_____

15. Someone should pick up their phone and call the police.

_____

CHAPTER 17

Spelling Skills

17.0 Introduction

In this chapter, you will learn how to write tricky plural nouns and verb endings, how to distinguish sound-alike words, and how to use the hyphen. A list of the words most frequently misspelled on beginning college students' papers is also included.

Some people are born as naturally good spellers; others are not. The writer of this text is not a naturally good speller. Once I sent a manuscript to a publisher with a reference to the parable of the shepherd who left his flock of ninety-nine sheep to find the one that had strayed. In my most solemn voice, I wrote that to seek the one that was lost, the shepherd had left the *"nighty and the nine."* I still cannot spell *accommodate*—or is it *accommodate* or *acomodate*? Nor am I ever quite sure when to insert a hyphen and when not to. Frankly I don't like hyphens. For example, I always resist using a hyphen with *first class* when it is used as an adjective, as in *first-class restaurant*. And I have just about given up trying to remember when to write *awhile* and when to write *a while*. But there is hope for the likes of me—the dictionary! Ask your instructor to recommend a dictionary that you can easily carry with you to check your spelling.

In addition to constant use of the dictionary, extensive reading will also help your spelling. Without even thinking about it, you will remember how various words are formed. The following suggestions will also help:

1. As you write, concentrate on each syllable of each word. You can usually avoid the following types of mistakes by carefully pronouncing each word as you write it:

   <u>necessry</u> for <u>necessary</u> (ne-ces-sa-ry)
   <u>practicly</u> for <u>practically</u> (prac-ti-cal-ly)

<u>goverment</u> or <u>govment</u> for <u>government</u> (gov-ern-ment)

<u>craddle</u> for <u>cradle</u> (cra-dle)

2. Begin your own dictionary, keeping a list of every word you ever misspell in any course in college. Anyone can misspell a word like *kindergarten* or *sacrilegious* or *shillelagh*, but you do not have to keep misspelling the same words. Before writing each of your essays, review your list.
3. Learn the rules for noun plurals and verb endings, which are given in Sections 17.1 and 17.2.
4. Learn the rules for contractions and how to distinguish them from the personal pronouns, such as *its*, that sound like contractions. (See Section 17.3.)
5. Learn to distinguish homonyms or sound-alike words, such as *there* and *their*. (See Section 17.4.)
6. Learn the rules on the use of the hyphen that are given in Section 17.5.
7. Study the list in Section 17.6 of the most commonly misspelled words in college writing. Even if you later forget how to spell some of these words, you will probably remember to look them up in your dictionary.
8. Proofread your papers carefully.

If you are still having problems, ask your instructor to suggest a spelling workbook. One that has helped many students is *College Spelling Skills* by James F. Shepherd (Boston: Houghton Mifflin Company, 1985).

17.1 Plurals of Nouns

Most noun plurals are made simply by adding an -*s* to the singular form: *experience* becomes *experiences*, *American* becomes *Americans*. Plurals formed in other ways can be tricky. Learn the rules below. As you read them, fill in the blanks.

1. Add -*es* to nouns that end in *x, ss, z, sh,* and *ch*:

   <u>box</u> becomes _____*boxes*_____   <u>church</u> becomes _____

   <u>sex</u> becomes _____   <u>business</u> becomes _____

   <u>bus</u> becomes _____   <u>rash</u> becomes _____

2. Add -*es* to a few nouns that end in -*o*. For example:

   <u>tomato</u> becomes _____*tomatoes*_____   <u>veto</u> becomes _____

   <u>hero</u> becomes _____   <u>Negro</u> becomes _____

   <u>potato</u> becomes _____

   Add -*s* to most other nouns that end in -*o*:

   <u>ego</u> becomes _____*egos*_____   <u>radio</u> becomes _____

zero becomes _____   two becomes _____

zoo becomes _____   tattoo becomes _____

3. Follow these rules for nouns that end in *y*:

   If the *-y* is preceded by a consonant (a letter other than *a, e, i, o, u*), change the *-y* to *-i* and add *-es*:

   cry becomes   *cries* _____   library becomes _____

   navy becomes _____   berry becomes _____

   If the *-y* is preceded by a vowel (*a, e, i, o, u*), add only *-s*:

   play becomes _____   journey becomes _____

   If a proper name ends in *-y*, add only *-s*; otherwise the name would be changed:

   Kennedy becomes _____   January becomes _____

4. Change *-f* or *-fe* endings of most nouns to *-ves*:

   self becomes _____   knife becomes _____

   life becomes _____   leaf becomes _____

   elf becomes _____   loaf becomes _____

   Note: *roof* becomes *roofs* and *belief* becomes *beliefs*.

5. The singular and plural for some nouns, especially animals that are hunted and certain fish, are the same:

   deer remains _____   elk remains _____

   trout remains _____   bass remains _____

6. Change the noun itself to form yet other plurals:

   man becomes _____   ox becomes _____

   woman becomes _____   mouse becomes _____

7. You may use *-'s* to form the plural of letters, numerals, and symbols. (Many publishers, however, omit the apostrophe.)

   the t becomes the t's

   1980 becomes the 1980's

   & becomes &'s

   Do *not* use *-'s* to form any other plurals.

If you are in doubt about a plural, look up the noun, designated *n*, in a dictionary, and you will find the plural, designated *pl*. If you look up *alumnus*, for example, you will see something like this:

a-lum-nus (ə-lŭm′nəs) *n., pl.* **-ni** (-nī).

You thus know that the plural is *alumni*. (The suffix *-ni* replaces *-nus*.) If two plural suffixes are given, always use the first alternative.

PRACTICE 1

Give the plurals for the following:

1. watch _____	ax	_____	first	_____
2. candy _____	sash	_____	two	_____
3. potato _____	Kennedy	_____	woman	_____
4. leaf _____	hero	_____	lady	_____
5. life _____	Negro	_____	honey	_____
6. 1990 _____	deer	_____	i	_____
7. roof _____	policeman	_____	bath	_____
8. self _____	stereo	_____	Monday	_____

9. hippopotamus _____ (Use your dictionary.)

10. analysis _____ (Use your dictionary.)

PRACTICE 2

Correct the noun plurals in the following paragraph. (Six plural endings have been omitted; two have been misspelled.)

The area where I live is called Graveyard because of the two graveyard located nearby. I have lived in Graveyard for twelve year now and know all the thing that go on there. I get tired of seeing the same people standing on the corner talking to each other all day long. They try to start conversation with the ladys who pass by, and they try to bum money from you so that they can buy beer, soft drink, and various kind of candys from the store down the street.

17.2 Verb Endings

The rules governing verb endings are given in Chapters 13–15. Here is a summary:

1. Add *-s* to most verbs to form third-person singular constructions in the present tense:

He, she, or it <u>loves</u>

He, she, or it <u>walks</u>

2. Add *-es* to verbs to form third-person singular constructions in the present tense if the verbs end in *-o, -x, -ss, -z, -sh,* or *-ch*:

He, she, or it <u>does</u>

He, she, or it <u>reaches</u>

3. If the verb ends in a *-y* that is preceded by a consonant, change the *-y* to *-i* before adding *-es* or *-ed*:

<u>spy</u> becomes <u>spies</u> or <u>spied</u>

<u>bury</u> becomes <u>buries</u> or <u>buried</u>

but

<u>journey</u> becomes <u>journeys</u> or <u>journeyed</u> (The *-y* is preceded by a vowel, *e*.)

4. When adding *-ed* or *-ing* to one-syllable verbs or verbs accented on the last syllable, double the final consonant if it is preceded by a single vowel. (See page 328 for more explanation.)

<u>drum</u> becomes <u>drummed</u> or <u>drumming</u>

<u>occur</u> becomes <u>occurred</u> or <u>occurring</u>

but

<u>happen</u> becomes <u>happened</u> or <u>happening</u> (The accent is on the first syllable.)

5. When adding *-ing* to verbs that end in *-y*, do not change the *-y*:

<u>fly</u> becomes <u>flying</u>

<u>satisfy</u> becomes <u>satisfying</u>

PRACTICE 3

Supply the correct verb forms below:

Base Form	Third-Person Singular, Present	Simple Past and Past Participle	Progressive Form
1. try	*tries*	*tried*	*trying*
2. comply			
3. hum			
4. bus			
5. bevel			
6. defer			
7. satisfy			

8. journey _____   _____   _____

9. open _____   _____   _____

10. jog _____   _____   _____

11. counsel _____   _____   _____

12. travel _____   _____   _____

13. study _____   _____   _____

14. refer _____   _____   _____

15. occupy _____   _____   _____

17.3 Contractions and Possessive Pronouns

Using Contractions

One meaning of *contract* is "to reduce in size." For example, ice contracts when it melts. To make a *contraction* in grammar, you join two words by reducing their number of letters:

> it is becomes it's
> there is becomes there's
> cannot becomes can't
> I would becomes I'd
> let us becomes let's
> Linda is going becomes Linda's going.

Notice that in each of the above an *apostrophe* (') replaces the missing letter or letters:

> it is becomes it's
> ↑
> omit
>
> cannot becomes can't
> ↑
> omit
>
> I would becomes I'd
> ↑
> omit
>
> Linda is becomes Linda's
> ↑
> omit

Except for *will not*, which becomes *won't*, all contractions are formed by using the apostrophe to *replace* the missing letter or letters.

Some tend to overuse contractions in their writing. It is fine to use some contractions, but give your papers variety by writing out *it is, will not, I would*, and the like most of the time. In formal writing—such as a research paper—use contractions seldom, if at all. Always avoid the following contractions:

> there's for there is (It is too easy to make a verb-agreement error, as in *There's two of us left*. Write out *There are two of us left*.)
>
> it's for it has (Save *it's* for *it is*. Write out *it has*.)
>
> Linda's going for Linda is going (The contraction is unnecessarily informal.)

Do not try to make a contraction of *there are*. Also, note that if you write out *can't*, you write *cannot*, not *can not*.

PRACTICE 4

Make contractions of the following:

1. who is _____
2. they are _____
3. cannot _____
4. let us _____
5. will not _____
6. would not _____
7. they would _____
8. should not _____
9. do not _____
10. you are _____

Contractions and Possessive Pronouns

Because some contractions sound like the possessive forms of certain pronouns, they are often confused with the pronouns in writing:

Contractions	*Possessive Pronouns*
It's (it is) raining	The dog went to its house.
They're (they are) ready.	Their knowledge is great.
There's (there is) the knife.	The knife is theirs.
Who's (who is) going to pass?	The ones whose papers are turned in on time are going to pass.
You're (you are) a pleasant person.	Your manner is pleasant.

To determine whether you need a contraction or the possessive pronoun, apply a simple rule: Try to convert the word in question into two words. If you can, the contraction is the correct form:

You can say, "It is raining." (Thus, *it's* is correct.)

You cannot say, "The dog went to <u>it is</u> house." (Thus, *its* is correct.)

You can say, "<u>They are</u> ready." (Thus, *they're* is correct.)

You cannot say, "<u>They are</u> knowledge is great." (Thus, *their* is correct.)

You can say, "<u>Who is</u> going to pass?" (Thus, *who's* is correct.)

You cannot say, "The ones <u>who is</u> papers are turned in on time are going to pass." (Thus, *whose* is correct.)

PRACTICE 5

Choose either the contraction or the possessive pronoun for each of the following:

1. I began to work there in 1977. (It's, (Its)) location was on Tanis Drive in Lexington.

2. If (you're, your) lucky, you might find peace.

3. When (you're, your) living at home, you cannot leave when you want to, as you can when you are staying in the dorm.

4. You can count on Mama Linda's cooking because you know (it's, its) going to be good.

5. Sometimes you can't even tell what (they're, their) talking about.

6. (There's, Theirs) is the least costly way.

7. (There's, Theirs) only one of us left.

8. (It's, Its) not a question of whom you are serving: You must always be polite. (You're, Your) reputation is at stake.

9. There are so many people that (it's, its) impossible to know them all.

10. (Who's, Whose) going to be the first to jump in?

11. Most of the classes are large, although (there's, theirs) at least one small one.

12. (Who's, Whose) child was that?

13. She's the one (who's, whose) watch was stolen.

14. Did the parrot say what (it's, its) name was?

PRACTICE 6

Write sentences using each of the sound-alike words below:

1. (its, it's) a. *It's a bad day for Black Rock.*

   b. *The train stopped at its destination.*

2. (your, you're) a. _____

   b. _____

3. (theirs, there's) a. _____

   b. _____

4. (whose, who's) a. _____

   b. _____

5. (its, it's) a. _____

   b. _____

6. (their, they're) a. _____

   b. _____

17.4 Other Sound-Alike Words

Besides pronouns and contractions that sound alike, there are a number of other words that sound similar. For example, read the definition of each of the following sound-alike words:

1. accept—a verb that means receive. (I accept your offer.)
   except—a preposition that means not including. (She likes everything except meatloaf.)

   If everyone is going except you, you are Xed out, poor you.

2. affect—a verb that means influence. (The storm affected the crop.)
   effect—a noun that means result. (The effect of the storm was great.)

   Say to yourself, "The affair affected her." The noun effect is usually preceded by an, the, or in.

3. choose—a verb that means decide for. (I choose to go this way.)
   chose—a verb that means decided for. (Yesterday, I chose to go that way instead.)

   Say to yourself, "Last night at the circus the clown chose a big, funny nose."

4. hear—a verb that means listen. (I hear with my ear.)
   here—an adverb that means place. (Bring the luggage here.)

   Here, there, and where are all place words.

5. whole—entire. (The whole class sent her a get-well card.)
   hole—a noun that means a round opening. (He dug a hole in the ground.)
   hold—a verb that means to grasp. (I hold on tightly.)

6. <u>new</u>—an adjective that means the opposite of old. (She welcomed the <u>new</u> day.)
<u>knew</u>—the past tense of know. (I <u>knew</u> better than that.)

7. <u>loose</u>—an adjective that means not tight. (The knot is <u>loose</u>.)
<u>lose</u>—a verb that means to misplace. (I might <u>lose</u> my hat.)

 To make <u>loose</u>, you loosen up <u>lose</u> to make room for an <u>o</u>.

8. <u>may be</u>—a verb that shows possibility. (You <u>may be</u> president someday.)
<u>maybe</u>—an adverb that shows possibility. (<u>Maybe</u> you will go with him.)

9. <u>of</u>—a preposition that means belonging to. (She is a member <u>of</u> the club.)
<u>off</u>—an adverb that means from or away. (It fell <u>off</u> the shelf.)

 You leave <u>f</u> off of <u>off</u> to form <u>of</u>.

10. <u>pass</u>—a present tense verb that means to successfully complete. (I hope you <u>pass</u> the test.)
<u>passed</u>—the past tense of pass. (You <u>passed</u> the test!)
<u>past</u>—a noun or adjective that means at an earlier time. (In the <u>past</u> week, you have taken three tests.)

 Say to yourself, "In the past, I passed, but now I can't seem to pass."

11. <u>quiet</u>—an adjective that means free of noise. (I like a <u>quiet</u> park.)
<u>quit</u>—a verb that means to stop doing something. (He <u>quit</u> his job.)
<u>quite</u>—an adverb that means completely. (He was <u>quite</u> alone.)

 It is not quite right to leave the <u>e</u> off of <u>quite</u>; in fact, it is quite wrong.

 If you are very quiet, you can hear the two syllables in <u>quiet</u>.

12. <u>read</u>—a verb that means to understand printed words (rhymes with <u>bead</u> in the present tense and <u>bed</u> in the past tense). (I <u>read</u> to my children every day when they come home from school. My parents <u>read</u> to me every day when I was a child.)
<u>red</u>—an adjective that refers to a color. (She photographed the <u>red</u> evening sky.)

13. <u>sense</u>—a noun that means understanding. (He has good <u>sense</u>.)
<u>since</u>—a preposition that means after a certain time. (She has been waiting for him <u>since</u> daybreak.)

 If you can spell exp<u>ense</u> you have the sense to spell <u>sense</u>.

14. <u>then</u>—an adverb that means afterward. (We ate dinner and <u>then</u> we left.)
<u>than</u>—a conjunction that is used to compare two things. (This car is bigger <u>than</u> the other.)

 When you use <u>than</u> to compare two things, think of one thing <u>an</u>d another.

15. there—an expletive or adverb that means a place not so close by. (He flew out <u>there</u> for vacation.)
    <u>their</u>—a possessive pronoun that shows ownership. (<u>Their</u> house is on fire.)

    <u>There</u> is farther away than <u>here</u>. (<u>There</u> she goes. <u>Here</u> she comes.)
    <u>Their</u> is used only as a possessive.

16. <u>though</u>—a conjunction that means in spite of. (He was able to walk <u>though</u> it was painful for him.)
    <u>thought</u>—the past tense of think. (I <u>thought</u> I saw her.)

    Though the two words may look alike, <u>though</u> does not have a <u>t</u> at the end.

17. <u>threw</u>—the past tense of throw. (I <u>threw</u> the javelin in high school.)
    <u>through</u>—a preposition that means into and out of. (We rode <u>through</u> the forest.)

    Say to yourself, "My engine threw a screw. I'm through with it."

18. <u>too</u>—an adverb that means also or the extent to which. (I am going <u>too</u>. The dog was <u>too</u> sick and <u>too</u> small.)
    <u>to</u>—a preposition with several uses. (They went <u>to</u> the store in order <u>to</u> buy a camera.)
    <u>two</u>—a noun or adjective that is the written form of the numeral 2. (I have <u>two</u> sisters.)

19. <u>weather</u>—a noun that means temperature or climate. (How is the <u>weather</u> in the mountains?)
    <u>whether</u>—an adverb that means condition. (<u>Whether</u> or not you should go, I don't know.)

20. <u>were</u>—the third-person plural, past tense, of the verb <u>to be</u>. (The skiers <u>were</u> cold at the end of the day.)
    <u>where</u>—an adverb that means <u>at the place of</u>. (Those fish live <u>where</u> the water is cold.)

17.5 Using the Hyphen

One of the most difficult elements in spelling is the use of the hyphen (-). The following rules will help, but if you are in any doubt as to whether a hyphen is necessary, look up the word in your dictionary. Use the hyphen:

1. To carry a word from one line to the next:

                                                              . . . an unnec-
essary remark.

Avoid breaking a word between lines, but if you must, divide it with a hyphen between syllables. Do not divide short words like *also* or *into*. A dictionary will show the breakdown of a word by syllables.

2. To write compound numbers from *twenty-one* to *ninety-nine*.
3. To write fractions such as *three-fifths, two-thirds, one and one-half*.
4. After a prefix that is joined to a proper name, such as *non-European, un-American*.
5. After certain other prefixes, such as *ex-wife, semi-invalid*.
6. To write certain compound nouns, such as *secretary-treasurer*, a *two-year-old, mother-in-law, president-elect*. Consult a dictionary. *If the compound noun is not listed, write it as two separate words*.
7. To join two words used as a single adjective, such as *first-place team, horn-rimmed glasses, warm-hearted coach*. Some compound adjectives, such as *high school* (as in *high school team*) are so familiar that many professional writers omit the hyphen.

17.6 Words Often Misspelled

In addition to the words you have already studied, the following are among those most often misspelled by beginning college students. If you are not sure of what any of the words mean, look them up in the dictionary. Try to learn to spell them all.

Single and Compound Words

almost	everything	something	a lot
already	forever	themselves	all right
altogether	itself	throughout	each one
always	meantime	weekday	each other
anyway	meanwhile	weekend	even though
anywhere	nevertheless	whenever	every time
apart	nowadays	whereas	high school
awhile	nowhere	wherever	in order that
cannot	someday	whoever	no one
everyone	somehow	without	one day
			post card

Numbers, Days, and Months

one-half	eighth	nineteenth	ninety-one	Saturday
fourth	ninth	twentieth	ninetieth	
sixth	twelfth	forty		January
eight	thirteenth	ninety	Wednesday	February

Others (See the rule below on when to use ie *and* ei.*)*

A

absence
academic
accidentally
accommodate
accumulate
achieve
across
advice (n)
advise (v)
agreeable
amateur
analysis
analyze
apologize
apology
apparent
appearance
argument
ascend
athlete
attendance
average
awful

B

bath (n)
bathe (v)
beautiful
beginning
belief (n)
believe (v)
bookkeeping
boundaries
breath (n)
breathe (v)
Britain
buried
bury
business
businesslike

C

calendar
category
ceiling
certain
college
coming
commission
commitment
committed
committee
competent
conceivable
conscience
conscious
council (n)
counsel (v)
counselor
criticize

D

deceased
decision
develop
dictionary
difference
dilemma
discussed
disgust
dormitory

E

earliest
either
embarrass
emphasis
emphasize (v)
employee
envelope
equip
equipment

equipped
especially
existence
expense
explanation
extraordinary

F

familiar
fascinate
fiery
foreign
freight
fulfill

G

gauge
generalize
government
grammar
grateful
guess (n, v)
guest (n)

H

handicapped
handkerchief
handsome
height
hoping

I

identical
illegible
immediately
incident
incompetent
inconceivable
independence
independent
intelligence
interest

J, K

jewelry
judgment
know
knowledge

L

later
latter
leisure
library
license
literature
loneliness
lounge

M

machinery
maintain
maintenance
marriage
mathematics
miniature
mischief
mischievous
misspell
moderate

N

necessary
Negroes
neither
niece
northeast
noticeable
nowadays

O

occasion
occur
occurred
occurrence
o'clock
okay (O.K.)

omitted
organization

P

paid
parallel
participant
pastime
peace (not war)
perceive
percent
permanent
permitted
personal
personnel
physical
piece (part of)
possession
potatoes
practical
precede
prejudiced
pressure
principal (one in
  charge)
principle (a rule)
privilege
proceed

R

realize
receive
recognize
recommend
referred
relieve
rhyme
rhythm
ridiculous

S

salary
secretary
seize
sense

sensible
separate
sergeant
similar
sophomore
succeed
successful
suppose
supposed to
surprise

T

taxable
technical
thorough
till (or until)
tragedy
traveled

U, V

used to
useful
valuable
vein
vice versa

W

wage
weird
while
women
writing
written

Y, Z

yearbook
yield
zealous

The *ie, ei* Rule

Use *i* before *e*, except after *c*, or when sounded as *a*, as in *neighbor* and *weigh* (*nay-bor* and *way*):

1. Use *i* before *e*:

achieve	conscientious	niece	thief
believe	earliest	piece	twentieth
conscience	mischief	relieve	yield

2. Except after *c*:

    ceiling   conceivable   perceive   receive

3. Or when sounded as *a*:

    freight   neighbor   sleigh   vein   weigh

4. Memorize these exceptions:

either	height	neither	their
foreign	leisure	seize	weird

PRACTICE 7

Correct the one misspelled word in each of the following:

1. almost, always, alright, altogether, already
2. apart, awhile, alot, nowhere, no one
3. everything, someday, throughout, weekend, highschool
4. anywhere, mean time, whereas, without, meanwhile
5. when ever, whoever, cannot, post card, somehow
6. one-half, fourth, twelth, ninetieth, ninety
7. January, Febuary, Wednesday, thirteenth, nineteenth
8. appearance, accidentally, accommodate, agreeable, absense
9. achieve, arguement, apology, apologize, analysis
10. attendence, agreeable, accumulate, across, athlete
11. businesslike, buried, Britain, bookeeping, breathe
12. begining, boundaries, beautiful, business, believe
13. committed, commitment, commitee, conceivable, counselor
14. ceiling, commission, counsel, coming, competant
15. develope, dilemma, disgust, dictionary, dormitory
16. existence, equipped, especially, emphasize, earlyest

17. envelope, emphasis, embarrass, explanation, existance
18. fiery, familiar, freight, fulfill, foriegn
19. guest, goverment, grateful, gauge, generalize
20. hoping, height, handsome, handkercheif
21. incompetent, independant, intelligence, illegible, inconceivable
22. judgment, jewelry, know, knowlege
23. leisure, loneliness, license, libary, literature
24. miniature, misspell, mathmatics, mischievous, maintenance
25. northeast, necessary, neither, neice, noticeable
26. o'clock, occurrence, okay, occured, occasion
27. percent, personnel, preceive, parallel, principle
28. potato, physical, possession, pastime, privilige
29. participent, permitted, precede, proceed, piece
30. rhyme, rhythm, relieve, rediculous, realize
31. seize, separate, sergeant, sensable, sophomore
32. suppose, supprise, similar, succeed, successful
33. traveled, tragedy, til, taxable, technical
34. use to, vice versa, useful, vein, valuable
35. yield, weird, writing, writen, wage

17.7 Review Exercise

Choose the correctly spelled words in each sentence below:

1. After they had (carried, carryed) the (radioes, radios) upstairs, they began bringing in the other furniture.

2. The travelers (journied, journeyed) to the remote wilderness of (their, there) dreams.

3. The people gave the space travelers a welcome reserved for (heros, heroes), and then one of the (Kennedys, Kennedies) made a speech.

4. I (studyed, studied) a book on the (lives, lifes) of the saints.

5. It (occurred, occured) to Henry Ford that he could make cars more cheaply on an assembly line. He thus (opened, openned) a new factory.

6. You (cannot, can not) have both of your (wishs, wishes).

7. (Let's, Lets) not (deceive, decieve) ourselves.

8. (Its, It's) a shame (your, you're) paper was late.

9. (Who's, Whose) children were they? Did they (appologize, apologize) for what they did?

10. I'd rather have (to, too) much (then, than) too little.

11. (Their, There) was no reason for (their, there) misbehavior.

12. They (threw, through) her into the (hole, hold) in the ground.

13. When my father turned (forty-five, forty five), he said that his life was (one-half, one half) over.

14. We (almost, allmost) forgot to include the (secretary, secretery).

15. You (all ways, always) (achieve, acheive) what you set out to accomplish.

16. His (appearence, appearance) before the (counseler, counselor) left much to be desired.

17. Our nation faces a (dilema, dilemma) in dealing with workers from (foreign, foriegn) countries.

18. The (mischievous, mischeivous) child did (permenent, permanent) damage to the house.

19. Our (handicapt, handicapped) students have not lost (interest, intrest) in trying to make the campus barrier-free.

20. (Now a days, Nowadays) there is no (occasion, ocassion) to rebel.

CHAPTER 18

Capitalization, Punctuation, and Numbers

18.0 Introduction

In this chapter you will learn the basic rules of capitalization and punctuation. A special section on writing numbers and numerals is also included.

Punctuation refers to all the marks and symbols used in writing: the period, the apostrophe, the comma, the hyphen, and so on. Punctuation is used to clarify the meaning of writing. In the words of the popular novelist Kurt Vonnegut, "If I broke all the rules of punctuation, had words mean whatever I wanted them to mean, and strung them together higgledy-piggledy, I would simply not be understood." This chapter should help you to be understood better in your writing.

It is difficult to learn all the rules of punctuation in a short time. But you can improve your use of punctuation if you consult this chapter while you are editing your writing. The more often you check your punctuation, the more quickly you will master the rules.

18.1 Capitalization

Since many tend to overuse capital letters, the first rule for capitalization is *do not use a capital letter unless you have a particular reason to do so.* Here are twelve reasons for using capital letters:

1. Capitalize the pronoun *I*.
2. Capitalize the beginning of every sentence.

3. Capitalize the first word of a quoted sentence or part of a sentence:

   She said, "You are not too young for Geritol."

   Hamlet said, "To be or not to be?"

4. Capitalize proper nouns (names of particular people, places, and things) but not general nouns:

Capitalize	Do Not Capitalize
Kennedy High School	my high school
Minneapolis, Minnesota	my home city and state
Labor Day	a holiday
Edward Manly Royall	my grandfather
the United States Constitution	a treaty
Mississippi River	the river
The Institute of Growth	

   (Capitalize *t* only if *The* is part of the official name.)

5. Capitalize titles when they are used with proper names:

Capitalize	Do Not Capitalize
Dr. Anita Zervigon	our family doctor
Senator Barry Goldwater	one of the senators
Mr. and Mrs. Johnson	the family next door
Peter B. Morial, Ph.D.	a professor of math

6. Capitalize the days of the week and the months, but not the seasons:

Capitalize	Do Not Capitalize
Sunday	summer
Monday	autumn
February	weekend
January	month

7. Capitalize the names of specific courses and language courses:

Capitalize	Do Not Capitalize
Mathematics 102	math
English	physics
Spanish	political science

8. Capitalize the names of relatives when used as proper nouns:

   My sister calls our mother Mom.

9. In all titles capitalize the first and last word and all other words except articles (*a, an,* or *the*), short prepositions (*of, in, on,* and the like), and short conjunctions (*and, or, but,* and so on):

   Professor Kahn assigned *The Protestant Ethic and the Spirit of Capitalism.*

10. You may (but do not have to) capitalize the titles of heads of nations:

    You May Capitalize | *Do Not Capitalize*

    the President of the United States | the president of the college
    | the chairman of the board
    | the senators in the United States Congress

11. Capitalize *north, east, northwest,* and the like when these words are used to designate recognized geographical areas, but not when used to show direction. *Deep South* is also capitalized.

    You must travel east from Hawaii to reach the West.

12. Capitalize words referring to a particular deity, belief, or religious object:

    Capitalize | *Do Not Capitalize*

    God | the gods are angry
    Trinity | divine
    Ten Commandments | deity
    Hinduism | holy
    B.C. (before Christ) | a church
    Bible | religion
    Torah |
    Jehovah |

    Pronouns referring to deity are often capitalized:

    Jehovah, as presented in the Bible, sometimes shows His anger.

PRACTICE 1

Capitalize as necessary in the sentences that follow:

1. The rules that govern our electoral politics need to be changed.

2. President jimmy carter lost his attempt for a second term after wasting time, money, and energy working for his reelection.

3. In an article in *newsweek* entitled "the six year presidency," Jack Valenti wrote, "a president's noblest stirring is toward his place in history."

4. willie morris, who wrote *north toward home*, moved to the north but now lives in oxford, mississippi, the deep south.

5. The torah is the name of the first five books of the bible.

6. One wednesday last fall, i began sitting in on a world history class and found it so interesting that i signed up for history 102.

7. My five-year-old son, ted, asked me, "what makes a car run, dad?"

8. I told him, "gasoline, sonny boy."

9. My favorite teacher at carver high school was mr. harry berger, but he is teaching at some junior high school now.

10. She asked us to write an essay entitled, "a time I would like to forget."

18.2 End Punctuation

Use either a period (.), question mark (?), or exclamation point (!) to end all sentences:

1. Use a period to end a sentence that makes a statement or expresses a command:

> Capital punishment is a controversial issue.
> Turn in your papers by Friday.
> Instead of saying "I do," the bride said, "I don't."

Note that the period is placed inside the quotation marks.

2. Use a question mark to end a sentence that asks a question:

> Will you come with me?
> "Will you come with me?" he asked.

Note that the question mark is placed inside quotation marks.

3. Use an exclamation point to end a sentence that expresses strong emotion:

> Stop that fighting!

An exclamation point is also used to indicate an interjection, which may not be a sentence:

> Ouch!
> Nonsense!

A period is also used to indicate most abbreviations:

> Mr. (mister)
> M.D. (medical doctor)

M.A. (Master of Arts)

P.M. (post meridian)

B.C. (before Christ)

PRACTICE 2

Insert periods, question marks, and exclamation points in the following sentences as necessary:

1. Dr. Sosnoski didn't say, "Will you stop smoking?"

2. He said, in a quiet voice, "Stop smoking right now"

3. "Ouch" I said, "That hurts"

4. I have been smoking for twenty years

5. "May I wait until after Christmas" I asked

6. "No" he almost shouted "Now"

7. Are the surgeon general and Dr. Sosnoski right about smoking

18.3 The Apostrophe

The apostrophe (') has varied uses: to mark the omission of one or more letters or numbers; to form plurals of letters, numerals, and symbols; and to show possession or ownership:

1. Use the apostrophe' to mark the omission of one or more letters in contractions:

   <u>cannot</u> becomes <u>can't</u>

   <u>let us</u> becomes <u>let's</u>

   <u>that is</u> becomes <u>that's</u>

   <u>it is</u> becomes <u>it's</u>

   See pages 397–399 for more examples and practice.

2. Use the apostrophe to mark the omission of letters and numbers in the following:

   <u>of the clock</u> becomes <u>o'clock</u>

   <u>the class of 1984</u> becomes <u>the class of '84</u>

3. Use the apostrophe to mark the omission of letters in quoted dialogue:

   He said, "I've just been <u>sittin'</u> and <u>waitin'</u> for my dinner."

4. Use the apostrophe to form the plurals of letters, numerals, and symbols:

   <u>one *t*</u> becomes <u>two *t*'s</u>

one <u>5</u> becomes two <u>5's</u>

one <u>$</u> becomes two <u>$'s</u>

(Many publishers have dropped the apostrophe in such uses and print the above plurals as *two ts, two 5s, two $s*.) *Note*: Do *not* use the apostrophe to form any other plurals.

PRACTICE 3

Supply the necessary apostrophes in the following sentences:

1. Its a long way to Maxine's house, but well go there anyway before it is too late.

2. The womens movement began in about 63 or 64 and is still strong in the 80s.

3. "Havent you ever eaten Mama Linda's chicken? Im tellin you; its better than finger lickin good."

4. Its theirs; you cant have it.

5. My children are sick of my telling them to dot their *is* and cross their *ts*.

Using the Apostrophe to Show Ownership

Use the apostrophe to show ownership:

1. Add *'s* to a singular noun or indefinite pronoun (*anyone, everyone,* and the like):

   <u>the house of Barry</u> becomes <u>Barry's house</u>

   <u>the house of Bess</u> becomes <u>Bess's house</u>

   <u>the opinion of everyone</u> becomes <u>everyone's opinion</u>

   <u>the trials of today</u> becomes <u>today's trials</u>

   Do *not* use the apostrophe for the possessive case of personal pronouns:

   The new car is <u>ours</u>.

   The choice is <u>theirs</u>.

   The computer can't make up <u>its</u> mind.

2. Add *'s* to a plural noun that does not end in *-s*:

   <u>the play of the children</u> becomes <u>the children's play</u>

   <u>the will of the people</u> becomes <u>the people's will</u>

3. Add just the apostrophe to a plural noun that ends in *-s*:

   <u>the home of the boys</u> becomes <u>the boys' home</u>

   <u>the blades of the propellers</u> becomes <u>the propellers' blades</u>

4. If there is joint ownership between two or more nouns, the final noun takes the apostrophe:

> the house of my mother and father becomes my mother and father's house

But notice how the apostrophe is used in the following cases:

> Rico's and Donna's watches were stolen. (Here the ownership is not joint because Rico and Donna own their watches separately.)

> Gladys's and my house is up for sale. (When the pronoun *my* or *our* is used in such compounds, the apostrophe is added to the noun even though the noun comes first. Note also that *mines* and *my's* are not words.)

5. Add *'s* or just the apostrophe to the last element in a compound word:

> the demands of a mother-in-law becomes a mother-in-law's demands

PRACTICE 4

Form the possessive of each of the following:

1. the room of the teachers *the teachers' room* _____
2. the address of the Smiths _____
3. the address of Charles _____
4. the events of today _____
5. the activities of the ladies _____
6. the husband of a woman _____
7. the relationship of a man and a woman _____
8. the good fortune of a son-in-law _____
9. the attitude of the boy _____
10. the attitude of the boys _____
11. the attitude of the people _____

PRACTICE 5

Write sentences using the possessive form of the following nouns:

1. (lady) *The lady's child was lost.* _____
2. (ladies) _____
3. (child) _____
4. (children) _____
5. (flowers) _____

6. (people) _____

7. (the Smiths) _____

8. (Ms. Marle Hass) _____

9. (birds) _____

10. (sons-in-law) _____

11. (women) _____

PRACTICE 6

Correct the errors in apostrophe use in the sentences below. Some of the apostrophes have been misused; others have been omitted, along with the -*s*. (One sentence is correct.) Remember: Do not use an apostrophe when you are simply adding an -*s* to make a plural.

1. President Carter recognized the ~~Peoples~~ *People's* Republic of China.

2. Her ~~sons~~ *sons'* wives all call her Mother, and she calls them her daughters.

3. His victory was everyones victory.

4. Sandra many boyfriends got together for a reunion.

5. The childrens constant crying is driving me insane.

6. The peoples' fear of crime is increasing.

7. My daughter Marys name for ballet is *baleg*.

8. Her two boys' call a window a *windoor*.

9. I like to shop at Natures Way.

10. The Joneses rent is due.

11. Pierre's and Violet's car is in the shop.

12. Uz's and Buzz's names come from the Bible.

13. There is so much smoke from the factories that the air smells as though someone house is on fire.

14. My neighbors lawns have almost been ruined by that garbage truck.

15. In our neighborhood we have different committee's to keep things running smoothly.

16. About seven o'clock you can hear the children mother screaming, "Tommy, Angela, come in! It's time to eat."

17. Next to Saint Raymonds Catholic Church is the priests home, where eight of these padres live.

18.4 The Comma

Conventional use of the comma (,) is perhaps the most difficult punctuation skill to master. Professional writers themselves often disagree about certain uses of the comma. Students tend to overuse commas, perhaps because they were taught to use a comma any time they wanted to indicate a pause in a sentence. To avoid comma errors, it is best to learn the general rules for comma use and to follow the advice of the old saying: *When in doubt, leave it out.* As you learn the ten rules given in this text, you can begin to insert commas. Refer frequently to these rules when you are editing your papers.

Rule 1   Use a comma before a coordinating conjunction when it joins two independent clauses. The coordinating conjunctions are *and, but, for, yet, so, or,* and *nor*:

> The weather was stormy, and it was very late.
>
> The weather was stormy, but I was not cold.

Do *not* use a comma before a coordinating conjunction when it joins two words, two phrases, or two dependent clauses:

> Carlos and Lucia are going swimming. (two nouns)
>
> At lunchtime we were throwing our food away and were creating quite a disturbance. (two verb phrases)
>
> When you see those things happen, you will know that the prophecy has been fulfilled and that the world is doomed. (two dependent clauses)

PRACTICE 7

Supply the necessary commas.

> Joseph's brothers took his coat of many colors and then threw him into a pit. Later, they saw a company of Ishmaelites and they lifted Joseph out of the pit and sold him to the Ishmaelites. Joseph was taken to Egypt in slavery but he eventually gained the Pharoah's confidence and became the prime minister. Many years later he saved his brothers from starvation and he told them, "What you meant for evil, God used for good."

Rule 2   Use a comma after a subordinate clause when it begins a sentence. Subordinate clauses begin with such conjunctions as *when, if, because, after, although, as, while, since, even though, before,* and *whenever*:

> While the girl pushed the car, her father watched.

However, when the dependent clause comes at the end of the sentence, you do not ordinarily need a comma. (See Rule 10 below for exceptions.)

> Her father watched while the girl pushed the car.

PRACTICE 8

Supply the necessary commas.

We were greatly surprised when we found out that Mr. Morales had cancer. But we are not depressed. While there is life there is hope. We know he will get well because he is such a fighter. If Mr. Morales will just do what the doctor says he will live many more years.

Rule 3   Use commas to set off an adjective clause if the clause is not *essential* to the meaning of the sentence. Adjective clauses usually begin with *who, which,* or *that:*

My mother, who likes sardine sandwiches, is an unusual person.

You can omit the clause *who likes sardine sandwiches* and the sentence will still make sense. Therefore, you need the commas. But if the adjective clause is *essential* to the meaning of the sentence, do not use commas:

My mother is the only one in our family who likes sardine sandwiches.

This time if you omit the clause *who likes sardine sandwiches,* the sentence does not make sense.

Hint: Which clauses usually take commas; *that* clauses seldom do.

PRACTICE 9

Supply the necessary commas.

Great Britain who was our ally went to war with Argentina who was also our ally. Americans who sided with either Argentina or Britain were criticized. This war which caused many deaths was a tragedy and should never have happened.

Rule 4   Use a comma or commas to set off most conjunctive adverbs (words and phrases like *however, for example, on the other hand, nevertheless, moreover, particularly, especially, therefore,* and *consequently*):

I know I said I would go; however, I have since changed my mind. (Here *however* follows a semicolon.)

I agree that is what I should do. However, I just cannot bring myself to do it. (Here *however* begins a new sentence.)

Children learn to read, however, in spite of poor teaching. (Here *however* comes in the middle of a simple sentence.)

You usually do not use a comma to set off *then* and *also,* although if you want to indicate a significant pause, you may.

PRACTICE 10

Supply the necessary commas.

Joseph's brothers had sold him into slavery; however he not only forgave them but also extended to them the hand of friendship. When his father Jacob heard the news, he decided to travel to Egypt. Jacob was an old man; nevertheless he was determined to see his son. When his father arrived, Joseph fell at his knees; then he wept. Joseph had many fine qualities for example his courage, his determination, and his love.

Rule 5   Use a comma or commas to set off an appositive. An appositive is a word, phrase, or clause used as a noun that identifies or explains another noun or pronoun:

Those were the happiest days in my life, the days when I was young and foolish. (The noun *days* is repeated and then explained.)

One of their neighbors, Boo Radley, was a very mysterious person. (The pronoun *one* is identified as Boo Radley.)

We like starches, especially grits, rice, and barley.

PRACTICE 11

Supply the necessary commas.

She lived her entire life in that house a house that had once been admired by all. When I knew her, the building was dilapidated. The porch a beautifully constructed work of art was now rotting. The front door, which had been brought over from England, was nailed shut. Curtains now nothing but rags hung wearily behind cloudy windows. Aunt Kathleen, however, a woman up in her eighties did not change. She was poor but still proud.

Rule 6   Use commas between items in a series (words, phrases, or clauses). Unless your teacher instructs otherwise, use the comma before the conjunction that connects the last item to the others:

She bought apples, oranges, and bananas. (nouns)

Chitty Chat likes to eat tuna, climb Christmas trees, and chase Hubert. (infinitive phrases)

We went home, we took a dip in the pool, and then we ate breakfast. (independent clauses)

The use of commas between adjectives in a series is more complicated. In such cases, use a comma between the adjectives *only* if you could replace the comma with the word *and*. For example:

He was a tall, lean man.

The comma is correct because you could write, *He was a tall and lean man.*
But look at the next sentence:

> He was a nice old man.

A comma is not correct because you would not be apt to write, *He was a nice and old man.*

PRACTICE 12

Supply the necessary commas.

> You are so civilized so intelligent and so self-possessed that you ought to be *Time's* "Man of the Year." But *Time* named that determined courageous man from Poland instead.

Rule 7   Use a comma or commas with direct quotations:

> The prophet said, "Go in peace."
> "Go in peace," the prophet said.
> "Go in peace," the prophet said, "and others will follow you."
> The prophet said, "Go in peace," and then he left them.

Note: The comma is always placed inside the quotation marks.
Do not use commas with indirect quotations:

> The prophet said to go in peace.
> The prophet said that we should go in peace.

PRACTICE 13

Supply the necessary commas.

> "If I were you" my dad said "I wouldn't go out in the rain." I told him that I was glad he wasn't me.

Rule 8   Use a comma or commas to set off items in dates and addresses, but not ZIP codes:

> I was born Friday, October 12, 1938, in Charleston, South Carolina.
> His address is Apt. A, 1426 M Street, Washington, D.C. 20012.

Do not use commas when prepositions introduce places and dates:

> He was born in Chicago in 1926.

PRACTICE 14

Supply the necessary commas.

> Abraham Lincoln was born in Hardin County Kentucky February 12 1809. He died in 1865.

Rule 9   Use a comma after an introductory phrase if the comma makes the meaning of the sentence clearer:

> After eating, my horse and I set out on our lonesome trip.
>
> In the still of the night, groans can sometimes be heard from the chest in the attic.

Avoid using commas after short introductory phrases if the meaning of the sentence is clear without the comma:

> Later that day they came to our rescue.

PRACTICE 15

Supply the necessary commas.

> While visiting Mary suddenly became ill. After trying for hours to locate her
>
> husband my sister and I took her to the hospital. At about ten o'clock her
>
> husband finally arrived.

Rule 10   Use a comma or commas to set off words, phrases, or clauses if they *clearly* break the flow of the sentence. Sometimes the words or words will be at the beginning of the sentence:

> Darren, please drop what you are doing and give me a hand.

Sometimes the word or words will be in the middle of the sentence:

> My grandmother, known for her habit of chewing tobacco, is nearly ninety. (This break in the middle of a sentence is often a nonessential adjective clause. See Rule 3 or Rule 5 above.)

Sometimes the words or words will be at the end of the sentence, almost as an afterthought:

> Anthony was completely honest about what he had done, not that I would have expected him to act any differently. (You are safe using a comma before all such constructions with *not*.)
>
> You do agree with me, don't you?
>
> I think we should do everything possible to find a peaceful solution, although I must say that I am not optimistic. (Even though the dependent clause comes at the end of a sentence, the comma is necessary because the clause is clearly an afterthought.)
>
> They ended the day in complete silence, knowing that any sound would give them away.

PRACTICE 16

Supply the necessary commas.

> Bob said to me, "Carlos that game was the greatest wasn't it?" I turned to my
>
> friend who was grinning at me devilishly and said, "Great for you my friend

not for me." One of these days I am going to beat Bob in Scrabble although lately I haven't even come close.

PRACTICE 17

Using Rules 1 and 2, supply commas as needed in the sentences below, citing the rule that applies in each case (not all sentences need commas):

1. My name is Bobby Carter, and I'm looking forward to writing this paper. *Rule 1*

2. As I have already said, job opportunities in my field are not good. *Rule 2*

3. I will know how to handle my clients and will be able to represent them well. _____

4. If you can survive this college you will do well in your chosen career. _____

5. I may never become rich but I will be able to acquire the things I want. _____

6. If I were to study nursing I know I would like it. _____

7. She wants to complete college but does not know for sure what the future holds for her. _____

8. My aunt wants to help open the day care center but she does not want to work there. _____

9. I wanted to be a bank robber when I was young. _____

10. Although a degree is not needed to open a nursery school it would help. _____

11. Because you work hard you will succeed. _____

12. You will succeed because you work hard. _____

13. It rained forty days and forty nights and the whole world was destroyed. _____

14. While the earth lasts seedtime and harvest will not cease. _____

15. Seedtime and harvest will not cease while the earth lasts. _____

16. When you see those things happening you will know that the end has come and that the world is no more. _____

17. It is a two-year course and will prepare me for an office management position. _____

18. I talk to my friends often and I try to help them. _____

19. I talk to my friends often and try to help them. _____

20. She would enjoy helping others as a doctor but she cannot stand the sight of blood. _____

21. She would enjoy helping others as a doctor but cannot stand the sight of blood. _____

22. Some social workers specialize in psychiatric social work because they want to become professional counselors. _____

23. More businesses are opening than ever before and they will all need to purchase insurance. _____

PRACTICE 18

Using Rules 3–5, supply commas as needed in the sentences below, citing the rule or rules that apply in each case. (One sentence does not need a comma.)

1. Sybil, who is a member of the Symphony Club, gave us two tickets for the performance. _*Rule 3*_____

2. Joe registered late; consequently, he will have to pay a five dollar fine. _*Rule 4*_____

3. Edgar Allen Poe the master writer of horror stories did not enjoy great popularity during his lifetime. _____

4. Only one person a carpenter was injured. _____

5. My English textbook which had been lost all semester turned up the day classes ended. _____

6. Luckily our family lives near the coast because we all love fresh seafood especially shrimp, redfish, and crab. _____

7. Many plants are killed by owners who pay too much attention to them; for example overwatering has killed many a plant. _____

8. André who had been cramming the whole night slept through the test. _____

9. We rushed to the theater to see the movie from the beginning; however it had already started when we arrived. _____

10. Chico our eccentric next-door neighbor is the only person I know who mows his lawn in a bathing suit. _____

11. Immunization is now available for three of the most dangerous childhood ailments diphtheria, typhoid, and measles. _____

12. My aunt spends most of her free time involved in outdoor activities particularly fishing, hunting, and camping. _____

13. Any student who has placed all the commas correctly in this exercise deserves a pat on the back.

PRACTICE 19

Using Rules 6–10, supply commas as needed in the sentences below, citing the rule or rules that apply in each case:

1. I told her not to worry but to stay cool, calm, and collected. _*Rule 6*_

2. It was a dark rainy spring day when we first met wasn't it? _____

3. Before riding in the automobile with my father my sister always takes a tranquilizer. _____

4. The City Council voted yesterday to increase the sales tax although they know the citizens will rise up in protest. _____

5. As director you will be responsible for the management of the center the hiring and training of the personnel and the development of new programs. _____

6. "Ask not what your country can do for you" President Kennedy said "but ask what you can do for your country." _____

7. In the middle of the night time stands still, and you can hear the lonely sound of a hoot owl. _____

8. Make love not war. _____

9. "War is not what I want" he said "but peace." _____

10. I left home suitcase in hand not knowing what I would do next. _____

11. Malcolm X, the controversial leader of a movement to unite black people throughout the world, was assassinated in New York City on February 21 1965. _____

PRACTICE 20

Using Rules 1–10, supply commas as needed in the sentences below, citing the rule or rules that apply in each case. (Some sentences are correct.)

1. *Dictionary* spelled backwards is *yranoitcid* but *madam* spelled backwards is *madam.* _____

2. We ended up walking in circles and bumping into the same security officer. _____

3. As the three of us walked outside we argued about where we had parked the car. _____

4. He said that he wanted the choir to sing at his wake and that he wanted to be buried in his choir robes. _____

5. That afternoon we divided into groups and searched the library for the items on the list. _____

6. All the girls wanted the leading part because it was that of a glamorous woman. _____

7. After we unloaded the bus our next task was to pitch the tent. _____

8. I tried to light the stove but I was unsuccessful because the matches were wet. _____

9. I tried to light the stove but was unsuccessful because the matches were wet. _____

10. Finally when we arrived at the Rivergate the people applauded us and the whole effort seemed worthwhile. _____

11. I love seafood especially crab shrimp and oysters. _____

12. I was guarding Tim Owens a 6'6" guard and I am only 6'. _____

13. If you look back you will turn into a pillar of salt. _____

14. You will turn into a pillar of salt if you look back. _____

15. Dwight Eisenhower the thirty-fourth president of the United States was born in Denison Texas on October 14 1890. _____

16. As I continued to walk down the road I noticed a small inviting brown cabin with smoke coming from the chimney. _____

17. We shared some very hard times but through it all we stuck together and became like sisters. _____

18. "Life is like walking in the snow" Granny used to say "because every step shows." _____

19. In October 1975 the Navy sent our family to Los Angeles California where I attended Grossmand High School and met Kim Steve and Colleen. _____

20. Honestly I am about ready to scream; these commas are too much! _____

18.5 The Semicolon

The semicolon (;) can be used to join independent clauses in compound sentences. Sentences take semicolons when:

1. The pronoun subject of the second independent clause refers to a noun in the first independent clause:

The prisoners at the penitentiary are rioting; they claim that the new warden has been unfair.

After just three days Gina quit her job; it didn't hold her interest.

2. One independent clause is related to another by a conjunctive adverb, such as *then* or *however*:

We first tried giving money to that country; then we sent soldiers.

The governor refused to grant the pardon; however, he did say he might consider the case again next year.

Use the semicolon to make a compound sentence *only* if the two independent clauses are closely related in content and *only* if a period could be substituted for the semicolon. The following sentence is incorrect:

In those days he tried various drugs; for example, marijuana, LSD, and cocaine.

If you substituted a period for the semicolon, the last part of the sentence would be a fragment:

For example, marijuana, LSD, and cocaine.

The semicolon is also used to set off items in a series if any one of the items has internal punctuation:

For the climb up Long's Peak we took a tent, which only weighed five pounds; two very light goose-down sleeping bags; and enough food for a large, hungry army.

PRACTICE 21

Correct the misused semicolons in the sentences below. (Five sentences are correct.)

1. Chief Donald Sartisky completed twenty years in the Coast Guard; and then decided to go back to college to finish his degree.

2. He found college quite different from the way he remembered it; however, he adjusted quickly to the new atmosphere.

3. He likes to say, "It is even more difficult; than I remember, but I like the challenge."

4. To his surprise, he found that he had much in common with quite a few of the students; many of them were as old as he.

5. The chief was a hospital corpsman in the Coast Guard; and he wants to pursue a career in nursing when he finishes college.

6. Bridge is more than a game of cards; it is a science.

7. Vacations are not a luxury these days; they are a necessity.

8. Marlene is pleased with the pay at Hibernia National Bank, moreover; she likes the people.

9. The president is correct about inflation being an immense problem, however; he doesn't know what to do about it.

10. I wish everyone would hike in the Smoky Mountains; they are indeed spectacular.

18.6 The Colon

The colon (:) can be used in various situations:

1. After the salutation in a business letter:

> Dear Dr. Rittenberg:

Note: A comma is used after the salutation in a personal letter.

2. To separate numbers in the time of day and in biblical passages:

> 1:15 A.M.
>
> Exodus 3:15 (chapter 3, verse 15)

3. Before items in a series that follow what could be written as a grammatically complete sentence:

> Be sure to buy the following: dates, pecans, raisins, and honey.

But do not use a colon when the items in the series are necessary for the sentence to be complete:

> As for me, I like sugar, canned foods, and lots of meat.

4. To introduce indented quotations and quotations that are preceded by grammatically complete sentences:

> Dr. Hume wrote the following in his book *Doctors East, Doctors West*: "Only those can enter into her life who approach China's citadel by way of friendship."

When you introduce a written quotation with words like *write, says,* and *said,* it is usually appropriate to use only a comma:

> In his book Dr. Hume writes, "Only those can enter into her life who approach China's citadel by way of friendship."

18.7 Quotation Marks and Underlining

Quotation marks (" ") are always used in pairs. (Do not allow end quotation marks to carry over to the beginning of a new line, and do not end a line with beginning quotation marks.) Quotation marks have several functions:

Direct Quotations

Quotation marks are used to set off direct quotations, which are the exact words someone says or writes. The quoted words are often a sentence within a sentence:

The prophet said to his disciples, "Go in peace."

Note the following about this sentence:

1. The words the prophet said, *Go in peace*, can function as a complete sentence. (The subject *you* is understood.)
2. The comma comes before the direct quote.
3. The second set of quotation marks comes after the period.

Here are four variations of the above quotation. Notice the position of the quotation marks, commas, and question marks and the use of capitalization:

"Go in peace," the prophet said to his disciples.
"Go in peace," the prophet said to his disciples, "and Allah will be with you."
"Will you go in peace?" the prophet asked. "Allah will be with you."
"Will you go in peace? Allah will be with you," the prophet said.

Notice that in the last example quotation marks are used only at the beginning and end of what the prophet said, not at the end of each sentence.

If you must use a quotation mark within another quotation, use a single mark (') to indicate the inside quotation:

The speaker stated his position as follows: "I firmly believe that fantasy is an important part of life. I always think of the newspaper editor who answered the letter of a young girl by writing 'Yes, Virginia, there *is* a Santa Claus.'"

PRACTICE 22

Supply quotation marks, other punctuation, and capitalization as needed below:

1. What's the matter Richard's mother asked. *"What's the matter?" Richard's mother asked.*

2. It's those same boys he said. They'll beat me. _____

_____

3. You've got to get over that. Now go on she said. _____

_____

4. Richard replied but I'm scared. _____

_____

5. She said how can I let you back down now. _____

_____

6. Please Momma he said don't make me fight. _____

_____

Indirect Quotations

Do not use quotation marks to set off indirect quotations, which are *not* the exact words that someone says or writes. For example:

> She said she would try harder next time.

The words she actually used were these: "I will try harder next time." She did *not* say, "She would try harder next time." The writer used these words to tell what she said. Here are two more examples of indirect quotations:

> Dr. Hume wrote that to enter into the life of China one must approach that nation by way of friendship.

> The union members carried signs saying that they would not compromise.

PRACTICE 23

Rewrite the following direct quotations as indirect quotations. Change verbs to the past tense as necessary.

1. The school board said to the union, "You are demanding far too much money." *The school board said to the union that they were demanding far too much money.*

2. The union replied, "We only want a fair wage." _____

_____

3. The school board said, "Take your case to the taxpayer." _____

_____

4. The union then said, "The school board is responsible for the wages of teachers." _____

_____

PRACTICE 24

Rewrite the following indirect quotations as direct quotations. Change verbs to the present tense as necessary.

1. The police chief said that he needed more cooperation from the judges.

   The police chief said, "I need more cooperation from the judges."

2. The judges said that they were already giving out much stiffer sentences.

   _____

   _____

3. The police chief responded that dangerous criminals were still being allowed to roam the streets. _____

   _____

4. The judges said that they could not be blamed for the amount of crime in the streets. _____

   _____

5. The police chief said that the judges could help. _____

   _____

Other Uses of Quotation Marks and Underlining

Quotation marks have other uses as well:

1. To set off words used as words:

   Students often confuse "their" with "there."

   It is just as correct, however, to underline such words:

   Students often confuse their with there.

   However, use underlining, not quotation marks, for foreign words:

   coup de grace
   femme fatale

   Note: In print, italics replace underlining.

2. To set off the titles of short published works:

   a magazine article—"The Power of Islam"
   a book chapter—"A Time to Laugh"
   a poem—"Freedom"
   an essay—"The Time I Learned Humility"

   Longer works are underlined (italicized in print):

   a book—To Kill a Mockingbird

a play—<u>Macbeth</u>

a magazine—<u>Newsweek</u>

Longer works (which are underlined) often contain shorter works (which take quotation marks). A book, for example, contains chapters, and a magazine contains articles.

3. To set off the titles of television programs and songs:

"Sixty Minutes"

"Hey Jude"

However, the titles of movies are underlined:

<u>E. T.</u>

18.8 Other Punctuation: The Hyphen, the Dash, and Parentheses

Since the hyphen is an important part of spelling, it is discussed in Chapter 17.5. Use the dash (—) and parentheses [( )] as follows:

1. Use the dash to emphasize certain words, usually at the end of the sentence:

One punctuation mark is misused more than any other—the comma.

There is just one course that I can never seem to pass—Math 1111.

2. Use the dash to indicate an aside to the reader:

She said the "girls"—they are all over sixty—would play bridge tonight.

The game between Alabama and Michigan—it is sure to be close—will be played in the Superdome.

Note: When typing, use two hyphens for a dash and do not leave a space on either side of it.

3. You may substitute parentheses for the dash when you make an aside to the reader:

She said the "girls" (they are all over sixty) would play bridge tonight.

The game between Alabama and Michigan (it is sure to be close) will be played in the Superdome.

4. Use parentheses to indicate a span of dates:

Booker T. Washington (1856-1915) was a black American educator.

In her article in the *Atlantic Monthly* (May 1986), Barbara Wallraff wrote about the various kinds of pens.

18.9 Numbers and Numerals

Numbers can be either spelled out or written as numerals. As a general rule, spell out numbers that can be written as one or two words: *forty, sixty-three, five hundred, two million, three-fourths.* Use numerals for all other numbers (*10,401, 325, 6,174*).

Exceptions

1. Spell out all numbers that begin sentences:

> Two hundred forty-one people are still missing.

2. Use numerals for the following:
    a. Most dates:

    > October 12, 1938

    But spell out *the twelfth of October.*

    b. Most dollar amounts:

    > $10.51 $3.01 $17.00

    But spell out numbers used to indicate general amounts (*a hundred dollars, five millions dollars*).

    c. Street numbers:

    > 42 Legare Street

    d. Percentage amounts:

    > 20 percent of your earnings

    e. Times used with A.M. and P.M.:

    > 8:00 A.M.

    But spell out *five o'clock* and *six-thirty* when used without A.M. and P.M.

    f. Page and line numbers:

    > page 42, line 15

    g. Numbers in a list, set off by indention:

    > You will need the following:
    > 5 lbs. chicken   3 onions
    > 2 cups cream   1 lb. bacon
    > 1½ cups flour   ½ lb. mushrooms

3. If you must write one number in a sentence as a numeral, write all the others numbers as numerals: "I caught 416 pounds of fish, 50 pounds of shrimp, and 91 dozen crabs last summer."

Hyphens

Use a hyphen (-) with all two-word numbers from twenty-one to ninety-nine and with all fractions (three-fourths, nine-tenths, and so forth).

PRACTICE 25

Correct the use of numerals and words in the following. (Five are correct.)

1. Nineteen hundred and one (a date)
2. Six o'clock
3. 5:30 P.M.
4. Five dollars and fourteen cents
5. Page sixteen
6. 51 Canal Street
7. 8 o'clock
8. 56 percent
9. $10,550.00
10. Two-thirty P.M.

18.10 *Review Exercises*

REVIEW EXERCISE 1

Choose the correct alternative in the following sentences. (NP means no punctuation is needed.)

1. Stop that fighting (! *or* .)
2. She said, "Will you help me with my car ("? *or* ?")
3. (Let's *or* Lets) be on our way.
4. Our (children's *or* childrens') friends fill our house with excitement.
5. We now have diplomatic relations with the (Peoples' *or* People's) Republic of China.
6. It was the hottest day of the year (, *or* ;) but we were comfortable inside with our air conditioning turned on.
7. We became stuck on the mud bank (, *or* NP) because the tide fell several feet.
8. When I knew her (, *or* NP) she was already eighty years old.
9. "Give me cold weather any time (", *or* ,") she said.
10. Be sure to include the following (: *or* ;) a purpose statement, good transition sentences, effective detail, and a conclusion.
11. They said that (" *or* NP) they would try harder next time (." *or* .)
12. My favorite movie of all time is ("The African Queen" *or* The African Queen).
13. "If you come to work with me," he said, ("You *or* "you") will be rich.
14. (Everyones' *or* Everyone's) opinion has changed since the last election.
15. Mona was (president *or* President) of her high school class.
16. Kyle said that he was angry about the sale (, *or* NP) and that he would protest.
17. People (, *or* NP) who need people (, *or* NP) are the luckiest people in the world.
18. We first tried to make peace (, *or* ;) then we sent in soldiers.
19. He looked up the article in ("Newsweek" *or* Newsweek).
20. At the last count (46 *or* forty-six) people were still missing.

REVIEW EXERCISE 2

Choose the correct punctuation in the following letter, which was written as a student assignment. (See page 185.) (*NP* means no punctuation is needed.)

Dear Gina (, or :)

When I received your letter (; or ,) it made me glad to know you consider me such a close friend. (I'm or I'am) sorry you had to contact me under such difficult circumstances. After reading your letter (, or :) I thought about your problem for a very long time (*NP* or ,) and I realized that it has no easy solution. The final decision will be yours (, or ;) but I will do all I can to give you helpful suggestions. Gina (, or *NP*) I think you should not have the abortion. You (should'nt or shouldn't) have it because you are blessed with the love of your family and friends (, or ;) moreover (, or ;) a child can be instrumental in helping you reach your goals.

I realize that you have many reasons you think are valid for wanting· to have an abortion. I understand that people expect a lot from you (, or *NP*) for you were what you call a (''hot-shot'' or hot-shot) student in (high-school or high school). I also (, or *NP*) understand that having this baby will possibly lessen your chances of graduating from college and going to law school. Moreover (, or ;) I realize there is another problem to be faced (— or *NP*) how your parents will take the news.

Gina (, or :) your mother and father love you very much (, or *NP*) and will understand. They may be upset at first (*NP* or ,) but they will stand beside you (. or ,) I know they will. I know them well (, or *NP*) you know (, or *NP*) and am confident they won't let you down (; or *NP*) when you need them the most.

Gina (*NP* or ,) you are experiencing one of the great miracles of nature (, or ;) giving birth to a child. You are carrying what may seem to be a burden but what really is love in the true sense of the word. A baby brings out emotions and feelings that we often lose touch with. A baby teaches us to share (, or *NP*) care (, or *NP*) and be responsible. The child may be just what you need to help you get your priorities in order. There is never any shame in having a baby (, or ;) and a person can still excel with a child (, or ;) it will just be harder. I realize that you are thinking that the child will have a negative effect on your future (, or *NP*) but I don't think it will (*NP* or ,) not in the long run.

Since I am a man (, or *NP*) I can give you a man's view of your relationship with your boyfriend. Don't be too dependent on him (! or .) He may let you down. Wait a while before you marry him. If he really loves you (, or *NP*) he will wait. I love you very much (, or *NP*) and hope I have given you good advice.

With love,

Randy

APPENDIX A

Preparing the Research Paper

The Research Paper

A research paper differs in two respects from other essays you have written: (1) it is generally longer, and (2) it makes extensive use of information sources beyond the writer's personal experience: books, magazines, and newspapers. Because this type of paper relies so heavily on outside research, the writer is responsible for accurately quoting the words of other people and giving them credit for what they have said. This involves learning the correct way of citing the sources consulted.

On the other hand, the research paper also resembles in important ways other essays you have written. It consists of an introduction, which gives necessary background information and states the purpose or thesis; a body, which develops the thesis in more detail and provides evidence to support it; and a conclusion, which sums up the main ideas presented in the paper. Even when you are writing a ten- or twenty-page research paper, you can still use the same six-step method that you used for shaping much shorter essays. Here is how to adapt the six-step method to your research paper.

Step One: Gathering Ideas and Information

In most cases, you will be given a general topic to research—the American education system, for example. Part of your job will be to narrow down the topic into a thesis of suitable scope for the length of the assigned paper. For instance, in a ten-page paper, you really could not hope to cover every important issue connected with the American education system, but you could examine a more limited question, such as *one* of these: How do students pass through the system without learning to read and write? How does our system compare with that of another country? In what ways can we improve the system without destroying it altogether?

The best way to begin your research is to assess how much you already know about the subject and then make a list of questions about the topic

437

that you would like to find answers to. Brainstorming works well for this step. For example, given the topic of the American education system, you might come up with questions such as these:

1. What are the differences between private and public schools in this country?
2. Why do so many students drop out of school?
3. Does a system that encourages students to think and ask questions work better than a system that requires mostly memorization?
4. Does the American curriculum teach students what they need to know in the outside world?

Of course, you are not under any obligation to answer all of these questions in the course of your research. However, making the list will help you to get a better focus on what interests *you*. That is the first rule for writing a good research paper: *Choose a part of your topic that you genuinely would like to find out more about.* If you set off with gritted teeth to spend hours in the library researching some topic you don't care about at all, the paper is bound to be a painful experience for you—and for your reader as well.

In addition to your interest in the topic, another very important consideration is the workability of the subject. Is there enough resource material available for you to base a paper on? How much has been written on the subject, and how much of what has been written does your library have? To answer these questions, you will need to head for the library. Your time there will be spent in making a working bibliography, reading and scanning, and taking notes.

Making a Working Bibliography   This is a list of the books and articles that might be useful to you in writing your paper. Your first stop in the library will most likely be at the card catalogue, to see what books have been written on your topic. As you do this preliminary research, it is a good idea to keep a record of both the titles of books you find included in the catalogue and also their call numbers, so that you can easily go back to them later. The best way to do this is to keep a stack of 3″ × 5″ index cards that give the author, title, publishing information, and call number, and perhaps a note concerning the subject of the book or chapter in it. A sample card is shown at the top of the next page. Keeping such a record will help you at several stages of your research: while you are looking up and reading the books, when it is time to quote from the material and cite the source, and again when you are preparing the final bibliography.

While you are compiling your working bibliography, strive whenever possible to have a balance of both books *and* articles on your topic. Don't stop with just the card catalogue, even though it may yield a long list of books. Check out the resources available to you in the reference room: first the *Readers' Guide* and the *Magazine Index*, and then any specialized

| 320.9 | has an interesting chapter explaining why |
| C363h | students drop out of school |

<u>An Introduction to the Foundations</u>
<u>of Education</u>, Third Edition

Allan C. Ornstein and Daniel U. Levine
Boston : Houghton Mifflin Company, 1985

indexes that might prove helpful. (See Chapter 8, "Finding Resource Material in the Library.")

Reading and Scanning   Now you are ready to begin investigating the books and articles that look the most promising. Try scanning the books rather than reading each of them all the way through. First, look at the date the book was written. (If you are writing a paper on recent student drop-out rates, you can eliminate a book that was written in 1950.) Then look through the table of contents to see what areas of the topic the writer has examined. By reading a few paragraphs in one of the chapters, you will get a sense of the level of difficulty of the writer's style. Then flip to the index at the back of the book to see how often your area of interest is mentioned. (For example, you might look in the index under the heading "School drop-outs." Is the term mentioned once, twice, six times in the book? Do any of the page references represent long segments of the book?) If you do this at the outset, you usually can determine which books or chapters of books warrant a closer reading. Begin by reading the material that is most likely to provide you with an overview of the subject.

Taking Notes   If any articles or sections of books are brief enough and are particularly important to you, you may want to photocopy these for your own use. For the most part, though, you will need to make an accurate written record of the ideas and information you may want to use later and to keep track of where they came from. Strive for accuracy when you write down someone else's words. Also write down the author, title, and the page number where the quotation was found. Your task will be simplified if you have already made out bibliography cards. If you have, all you need to put in the way of documentation on your notes is the author's last name and the page numbers used. Remember, you will have access to the book only for a limited amount of time, and you may not have it in your hands during the final stage of writing your paper.

Some writers prefer to use loose-leaf paper or notebooks for their note taking, but the most generally accepted technique is to use index cards or half-sheets of paper. If you limit the amount of material on each card to one subject, and put a subject heading in the upper right-hand corner, then you will be able to shift and rearrange cards as needed, keeping together all the material on a particular subject.

One final note about the information-gathering stage: As you can see, it is much more involved and time-consuming than any information gathering you have done in the past. Yet it is crucial that you give yourself the time to do it thoroughly, because the information you collect is the foundation upon which your research paper will rest. Therefore, be sure to begin well in advance of the date when the paper is due.

Step Two: Analyzing the Ideas and the Information

At this point, you need to take a step away from all your reading and note taking to ask, "What part of this subject am I most interested in pursuing?" You will probably want to expand upon (or alter) your original list of questions. Then select from the list the question (or group of questions) you want to look at more closely. Do you already have enough information on this limited part of your topic, or do you need to find out more? How can you put together in a meaningful way the information you have? (For example, given the issue of the student drop-out rate, do you want to concentrate primarily on the causes or on what you think can be done to help keep students in school?)

Step Three: Stating the Purpose

Your purpose statement (thesis) will come out of the questions you answer in Step Two. The thesis is simply a more explicit statement of the main idea that you want to examine in your paper. Try to say in a sentence or two what you want to prove or show. For example, if you choose to concentrate on what causes students to drop out of school, you might begin with the following purpose statement:

> Students drop out of school because they cannot make a direct connection between the subjects they study in class and the jobs they expect to have later in life.

See page 84 for help in writing the purpose or thesis statement.

Step Four: Planning the Paper

The longer the paper is, the more attention you need to pay to the way it is structured. This is especially true of the research paper, because you so often need to refer to outside sources as you write. Each paragraph must follow logically and consistently from the part before it—and relate clearly to the thesis—or your readers will be lost from the start.

A tight, clearly stated thesis is your best insurance against a weakly structured paper. Notice that the thesis statement above is limited and exact enough to give directions to the writer in planning the paper.

Look at your own thesis statement. Does it indicate the focus of your paper and help you in planning the body? If not, rewrite it, keeping in mind the criteria of a good thesis: It must be clearly stated and sufficiently limited; it should assert an opinion.

When you are satisfied that your thesis statement is as good as possible, you are ready to make an outline. Here is an example of the form your outline might take:

Title of Research Paper

I. Introduction

    A. Necessary background information or explanation of the issue
    B. Key terms that need to be defined

    C. Thesis statement: _____

_____

_____

II. Body

    A. Main idea of first part of body: _____

_____

    B. Evidence from outside sources that supports and reinforces this idea:

        1. Writer's name, pp. _____
        2. Writer's name, pp. _____
        3. Writer's name, pp. _____
        4. Writer's name, pp. _____

    C. Main idea for next section of the body: _____

_____

    D. Evidence from outside sources that supports and reinforces Idea C:

        1. Writer's name, pp. _____
        2. Writer's name, pp. _____
        3. Writer's name, pp. _____
        4. Writer's name, pp. _____

(Repeat the procedure of stating the main idea for each major portion of the body and give the sources you will use for support.)

III. Conclusion

   A. Sum up the main ideas presented in the paper.
   B. Close the paper by using one of the techniques discussed in Chapter 4.

Step Five: Writing the Paper

With your purpose statement in front of you, begin to write. Consider this writing effort a rough draft, and don't be concerned if every detail is not perfect. Just concentrate on writing an essay that is coherent (that is, one in which the ideas are closely and logically related) and on using the information you have found to reinforce your main ideas.

Many research papers suffer from an overdependence on long quotations from outside sources. Even though you do need to borrow the ideas of others from time to time, it is still *your* paper. Let your own voice be heard. Many students find that they can resist more successfully the temptation to let other writers' voices "take over" if they put aside their notes and try first to freewrite a two- or three-page paper on the subject. Then they can go back and fill out the body paragraphs more fully by using their outside sources. Whatever technique you favor, don't let your paper degenerate into a long string of quotations that are connected loosely by a few words of your own.

Four ways to quote other sources are described in detail on pages 443–445. They are: making the quotation flow grammatically into your own sentence; making the quotation stand by itself, in quotation marks, as one full sentence; indenting longer quotations and omitting the quotation marks; and paraphrasing—that is, putting the thought into your own words. As a general rule of thumb, most of the time you will want to paraphrase and to integrate short quotations into your own sentences. Save longer quotations for those occasions when it is especially important to preserve the original words intact.

All four methods, including paraphrasing, require citing your sources. This is a way of giving credit to the writers whose ideas you quote. The simplest way to do this is to give the author's name and the page number of the book or article in parentheses, at the end of the quote.

> In his article, "The Japan Gap," Herman Arthur explains that "many Japanese students attend cram schools, which cost about $500 a year" (Arthur 6).

When you have finished writing the paper and citing the sources, one final task remains in the writing stage: compiling the bibliography. The bibliography is an alphabetized listing of the sources you have consulted. It is placed at the end of the research paper, on a separate page. The bibliography should be entitled "Works Cited." See page 450 for sample entries in a "Works Cited" section.

Step Six: Revising and Submitting the Paper

After you have completed your rough draft, let it rest for a day or two, if at all possible, before you begin the revision process. When you have made all the necessary changes, proofread the final copy carefully for mechanical and grammatical errors. Submit your research paper with a title page, which gives the title of your paper (do not use quotation marks around it), your name, the course title, and the date. (Follow the sample on page 447.)

Quoting Published Material

When quoting published material, observe the following key rule: Use quotations to support or further explain your points, but do not depend on them too heavily. Quotations are generally used to give an expert's opinion or to pass on a particularly important or well-written phrase or sentence. In short papers, quotations should be brief. Experiment with using quotations from time to time until you master the art. When you do quote, give the author's full name and the source of the quotation, such as the name of the magazine or the title of the book from which it was taken. If you then use the author's name again, you only have to give his or her last name. Here are four ways of quoting published material:

Method 1   Incorporate the quotation into the grammar of your sentence:

> In his article, "The Japan Gap," Herman Arthur discusses the Japanese educational system, which produces a "highly literate population of avid readers."

RULES ON FORM

1. When the quotation is part of the grammar of your sentence, do not capitalize the first word of the quote, unless of course it should be capitalized anyway. The beginning word *highly* in the quotation above is not capitalized because it does not begin a whole sentence.
2. Use quotations marks only if you quote the *exact* words of the author.

Method 2   Let the quotation stand by itself as at least one full sentence:

> In his article, "The Japan Gap," Herman Arthur states, "If the statistics are accurate, America's economic capacity is being sapped by its 25 million illiterates and 35 million semi-literates."

RULES ON FORM

1. If the quotation can stand by itself as a full sentence or more, capitalize its first word.
2. Use quotation marks.
3. When using a verb such as *said, wrote,* or *stated* to introduce a direct quotation, insert a comma after the verb:

> Herman Arthur wrote, "Whatever the numbers . . ."

4. When introducing a direct quotation with expressions such as *the following*, use a colon after the introductory phrase:

> Arthur wrote the following: "Whatever the numbers . . ."

Note that the quotation is introduced by a statement that is a grammatically complete sentence.

Method 3   Indent quotations of five or more lines:

> Admissions data gathered at the University of California's Berkeley campus show just how well Asian-American students have fared:
>
>> In California . . . Asian-Americans make up only 6 percent of the state's population but accounted for 24.7 percent of the undergraduates and 27 percent of the freshman class last year at Berkeley, the most prestigious campus of the state university system. By contrast, Hispanics form 19 percent of California's population but only 7.1 percent of Berkeley's undergraduates, while blacks were 7.7 percent of the state population and 5.1 percent of the school's undergraduates.

RULES ON FORM

1. Set off a quotation of five or more lines by indention, not quotation marks. Indent the entire quotation five spaces from the left-hand margin if you are typing, or an inch if you are writing by hand.
2. Skip a line above and below the indented quotation. If you are typing, single-space the quotation.
3. Do not indent further to show the beginning of *any* paragraph. But if you quote two or more paragraphs, skip a line between them.
4. Introduce quotations such as the one above with a colon.
5. Use an *ellipsis* (. . .) to indicate omitted material. However, when you use an ellipsis, make sure the quoted material moves smoothly from the last words before the ellipsis to the first words after it, as though the thought was continuous. (See the ellipsis in the quotation above.)

Method 4   You can make the quotation indirect, as follows:

> In his article, "The Japan Gap," Herman Arthur states that many American high school students are unable to read and write.

Here you *paraphrase,* or rewrite, the author's statement in your own words. The advantage of using indirect quotations is that you have much more flexibility. Often your quote can be a lot shorter as you summarize the author's point of view.

RULES ON FORM

1. Do not use quotation marks for a paraphrased or indirect quotation, but you must use quotation marks for the *exact* language of the author. (See Method 1.)
2. Indirect quotations are often introduced by the word *that*, as in the sample above.

OTHER RULES ON FORM

1. Give the full name of the author of the material you are quoting the first time you quote, but then only give the last name:

   Herman Arthur wrote in his article. . . . Arthur went on to say. . . .

2. Give the source of the quoted material with the first quotation from that source. Put quotation marks around the titles of short pieces, such as articles, essays, poems, songs, and television programs. Underline the titles of longer works, such as magazines, books, plays, and movies.
3. A convenient way to give the date of a periodical is to place it in parentheses immediately following the periodical's title:

   . . . in The American Educator (August 1983) . . .

4. Avoid quotations within quotations (they can be very awkward), but if you must use them, use a single quotation mark (') around the inside quotation:

   Arthur describes the Japanese philosophy of work the following way: "A house rule of Japan's largest ad agency reads: 'Once you have chosen a task, never give up—no matter what.'"

Notes and Works Cited

NOTES

The Modern Language Association, which sets the standard for documentation used by most English instructors, encourages citing sources within the paper itself (see the examples on pages 442 and 449). If, however, you wish to provide further information about a topic but feel that it will take away from the point you are making in the paper itself, it is a good idea to use a note. Notes are numbered consecutively, starting with 1, throughout the paper. Place note numbers slightly above the line, and place the notes themselves in a section called "Notes" at the end of the paper, before the section "Works Cited." Here is an example of a note:

   [1] For further information on this study, see Fox Butterfield, "Why Asians Are Going to the Head of the Class," New York Times 3 August 1986: 18–23.

WORKS CITED (BIBLIOGRAPHY)

FORM FOR ARTICLES IN NEWSPAPERS OR MAGAZINES

Butterfield, Fox. "Why Asians Are Going to the Head of the Class," New York Times 3 August 1986: 18-23.

FORM FOR BOOKS

Ornstein, Allan C., and Daniel U. Levine. An Introduction to the Foundations of Education, Third Edition. Boston: Houghton Mifflin Company, 1985.

In the "Works Cited" section, entries always appear in alphabetical order by author. (If you are citing an unsigned article from a newspaper or magazine, alphabetize the entry by the name of the newspaper or magazine.) Note that titles of articles appear in quotes; titles of books, magazines, and news-papers are underscored.

Sample Research Format

The following few pages show you how to set up and begin your research paper. Page 447 gives an example of a title page; pages 448–449 show the opening pages of the paper itself; and the last sample page shows you how to set up your "Works Cited" section.

A Research Assignment

The article "The Japan Gap," by Herman Arthur, on pages 451–456, is designed to give you a starting point for your own research. Start by reading this article; then read and discuss the Questions for Discussion with your classmates. Finally, using what you have learned in this course and in this appendix, complete one of the two Research Writing Assignments that appear at the end of this appendix.

About the Reading Selection

"It is no longer news that many high school graduates are unable to read or write," Herman Arthur observes in this selection. He first describes the social setting in America that has created the conditions for such wide-spread illiteracy. He then examines the educational philosophy of the Jap-anese, who, as a nation, boast one of the highest literacy rates in the world. Why do the Japanese value work for its own sake and obedience more highly than Americans do? How do their schools differ from ours? What are their attitudes toward teachers, test taking, failure, and learning in general? These are some of the questions Arthur addresses as he probes into the reasons for Japan's success in producing a nation of avid readers.

Whereas Arthur obviously approves of much about the Japanese system,

Education and the Asian-American Culture

By

Sarah Walsh

English 101

The American school system is failing its students, and so its students are failing—that's been the sorrowful refrain of parents and teachers for years. No one can deny that illiteracy and ignorance have reached appalling depths, nor that our school systems are in need of improvement. However, the success of one ethnic group, Asian Americans, seems to indicate that at least part of the problem lies in American culture. Asian Americans are highly motivated students whose parents respect and encourage scholarship and hard work. Their short-term goals are clearly set out, and they work toward long-term goals of college and a professional career. American students, in contrast, often come from homes in which the parents are ambivalent about the value of education and are as concerned about their children's social success as they are about academic success. American society places a higher value on the ability of children to "get along," to be popular and self-assured, than on the ability to concentrate, to learn, and to work hard.

Educators across the country have become interested in the question of why Asian-American students have performed so well despite the barriers for many of them of language, recent emigration, and lack of finances. Consistently, throughout the school system and from elementary school through graduate school, Asian-American students have gotten the highest grades, the highest scores on standardized tests, and the highest awards. Admissions data gathered at the University of

California's Berkeley campus show just how well Asian-American students have fared:

> In California . . . Asian-Americans make up only 6 percent of the state's population but accounted for 24.7 percent of the undergraduates and 27 percent of the freshman class last year at Berkeley, the most prestigious campus of the state university system (Butterfield 2).

The success of the Asian-American culture has been found to be due to its values and its emphasis on the importance of education. In these families, each member's success gains honor for the family, especially for the parents, who are highly respected. As Allan C. Ornstein and Daniel U. Levine say in their text, An Introduction to the Foundations of Education, "Because the family is the whole world to the very young child, its members teach children what matters in life, often without realizing the impact they are having. The desire to achieve popularity, the belief that a girl should be docile, the motivation to excel in school, and other beliefs and values are passed from parent to child" (326). The importance Asian parents place on school work shows up in the attitude of schoolchildren toward homework: Asian children, researchers have found, spend at least twice the time American children do on homework, and enjoy it, while American children dislike it (Ornstein and Levine 129). American culture is generally far more concerned with social achievements and "extra-curricular activities" than with scholarship and grades. . . .

Works Cited

Butterfield, Fox. "Why Asians Are Going to the Head of the
Class," <u>New York Times</u> 3 August 1986: 18–23.

"Confucian Work Ethic," <u>Time</u> 28 March 1983: 52.

Davis, Kingsley. "The Child and the Social Structure," <u>Journal of
Educational Sociology</u> December 1940: 217–229.

Friedenberg, Edgar Z. <u>Coming of Age in America</u>. New York:
Random House, 1965.

Ornstein, Allan C., and Daniel U. Levine. <u>An Introduction to the
Foundations of Education</u>, Third Edition. Boston:
Houghton Mifflin Company, 1985.

Otto, Luther B. "Extracurricular Activities in the Status Attain-
ment Process," <u>Rural Sociology</u> Summer 1976: 217–233.

Williams, D. A. "A Formula for Success," <u>Newsweek</u> 23 April
1984: 77.

his assessment of it is not altogether complimentary. He reveals an educational climate that stifles individuality, discourages question asking, and even drives some failing students to suicide. As you read, keep a balanced view of both sides of the issue.

The Japan Gap

Remember Sputnik? Remember the panic that swept the United States when it fell for the gospel of Soviet scientific superiority? Remember the ominous news about the purported excellence of Soviet schools? That scare shook a billion dollars out of Congress for upgrading education—the first of many installments.

Then Wernher von Braun and his emigre team salvaged the reputation of American rocketry, John Glenn made his circuit of the earth, and John Kennedy promised us the moon. Soon afterward, the experts told us that Soviet schooling wasn't that great. Huge defense and space outlays actually siphoned off the people the schools needed. Those who could have taught science and math have taken jobs in high technology industries.

When the dust settled, American schools retreated gratefully into preoccupation with self-discovery, driver education, and baton-twirling. Subsequent earthquakes—Vietnam, Watergate, and domestic turmoil—helped divert youth from the pursuit of scholarship.

Far more serious concerns than Sputnik are upon us now: creeping "Japanization" and creeping illiteracy. Crushed in World War II, Japan turned its energies from militarism to industrial growth. Japan's production machine has upended one American industry after another as Japanese products have replaced American ships, steel, autos and motorcycles, cameras, pianos, copying machines, wristwatches, television sets, and stereos. After humbling GM, U.S. Steel, and RCA, the Japanese are now probing fortress IBM. The United States and Canada are declining into quasi-colonies—suppliers of natural resources to Japan and markets for Japanese manufactures.

If the statistics are accurate, America's economic capacity is being sapped by its 25 million illiterates and 35 million semi-literates.

Whatever the numbers, nobody doubts that illiteracy is widespread. Anyone teaching for the past two decades recognizes the slippage. It is no longer news that many high school graduates are unable to read or write.

The contrast with other nations is startling. Among those that boast high literacy levels are the Scandinavian countries, the Low Countries, and three others of particular interest—Barbados, Iceland, and Japan—nations with black, Caucasian, and Oriental populations, respectively.

The combined populations of Barbados and Iceland could be absorbed by Cleveland. Japan, with 120 million people, is another story. But the three countries share common characteristics. They are island nations, their populations are strikingly homogeneous, and they have a long tradition of valuing the written word.

Most researchers seeking the causes of illiteracy tend to look through the wrong

---

Herman Arthur, "The Japan Gap," *The American Educator* August 1983. Reprinted by permission.

end of the telescope. They focus narrowly on teaching methodologies instead of on the entire social scene. It may well be that the roots of American illiteracy lie in our attitudes, values, and practices. If it is true that literacy levels are factors in Japan's success and America's malaise, it is appropriate to examine the total setting, beginning with historical attitudes toward book learning.

Thomas Jefferson and Benjamin Franklin both viewed universal education as essential to our system. The people, Jefferson said, are the only safe depositories of government power, "and to render them superior, their minds must be improved." Consequently, he designed the University of Virginia to create a new breed of Renaissance men. Franklin, more of a blue-collar type, promoted free public libraries and newspapers as a way of educating working people.

But while they and subsequent American leaders were encouraging learning, a powerful contrary force emerged in the form of an American hero—part mythic, part genuine—who was uncouth and unlettered, yet enormously capable. He had "street smarts" and inborn ingenuity adequate to any situation. The learned man, on the other hand, began to be patronized as a quaintly comic dreamer. These images were most satisfying to the millions of unlettered immigrants who poured in from Europe. They are still a staple of popular entertainment.

Alexander Hamilton, the prophetic genius of American capitalism, had a practical solution for illiteracy. He proposed that production be subdivided into simple, repetitive steps that even children could handle, "thus rendering them more useful at an early age." No need, then, to waste time and money educating any but a small, privileged elite.

A sizable segment of America's work force functioned for decades on this principle. Illiterates could prosper by performing easily learned tasks such as bolting bumpers to automobile frames. (When Ford closed its Rahway, New Jersey, plant recently, a newspaper profiled one of the workers who for twenty years had been paid extremely well to drive cars from an assembly line to a storage lot. Now he was astonished to discover he couldn't get a job for more than $4 an hour.) Our present concern about illiteracy may well be prompted by the shrinkage of these simple jobs.

Japan, unlike the United States, is a latecomer to the modern world, yet it has achieved a high rate of literacy. What cultural forces made this possible? Does the Japanese experience offer us any useful lessons?

Two Japanese characteristics are particularly striking. One is the extraordinary durability of its centuries-old traditions. The second is the unique homogeneity of its population. Of its 120 million people, three million are *burakamin*, an outcaste group resembling India's untouchables. Another 600,000 are Koreans. The rest are mainstream Japanese.

The result is a monolithic society with universally shared values and an attitude toward other social systems that borders on contempt. Among these shared values are the worship of work and thrift, the imperatives of obedience and conformity, and a belief in learning as the key to success. Group effort and relentless persistence are valued greatly. The Japanese have very little tolerance for failure and no tolerance at all for lack of effort. From kindergarten to the work place, it is assumed that success comes from sustained effort, failure from not trying hard enough. A house rule of

Japan's largest ad agency reads: "Once you have chosen a task, never give up—no matter what."

The Japanese have been workaholics for centuries, since work and thrift were essential survival skills in a poverty-striken feudal society. Today, social pressure and overpowering conformity enforce the desired behavior. Individuality and eccentricity are strongly disapproved. As a well-known Japanese maxim puts it, "The stake that sticks up is hammered down." It would be hard to conceive of eccentric achievers such as Hyman Rickover, Robert Goddard, Glenn Gould, or Isadora Duncan flourishing in a Japanese milieu.

An in-depth description of Japanese education is beyond the scope of a magazine article, but the following observations may offer some insight into how these values affect the educational process.

Schools in Japan are under central control, with standardized curricula, textbooks, and course content. The American occupation decentralized this structure by creating American-style local school boards, but this change was abandoned, as was the attempt to encourage student questioning and independent thinking. The learning process is based on rote memorization and teacher-directed learning from textbooks.

Funding and facilities are reasonably uniform throughout the country. There are none of our deplorable discrepancies between wealthy and poor districts.

Japanese teachers gain lifetime tenure when hired, as do most other employees in Japan. It is assumed that, having met the qualifications, they can see the job through, "never giving up, no matter what." Principals have very little to say about teaching practices. Teachers enjoy great prestige. They rank high in career choice surveys of Japanese students. They were unionized under the occupation, long before American teachers.

Classes are huge—forty to forty-five students—but behavior problems are minor, although teachers complain about the erosion of traditional discipline. Students spend a large part of the first year becoming acclimated to rules and procedures. Incoming students keep the same teacher and classmates for two years. By then, group discipline and group loyalty have been instilled in them.

Japanese society is male-dominated. Working mothers are uncommon, single-parent families extremely rare. Mothers are child-centered and deeply involved in their children's schooling. The "education mama," roughly comparable to the American stage mother, is a Japanese stereotype. To her is attributed the saying: "Four hours sleep, pass; five hours sleep, fail," mocking her fixation on success in school. All parents join the local PTA, and practically all attend the monthly "open school" day. In turn, teachers visit each child's home at least once a year and often host social get-togethers for their classes.

Teachers expect all students to participate actively and all to learn. They largely disregard differences in ability on the assumption that sufficient effort will dissolve all difficulties. As a Japanese educator put it: "Is it not the responsibility of the teacher to push the students as much as possible?" The formula is "encourage, prod, assist, repeat, and repeat."

Promotion is automatic at all levels. Dropouts are extremely rare. Although compulsory education ends at the ninth grade, 92 percent of middle school graduates attend high school. Failure in school, as elsewhere, is unacceptable. The other side of the coin is that exceptional talents can be stifled: "The stake that sticks up is hammered down."

Children play a major role in the schools' daily operations. Adults do not pick up after them. Students serve lunches on a rotating schedule, operate the public address system, take attendance, run school libraries, care for animals, plant and maintain flowers and shrubs, and keep classrooms spic and span. At periodic intervals, the principal, teachers, and children come to school in old clothes and give the building a scrubbing.

No local pressure groups attempt to censor books, oversee teaching methods, or dictate course content. Such activities would be pointless in a centrally controlled system. Japanese believe fervently that success in school guarantees success in life; therefore schools must be supported. Any shortfall is blamed on lack of student effort—"five hours sleep, fail." Responsibility is personal, not passed off on "the system."

Delinquency and crime are rare, and truancy is almost nonexistent. Traditional drug problems, such as heroin or excessive use of amphetamines, are adult practices to the extent they exist. (If Japanese celebrities use cocaine, they would never flaunt it.) To cite one statistic, in 1970, *before* U.S. crime rates exploded, New York City reported 74,000 holdups; Tokyo, a much larger city, had 472. Conformist children grow into law-abiding adults.

With more time at their disposal, Japanese schools offer more science, music, art, and physical education than their American counterparts. Most sixth graders can play two or three musical instruments. By grade seven, English instruction begins. Since 92 percent of Japanese students attend high school and one-third of these go on to college, millions of Japanese study English for as long as ten years. In fact, they use English as the language of computer programming. If we project existing literacy trends into the future, at some point there would be a greater percentage of Japanese than Americans capable of reading English!

A major motivational force pervades the entire educational process—the national testing system. Ninth graders who apply to high school must take entrance exams. If they seek higher education, they take college tests of several days' duration, and each college administers its own tests. There is no Japanese SAT. Once students finish college and apply for a salaried job—you guessed it—many companies require an exam. The elite private schools, which supply many national leaders, give exams for admission to kindergarten and subsequent tests at every level.

Since college is the avenue to job security, successful test-taking is the key to a student's future. Once the test hurdle is overcome, students can complete course requirements, since the same rote regurgitation called for by the tests is required in the classroom. In that respect the admission test is a valid selection device.

The Japanese test gauntlet is a clear-cut merit system. "How else," one Japanese educator said, "are you going to give everyone an equal chance?" Combined with universal education, this merit system does open the doors to all equally—with one significant qualification. Just as American students take SAT cram courses and would-be lawyers cram for the bar, many Japanese students attend cram schools, which cost about $500 a year.

Somehow, the Japanese "education mama" squirrels away enough yen to pay for cram school (provided her child passes the cram school entrance test). One out of three urban sixth graders attends cram school ten hours a week; four out of ten attend by the ninth grade.

In fact, the entire ninth year of school is devoted to preparing for the high school test. The students' schedule consists of an eight-hour day, two hours of cram school, and four hours' homework. "Five hours sleep, fail."

The college tests are intimidating; they include Japanese and English languages, math, science, and social studies, with each series lasting several days. It's not uncommon for high school graduates to spend a year preparing for college admission.

The failures help boost the suicide rate. Failing applicants are called *ronin*, which originally meant a leaderless samurai, an outcast without a master. Students cast out by test failure feel similarly ostracized.

Despite its obvious shortcomings, the test system has positive aspects. It provides a momentous, ever-present target for all students from the moment they enter school. Even students who fail have succeeded, because in striving for that all-consuming goal they acquire literacy and other survival skills. They can be compared to marathoners who achieve great heart-lung capacity, whether or not they complete twenty-six miles. And since all Japanese high school students have passed the exam, every single high schooler is fully literate.

One would expect Japanese children to be miserable and anxiety-ridden. On the contrary, they are described as cheerful, eager, and docile—not as docile as the less-affluent students of years past but far more so than their peers elsewhere.

How can this be explained? Bruno Bettelheim, writing in the Winter 1979 *American Educator*, argued that postponing gratification is essential to learning. "Present pleasure," he wrote, "must be largely foregone for greater gains in the future." Normally, a child's sense of self-interest is not strong enough to disregard immediate pleasure (i.e., watching television, playing, hanging out) to complete school work. There is usually a heavy dose of anxiety prompting children (paternal, teacher, or peer disapproval; fear of some unpleasant consequence). Bettelheim concluded that only the mature individual is capable of making a rational decision to postpone gratification. (Putting money in the bank each week will enable me to buy a car next year.)

The test bugaboo presents these students with an enormous burden of anxiety, but despite this burden they do gain immediate gratifications. Acceptance by peers and the teacher is an important source of self-esteem. Participation in real-life tasks of running the school provides them with a sense of achievement. An elaborate array of after-school clubs caters to every interest. Mastering subject matter brings rewards, even if other students help out. Students receive approval on all sides from parents and the community.

In workaholic Japan, *work itself is a source of gratification*. Excessive devotion to work brings credit; it is not considered the sign of a personality disorder. Preparation for tests looming in the distance is gratifying in itself; anxiety about the tests comes later.

Student rebellion emerges among collegians *after* they have surmounted the test barriers. Jack Seward in his interesting book, *The Japanese*, attributes organized student violence to young people's resentment at the prospect of spending their working years being obsequious to their superiors in an industrial bureaucracy while making herculean efforts to succeed at assigned tasks. Only on retirement can they regain the freedom they enjoyed in their preschool days.

Whatever the faults of the Japanese system, it does produce a highly literate population of avid readers. (There are 100 newspapers in Tokyo alone.) Are there any aspects of the Japanese experience that would be useful in attacking America's problem of illiteracy?

Most Americans would reject out of hand the stifling conformity, rote regurgitation, and totally centralized direction of Japanese schools. Such a structure would smother the idiosyncratic, innovative individuality and the group diversity that are among America's greatest strengths. Nevertheless, Japan offers us some useful lessons, if only by contrast.

–Herman Arthur

QUESTIONS FOR DISCUSSION

1. One of the basic assumptions behind Herman Arthur's essay is that America as a nation prizes "self-discovery, driver education, and baton-twirling" more than scholarly pursuits. On the whole, do you think he is right? What was emphasized in your high school? How much emphasis was placed on "scholarly pursuits"? Explain.
2. What do you think accounts for the high rate of illiteracy in America? Name as many reasons for it as you can. Why do you think Arthur says it is necessary to examine the "entire social scene" to discover the roots of American illiteracy?
3. What shared values do the Japanese have that may account for their high rate of literacy? Should we develop any of these values in this country? Explain.
4. "The stake that sticks up is hammered down." Discuss both the positive and negative effects of this philosophy of education.
5. Arthur states that in Japanese schools the stigma of failure falls on the student rather than on the system. In this country we tend to put little blame on the individual student. Think of your own high school experience. How much responsibility did you have for the problems, and how much responsibility did the system have? Explain.
6. Discuss both the good and bad effects of the following features of Japanese education and society:

   a. centrally controlled schools with standardized texts and course content
   b. emphasis on rote memorization and teacher-directed learning from textbooks
   c. lifetime tenure for teachers
   d. emphasis on conformity and group loyalty, which are instilled in students at an early age

    e. male-domination of society, with few working women

    f. student participation in the daily functioning of the schools

    g. the national testing system

7. What does Arthur mean when he says that the ability to postpone gratification is essential to learning? Do you think American schools (or American society) foster this ability? Why does Arthur suggest that this attitude is more easily grasped by the Japanese?

RESEARCH WRITING ASSIGNMENT 1

If you were on the school board of your city or county, how would you try to improve the public education system? Write a research paper (of a length designated by your instructor) that describes the present failures of the public schools and suggests a remedy. Research the issue thoroughly, gathering information from these sources:

1. Your own experience. (If you did not go to public school, think of what worked well in your school and ask yourself what ideas you might offer from your education to the public school system.)
2. Interviews with your classmates and others who did attend public schools.
3. Interviews with public school teachers.
4. The library. Read Chapter 8 and check the appropriate indexes in the reference section of your library.

Research magazine and newspaper articles as well as books, and keep track of the publishing information on the sources you use. An excellent place to begin is to read the report of the National Commission on Excellence in Education (April 1983).

Analyze the information and ask yourself this question: What does public education need most of all?

State your purpose. If you were getting ready to run for another term of office on the school board, how would you state your position, in a campaign slogan of one or two sentences, on what needs to be done? For example: "Our schools need discipline, dedication, and diversity." As you make your outline, think of three or four changes you would make to carry out your slogan. What reasons can you give to show why these are such important changes?

RESEARCH WRITING ASSIGNMENT 2

Use the library to find out about the public school system in another country, such as Germany, Sweden, or England. Find out exactly how that system works and whether it succeeds. Then write a research paper (of a length designated by your instructor) comparing that country's school system with the American system. You can use Arthur's article, "The Japan Gap," to make a brainstorming list of questions about the other country's school system that you will want to answer during the information-gathering stage.

APPENDIX B

Reading for Pleasure

When Richard Wright, in his book *Black Boy,* told his story of growing up in the midst of poverty and oppression in the first part of this century, he said over and over again that what enabled him to free himself from the bondage of his youth was, more than anything else, *reading.* Reading novels, especially, allowed him to enter new worlds and transcend the crippling world into which he had been born:

> Reading grew into a passion. My first serious novel was Sinclair Lewis's *Main Street.* It made me see my boss, Mr. Gerald, and identify him as an American type. I would smile when I saw him lugging his golf bags into the office. I had always felt a vast distance separating me from the boss, and now I felt closer to him, though still distant. I felt now that I knew him, that I could feel the very limits of his narrow life. And this had happened because I had read a novel about a mythical man called George F. Babbitt.

Although you may not face the same difficulties Wright faced in growing up, reading for pleasure can be just as liberating for you. Furthermore, the more you read, the better you will write. Without even thinking about it, you will learn how to give variety to your sentences, you will greatly increase your vocabulary, and you will learn to avoid mechanical errors.

The following books are popular among beginning college students. Read as many of these books as you can—and more.

The Adventures of Huckleberry Finn, by Mark Twain   Thought by many to be the "great American novel," this wonderfully funny yet deeply serious book tells of the adventures of Huck, a runaway teenager, and Jim, a runaway slave, as they float down the Mississippi River on a raft toward freedom.

Black Boy, by Richard Wright   This autobiography is an American classic, for it is the story of a person who triumphs even though everything seems to work against him.

Blue Highways, by William Least Heat Moon   This is the true account of a man who has lost his job and whose wife has left him. He buys a van, outfits it for travel, and takes off on a journey around the country in search of his own identity—and the best diners in America.

The Boys of Summer, by Roger Kahn   If you are a sports fan, you will enjoy this book: it is the story of the author's love for the great Brooklyn Dodgers' teams of the 1950s.

Bread Givers, by Anzia Yezierska   This is an autobiographical novel of a young immigrant growing up in New York City at the beginning of the twentieth century. If you or close family members are immigrants, be sure to read this novel. Even if you and your family are not immigrants, you will find it hard to stop reading this novel.

The Catcher in the Rye, by J. D. Salinger   A long-time favorite among college students, this novel is the story of Holden Caulfield, a prep-school dropout, and his frantic search for meaning in a world where everything seems phony.

Clan of the Cave Bear, by Jean Auel   This is an amazing and beautiful long novel about a tribe of prehistoric Neanderthals who adopt the young girl named Ayla. Ayla is strange to the tribe but familiar to us since she is what we call a "human being."

The Color Purple, by Alice Walker   This is a novel about a badly abused, young black woman who gradually learns how to take care of herself in a "man's world." It is also a book about the power of love to reconcile and change.

The Member of the Wedding, by Carson McCullers   Frankie Addams, a twelve-year-old girl and the main character in this novel, is a member of no peer group and feels quite alone. Wanting desperately to belong to someone, she takes part in the plans for her brother's wedding, imagining that she will be with them when they go away on their honeymoon.

Of Mice and Men, by John Steinbeck   This novel is most of all a story about the friendship of Lennie, a simple-minded giant, and George, a ranch hand. It is also the story of a hope that will not die.

To Kill a Mockingbird, by Harper Lee   This all-time favorite is the story of one person's willingness to stand up for what is right, even though his cause is unpopular.

One Flew over the Cuckoo's Nest, by Ken Kesey   This novel opens in a mental institution where the Big Nurse has reduced her patients to passive robots. Then McMurphy, a brawling, fun-loving, highly intelligent rebel, appears on the scene and challenges Big Nurse's authority. Whether or not you have seen the film, be sure to read this novel.

Never Cry Wolf, by Farley Mowat   A young zoologist is dropped off in the Yukon to spend a year alone, studying the habits of wolves. He meets a few natives living in the wilderness and encounters sport hunters; he also meets the wolves. He learns about the Yukon wilderness and about the wolves; he also learns about himself.

APPENDIX C

Answers to Practice Exercises in Part Three

Chapter 10

PRACTICE 1

1. P
2. C
3. S
4. S
5. C

6. S
7. P
8. P
9. C
10. P

PRACTICE 2

1. essay, test, task
2. students, thoughts, time, outline
3. ideas, order

4. sentences
5. time, essay

PRACTICE 3

1. Richard Wright, *Black Boy*
2. American, Deep South

3. Memphis, Jackson
4. Wright

PRACTICE 4

1. Richard Wright, obstacles
2. education, schools, blacks, whites
3. family, Wright, bed
4. clothes, books, food
5. Wright, hardships

6. things, reading, defiance, learning, determination
7. way, magazines, books
8. struggles, Wright, youth, world, man
9. struggles, youth, scars
10. students, book, *Black Boy*

PRACTICE 5

1. men
2. Cavemen
3. women

4. men
5. women

PRACTICE 7

1. I do believe
2. testimony could hurt
3. troop should go

4. minutes should have made
5. Marines want
6. David should have been chosen

PRACTICE 9

1. Yesterday was, day
2. movies were, films
3. Mr. Reynolds has been, chairman

4. solution seems, one
5. painting is, example
6. Tom was, member

PRACTICE 10

1. The teller will cash our check. (teller will cash)
2. Mary and Martha are the sisters mentioned in the story. (Mary and Martha are)
3. The employees should insist on collective bargaining. (employees should insist)
4. Physics is the most difficult course. (Physics is)
5. We should have listened to Einstein when he warned against atomic power. (We should have listened)

PRACTICE 11

1. bug is
2. volunteers are
3. change is
4. examples are

5. one is
6. three are
7. day was

PRACTICE 12

1. television will replace
2. children watch
3. programs will occupy

4. Neil Armstrong did say
5. advantages are
6. Students learn

7. no one feels
8. person can progress
9. drawback is
10. program will survive

11. opportunities are
12. team should have chosen
13. couple has
14. techniques should combine

PRACTICE 13

1. We watched television (tells what)
2. girls baked cookies (tells what)
3. Andy asked Melissa (tells whom)
4. Andy ate cookies, drank quart (tells what)
5. Andy had stomach ache (tells what)
6. instructor returned tests (tells what)
7. Karen defeated Janice (tells whom)
8. She finished problems (tells what)
9. she passed test (tells what)
10. teacher wrote comment (tells what)

PRACTICE 15

1. (During the sixties), (in drugs)
2. (of particular drugs), (such as LSD and marijuana), (on the news)
3. (with drugs), (at this time)
4. (With the increase), (of drug use), (of drug use)
5. (to an early death), (for some)
6. (by drugs)
7. (in large cities)
8. (For some people), (on the street)
9. (for Ecstasy), (of the most dangerous drugs), (on the American scene)
10. (at our university), (to the drug problem), (to their children)

PRACTICE 16

1. Tom brought his friend a basket of fruit.
2. Elizabeth gave her instructor some free advice.
3. The news gave the family a shock.
4. The real estate agent offered her clients a special deal.
5. The thief sold a stolen car to my husband.
6. She made her daughter a beautiful dress.

PRACTICE 18

1. he
2. I
3. me
4. I
5. me
6. its

7. we
8. them
9. whom
10. they
11. my

PRACTICE 19

1. I
2. me
3. us
4. she
5. she
6. me
7. him and me
8. me
9. I
10. me
11. I
12. Who
13. Whoever
14. whomever
15. whom
16. she

PRACTICE 20

1. who (rel)
2. She (per)
3. you (per)
4. her (per)
5. She (per)
6. herself (reflex)
7. her (per)
8. Her (per)
9. which (rel)
10. her (per)
11. that (rel)
12. her (per)
13. She (per)
14. that (rel)
15. her (per)
16. she (per)
17. she (per)
18. anyone (ind)
19. her (per)
20. She (per)
21. everything (ind)
22. herself (reflex)
23. that (dem)
24. she (per)

PRACTICE 21

1. herself (reflex)
2. This (dem)
3. what (rel)
4. she (per)
5. She (per)
6. her (per)
7. which (rel)
8. What (inter)
9. you (per)
10. she (per)
11. She (per)
12. She (per)
13. her (per)
14. she (per)
15. that (dem)
16. she (per)
17. she (per)
18. she (per)
19. her (per)
20. her (per)
21. whom (rel)
22. she (per)
23. this (dem)
24. she (per)
25. her (per)
26. She (per)
27. everything (ind)
28. she (per)
29. everyone (ind)
30. everyone (ind)
31. her (per)

PRACTICE 22

1. The (Kool Jazz Festival), <u>a</u> (mixture), <u>jazz</u>, <u>soul</u> (music)
2. These (concerts), <u>different</u> (types)
3. <u>the</u>, <u>rowdy</u> (ones), <u>the</u>, <u>dreamy</u> (lovers), <u>the</u> (smokers), <u>the</u> (ones), <u>the</u> (walls), <u>the</u>, <u>whole</u> (night), <u>the</u> (people), <u>profane</u> (language)
4. <u>the</u>, <u>rowdy</u> (ones), <u>young</u> (ones)
5. <u>those</u>, <u>loud</u> (whistles)
6. <u>the</u>, <u>dreamy</u> (lovers), <u>the</u>, <u>whole</u> (concerts), <u>moony</u> (eyes)
7. The (smokers), <u>the</u> (air), <u>the</u>, <u>disgusting</u> (smell)
8. The, <u>unfriendly</u> (wall-standers)
9. The (cursers), <u>any</u> (respect), <u>the</u>, <u>older</u> (people)
10. <u>the</u>, <u>terrific</u> (Kool Jazz Festival)

PRACTICE 24 (Examples of comparative and superlative adjectives)

1. prettier, prettiest
2. more difficult, most difficult
3. colder, coldest
4. worse, worst
5. less, least
6. better, best
7. tastier, tastiest
8. worse, worst
9. less, least
10. more fulfilling, most fulfilling

PRACTICE 26

1. <u>so</u> (dark), <u>noisily</u> (fell)
2. <u>so</u> (beautifully), <u>beautifully</u> (arranged)
3. <u>very</u> (incompetently), <u>incompetently</u> (conducted), <u>quietly</u> (had been stealing)
4. <u>just</u> (too), <u>too</u> (noisy)
5. <u>generously</u> (gave), <u>most</u> (lovely)
6. <u>most</u> impatiently, <u>impatiently</u> (has been waiting)
7. <u>triumphantly</u> (entered), <u>very</u> (slowly), <u>slowly</u> (riding)
8. <u>extremely</u> (hard), <u>not</u> (complain)
9. <u>always</u> (begins), <u>unnecessarily</u> (long)
10. <u>never</u> (admits), <u>not</u> (has been screened), <u>carefully</u> (has been screened)

PRACTICE 27

1. both/and also (cor)
2. When (sub)
3. because (sub), while (sub)
4. and (cc)
5. If (sub)
6. where (sub)
7. but (cc), or (cc)
8. either/or (cor)
9. Because (sub)
10. when (sub)
11. and (cc), while (sub)

Chapter 11

PRACTICE 2

1. S
2. S
3. N
4. N
5. N

6. N
7. N
8. S
9. N
10. N

PRACTICE 6

1. One day she was running and playing in the corn field.
2. Every day from then on the crow and my mother would meet in the corn field.
3. They walked together that way all over the corn field.
4. That night her uncle, Al Reynolds, died of a heart attack.

PRACTICE 7

1. This past Tuesday night, my husband and I were shopping at Maison Blanche, and we were about to call it a night.
2. I have come across this unhappy situation many times before, but each time it shocks and saddens me.
3. The rising divorce rate is especially distressing, for many of the marriages could have been saved.

PRACTICE 8

1. . . . shark-infested waters, for the movement . . . .
2. . . . on the tenth, and we will be gone . . . .
3. . . . and dark, but I like it.
4. . . . decision quickly, for time is running out . . . .
5. . . . movie tonight, or we may . . . .
6. . . . by 10:00 P.M., but my roommate . . . .
7. . . . late afternoon, and we plan . . . .
8. . . . another year, or I may cancel it now.

PRACTICE 9

1. . . . raw oysters, nor does she like any other shellfish.
2. . . . is rated PG, so we probably . . . .
3. . . . odd-looking character, yet many women . . . .
4. . . . next month, so she . . . .
5. . . . friends' advice, nor does he pay attention . . . .
6. . . . his sixties, yet he still . . . .

PRACTICE 13

1. I must study first, and then I may go to the movies with you.
2. I was not sick after eating the pizza and marshmallows; however, Helen and Tom . . . .
3. We had many things to talk about; therefore, the time passed quickly.
4. The poet Keats died in his mid-twenties; nevertheless, his poetry . . . .
5. The barbeque restaurant will probably be more successful now that it is in a better location; moreover, its new management is first-rate.
6. Paula knows how to fix everything; for example, she even fixed her grandfather's cuckoo clock.
7. It was only a small, inexpensive gift; however, it was a well-chosen one.
8. I enjoy working in the early morning because I feel rested then; moreover, it is the only time the house is quiet.
9. Every day Mrs. Carr picks whatever is ripe, and then she feeds the chickens.
10. Christy Brown was an Irish writer who was severely brain damaged from birth; nevertheless, he published . . . .
11. The day was clear and sunny; therefore, we decided . . . .
12. Thousands of people greet each other every day at the Los Angeles airport; however, it is not . . . .

PRACTICE 15

1. As I walked up the gravel road, I looked up at the morning sky.
2. The leaves on the trees were trembling because the wind was blowing slightly.
3. I continued walking until I saw a child with light brown hair.
4. She acted as though she did not have a care in the world.
5. They were the same color as my eyes when I was young.
6. As she looked up, she asked what I was doing there.
7, 8. When she spoke, I realized I was seeing myself when I was young.
9. While I was turning to leave, I changed my mind.
10. But she was gone, just as the past has been gone from my memory, until now.

PRACTICE 16

1. When — time
2. Although — contrast
3. While — time
4. If — condition
5. Because — reason
6. Unless — condition

PRACTICE 17

1. after — time
2. because — reason
3. while — time
4. before — time
5. unless — condition

PRACTICE 20

1. The president stood by what he said because he was a man of great conviction.
2. I am leaving because I am afraid I will get caught in the rain.
3. It is easy to see a glass as half-empty, although it is better to see it as half-full.
4. When the terrorists attacked the embassy, two people were killed.
5. Eighteen-year-olds should be able to buy alcohol because they are old enough to fight and vote.
6. Although eighteen-year-olds are old enought to fight and vote, they should still not be able to buy alcohol.

PRACTICE 21

1. We moved to a new town when I was five years old.
2. Because Josh does not have enough money to live comfortably, he is looking for a new job.
3. When I moved to Jefferson City about five years ago, I was puzzled by certain words I heard.
4. Some of the words were very hard to understand because the people pronounced them in a funny way.
5. I frequently had to ask people to repeat themselves since (or because) I could not . . . .
6. Although some words, like *yat*, were clearly pronounced, they were so odd . . . .
7. When I finally asked someone what *yat* meant, I was told . . . .
8. Because some people in the city use *yat* all the time, they are called *yats*.
9. While many *yat* mothers call their children by names such as Precious, Sweetheart, and Dawlin', angry *yat* mothers call . . . .

PRACTICE 22

1. that is filled with good friends and good times (life)
2. who is usually the last to leave a party (Joe)
3. which has not been washed in two years (car)
4. where I grew up (town)
5. who is very tall for her age (Anita)
6. who did not have a way to get to school (Karen)
7. [that] I would like to see run for office (one)
8. when President Kennedy was assassinated (1963)

PRACTICE 23

1. Jennifer, <u>who is a very neurotic person</u>, still . . . .
2. . . . experience <u>that he will never forget</u>.

3. The plan <u>that we finally decided upon</u> was . . . .
4. My typewriter, <u>which has not been cleaned in eight years</u>, is in poor condition.
5. . . . the celebrity, <u>who was doing his best to avoid the crowd</u>.
6. The film <u>that Altman directed</u> was the best.
7. Friends <u>who talk behind your back</u> are no friends.
8. I moved to California, <u>where the grass</u> . . . .

PRACTICE 27

1. The hillsides, which extended as far as the eye could see, were covered . . . .
2. My parents, who have never been to New England, would love to see . . . .
3. Our decrepit Volkswagen, which was loaded down with luggage, did its best on the mountain roads.
4. We finally arrived at the ski lodge, which was to be our home for the next few months.
5. The owner of the lodge, who looked like an aging Woody Allen, helped us unload.
6. I remember watching the first snowfall, which was a sight . . . .
7. The local people, who have experienced icy roads and snow-shoveling all their lives, probably would not . . . .

PRACTICE 29

1. The puppy chewed up everything in sight, for example, shoes, newspapers, and even the corner of the couch.
2. Greece, a land of blue skies and whitewashed houses, is a popular vacation spot.
3. Updike's latest novel, a book about failing relationships, is supposedly his best.
4. The defensive-driving coach was a little nervous about his new pupil, a man convicted . . . .
5. Maria, now eight months pregnant, decided not to join the neighborhood softball team.

PRACTICE 31

1. Paco brought everything he thought he might need for a weekend visit, everything from five outfits . . . .
2. I have three favorite politicians, Ted Kennedy, George Bush, and Clint Eastwood.
3. Movies rated *R* may include controversial material, both sex and violence.
4. Choon Jai likes horror films, especially the old-fashioned . . . .

5. Joan gave me a Christmas present that I really needed, a heavy wool sweater.
6. He reads magazines every chance he gets, everything from . . . .

Chapter 12

PRACTICE 1

1. F
2. S
3. F
4. S
5. F
6. F
7. F
8. S
9. F
10. F
11. S

PRACTICE 3

1. . . . in the right manner, even if they are hard to handle.
2. . . . a certain type of person, whether that person is a sportsman, a swinger, or a conservative.
3. . . . all the customers because some of them are crazy.

PRACTICE 4

1. . . . no one to react, no one to care.
2. . . . and put on a tie when he could take it no longer.
3. . . . so he gave up and lost himself and was dead before he died.

PRACTICE 5

1. There are two distinct areas within this room.
2. The other area contains a sixty-inch . . . .
3. . . . the kitchen. It contains shelves . . . .

PRACTICE 6

1. . . . "easy to open" boxes, all tagged with labels . . . .
2. . . . simple way of life, while in reality our lives . . . .
3. . . . many problems, such as how to operate . . . .

PRACTICE 7

1, 2, 3. . . . in 1939, but did not achieve widespread popularity until the 1950s, which was television's golden era and a time of continued experiments, all of which were done live.
4. . . . children's shows, "Howdy Doody," "Lassie," "The Wonderful World of Disney," to name a few.
5. . . . expanded its scope and added bigger and better . . . .

PRACTICE 8

1. I had the hours and the instructors I wanted . . . .
2. I was even early that day because I knew registration would be crowded.
3, 4. People were running around like chickens with their heads cut off, frantically searching for answers.
5. Some were lying on the floor in a daze, others leaning . . . .
6. . . . across the floor, an area littered . . . .
7. . . . a registered college student, not a happy one, but registered, nevertheless.

PRACTICE 9

1. . . . on their watches. They would be . . . .
2. . . . check the water. It looks good to me.
3. Shut the door. It is cold in there.
4. . . . which one you take. Both roads will . . . .
5. . . . woman. Your past . . . .
6. . . . my imagination. It was a little girl.
7. . . . people. Someone will surely help us.
8. . . . the university. The blocks are not long, and each . . . .
9. . . . for instance. I am not . . . .

PRACTICE 10

1. . . . a new dress, and I . . . .
2. . . . summer, but he . . . .
3. . . . worry, for we . . . .
4. . . . telling me, yet I knew . . . .
5. . . . to rain, so we had . . . .
6. . . . to Seattle, or I am not . . . .
7. . . . to school, nor will he look . . . .

PRACTICE 11

1. . . . was cold, and there was . . . .
2. . . . man, but I liked him.
3. . . . shove, and I fell . . . .
4. . . . sometimes, but it has been . . . .
5. "Marry me, or I will not . . . . "
6. . . . well fed, yet she is still skinny.
7. Let me go, for I have . . . .
8. . . . home, for she had . . . .
9. . . . Academy, so now I am here . . . .
10. He will not sleep, nor will he eat.

PRACTICE 12

1. . . . his health; then he . . . .
2. . . . person; however, she is . . . .
3. . . . inexpensive; for example, you . . . .
4. . . . strict; however, college . . . .
5. . . . cream sauce; then you . . . .
6. . . . was dead; then it . . . .
7. . . . would decline; moreover, young people . . . .
8. . . . our goal; however, it did . . . .
9. . . . against cigarette smoking; consequently, 30 percent . . . .

PRACTICE 13

1. . . . with Joyce because she . . . .
2. When he graduates this May, I am going to miss him.
3. If you study in our room, I will study in the library.
4. While the states of our nation are different in most ways, they do . . . .
5. . . . will eventually pass, although it will take many years.
6. Since kids are playful, joyful, and bright, that is why . . . .

PRACTICE 14

1. . . . my eyes. The car was . . . .
2. . . . the door. Let's keep . . . .
3. When the rock hit him beneath his eye, it taught him a lesson.
4. . . . the problem; however, they do . . . .
5. I need those notes, so please give them to me.
6. . . . your poor, and I will make . . . .
7. . . . very friendly; in fact, they . . . .
8. . . . of 1981. In so doing . . . .
9. Russell is 6'5", and he weighs 175 pounds.
10. Correct
11. . . . college men because I know . . . .
12. . . . of teaching; moreover, she . . . .
13. . . . to yourself because there is one more ball left to play.
14. Correct
15. . . . really wins. It eats your money.
16. . . . their own actions; however, adults . . . .
17. . . . hard to detect because sometimes they . . . .
18. . . . as a nation; moreover, we seem . . . .
19. . . . once was because it has lost . . . .
20. . . . our enemy; however, its people . . . .

PRACTICE 15

1. . . . it was Sunday, and people were still . . . .
2. . . . usual attire; however, the . . . .

3. . . . seen the Klan before, and I wanted . . . .
4. . . . "White power." It struck me funny . . . .
5. . . . the Liberty Monument. Their leader . . . .
6. . . . NAACP button. Every now and then . . . .
7. . . . them; however, after seeing what I saw . . . .
8. Do not get me wrong though. I have not . . . .

PRACTICE 16

1. . . . dangerous illness. It is . . . .
2. . . . defensive because he could not . . . .
3. . . . on the bill, and then it . . . .
4. . . . the information, and then . . . .
5. . . . ferocious; however, he is . . . .
6. . . . for our country; therefore, they . . . .
7. When we began climbing to the top, the wind . . . .
8. . . . any further, so we . . . .
9. . . . "Will you just listen to me? I have something to say . . . ."
10. "What do you want from me? I can no longer . . . ."

PRACTICE 17

1. . . . two years ago, and she is . . . .
2. . . . one elderly couple, who accepted her . . . .
3. . . . on holidays. She had only . . . .
4. . . . dart tournaments. Darts is a game . . . .
5. . . . of the people, for it is a land . . . .
6. . . . small farms, and one can see . . . .
7. . . . and Italy. She loved . . . .
8. . . . friendly, too. There are . . . .
9. . . . Switzerland. It has breathtaking . . . .
10. . . . especially lovely. It is located . . . .
11. . . . the Alps; however, the snow . . . .
12. . . . the lodge, and then they . . . .
13. . . . on the glacier, and the sun . . . .
14. . . . by ropes; however, no one slipped.

PRACTICE 18

1. . . . sleeping bags. They had nothing . . . .
2. . . . we roughed it. We slept in a tent . . . .
3. . . . no shade because the tallest tree . . . .
4. . . . in the wilderness. This time we . . . .
5. There was no tent, but we had . . . .
6. . . . of life. They brought . . . .
7. . . . in camping, and we have . . . .
8. . . . pantry. The trailer even has . . . .
9. . . . back to nature. I recommend . . . .

PRACTICE 19

1. carefully (carry)
2. curiously (looked)
3. nicely (has fixed up)
4. rapidly (were moving)
5. beautiful (She)
6. loudly (bark)
7. well (did)
8. well (plays)
9. good (she)
10. frequently (frowns)
11. crazily (have been carrying on)

PRACTICE 22

1. . . . all their money, they headed . . . .
2. . . . foundation, a house will not fall down.
3. . . . father, you [or one] must spend a lot of time with the children.
4. . . . in the river, we were scared by a bad thunderstorm.
5. . . . your best, you must stay in good shape.
6. The squirrel ran across the hunter's plate while he was eating his supper. [Or: While eating his supper, the hunter was surprised to see a squirrel run across his plate.]
7. Convicted of a third felony, the man was sent to prison for life.
8. Having awoken early, they could not be found.
9. . . . is planted, one must make the best . . . .

PRACTICE 23

1. My aunt, with a failing heart, was rushed . . . . [Or: With a failing heart, my aunt . . . .]
2. The interns on duty in the emergency room were . . . .
3. . . . cost her almost three hundred . . . .
4. . . . testified on behalf of neglected children before the . . . .
5. . . . listened with great interest to her appeal . . . .
6. . . . passed the bill to appropriate almost one hundred . . . .
7. The children who have been neglected will now be helped . . . .
8. With their determined leadership, Dr. Watts and . . . .
9. . . . has recruited nearly three hundred . . . .
10. The members argue convincingly for various . . . .
11. . . . what one person with a dream can do to change things.

PRACTICE 24

1. . . . could be classified as friendly, indifferent, and just plain mean.
2. . . . does not deter crime, it is used only against the poor, and it is cruel and unusual punishment.
3. . . . his nap in the afternoon, his bike ride in the early morning, and his novels at night.
4. Manning watches the soap operas in the morning, news programs in the late afternoon, and television movies at night.

5. . . . to make the customers feel welcome, to show them to a table, and to find them a waiter.
6. . . . I am going to save some money, then open my own business, and finally sit back and get rich.

Chapter 13

PRACTICE 1

1. boys, sew
2. sisters, run
3. fists, ask
4. risks, risk
5. plays, play
6. dreams, dream

PRACTICE 2

1. cat, hits
2. box, costs
3. bus, loves
4. bill, bills
5. dance, dances
6. type, types

PRACTICE 3 (Examples)

1. instructor (S), involves (S)
2. Musicians (P), play (P)
3. sisters (P), make (P)
4. dances (P), seem (P)
5. Maria (S), dances (S)
6. mother (S), whacks (S)
7. fans (P), watch (P)
8. aunt (S), fans (S)
9. dresses (P), seem (P)
10. Jimmy (S), dresses (S)
11. It (S), seems (S)
12. Robin Hood (S), robs (S)

PRACTICE 4

1. apples (they) cost
2. Robin Hood (he) robs
3. police (they) complain
4. Mrs. Thatcher (she) complains
5. program (its) consists
6. Love (it) makes
7. Happiness (it) seems
8. daughter (she) seeks
9. mother and father (they) keep
10. Grandfather (he) becomes

PRACTICE 5 (Examples)

1. We hope . . .
2. Our mayor involves
3. You practice
4. You spend
5. Anton and Molly sew
6. It consists
7. I give
8. The dream becomes
9. The people say
10. They use
11. She seems
12. The nations seem

PRACTICE 6

1. police raid
2. United States experiences
3. jury eats
4. poor pay, rich pay
5. class gives
6. family acts
7. Politics makes
8. experienced (people) make
9. people need
10. pants show
11. handicapped demand
12. jury argue
13. police support
14. The U.S.S.R. wants
15. Saints quit
16. Republican party supports
17. United States gives
18. powerful control

PRACTICE 7 (Examples)

1. My wife preaches
2. The child pinches
3. My father fusses
4. It costs
5. Apples cost
6. Fools rush
7. The Bears crush
8. The police officer asks
9. The priest blesses

PRACTICE 8

1. Dr. Greenway doesn't
2. instructor does (or doesn't)
3. city does
4. noise does
5. woman doesn't
6. They do
7. Santa doesn't
8. It doesn't
9. English do (or don't)
10. She does (or doesn't)
11. Does (or Doesn't)

PRACTICE 9

1. Mary carries
2. Ben defies
3. She tries
4. Mia travels
5. bird flies
6. The team journeys
7. It buries
8. It does
9. It doesn't
10. The van goes

PRACTICE 10

1. City of Detroit has
2. Everyone has
3. You have
4. China has
5. They have
6. soldier has
7. The United States has
8. scissors have
9. police have
10. People have
11. The class has

PRACTICE 11

1. People are
2. My husband and brother-in-law were
3. The jury is (or *are* if used for individual jury members)
4. Uncle Mac wasn't
5. They weren't
6. Congress was
7. Rams aren't
8. Police are
9. You weren't

PRACTICE 12

1. Does he need more money for the trip? (he does need)
2. Is she going to dance with you? (she is going)
3. Do those children need heavier jackets? (children do need)
4. Were they the ones we were looking for? (they were)
5. Has the leg healed completely? (leg has healed)
6. Doesn't the senator deliver on his promises? (senator does deliver)

PRACTICE 14

1. deer were
2. something is
3. fighting is
4. survivors were
5. use wasn't
6. thing wasn't
7. alternatives are
8. crime has been
9. reason hasn't been
10. murders have been
11. concern has been

PRACTICE 15

1. problem is
2. hope is (correct)
3. reason is (correct)
4. essays are (Here are the essays . . . .)
5. changes haven't been (There haven't been . . . .)
6. anything hasn't been (There hasn't been . . . .)
7. thing wasn't (There wasn't a thing . . . .)
8. reasons are (There are several reasons . . . .)
9. no point is (correct)
10. reasons are (correct)
11. some are (There are some . . . .)

PRACTICE 16

1. Mother and I sew
2. Gas and oil cost

3. What I want and what she wants aren't
4. what is
5. This man and this woman give
6. Getting better grades is
7. Getting better grades and playing more tennis are
8. My aunt and uncle buy
9. potatoes, corn and spinach seem
10. The Bill of Rights and the Constitution protect
11. Making clothes for her children is

PRACTICE 17

1. Mrs. Appleby or Mrs. St. John comes
2. Neither you nor they are
3. Abraham and his son, Isaac, are
4. Either Abraham or his servants are
5. A ram or other animal appears
6. Isaac but also Abraham is
7. Not only the grandfather but also the children jog
8. Not only the children but also the grandfather jogs
9. Either Sophia or you have
10. Both the cat and the dog sleep
11. Neither Russia nor the United States experiences

PRACTICE 18

1. Some are
2. Everything costs
3. Anyone is
4. Some was
5. All are
6. Everything involves
7. Half tells
8. Does everyone
9. Most have
10. Much is
11. Does anyone

PRACTICE 19

1. (choice) is
2. (names) were
3. (agenda) is
4. (one) is
5. (winner) was
6. (winners) were

PRACTICE 20

1. friends who were
2. nations that break
3. one who minds
4. ones who care
5. coins that turn
6. People who need
7. police who believe
8. date who talks
9. those who know
10. gifts that cost
11. scissors that are

PRACTICE 21

1. is
2. is
3. is
4. are
5. is

PRACTICE 22 (Examples)

1. typewriter that skips
2. Automobiles that last
3. A family who live
4. People who know
5. The reasons that come

Chapter 14

PRACTICE 1

1. begun
2. loved
3. beginning
4. walked
5. begin
6. was
7. drowned
8. seemed
9. asked
10. pleaded
11. having

PRACTICE 2

1. broken
2. laid
3. lay
4. set
5. lain
6. laid
7. set
8. drowned
9. cost
10. gone
11. begin
12. saw
13. beginning
14. laying
15. hurting
16. breaks
17. being
18. been
19. were
20. are
21. done

PRACTICE 3 (Examples)

1. can
2. might
3. will
4. should
5. shall
6. would
7. may
8. could
9. must

PRACTICE 4

1. could		9. would	
2. can		10. will	
3. could		11. would	
4. can		12. may	
5. could		13. might or may	
6. would		14. might	
7. will		15. may	
8. would		16. might, might	

PRACTICE 5

1. a. dresses	b. dressed		
2. a. cuts	b. cut		
3. a. begin	b. began		
4. a. choose	b. chose		
5. a. reads	b. read		
6. a. costs	b. cost		
7. a. drowns	b. drowned		
8. a. wakes	b. woke		
9. a. has	b. had		
10. a. feel	b. felt		
11. a. gets	b. got		

PRACTICE 6

1. a. Marlon tears	b. he tore
2. a. I lay	b. I laid
3. a. Grandfather says	b. Grandfather once said
4. a. I ask	b. One time I asked
5. a. They use	b. my sisters used
6. a. She looks	b. Cindy looked
7. a. I quit	b. I quit
8. a. Kirby hits	b. Kirby later hit
9. a. you begin	b. she began
10. a. lawyer pleads	b. the lawyer pleaded

PRACTICE 7

1. *help*: it ends in a double consonant
2. *loom*: the final consonant is preceded by a double vowel
3. *enjoy*: it ends in -*y*
4. *differ*: the accent is on the first syllable
5. *return*: it ends with a double consonant

PRACTICE 8

1. enjoyed
2. preferred
3. gassed
4. stepped
5. supposed
6. hummed
7. counseled (counselled is also correct but not preferred)

PRACTICE 9

1. cried
2. fried
3. obeyed
4. married
5. buried

PRACTICE 10

1. taught
2. risen
3. begun
4. chosen
5. sat
6. come
7. become
8. run
9. quit
10. put
11. hit
12. led
13. laid
14. lain
15. rung
16. begun
17. seemed
18. involved
19. gone
20. done
21. seen

PRACTICE 11

1. have loved, had loved
2. has happened, had happened
3. have legalized, had legalized
4. have guessed, had guessed
5. have finished, had finished
6. have built, had built

PRACTICE 12

1. have broken, had broken
2. have or has lifted, had lifted
3. have or has begun, had begun
4. have or has shown, had shown
5. have or has found, had found
6. have or has set, had set
7. have or has lain, had lain
8. have or has laid, had laid
9. have or has become, had become

PRACTICE 13

1. I had
2. . . . I still kept to myself because I made . . . .

3. . . . I soon got . . . who had taken . . . .
4. She had . . . and asked . . . .
5. I could soon say that I had made . . . .
6. I have [or had] . . . .

PRACTICE 14

1. The bridge was built by them to withstand hurricanes.
2. My shirt is torn every time I play football.
3. My shirt was torn . . . .
4. His knee was split wide open by the glass.
5. Their house was built upon a rock.
6. That song was first sung by the Jackson Five.

PRACTICE 15

1. You are supposed
2. It is written
3. They were used
4. I was sworn
5. My finger was hurt
6. It is said
7. Alvina was driven
8. Nantucket is known
9. I will never get used to
10. The lakes were frozen
11. My alarm clock is set

PRACTICE 16

1. I greatly appreciate what you have done.
2. We really needed the supplies.
3. They will use the money to buy a car.
4. Her father called the doctor.
5. I understood the lecture.
6. You have carefully learned the various verb forms.

PRACTICE 17

1. You are looking
2. we were beginning
3. She was helping
4. they are asking
5. Dr. Ward is quizzing
6. I was dyeing
7. We were traveling
8. The old man was lying
9. I am laying
10. she is saying
11. she was hitting
12. I was beginning

PRACTICE 18

1. crept, crept, creeping
2. wove, woven, weaving
3. mowed, mowed (or mown), mowing
4. bent, bent, bending
5. shone, shone, shining
6. forbade, forbidden, forbidding

7. shouldered, shouldered, shouldering
8. hanged, hanged, hanging
9. harkened, harkened, harkening
10. happened, happened, happening
11. spayed, spayed, spaying

PRACTICE 19

1. They surprised us when they came to our school.
2. When I was young, I used to tear . . . .
3. She got so mad that she turned red.
4. They always dressed up when they went out to eat.
5. We worked, we worked, and we worked, but we got nowhere.
6. When we returned, we freed the prisoners.
7. My wife said you advertised . . . .
8. They acted as if they had never seen . . . .
9. Maria said that she would study . . . .
10. The president told the nation that he could balance the budget.
11. We came home after the war, just as we said we would.

PRACTICE 20

1. It was; the year was 1977; I knew once I got; this Christmas was going
2. The morning went; everybody was complaining; But the fussing really started; man I had never seen before came; I was puzzled; mother knew him; Everybody thought he was; although he was; as I was; My mother didn't say
3. When I went into the kitchen; Sidney followed and started telling; man was entirely too old; That was; We threw harsh words; I told him that he was as crazy as he looked; he told me that I was headed for trouble; I became very upset.
4. When I went; Momma and the man were just sitting; tears rolled; she looked; reason that I was so upset was; strange man and Momma kept looking; I made; Finally, I could; I turned; and asked; who in the world he was; The man, whom my mother called Robert, turned; got up slowly, and told me that he was; family began
5. I was very shocked and couldn't; My mother cried; and said, "Don't laugh . . . ."; I would never forget; I ran; and wept; My mother then came out; I had; I was ashamed; I couldn't bring; I certainly couldn't; I loved
6. But things worked; We went on; I felt funny; I told; I never wanted; Sidney was

PRACTICE 25

1. Seeing
2. loved
3. begun

4. Shocked
5. Beginning

PRACTICE 27

1. shocking
2. beginning
3. doing, being

4. giving
5. waiting

PRACTICE 28

1. makes
2. is
3. are

4. is
5. are
6. prepare

Chapter 15

PRACTICE 1

1. We refuse, we keep
2. you say, you love, you act
3. I say
4. They like, they love
5. We do
6. I don't care, we do, I don't care, you do, I don't care, they do, I do care, what He does.
7. They love

8. They seem, they believe
9. We carry, we don't
10. They cost
11. They haven't had
12. You and your family have
13. days haven't been
14. You have, I have
15. We have
16. We ask, we do receive

PRACTICE 2

1. police (P) ask, he (S) gives
2. Mary (S) doesn't
3. husband (S) tries, he (S) buys
4. What (S) interests, is
5. She (S) cleans, daughters (P) sit
6. It (S) doesn't
7. Mia (S) fixes
8. she (S) does
9. government (S) employs (correct)

10. Stan (S) pushes, he (S) is going
11. Ferdinand (S) sleeps, eats, and watches
12. class (S) sings, teacher (S) asks
13. people (P) come and climb
14. Mama Linda (S) is, cares
15. recipe (S) doesn't
16. It (S) seems
17. comet (S) doesn't appear

PRACTICE 3

1. we were
2. I am, you are, we are
3. we were
4. they weren't
5. truth isn't

PRACTICE 4

1. governments (P) weren't
2. fish (P) were
3. soldiers (P) weren't
4. students (P) were
5. chance (S) isn't
6. more (P) aren't going
7. people (P) died or were brought
8. nations (P) met, who [nations] (P) were gathering
9. police (P) weren't
10. United States (S) isn't trying
11. Red nor his parents (P) were

PRACTICE 5

1. were
2. is
3. is or was
4. is or was
5. are or were
6. are or were

PRACTICE 6 (Examples)

1. She does
2. I feel
3. She has
4. radio and television make
5. people say
6. husband tells

PRACTICE 8

1. She and I were
2. paper helps
3. They were serving
4. reporter faces
5. (Correct)
6. (Correct)
7. he catches
8. (Correct)
9. April takes
10. (Correct)
11. they plan

PRACTICE 9

1. sounds (of my neighborhood) change
2. houses (on my block) are
3. Everybody (in my classes) is working
4. years (of school) were
5. sounds (in my neighborhood) are
6. great-grandmother (in most people's eyes) seems
7. thought (of her children) is satisfying
8. work (on the houses) begins
9. One (of us) is
10. Harold Muskie (of Chase Metropolitan Bank) recommends
11. dreams (for a better life) were fulfilled

PRACTICE 10

1. children (who are not in school) have
2. Those (who don't have the money) get

3. things (she has left behind) mean
4. children (who live in my neighborhood) play
5. school (where my mother taught for the last seven years) is closing
6. gifts (he brings to my son) come

PRACTICE 12 (Examples)

1. I am loving
2. they are loved
3. The captain had loved
4. The child was drowned
5. We have found
6. She flies
7. The pond is frozen
8. They had gone
9. It was happening
10. I laid down my watch
11. We led
12. You are lying out in the sun (not *laying* out in the sun)
13. I did lose my watch
14. We had paid for the ticket
15. They saw
16. The sun is setting
17. The choir sang
18. The car was stolen
19. It was taken
20. The instructor taught
21. The pitcher has thrown

PRACTICE 13

1. mother beat
2. he lied, stole, and struggled
3. (Correct)
4. He went, stayed, and tried to impress
5. he stood and watched
6. he felt and wanted
7. he lied and said
8. (woman) who hired
9. Richard had struggled and worked
10. he had finished
11. he used
12. he had given, principal wrote
13. (things) that enabled
14. (Correct)
15. he had
16. he managed
17. (Correct)
18. He had hidden, he learned
19. He took and ran
20. he went and escaped
21. conditions began

PRACTICE 14

1. it means
2. they seemed
3. woman asked
4. she would vote
5. he loved
6. we used
7. we had, we could
8. Neddie came
9. grandfather said
10. We used
11. He asked

PRACTICE 15

1. She told
2. father stayed and rubbed
3. mother told
4. pains began
5. Mother had called
6. we arrived
7. doctor examined
8. I started
9. I told
10. Lynette had
11. doctor left and told
12. He asked me
13. I stood
14. I was supposed
15. They would have to do
16. they changed and took
17. I said to myself
18. I left to sit
19. she joined
20. doctor came
21. I named
22. I named
23. we have learned

Chapter 16

PRACTICE 1

1. about Troy and me
2. older than I
3. Michael and I
4. (Correct)
5. between you and me
6. It was she

PRACTICE 2

1. my friend Regina and I traveled
2. Someone told Regina and me
3. as much luck as she
4. brought Regina and me
5. Regina and I did not have
6. to give either her or me
7. know to whom
8. Just between you and me
9. "Who do you girls think you are?"
10. But we "girls"
11. Regina and I were completely crazy
12. Regina and I ever had
13. Whoever said

PRACTICE 3 (Examples)

1. their children
2. ball carrier
3. the authorities
4. the waiters
5. this situation
6. the mechanic (the office manager)
7. the department is
8. this problem
9. the repair clerk said that he
10. The landlord is charging too much rent and does not want
11. the staff

PRACTICE 4

1. we
2. it
3. it
4. it
5. we

6. you
7. they
8. she
9. they
10. they

1. us
2. it
3. it
4. it
5. us

6. you
7. them
8. her
9. them
10. them

PRACTICE 5

1. they (movies) contain
2. it (world)
3. him (son)
4. it (Hawaii) has
5. her (lady)
6. his or her (reader)

7. them (stories)
8. it (government) wastes
9. it (Mexico)
10. his or her (patient)
11. him or her (person)

PRACTICE 7

1. without them
2. than it can, it has to import
3. in its own culture
4. she loved them
5. (Correct)
6. return them

7. they found
8. they found him
9. it imported too much of its oil
10. they need a lot more help from their husbands
11. one helps

PRACTICE 8 (Examples)

1. a hard time keeping a job
2. available to patients
3. to help patients with any problems they may have
4. There are nurses who are concerned about their work only when someone is watching them.
5. These people are at the bottom; they live
6. Both of my parents have helped me in their own ways, and I am grateful for what both have done.
7. parents to relate to their children
8. People with problems should make sure that they see somebody trained to help.
9. A teacher should be completely fair to students.
10. A teacher should plan all classes carefully.

PRACTICE 10 (Examples)

1. if you have moved
2. When you go to see her
3. whether one has good grades or not
4. Your social class
5. always talk to me
6. (Correct)
7. that I should forgive
8. one is moved
9. dangerous to them
10. what they tell us
11. to all one hears

Chapter 17

PRACTICE 1

1. watches, axes, firsts
2. candies, sashes, twos
3. potatoes, Kennedys, women
4. leaves, heroes, ladies
5. lives, Negroes, honeys
6. 1990's, deer, i's
7. roofs, policemen, baths
8. selves, stereos, Mondays
9. hippopotamuses
10. analyses

PRACTICE 2

1. two graveyards
2. twelve years
3. all the things
4. conversations
5. ladies
6. soft drinks
7. various kinds
8. candies

PRACTICE 3

1. tries, tried, trying
2. complies, complied, complying
3. hums, hummed, humming
4. buses, bussed, bussing
5. bevels, beveled, beveling
6. defers, deferred, deferring
7. satisfies, satisfied, satisfying
8. journeys, journeyed, journeying
9. opens, opened, opening
10. jogs, jogged, jogging
11. counsels, counseled, counseling
12. travels, traveled, traveling
13. studies, studied, studying
14. refers, referred, referring
15. occupies, occupied, occupying

PRACTICE 4

1. who's
2. they're
3. can't
4. let's
5. won't
6. wouldn't
7. they'd
8. shouldn't
9. don't
10. you're

PRACTICE 5

1. Its
2. you're
3. you're
4. it's
5. they're
6. Theirs
7. There's
8. It's, Your
9. it's
10. Who's
11. there's
12. Whose
13. whose
14. its

PRACTICE 7

1. all right
2. a lot
3. high school
4. meantime
5. whenever
6. twelfth
7. February
8. absence
9. argument
10. attendance
11. bookkeeping
12. beginning
13. committee
14. competent
15. develop
16. earliest
17. existence
18. foreign
19. government
20. handkerchief
21. independent
22. knowledge
23. library
24. mathematics
25. niece
26. occurred
27. perceive
28. privilege
29. participant
30. ridiculous
31. sensible
32. surprise
33. till
34. used to
35. written

Chapter 18

PRACTICE 1

1. (Correct)
2. Jimmy Carter
3. *Newsweek*, "The Six Year Presidency," "A president's . . . ."

4. Willie Morris, *North Toward Home*, North, Oxford, Mississippi, Deep South
5. Torah, Bible
6. Wednesday, I, I, History 102
7. Ted, "What . . . , Dad?"
8. "Gasoline, Sonny Boy."
9. Carver High School, Mr. Harry Berger
10. "A Time I Would Like to Forget"

PRACTICE 2

1. . . . smoking?"
2. . . . right now."
3. "Ouch!" I said, "That hurts."
4. years.
5. . . . Christmas?" I asked.
6. "No!" he almost shouted. "Now!"
7. . . . smoking?

PRACTICE 3

1. It's, we'll
2. women's, '63 or '64, '80's
3. Haven't, I'm tellin', it's, lickin'
4. It's, you can't
5. i's, t's

PRACTICE 4

1. teachers' room
2. Smiths' address
3. Charles's address
4. today's events
5. ladies' activities
6. woman's husband
7. a man and a woman's relationship
8. son-in-law's good fortune
9. boy's attitude
10. boys' attitude
11. people's attitude

PRACTICE 5

1. lady's
2. ladies'
3. child's
4. children's
5. flowers'
6. people's
7. the Smiths'
8. Ms. Marle Hass's

9. birds'
10. sons-in-law's

11. women's

PRACTICE 6

1. People's
2. sons'
3. everyone's
4. Sandra's
5. children's
6. people's
7. Mary's
8. boys
9. Nature's Way

10. Joneses'
11. Pierre and Violet's
12. (Correct)
13. someone's
14. neighbors'
15. committees
16. children's
17. Raymond's, priests'

PRACTICE 7

1. Ishmaelites, and they
2. slavery, but he
3. starvation, and he told

PRACTICE 8

1. While there is life, there
2. doctor says, he

PRACTICE 9

1. Great Britain, who was our ally, went
2. Argentina, who
3. This war, which caused many deaths, was

PRACTICE 10

1. however, he
2. nevertheless,
3. qualities, for example, his courage

PRACTICE 11

1. house, a house that had once been
2. porch, a beautifully constructed work of art, was now
3. Curtains, now nothing but rags, hung
4. a woman up in her eighties, did not

PRACTICE 12

1. so civilized, so intelligent, and so self-possessed
2. determined, courageous

PRACTICE 13

1. "If I were you," my dad said, "I wouldn't

PRACTICE 14

1. Hardin County, Kentucky, February 12, 1809

PRACTICE 15

1. While visiting, Mary
2. husband, my sister

PRACTICE 16

1. "Carlos, that game was the greatest, wasn't it?"
2. friend, who was grinning at me devilishly, and said
3. my friend, not for me.
4. in Scrabble, although lately

PRACTICE 17

1. Carter, and I'm (Rule 1)
2. said, job (Rule 2)
3. (Correct)
4. college, you (Rule 2)
5. rich, but I (Rule 1)
6. nursing, I (Rule 2)
7. (Correct)
8. center, but she (Rule 1)
9. (Correct)
10. school, it (Rule 2)
11. hard, you (Rule 2)
12. (Correct)
13. nights, and the (Rule 1)
14. lasts, seedtime (Rule 2)
15. (Correct)
16. happening, you (Rule 2)
17. (Correct)
18. often, and I (Rule 1)
19. (Correct)
20. doctor, but she (Rule 1)
21. (Correct)
22. (Correct)
23. before, and they (Rule 1)

PRACTICE 18

1. Sybil, who is a member of the Symphony Club, gave (Rule 3)
2. consequently, he (Rule 4)
3. Poe, the master writer of horror stories, did (Rule 5)
4. person, a carpenter, was (Rule 5)
5. textbook, which had been lost all semester, turned (Rule 3)
6. seafood, especially shrimp (Rule 5)
7. owners, who pay too much attention to them (Rule 3); for example, overwatering (Rule 4)
8. André, who had been cramming the whole night, slept (Rule 3)
9. however, it (Rule 4)
10. Chico, our eccentric next-door neighbor, is (Rule 5)
11. ailments, diphtheria (Rule 5)

12. activities, particularly fishing (Rule 5)
13. (Correct)

PRACTICE 19

1. cool, calm, and collected (Rule 6)
2. dark, rainy (Rule 6); first met, wasn't it? (Rule 10)
3. my father, my sister (Rule 9)
4. tax, although (Rule 10)
5. management of the center, the hiring and training of the personnel, and the development (Rule 6)
6. for you," President Kennedy said, "but ask (Rule 7)
7. night, time (Rule 9)
8. Make love, not war (Rule 10)
9. "War is not what I want," he said, "but peace." (Rule 7)
10. in hand, not knowing (Rule 10)
11. February 21, 1965 (Rule 8)

PRACTICE 20

1. *yranoitcid*, but *madam* (Rule 1)
2. (Correct)
3. outside, we (Rule 2)
4. (Correct)
5. (Correct)
6. (Correct)
7. bus, our next (Rule 2)
8. stove, but I (Rule 1)
9. (Correct)
10. Finally, when (Rule 10); Rivergate, the people (Rule 2); applauded us, and the (Rule 1)
11. seafood, especially (Rule 5); crab, shrimp, and oysters (Rule 6)
12. Tim Owens, a 6'6" guard, and (Rule 5)
13. look back, you will (Rule 2)
14. (Correct)
15. Eisenhower, the thirty-fourth president of the United States, was (Rule 5); Denison, Texas, on October 14, 1890 (Rule 8)
16. the road, I noticed (Rule 2); small, inviting brown cabin (Rule 6)
17. times, but through (Rule 1)
18. in the snow," Granny used to say, "because (Rule 7)
19. October, 1975, the Navy sent our family to Los Angeles, California, where (Rule 8); and met Kim, Steve, and Colleen (Rule 6)
20. Honestly, I am (Rule 10)

PRACTICE 21

1. in the Coast Guard and then decided
2. (Correct)

3. difficult than I remember
4. (Correct)
5. Coast Guard, and he
6. (Correct)
7. (Correct)
8. Bank; moreover, she
9. problem; however, he
10. (Correct)

PRACTICE 22

1. "What's the matter?" Richard's mother asked.
2. "It's those same boys," he said. "They'll beat me."
3. "You've got to get over that. Now go on," she said.
4. Richard replied, "But I'm scared."
5, She said, "How can I let you back down now?"
6. "Please Momma," he said, "don't make me fight."

PRACTICE 23

1. The school board said to the union that they were demanding far too much money.
2. The union replied that they only wanted a fair wage.
3. The school board said that the union should take its case to the taxpayer.
4. The union then said that the school board was responsible for the wages of teachers.

PRACTICE 24

1. The police chief said, "I need more cooperation from the judges."
2. The judges said, "We are already giving out much stiffer sentences."
3. The police chief responded, "Dangerous criminals are still being allowed to roam the streets."
4. The judges said, "We cannot be blamed for the amount of crime in the streets."
5. The police chief said, "The judges can help."

PRACTICE 25

1. 1901
2. (Correct)
3. (Correct)
4. $5.14
5. Page 16
6. (Correct)
7. eight o'clock
8. (Correct)
9. (Correct)
10. 2:30 P.M.

Index

Active voice, 334
Addresses, punctuation of, 420
Adjectives, 224–228
  articles as, 224–225
  clauses as, 249–255, 361–362, 418
  comparative and superlative, 226–228
  confused with adverbs, 280–281
  demonstrative, 225
  indefinite, 225
  predicate, 225
  special types of, 224–225
  workbook practice on, 225–226, 227–228
Adverbs, 228–230
  confused with adjectives, 280–281
  conjunctive, 242–243, 418
  workbook practice on, 229–230
Agreement. *See* Antecedents of pronouns; Subject-verb agreement
Analysis
  of ideas and information, 61, 67, 77
  of writing. *See* Evaluation of writing
Angelou, Maya, 52–53
Antecedents of pronouns, 377
  agreement with, 378–385, 386, 387
  unclear, 377–378, 386
Apostrophe use, 396–399, 413–416
  in contractions, 396–399, 413
  showing ownership, 414–416
Appositives, 255–259
  punctuation of, 255, 419
Argument essays, 187–202
  description of, 190–191
  exercises on, 187–190
  forming argument in, 187–190
  guidelines for writing of, 191–193
  samples of, 193–195, 199–200
  six-step method for writing of, 195–198
  writing assignments on, 195–202
Arthur, Herman, 446, 451–456

Articles, as adjectives, 224–225
Auden, W. H., 32
Audience
  of argument essay, 193, 198
  of letter to classmates, 3–8

Base form of verbs, 318, 323–325, 363
  irregular, 319–322
Bibliography, 438–439, 442, 445–446
  sample of, 450
Brainstorming, 31–37
  assignments on, 33–37
  for classification essay, 152–153
  as first step to writing well, 60, 64–66, 75–77
  sample of, 33

Call numbers in card catalog, 178–179, 438
Capitalization, 409–412
  rules on, 409–411
  of title of paper, 91
Card catalog in library, 178–179, 182, 438
  call numbers in, 178–179, 438
Case of pronouns, 219–221, 375, 397–399, 414
  errors in, 375–377, 386
Citation of sources, 437, 438–439, 442, 445–446, 450
Classification essays, 145–155
  description of, 145–146
  guidelines for writing of, 146–147
  persuasive, 192
  samples of, 148–150
  six-step method for writing of, 151–155
  transition sentences in, 147–148
  writing assignment on, 151–155
Classrooms
  discussions in, 50–54
  interview of classmate in, 8–12
  letter writing to classmates in, 3–8
  reading aloud of writing in, 8, 12, 72, 81–82

Clauses in sentences, 207, 208
  adjective, 249–255, 361–362, 418
  in complex sentence, 243–244, 249–255
  in compound sentence, 238–239
  dependent, 236–237, 243–244, 249–255
  independent, 236–237, 238–239, 243–244, 426–427
  in simple sentence, 236–237
  subordinate, punctuation of, 417
Clincher statement ending paragraph, 23
  revision of, 26
Clustering method for gathering ideas and information, 75
  assignments on, 49–50
  samples of, 46–49
  Sign mind and Design mind in, 46
  technique of, 46
Colon, use of, 428
Comma, use of, 417–426
  rules governing, 417–421
  in run-on sentence, 270
  workbook practice on, 417–426
Comma-splice sentences, 270
Comparative and superlative adjectives, 226–228
  irregular forms of, 227
Comparison and contrast essays, 131–145
  description of, 131
  guidelines for writing of, 131–132
  persuasive, 192
  planning of, two methods for, 132–139, 141–143
  samples of, 135–138
  six-step method for writing of, 139–144
  writing assignments on, 139–145
Complex sentences, 243–244
  adjective clause in, 249–255
  subordinating conjunction in, 243–249
Compound sentences, 238–243
  conjunctive adverb in, 242–243
  coordinating conjunctions in, 239–241
  punctuation of, semicolon use in, 426–427
Compound subjects
  joining of, 305, 306
  verb agreement with, 305–307
Compound words, spelling of, 402
Conclusion of essay, 23, 89–90, 437, 442
  evaluation and revision of, 26, 92, 94
  ideas for, 89–90
Conflict situations, narrative writing on, 109–110
Conjugation of verbs, 293
  subject-verb agreement in, 293–295
Conjunctions, 230–232
  coordinating, 230, 239–241
  correlative, 231, 306
  punctuation of, 239, 417, 419
  subordinating, 230–231, 243–249
  workbook practice on, 231–232
Conjunctive adverbs, 242
  in compound sentence, 242–243
  punctuation of, 242, 418

Contractions, 396–399
  apostrophe in, 396–399, 413
  compared to possessive pronouns, 397–399
  use of, 396–397
Contrast and comparison essays, 131–145. *See also* Comparison and contrast essays
Conversation, writing dialogue based on, 54–58
Coordinating conjunctions, 230, 239–241
  in compound sentences, 239–241
  punctuation of, 239, 417
Correlative conjunctions, 231
  joining compound subjects, 306

Dangling modifiers, 281–283
Dash, in punctuation, 432
Dates
  punctuation of, 420
  spelling of, 402
Demonstrative adjectives, 225
Demonstrative pronouns, 221–222
Dependent clauses, 236–237, 243–244
  as adjectives, 249–255
Descriptive writing, 97–109
  in argument essay, 192
  assignments on, 101–107
  guidelines on, 98–99
  six-step method in, 102–106
  topic selection in, 102
  uses of, 97–98
  word selection in, 107–108
Dewey decimal classification system, 179
Dialogue writing, 54–58
  assignment on, 57–58
  evaluation and revision of, 106
  narrative, 110, 111, 115, 116
  rules on, 56–57
  sample of, 56
Dictionary use
  for selection of exact word, 107
  for spelling, 391
  for verb forms, 339–341
Direct objects, 215–216
Discussion, intentional, 50–54

Editing of writing, 91–96. *See also* Revision of writing
Education Index, 180
Elbow, Peter, 37
Ellipsis, use of, 444
Essay and General Literature Index, 180–181
Evaluation of writing, 26–27, 28, 91–96
  in argument essay, 198
  assignments on, 29, 96
  in classification essay, 155
  in comparison and contrast essays, 144
  in descriptive essay, 106
  in example essay, 130–131

example of, 26-28, 92-96
guidelines on, 72, 91-92
in narrative essay, 109, 116
in process essay, 124
as sixth step to writing well, 62-64, 72, 81-82
in summary of reading material, 166
Example essays, 125-131
description of, 125-126
guidelines for writing of, 126-127
persuasive, 192
sample of, 127
six-step method of writing, 128-131
writing assignment on, 128-131
Exclamation point, use of, 412
Expletives, reversed order of subject and verb with, 303-304

Footnotes, 445
Fragments of sentences, 265-270
Free writing
assignments on, 37-45
gathering ideas and information for writing from, 37-45
process of, 37, 41, 44-45
revision of, 41, 44-45
Fused sentence, 270

Gathering ideas and information for writing, 31-58
as first step in writing well, 60-61, 64-66, 75-77, 437-440
Gender confusion in pronoun use, 381-384, 387
Gerunds, 346-347
wrong personal pronoun used with, 385-386
Gipe, George, 164

Helping verbs, 212
Holt, John, 169, 172
Hot Topics: The Magazine Index, 180, 182
"How to" essays, 116-124. *See also* Process essays
Humanities Index, 180, 183
Hyphenation of words, 28-29, 391, 401-402, 432
rules on, 402

Ideas and information for writing
analysis of, 61, 67, 77
in argument essay, 196, 198
from brainstorming, 31-37
from class discussions, 50-54
in classification essays, 152-153
from clustering technique, 45-50
in comparison and contrast essays, 139-140
in descriptive writing, 102-103, 104
in example essay, 128-129
from free writing, 37-45
gathering of, 31-58, 60-61, 64-66, 75-77, 437-440
from interviews, 8-9, 10-11
in letter writing, 3-7, 184-185, 200-201, 202
from library research, 177-186, 438-440

from listening to others, 54-58
in narrative writing, 114-115
in persuasive writing, 187-202
in process essay, 120-121
from reading material, written summary of, 159-176
in research paper, 437-440
Indefinite adjectives, 225
Indefinite pronouns, 222
and gender agreement, 383-384
and verb agreement, 307-308
Independent clauses, 236-237, 238-239, 243-244
punctuation of, 426-427
Indirect objects, 217-218
Infinitives, 324, 344-345
Intensive pronouns, 222
Interjections, 232
Interrogative pronouns, 223
verb agreement with, 308
Interviews, 8-17
active listening in, 8, 9
in classroom, 8-12
development of ideas from, 10-11
gathering ideas and information from, 8-9
outside of classroom, 12-13
questions in, 9, 13-17
self-questioning in, 13-17
Introduction, in writing
in classification essay, 155
evaluation and revision of, 92, 94
in narrative writing, 109
suggestions for, 88-89
Italics, 431

Journals, 13-17

Letter writing, 3-5, 19-20
to classmates, 3-8
developing ideas for, 5-7
to editor of newspaper, 184, 200-201
gathering ideas and information for, 3-5, 184-185, 200-201, 202
library research for, 184-185, 200-201, 202
of personal letter, 185, 202
punctuation of, colon use in, 428
rules on, 7
samples of, 6-7
work sheets on, 4-5
Library of Congress classification system, 179
Library research
for argument essay, 189, 191, 195-202
exercise on, 181-183
locating resource materials for, 177-186
with periodicals, 179-180, 183-186
with publications on reserve, 181
reference tools in, 180-181
for research papers, 438-440
writing assignments requiring, 183-186, 195-202, 457-458

Linking verbs, 212–213
Listening skill
  and dialogue writing, 54–58
  in interviews, 8, 9

Magazine articles in library, 179–180
  assignments requiring use of, 183–186
Magazine Index, 180, 438
Margins of pages, 28–29
Metaphors, in descriptive writing, 99
Modal verbs, 324–325
Modifiers
  dangling, 281–283
  misplaced, 283–285

Narrative writing, 108–116
  in argument essay, 192
  assignment on, 112–116
  on conflict situations, 109–110
  exercises on, 112
  guidelines on, 109–110
  run-on sentences in, 116, 277
  six-step method in, 112–116
  topic selection in, 112–113
  uses of, 108–109
New York Times Index, 181
Newspapers
  letter writing to editor of, 184, 200–201
  locating articles in, 181
Nominatives, predicate, 213, 225
Nonstandard forms, 51, 353. *See also* Verb(s)
Notes, for citing sources, 445
Note-taking, 439–440
Nouns, 208–210
  adjectives modifying or describing, 224–228
  appositives describing, 255–259
  definition of, 208
  as direct objects, 215–216
  as indirect objects, 217–218
  as irregular third-person subjects, 295–297
  as objects of prepositions, 216–217
  plural forms of, 291–292, 392–394
  possessive forms of, 414–415
  pronouns substituting for, 218–224
  proper, 209
  singular forms of, 291–292
  as subjects of sentences, 210
  workbook practice on, 209–210
Numbers
  and numerals, 433–434
  spelling of, 402

Object(s), 215–218
  direct, 215–216
  indirect, 217–218
  of prepositions, 216–217
Objective case of pronouns, 219
O'Connor, Flannery, 108

Organizing principle of paragraphs, 19
  evaluation of, 64
  outline of, 69
Outline of writing
  in argument essay, 198
  in classification essay, 153–155
  in comparison and contrast essays, 132–139,
    141–143
  consistency of, 68–69
  in descriptive writing, 104–105
  in example essay, 129–130
  as fourth step in writing well, 62, 68–71, 79–80
  in narrative writing, 115–116
  in process essay, 122–123
  in research paper, 441–442
  in summary of reading material, 166

Paragraphs, 19–29
  on classroom interviews, 10, 11
  clincher statement in, 23, 26
  concluding, 89–90
  concluding sentence in, 23, 26
  in descriptive writing, 104–105
  details and examples in, 20–21, 26, 70, 72, 92, 93
  in dialogue writing, 56, 57
  evaluation and revision of, 12, 25–28, 62–64, 72,
    92, 93
  indentation of, 28
  introductory, 88–89
  length of, 26
  in letters, 3–5, 19–20
  organizing principles in, 19, 64, 69
  planning of, 62, 68–71, 79–80
  punctuation of, 29
  topic sentences in, 20, 21, 22, 23, 26
  transition sentences in, 21, 22, 23, 24–25, 74–75
  writing assignments on, 23–25
Paraphrasing. *See* Quotation(s), indirect
Parallelism in sentences, faulty, 285–286
Parentheses, use of, 432
Participles, 345–346
  past, 318, 329–337, 345, 363
  present, 345
Passive voice, 329, 334–337, 364
  use of, 335–337
Past participle, 318, 329–337, 345, 363
  with *am, is, are, was,* and *were,* 334–335
  with *have, has,* and *had,* 330–334
  irregular forms of, 319–322, 330
Past tense of verbs, 318, 325–329, 363
  irregular forms of, 319–322
  with past participle, 318, 329–337
  perfect, 331
  rules on verb endings in, 328–329
Perfect tense of verbs, 329, 363–364
  past, 331
  present, 331
Period, use of
  in abbreviations, 412–413
  ending sentence, 412

Periodicals in library, 179–180
  assignments requiring use of, 183–186, 457
Personal pronouns, 219, 221
  incorrect use of, 385–386
Persuasive writing, 187–202
Phrases, 208
  prepositional, 216–217, 361
  verb, 212
Plagiarism, 165
Plan of writing. *See* Outline of writing
Plural forms
  apostrophe use in, 413–414
  of nouns, 291–292, 392–394
Poetry
  class discussion on, 50–54
  examples of, 51–53
  nonstandard constructions in, 51
Possessive case, 414–415
Possessive pronouns, 219, 414
  compared to contractions, 397–399
Predicate adjectives, 225
Predicate nominatives, 213, 225
Prepositions, 216
  objects of, 216–217
  phrases with, 216–217, 361
Present participles, 345
Present tense of verbs, 323
  agreement with subject, 310–311
  perfect, 331
  with present participle, 345
Process essays, 116–124
  assignment on, 119–124
  guidelines for writing of, 117–118
  sample of, 118–119
  six-step method for writing of, 119–124
  topic selection for, 119–120
  uses of, 116
Progressive form of verbs, 318, 337–339, 363
  irregular, 319–322
  rule for construction of, 337–338
Pronouns, 218–224, 375–389
  adjectives modifying or describing, 224–228
  agreement with antecedent, 378–385, 386, 387
  case of, 219–221, 375–377, 386
  in compound constructions, 221
  demonstrative, 221–222
  indefinite, 222, 307–308, 383–384
  intensive, 222
  interrogative, 223, 308
  objective, 219
  personal, 219, 221, 385–386
  possessive, 219, 397–399, 414
  reflexive, 222–223
  relative, 223, 244, 249–250, 309–310, 386, 387
  reversed order of, 385, 387
  review exercises on, 389
  shifts in person of, 124, 384–385, 387
  as subject of sentence, verb agreement with, 307–310
  subjective, 219, 220

  unclear antecedents of, 377–378, 386
  used with gerund, wrong form of, 385–386
  workbook practice on, 220, 221, 223–224
Proofreading, 62–64, 72, 81–82, 106, 443
Proper nouns, 209
Punctuation
  of adjective clause, 251, 418
  apostrophe in, 396–399, 413–416
  of appositives, 255, 419
  colon in, 428
  comma in, 270, 417–426
  with conjunctive adverb, 242, 418
  with coordinating conjunction, 239, 417
  dash in, 432
  of dialogue, 56–57
  at end of sentence, 412–413
  evaluation and revision of, 106
  hyphen in, 28–29, 391, 401–402, 432
  of narrative writing, 116
  of paragraphs, 29
  parentheses in, 432
  of quotation, 412, 420, 428–431, 443, 444
  quotation marks in, 428–432, 443–445
  review exercises on, 433–434
  of run-on sentences, 270
  semicolon in, 426–428
  with subordinating conjunction, 244, 417
  of title of paper, 91
Purpose statement, 84–88
  in argument essay, 191, 196, 198
  in classification essay, 147, 148, 153
  in comparison and contrast essay, 131–132, 140–141
  in descriptive writing, 104, 106
  evaluation and revision of, 72, 81, 91, 93
  in example essay, 129
  exercises on, 86–88
  in narrative writing, 115
  outline of, 68
  in process essays, 117, 121–122, 124
  in research paper, 437, 440, 441
  suggestions for writing of, 84–86
  in summary, 165
  as third step in writing well, 61, 67–68, 77–79

Question marks, 412
Questions
  interrogative pronouns in, 223, 308
  in interviews and self-interviews, 9, 13–14, 17
  punctuation of, 412
  reversed order of subject and verb in, 302–303
  subject-verb agreement in, 302–303, 308
Quotation(s)
  in argument essay, 193, 198
  direct, 429–430, 443–444
  indirect, 430–431, 444–445
  punctuation of, 412, 420, 428–431, 443–444
  in research paper, 442, 443–445
  rules on form in, 443–445
  run-on sentences in, 277

Quotation marks, 428–432, 443–445

Readers' Guide to Periodical Literature, 179–180, 182, 438
  assignments requiring use of, 183–186, 195–202, 457
Reading aloud of writing, 8, 12, 72, 81–82
Reading for pleasure, 459–461
Reading material
  in library, methods of locating, 177–186, 438–439
  written summary of, 159–176
Reflexive pronouns, 222–223
Relative pronouns, 223, 244
  with adjective clause, 249–250
  incorrect use of, 386, 387
  with subordinating conjunction, 244
  verb agreement with, 309–310
Repetition in writing, 71, 72, 81
  evaluation and revision of, 72, 92, 94
Research, locating resource materials for, 177–186.
  See also Library research
Research paper, 437–458
  quoting published material in, 442, 443–445
  sample format for, 447–450
  six-step method for writing of, 437–443
  writing assignments for, 446, 457–458
Reserved publications in library, 181
Resources for writing, 157. *See also* Ideas and information for writing; Library research; Summary writing
Revision of writing, 12, 91–96
  in argument essay, 198
  assignments on, 29, 96
  in classification essay, 155
  in comparison and contrast essays, 144
  in descriptive essay, 106
  in example essay, 130–131
  examples of, 26–28, 92–96
  in free writing, 41, 44–45
  guidelines on, 72, 91–92
  in narrative essay, 109, 116
  in paragraphs, 12, 25–28
  in process essay, 124
  in research paper, 443
  as sixth step to writing well, 62–64, 72, 81–82
  in summary of reading material, 166
Rico, Gabrielle, 45–46
Run-on sentences, 270–280
  comma-splice, 270
  editing for, 81, 116, 124, 271–280
  fused, 270
  in narrative writing, 116, 277
  in process essays, 124
  types of, 276–277

Semicolon use, 426–428
  rules governing, 426–427

Sentences. *See also specific parts and types of sentences*
  adverb-adjective confusion in, 280–281
  appositives in, 255–259
  comma-splice, 270
  commas in, rules governing use of, 417–421
  complete, test determining, 235, 265
  complex, 243–255
  compound, 238–243, 426–427
  concluding, of paragraph, 23, 26
  conjunctions in, 230–232, 239–241, 243–249
  effective, writing of, 235–263
  end punctuation of, 412–413
  faulty parallelism in, 285–286
  fragments of, 265–270
  fused, 270
  modifiers in, dangling or misplaced, 281–285
  parts of, 207–208
  prevention of errors in, 265–289
  run-on, 116, 124, 270–280
  semicolons in, 426–428
  simple, 236–238
  subject of, 207
  topic, 20, 21, 22, 23, 26
  transition, 21, 22, 23
Serials Catalog, 180, 182, 183
Similes, in descriptive writing, 99
Simple past tense of verbs, 318, 325–329, 363
  irregular forms of, 319–322
  rules on, 328–329
Simple sentences, 236–238
  combining of, 247–249, 254–255
Simple verbs, 212
Single-paragraph essays, 20–24
SIRS (Social Issues Resources Series), 181, 182, 184
  assignments requiring use of, 184, 185, 200, 201, 202
Six-step method of writing, 59–96
  in argument essay, 195–198
  in classification essay, 151–155
  in comparison and contrast essay, 139–144
  in description essay, 102–106
  description of, 59–96
  in example essay, 128–131
  in narrative essay, 112–116
  in process essay, 119–124
  in research paper, 437–443
Skim, Read, and Review reading method, 161–162
Slang words, use of, 107
Social Issues Resources Series, 181, 182, 184
  assignments requiring use of, 184, 185, 200, 201 202
Social Studies Index, 180
Sound-alike words, spelling of, 397–401
Sources, citation of, 437, 438–439, 442, 445–446, 450
Speech, parts of, 207–233
  adjectives, 224–228
  adverbs, 228–230

conjunctions, 230-232
interjections, 232
nouns, 208-210
objects and prepositions, 215-218
pronouns, 218-224
review exercise on, 233
verbs, 210-215
Spelling, 391-407
of contractions and possessive pronouns, 396-399
editing for mistakes in, 106
and hyphenation of words, 391, 401-402, 432
ie and *ei* rule on, 405
list of words often misspelled, 402-404
of noun plurals, 391-394
review exercise on, 407
of sound-alike words, 397-401
suggestions for improvement of, 391-392
of verb endings, 297-300, 328-329, 337-338, 353-355, 394-396
Statement of purpose, 84-88. *See also* Purpose statement
Steps in writing. *See* Six-step method of writing
Storytelling. *See* Narrative writing
Subject of sentence, 207
agreement with verb. *See* Subject-verb agreement
compound, 305-307
dangling modifiers describing, 281-283
with expletives, 303-304
irregular forms of, verb agreement with, 295-297
misplaced modifiers describing, 283-285
nouns as, 210
placed after verbs, 213-214
pronouns as, verb agreement with, 307-310
in questions, 302-303
separated from verb, 360-363
Subject-verb agreement, 291-315, 353-363
with compound subjects, 305-307
in conjugation, 293-295
with expletives, 303-304
with irregular noun subjects, 295-297
in present-tense essays, 310-311
with pronoun subjects, 307-310
in questions, 302-303, 308
review exercises on, 313-315, 371-372
and separation of subject and verb, 360-363
with third-person endings, 310-311, 355-356
with two or more subjects, 305-307
with two or more verbs, 358-360
in use of *be* verbs, 301-305, 356-358
in use of *do* and *go*, 298-299
in use of *have* and *has*, 300-301, 354
and verb endings, 297-300, 310-311, 353-355
workbook practice on, 353-363, 371-372
Subjective case of pronouns, 219, 220
Subordinate clauses, punctuation of, 417
Subordinating conjunctions, 230-231
combining simple sentences with, 247-249
in complex sentence, 243-249

Summary writing, 159-176
assignments on, 160-161, 167-176
description of, 159-160
plagiarism in, 165
Skim, Read, Review method of, 161-162
suggestions for, 165-166
Superlative and comparative adjectives, 226-228
irregular forms of, 227

Tense of verbs, 80, 317-351
in base form, 318, 323-325, 363
dictionary entries on, 339-341
evaluation and revision of, 81, 106
forms of, 317-318, 363
irregular, 318-323, 363
and modal verbs, 324-325
in narrative writing, 116
and past participles, 318, 329-337, 363
perfect, 329, 331, 363-364
present, 310-311, 323, 331, 345
progressive form of, 318, 337-339, 363
review exercises on, 349-351, 373-374
shifts in, 341-343, 367-369
simple past, 318, 325-329, 363
spelling of, 395-396
workbook practice on, 363-369, 373-374
Thesaurus use, 107
Thesis statement, 84-88. *See also* Purpose statement
Thigpen, Robert, 175, 200
Third-person endings, subject-verb agreement in, 310-311, 355-356
Title of essay
rules for, 91
suggestions for, 90-91
Topic selection
for argument essay, 191, 195-196
for classification essay, 151-152
for comparison and contrast essay, 139
for descriptive writing, 102
for example essay, 128
for narrative writing, 112-113
for process essay, 119-120
for research paper, 437-438
Topic sentences
details and examples explaining, 20-21, 26
revision of, 26
in single-paragraph essay, 20, 21, 22, 23
Transition sentences
in classification essays, 147-148
in comparison and contrast essays, 134-135
evaluation and revision of, 26, 92, 94
joining paragraphs, 24-25, 74-75
in process essays, 118
in single-paragraph essays, 21, 22, 23
words or phrases in, 22-23
Twain, Mark, 54, 459

Underlining of words, 431–432, 446

Verb(s), 210–215, 291–374
  in active voice, 334
  adverbs modifying, 228–230
  agreement with subject. *See* Subject-verb
      agreement
  base forms of, 318, 323–325, 363
  conjugation of, 293–295
  definition of, 210
  dictionary entries on, 339–341
  endings of, 297–300, 310–311, 328–329, 337–338,
      353–356, 394–396
  helping, 212
  infinitive form of, 324, 344–345
  irregular, 318–323
  linking, 212–213
  modal, 324–325
  nonstandard, 353
  in passive voice, 329, 334–337, 364
  past participle, 318, 329–337, 363
  in perfect tenses, 329, 331, 363–364
  in phrases, 212
  in present tense, 323
  progressive form of, 318, 337–339, 363
  review exercises on, 313–315, 349–351, 371–374
  separated from subject, 360–363
  shifts in tense of, 341–343, 367–369
  simple, 212
  in simple past tense, 318, 325–329, 363
  singular and plural forms of, 291–293
  subjects placed after, 213–214
  tense of, 81, 106, 317–351, 363–369
  and use of *be*, 301–302, 322–323, 356–358
  and use of *have* and *has*, 300–301, 330–334, 354
  workbook practice on, 211–215, 363–369,
      373–374
Verbals, 343–347
  gerunds, 346–347, 385–386
  infinitives, 344–345
  participles, 345–346
Voice
  active, 334
  passive, 329, 334–337, 364

Williams, Vicki, 167, 169
Word selection
  in argument essay, 191
  in descriptive writing, 106
  evaluation and revision of, 92, 94
  in process essays, 121–122
  suggestions for using most exact word, 107–108
Works Cited, as section of research paper, 442,
      445–446
  sample of, 450
Wright, Richard, 110, 161, 459

The Resourceful Writer

To the Student:

One of the best ways for us to plan future editions of *The Resourceful Writer* is to get reactions and suggestions from you, the student. When you have used this book for a complete course, please take a few moments to answer the questions below. Then tear out this page and mail it to

William H. Barnwell
c/o Marketing Services
College Division
Houghton Mifflin Company
One Beacon Street
Boston, MA 02108

1. Is the writing style of the book clear?   Yes _____ No _____
   Are there any sections that you feel could be made clearer?

2. Did the student samples throughout the book help you with your own writing assignments? Were the samples clear examples of what you thought the author was trying to illustrate?

3. Did you find the writing assignments motivating? Why or why not?

4. Did you find Part Three, "A Writer's Workbook," helpful throughout the course? Were the explanations clear? If there were any places in which you felt the explanations could be clearer, please note them.

5. Were there enough exercises in Part Three? Were there any areas in which you felt you could have used more practice? Please note them.

6. Which chapters in the book did you find most helpful? (Please list them.)

7. Which chapters in the book did you find the least helpful? (Please list them.)

8. Please feel free to make any additional comments.